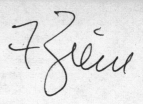

Nation-wide Critical Praise For *How to Win at Duplicate Bridge*:

"An Excellent Book" — B. Jay Becker, *King Features Syndicate*

"A fine new book . . . . One of the most interesting chapters is devoted to defense and gives a much-needed emphasis to this phase of play." — Florence Osborn, *New York Herald Tribune*

"For those who take bridge seriously." — *Chicago Tribune*

"Detailed and constructive." — *Los Angeles Mirror-News*

"Certain to help the reader in his quest for top scores." — *Cleveland Plain Dealer*

"Here is the book you've been looking for . . . . [It] contains the material to make a person a tournament player. Want to try?" — *Durham (N. C.) Herald*

D0889504

MARSHALL MILES

HOW TO
DUPLICATE

WIN AT BRIDGE

COLLIER BOOKS
NEW YORK, N.Y.

First Collier Books Edition 1963

This Collier Books edition is published by arrangement with Exposition Press, Inc.

The Macmillan Company, New York
Collier-Macmillan Canada Ltd., Toronto, Ontario
Divisions of The Crowell-Collier Publishing Company
Printed in the United States of America

Contents

Foreword

MARSHALL MILES has been developing ideas about duplicate bridge and guiding players to victory for over a decade. Many of us on the West Coast have had the opportunity to profit from detailed discussions with him on each phase of match-point bidding and play. In my own bridge development these discussions have been a most significant constructive factor. And now Mr. Miles has incorporated his ideas into a book, valuable both for its theoretical soundness and its provocative presentation.

In the introduction the author has clearly stated his principles, orientation and goals. Since I have played regularly with him for the past eight years, I shall say a word about him from my vantage point across the table.

Many players are able to conjure up sparkling ideas of bidding and play, especially while talking over hands at a midnight post-mortem session; some are able to write about them. Few are able to apply their ideas in the heat of battle. Mr. Miles can and does. When the bidding suggests an opening lead of low from K-x against a six bid, that lead is made; if percentages indicate a finesse holding A K Q J 9 opposite a singleton, the finesse is taken; and if the psychological moment has arrived for a bluff-play in no-trump, holding x x x opposite x x, that suit is played. The point is that at the table Mr. Miles makes, and in this book he recommends, the play or bid which has the best chance of producing a good result in match-point competition. Dogma and tradition do not cloud his reasoning.

If the reader wishes to become a consistently successful tournament player, be he an experienced dupliphile—perhaps a Lifemaster—or a rubber player first crossing the great divide, the means are in this book.

Now it is up to you.

WILLIAM HANNA

How to Win at Duplicate Bridge

Chapter 1

Introduction

THIS IS A BOOK for those who take bridge seriously. If you do not care particularly whether you win or lose so long as you have fun, I envy you. What an excellent attitude to take toward recreation! But this book is not for you. It is for greedy players who want to win far more than their fair share of the time. It is for players who are dissatisfied with coming in second when they should have come in first.

If you have never read a bridge book, put this one aside until you have read one by Charles Goren or Ely Culbertson. This book does not dwell on fundamentals. The emphasis is on exceptions and modifications rather than general rules. Basic knowledge on your part is assumed.

A good background in rubber-bridge technique is an aid at duplicate if you can break the bad habits acquired from rubber bridge. By bad habits, I mean playing safe for your contract at the cost of overtricks, or being too conservative in competitive situations. In duplicate one hand counts as much as another. It is just as important not to let the opponent make two hearts when you can make two spades as it is to bid a grand slam. Consequently, a high degree of aggressiveness is called for on part-score hands. As Culbertson states, in rubber bridge you consider the *amount* of gain as against the *amount* of loss. In duplicate you consider the *frequency* of gain as against the *frequency* of loss.

In rubber bridge an overcall conforms to the rule of two and three. There must be enough playing strength to limit the loss to a reasonable amount. In duplicate you do not worry about how much an overcall *might* go down. You are concerned with

11

how often it will result in a bad board, and how it is most likely to work out with this particular hand. Similarly, when you double the opponent's part-score contract at rubber bridge, you need a two-trick safety margin if the doubled contract would be enough for game, if made. A double for a one-trick set gives the opponents odds of six or eight to one. However, in duplicate, where total points do not count, you double very freely whenever you think the opponents are trying to steal the bid. In some situations, you have less to lose by an unsuccessful double than you stand to lose by not doubling if the opponents are too high. Nor do you differentiate between "light doubles" and "tight doubles," in Culbertson's terminology. In duplicate an unsuccessful double of two clubs is just as costly as an unsuccessful double of two spades.

Another result of the difference in scoring at duplicate is that you prefer a risky part-score contract which will pay more (no-trump or a major-suit contract with a 4–3 trump holding) to a safer minor-suit contract. At rubber bridge the difference between 40, 60, 70, or 90 part-score is negligible. You would rather get 40 points below the line for sure (with a probable 20 points above) than to speculate on a no-trump contract for 70 points. In duplicate you prefer two plus 120's, and a minus 200, to three plus 110's.

In rubber bridge you do not take a deliberate 500-point set when there is a chance to defeat the opponents' vulnerable game contract. Suppose your decision were right; you save very few points. If you were wrong, your loss would have been considerable. In duplicate you would gladly risk 600 points to gain 120 if the odds were 2 to 1 in your favor. Of course it is foolish to worry about whether 6 to 5 odds are good enough—it depends upon whether all the opponents will bid game, whether you need a good board or cannot afford a bad one—since you cannot forecast your chances with any such degree of accuracy.

Many players have the philosophy that you should try to bid as others will bid and pick up your points in the play. To me this seems like giving up your major advantage over the field. It is just as logical to play your hands "like everyone else" (if you can tell what "everyone else" will do) and pick up your points in the bidding. Where it pays most to consider what others will bid is in the field of sacrificing. Suppose good opponents reach a vulnerable small slam which you believe they can make, and you are contemplating a sacrifice bid which should be down 900 or 1100 points. If you believe that most of the opponents will bid a slam with the opponents' cards, you may sacrifice. But if only one or two other teams, at most, will reach the slam, your sacrifice would result in a bad board whether the slam is makable or not. Rather than try for a twenty per cent board, pass and hope for a set.

The major objective in rubber bridge is to reach game. The opening bids are keyed to this objective. Goren states that an opening bid opposite an opening bid with a fit equals game. Point-wise, an opening bid shows approximately 13 points minimum and 26 points are required for game. Since the objective in duplicate is to reach the best result, whether a game, part-score, or penalty on the maximum number of hands, you might expect the requirements for an opening bid to be decreased. But experience has shown that partner cannot handle lighter than normal opening bids. When both partners have 11 points, theoretically they would do well to open and reach a part-score contract. But when one opens light, a partner with reasonable aggressiveness will constantly push the bidding too high. Many times when a hand has been passed out, you will notice that North-South can make one no-trump, two hearts, or three clubs, while East-West can only make one spade or two diamonds. Does this mean a bad board for North-South? No, because the few times that North or South improperly opened the bidding, the final contract was two no-trump or three hearts, down one.

A further discussion of the difference between duplicate and rubber bridge in *general* terms would not be profitable. Each phase of bidding will be analyzed in detail, and the influence of match-point scoring as it applies to each phase will be emphasized.

In this introductory chapter, match-point philosophy, hand evaluation, and forcing bids will be discussed, since this knowledge must be applied to all phases of bidding. In the other chapters on bidding, I have rejected the orthodox approach. Instead of dividing the material into small sub-topics such as opening suit bids, opening no-trump bids, responses, re-bids, and second-round responses, I have attempted to show how you should plan to describe a hand, however many bids may be required. More space is devoted to slam bidding and competitive bidding than you will find in most bridge books. Competitive bidding is emphasized because of its increased importance at duplicate and because match-point scoring requires a new approach. Slam bidding is discussed in detail because I know of no single book that treats it adequately from an expert point of view.

In the United States, the best bridge literature for advanced players is to be found in *The Bridge World* magazine and in the bridge columns of newspapers.

Perhaps you wonder whether I am attempting to introduce a new system. The answer is emphatically *no*. Most of the suggestions which may seem new to you are accepted ideas *for duplicate* among top players, as can be seen by a perusal of tournament reports and experts' panels in *The Bridge World*. When I have a suggestion of my own, I have attempted to label it as such, and when there are several points of view, I have presented all sides while plugging the view which seems most logical to me. I may fudge a little here and there because of bias, conscious or unconscious.

In one respect this book may appear unrealistic. The opponents always bid logically. You can trust their bidding almost as much as your partner's. When you play hands, the opponents defend with imagination and precision. When you defend, declarer not only plays well; he is often diabolically deceptive. At what tournament can you find this caliber of play? Surely not in your typical weekly game. Should more space be devoted to "How to Steal Candy From a Baby"? Inexperienced players can often be stolen blind by psyching. Overbidding is rewarded rather than punished. If you bid two or three tricks too high to compete against a part-score, the opponents will fail to double and will lose a trick or two on defense. But is that what you want from bridge—to win every weekly game at all costs? You should set your sights a little higher.

Look at it this way. In your weekly game, they give out rating points. In a regional or national event they give out master points. Unless you are rich, retired, or professional, you are lucky to be able to attend two or three big events per year. If you can come in second or third in one event of one regional meet against good competition, it means more than 52 little victories, total rating points awarded notwithstanding. Would you jeopardize your chances in the big events by destroying partnership confidence and developing bad habits just to win a few more weekly games?

Why do we play bridge anyway? For relaxation? Don't kid yourself! A good game of bridge is more exhausting than anything you do for a living. The violent arguments which take place at the bridge table are a manifestation of the strain we are under. We play bridge largely to build up our ego. We want to convince others that we are intelligent and play a good game, and if enough people believe it, we ourselves are convinced. Master points are merely evidence with which we attempt to prove our contention—that we are good. There may be a few normal, well-balanced people who play bridge for fun. But these well-balanced people are seldom good players because they do not spend enough time and effort at bridge. I once knew a fellow who missed a two-session event just to take his family to a picnic! Obviously a hopeless case!

The desire for recognition is normal. The problem is to hold it within bounds. A child will misbehave, if necessary, to attract attention. When we get older we say to ourselves, "Let's attract *favorable* attention without being too obvious about it." The "child" at the bridge table tries to show how good he is by belittling the opponents. As he reaches adolescence, he realizes that the opponents are not considered fair game, and he confines his attention to his partner. When he reaches maturity, he seeks ways of attracting favorable attention without being too obvious. He may win friends, even though his bridge is not flawless. If he wants recognition through bridge, the best way, of course, is to win most of the time. But consistently winning is such a hard way to gain recognition!

Playing well is not enough; one must find ways of getting partner to play well, too. This involves applied psychology of the highest order. Just as it is vitally important to discuss hands with a regular partner, it is equally important not to try to "train" a casual partner. Don't give him anything new to worry about. If he doesn't play Stayman or the "weak two" bid, don't try to teach him so that he can use it with you for one session. The professionals often win important events with a very mediocre pupil. Good as the professional is, he cannot do it alone. The pupil has to play a fair game. Take this attitude: If your partner does not play his best game, it must be your fault.

Criticism of another's bridge game is always a touchy business. We all tend to forget that an accusation of a mistake at bridge is not an attack on character, or even intelligence. Never make any comments when partner makes an obvious mistake which he is aware of. A bridge discussion should not be for the purpose of humbling another, but merely for the purpose of avoiding a repetition of a mistake or misunderstanding. The proper way to approach the subject varies from person to person. Not many people are able to discuss bridge objectively, and the ability to take criticism is proportional to one's self-confidence.

The cocky individual who imagines that he is irresistible to women is the easiest to get along with. You can shout, "Butcher!", and he will grin from ear to ear. By a devious reasoning process, he considers your exclamation a compliment. Unless you thought he was pretty good, you would not get excited over a mistake! Furthermore, he will admit his mistakes readily with a "Caesar-has-fallen" attitude, since he knows that you know he only makes a mistake like this three or four times a year. The fact that he has made two years' worth this session is beside the point. You can relax and save your tact for someone else, since nothing you say will insult him. His optimism and good spirits are contagious, and you both start laughing over each other's wild bidding.

The other extreme is the timid soul who keeps asking, "Did I do the right thing, partner?" The truthful answer would be *no*, but the truth would be brutal to a sensitive person, and you must be very careful what you say.

The average partner falls somewhere between these extremes. He does not want any unfavorable comment right after a hand has been played, nor does he want any criticism in front of others. For that matter, no one likes angry or emotional criticism. Form the habit of keeping a private score and jotting down the hands you want to discuss later if you are afraid of forgetting them. Then discuss the hands in private. If your partner cannot discuss hands unemotionally the next day, change partners, because it is vital to a regular partnership to discuss hands where points were lost. It will be a great deal of help if you can start out by admitting a mistake you made on the same hand, even though you think your own mistake was insignificant. Remember, the purpose of the discussion is not to prove you played better than partner, but to avoid the recurrence of mistakes. Once partner says, "Yes, I should have played the queen of diamonds," drop the subject. Don't rub it in or remind him of the hand two years later when you have an argument. Don't make such an issue of any hand that neither you nor partner can ever give in without an injury to pride.

Enough on psychology. Back to the technical aspects.

A few top players, the "Four Aces," recommended a point count in 1935, but they were unable to sell their ideas or their book very well. Consequently, till around 1950, almost all bridge players used Culbertson's honor count and playing tricks in evaluating hands. Then, as one writer after another, including Culbertson, suggested point adjustments for distribution, the Work point count became popular.

Point count has two main advantages over honor count. Point count is a combination (in effect) of honor count and playing tricks; consequently, only one evaluation is necessary—only one at a time, anyway. More important, there are certain fixed goals such as 26 points for game or 33 for a slam. If you forget what you need to make a certain bid, you can figure it out anew, or you can subtract your points from 26 to see what partner needs in order for you to make game. This is easier (but less accurate) than trying to imagine various *hands* partner might have, consistent with his bidding, in order to determine how many tricks you could take. Point count is best with balanced hands, particularly for no-trump bidding. With distributional hands, honor count is better. Either method of evaluation needs adjustments. For example, using honor count, it is necessary to add a plus value for possession of several honor cards; using points, deduct for unsupported honors. The main trouble with a point-count evaluation is that, with corrections and adjustments, it purports to be extremely accurate and is taken too seriously. Despite ingenious suggestions for corrections, it is still misleading in many cases. With few corrections, there are many inaccuracies; with many corrections, it becomes too complicated.

For example, partner opens the bidding with one spade. You have ♠ K x x x, ♡ A J x x, ◇ x x x, ♣ x x. Admittedly, the king of spades is of more probable value to partner than any other king. But is this hand as good as it would be with the ace or king-jack of spades? Of course not, but that is the result you would get by following Goren's rule of promotion. Now change the hand to ♠ K x x x, ♡ A J x x x, ◇ x x, ♣ x x. Isn't this a better hand? Don't you prefer 4-5-2-2 distribution to 4-4-3-2 distribution? According to the Culbertson point count, both hands are worth ten points in support of spades. This is not a criticism of Culbertson or Goren. There are many factors of *some* value. One person assigns a point to this value; another disregards it. The more accurate evaluation might well be a fraction of a point, but the added complication of using fractions would outweigh the slight increase of accuracy.

In my opinion, the best solution is to learn where the point count is least accurate. Then, if there are several overvaluations, you may use your judgment and subtract a point or two. When there are several undervaluations, you may add a point or two. Furthermore, you do not have to be consistent throughout the entire hand. As the bidding develops, you can tell whether you have the "right" cards or the "wrong" cards. As for distribution, you can tell after a couple of rounds of bidding whether an unbalanced hand pattern means ruffing values and an establishable suit or a misfit and duplication. Following are several "evaluation factors" which you should consider.

(1) Aces are undervalued in relation to other honors in the 4-3-2-1 count, even for no-trump bidding. The undervaluation is more serious when you contemplate a suit bid. Most bridge writers recognize this fact in one way or another. Goren subtracts a point when opener has an aceless hand. Culbertson adds a point for possession of four aces and suggests passing all optional opening bids (at rubber bridge) containing no aces. Stayman counts an ace as 4½ points. Even kings are slightly undervalued in relation to the minor honors. Any time you have a borderline decision, bid more with strength concentrated in aces and kings; bid less with a preponderance of queens and jacks.

(2) Minor honors are worth more in combination than by themselves. Stated another way, when other things are equal, the greater the honor count, the better the hand. Over partner's opening spade bid, ♠ K x x, ♡ x, ◇ K x x x x, ♣ Q 10 x x, is just a sound raise to two spades, while ♠ K x x, ♡ x, ◇ A J 10 x x, ♣ x x x x, is too strong for an immediate spade raise. Remember that till the point count became popular, a queen was valued as one quarter of a trick (in effect) when it was accompanied by no higher honors, but when it was with an ace or king, it was worth a half trick. A jack by itself was a dubious value but always worth a plus or quarter value when accompanied by a higher honor. What was true for twenty years is true today. Honors are still worth more in combination so that they can support each other. This is particularly true when partner has, or may have, a weak hand. If he opens one no-trump, ♠ Q x x x x, ♡ J x x, ◇ K x x, ♣ A x, is just about as good a hand as ♠ K Q J x x, ♡ x x x, ◇ x x x, ♣ A x. But suppose you were defending against three no-trump. Naturally, you prefer the latter hand.

(3) It is better to have your strength concentrated in your long suits rather than in your short suits. Suppose partner opens the bidding one no-trump and you hold ♠ A J 10 x x x, ♡ x x, ◇ x x, ♣ x x x. You cheerfully raise to two no-trump because partner should have no worse than a finesse for six spade tricks. But suppose your hand were ♠ x x x x x x, ♡ x x, ◇ x x, ♣ A J 10. Now you must either bid two spades or pass because you can visualize how the play would go. It would take time and more entries than you have to establish and run the spades unless partner has a remarkably good spade fit.

Or suppose partner opens the bidding one spade and you hold ♠ A x x x, ♡ Q x, ◇ Q x, ♣ J x x x x. Your high-card total is nine points, and you get two more points for distribution, as will be explained later. Nevertheless, your correct bid is two spades, not two clubs. Why? In the first place, the honors are not in combination. Also, there will be too much wasted strength. The two points for distribution were awarded for ruffing values, one for each doubleton. But if partner is going to ruff the third round of the suit what good will the queen do him? If he has A J or K x x of hearts or diamonds, the queen might be of value, but it is quite likely that one queen will be completely valueless. The hand would be stronger with worthless doubletons and the four points somewhere else. Change the hand to ♠ K x x x, ♡ x x, ◇ x x, ♣ A J x x x, and it is too strong for a raise to two spades despite the reduced gross count. Now, the ten of clubs added to this hand would be of more probable value than the jack of hearts or diamonds. Since point count cannot take the place of judgment, it is better to combine the two.

How do other writers correct for these factors? Goren deducts a point for a singleton king, queen, or jack, or a doubleton queen-jack. Culbertson subtracts one point from *opener's* hand for one or more combinations such as Q x or J x. (But what about responder or overcaller?) Jacoby deducts a point for no small cards in a suit; consequently he deducts for a singleton ace, doubleton ace-king or king-queen. Everyone recognizes the problem, but all these rules do either too much or too little. Why not point out the problem and let the player use his own judgment? One bad feature can be cancelled out by a good one, or the good or bad features may be cumulative. It is much too difficult to reduce everything to a formula where you either subtract a point or not. If there is any hope for you as a bridge player, you must be able to make an on-the-spot decision.

(4) Honors in bid suits are of more probable value than honors in unbid suits. Suppose partner opens with one heart and re-bids diamonds. Any honors in the red suits will be useful to him. Aces in the black suits will be useful cards and kings may be useful. But in support of a heart or diamond contract, your queens and jacks in the black suits will usually be worthless. The more distributional your hand is, or the more distributional you suspect partner's hand is, the more you should promote your hand for the right cards or demote it for the wrong ones.

(5) Tenace holdings increase or decrease in value depending upon the opponents' bidding. K x is a better three points when the person on your right bids the suit than when the person on your left bids it.

(6) The points to be awarded for distribution should vary throughout the auction. Even for the first bid there may be a slight inaccuracy which you should take into account with a borderline opening bid. Since we wish to avoid fractions, it is

necessary to award the same number of points to hand patterns of slightly different strength. ♠ A 10 9 x, ♡ K x, ◇ A J x, ♣ x x x x and ♠ A 10 9 x x, ♡ K x, ◇ A J x, ♣ x x x count up to thirteen points for the dealer whether you use Culbertson's or Goren's point count. Yet the second hand is definitely stronger and is a compulsory opening bid. Similarly, ♠ A x x x x, ♡ K x x x, ◇ A x x, ♣ x, is better than ♠ A x x x x, ♡ K x x x, ◇ A x, ♣ x x. The difference is slight so far as opener is concerned. But suppose responder holds ♠ A x x x, ♡ x x, ◇ x x x x, ♣ x x x. He would have a very doubtful response to an opening bid of one heart, but he would have a much more reasonable bid with one more spade and one less diamond. Yet, if you apply either Culbertson's or Goren's point count automatically you get the same result, five points.

In general, a singleton or doubleton in partner's suit is a negative factor since it increases the probability of a misfit. You do not worry much about it on your first bid, but if partner re-bids his suit, it pays to become conservative. Or suppose you have a long suit. If partner raises or bids, or re-bids no-trump, your length is usually worth slightly more points than you assign to it. But if he continues to bid other suits, your length is worth nothing at all. In fact, it probably means that you are short in partner's suits and it is actually a disadvantage.

Of course evaluation factors can only be applied after you have made a rough determination of points based upon high cards and hand pattern. There is no problem in counting points for high cards. Just count four, three, two, and one for the ace, king, queen, and jack, respectively. At no-trump, you may count two tens as a point. The difficulty is in assigning the proper number of points to distribution. Despite the fact that points are a sort of combination of high cards and playing tricks when so used, you start out by counting high cards mostly, and revalue so as to count more for playing tricks on the later rounds, at least after partner has raised. Almost every bidding sequence calls for a slightly different evaluation, but Culbertson and Goren have found it practical to use just three different counts. The first is when you bid the first time (unless you raise partner or contemplate a later raise). The second count is for re-bidding after a raise. The third count covers the exception to the first. When you plan to raise partner either immediately or later, use the support count which is based largely upon ruffing values.

For the first count, Culbertson and Goren get exactly the same answer by different methods. Goren counts short suits; Culbertson counts long suits. I prefer the Culbertson method because it seems more natural and because it lends itself better to adjustments and revaluation. In addition to your high card points, add one point for every card over four in your "long suit" and for every card over three in the others. If you have two four-card suits, or two five-card suits, you may call either your long suit. For example: ♠ A x x x x, ♡ A x x x, ◇ K x, ♣ x x. Count one point for the fifth spade, one for the fourth heart, and you get two points for distribution, eleven for high cards. Goren gets the same answer by counting a point for each doubleton. One advantage in using the Culbertson method is that if you do not want to count the four-card side suit for any reason (perhaps because you are going to support a no-trump contract), you do not have to use a completely different system. Also, it seems weird to count up points for a void or singleton in partner's suit, although it may be necessary to do this in order to reflect the true value of your long suit in Goren's method. Take ♠ K x x x, ♡ A x x x, ◇ x x, ♣ A Q x. Even though you open the bidding with one club, you must still count hearts or spades as your long suit, giving you no points for distribution in your "long" suit and one point for the four-card "side" suit. After you use this count a short time, you will memorize the number of points to be awarded for all the common distributions.

After partner has raised your suit, you should revalue your hand. Your long cards are worth a trick (three points) each instead of one point each. Therefore add two points for each card over *five*. Why start with five? It is a complicated story, and don't worry if you miss the point. However, the explanation is as follows:

If you were to award the full trick-taking value to distribution in both hands, the same 26 points would be required for nine tricks, whether in no-trump, spades, or diamonds! Horrors, what a mess this would be! The authorities agree that 29 points are required for game in a minor suit—presumably the same 29 points to make eleven tricks in a major—but only 26 points for nine tricks at no-trump or ten in a suit. What is the catch? Either not enough points are awarded to distributional values, or 26 points are not enough for ten tricks. The answer is that not enough points are assigned to distributional values to reflect the increased trick-taking ability.

Whatever the logic may be, the main idea is to make the re-bids and responses mesh so that you arrive at the right contract. My suggestion is therefore to count two additional points each for the sixth and seventh cards of your suit, but to forget the fifth. Also, add one point for a singleton or two points for a void provided you have at least five trumps. Let us see how this works. You open one spade and get a raise to two. ♠ A K x x x x, ♡ A J x, ◇ x x, ♣ x x. You had 14 points when you opened, but you have 16 points upon revaluation. Normally, 17 points are required for a re-bid, but this is a borderline hand, since the evaluation factors are favorable; your honors are all in combination, and you have two aces. Change the hand to ♠ A K x x x x, ♡ A J x, ◇ x x x, ♣ x, and you have a clear-cut three-spade bid. One point was added for the singleton club.

The third point count is in support of partner's suit. Culbertson's system is the simplest but, in my opinion, not very accurate, so we shall use Goren's for the most part. Count one point for each doubleton, three points for a singleton, and four for a void. Deduct a point for possession of only three trumps. Goren's promotion of certain honor combinations has the effect of evaluating his supporting hands one point higher than this for a majority of the time. I will admit that my failure to go along with him results in a rather conservative evaluation, but if you know that is the case, you can be rather liberal in applying positive evaluation factors. In support of partner's spade bid, a 5-4-2-2 or 4-5-2-2 distribution is worth two points, one for each doubleton. A 4-4-4-1 or 4-5-3-1 distribution is worth three points. A 3-5-4-1 distribution is worth two points, since a point must be subtracted for the three-card trump support, and a 3-4-4-2 distribution is supposedly worth no points, although a raise is usually preferable to a no-trump bid.

Following are a few examples to show how the three point counts work. Partner opens the bidding with one heart. You have ♠ K J x x x, ♡ x x x, ◇ x x x, ♣ x x, four points in high cards and one for the fifth spade, giving you five points for a spade response.

♠ K J x x, ♡ x x x, ◇ x x x x, ♣ x x: According to the rules, you have a total of five points again, this time by counting your four-card diamond length. However, common sense should tell you that it will be hard to utilize your four-card diamond suit when you have so weak a hand; this hand is no better than ♠ K J x x, ♡ x x x, ◇ x x x, ♣ x x x, and surely not as good as ♠ K J x x x, ♡ x x x, ◇ x x x, ♣ x x.

♠ K J x x, ♡ K J x, ◇ Q x x x, ♣ x x: This hand adds up to 11 points for a one-spade bid, but sooner or later you expect to support hearts. In support of hearts, this is only a ten-point hand. The proper bid is an immediate raise to two hearts since you are slightly too weak to bid one spade and raise hearts later. Change the hand to ♠ A Q x x, ♡ K J x, ◇ x x x x, ♣ x x, and your evaluation factors should persuade you to take the more aggressive action.

Partner opens the bidding with one no-trump and you hold ♠ x x, ♡ x x, ◇ K Q x x x, ♣ Q 10 x x. In support of a no-trump contract, you should count a five-card suit for one point, but you should disregard side-suit length, since you do not normally have time to use both suits. Besides, a four-card side suit means a short suit or weakness somewhere else; consequently, the weakness and strength just about cancel each other out. You would count the club length, of course, in determining the value of your hand at a diamond contract.

Actually, only counting one point for long cards in support of a no-trump contract is an undervaluation in one respect. A long card is often worth a full trick or three points. However, when you count distribution to reach a certain total, you have fewer points in high cards, which means that the opponents will have more. The opponents' high cards help them to establish their long suits. If your strength is concentrated so that your tricks could be taken in a hurry, the suit length is really worth more than the values assigned to it. When your suit is not readily establishable and when your honors on the side are queens and jacks, one point for a long card is a liberal award. So one point is a compromise figure. A six-card suit is worth two or three points for no-trump, depending upon whether the suit is good or poor, and whether the strength is in aces and kings or in queens and jacks.

Experts do not have any serious disagreement on how to evaluate hands. In most cases the process is largely subconscious, and Goren, Schenken, and Culbertson would usually, in actual play, raise one spade to two spades with the same hands. The only disagreement is in reducing to a formula the considerations they take into account. The greatest actual differences in bidding today are in forcing bids and in what may be called style. Style will be discussed in detail in a later chapter, but now is a good time to decide what bids are forcing.

Culbertson recommends very few forcing bids, while Goren recommends a large number of forcing bids. In this respect, Goren's writing reflects the practice of a vast majority of the top American players. Both Culbertson and Goren have various inferential forces, but generally Culbertson requires an immediate jump or a subsequent jump in a new suit to force, while Goren plays any new suit bid or any jump (new suit or old) by responder as forcing. For example:

OPENER	RESPONDER
1 ♡	1 ♠
2 ♣	?

Culbertson says that three spades is a strong bid or "semi-force." Three hearts is merely a raise, since two hearts is a preference and no stronger than a pass. Two diamonds would not even be a strong bid and is less encouraging than two no-trump. Goren plays all three bids as forcing. Culbertson would argue that if you played three spades and three hearts as forcing, you would have the choice of overbidding or underbidding with many hands. What should responder do with ♠ A Q J x x x, ♡ x x, ◇ K x, ♣ J x x, or ♠ A J x x x x, ♡ K J x, ◇ x x, ♣ J 10 x? He is not strong enough to insist upon game; yet a two-spade or two-heart bid would not come close to describing his hand. Or if two diamonds were forcing, responder would have to pass with ♠ K Q x x x, ♡ x, ◇ Q J 9 x x, ♣ x x before getting into really serious trouble, since this could be a dangerous misfit. Besides, a forcing two-diamond bid has a constructive connotation responder cannot afford with this hand. Goren and an impressive array of experts would argue: Yes, with this particular hand we would like to be able to bid two diamonds as non-forcing or downright weak, but this does not look like a game hand, and in the long run we are willing to concede the part-score contracts with misfits in order to make the bidding easier with good hands. As for the first two hands, we must guess what to do— probably stretch and bid three spades or three hearts. If we wish to reach game on all close hands, we can find the *right* game contract better by treating all jumps by responder as forcing. The increased bidding accuracy with good hands makes up for a few lost part-scores. Suppose after

OPENER	RESPONDER
1 ♡	1 ♠
2 ♣	?

responder held ♠ A J x x x, ♡ K J x, ◇ A x, ♣ J 10 x, or ♠ A K x x x x, ♡ Q x, ◇ x, ♣ K Q x x. With the first hand he is strong enough to insist upon game somewhere, but is the proper spot three no-trump, four hearts, or four spades? A jump to three diamonds would paint a distorted picture of responder's hand. Unless there is some other forcing bid, responder must just guess what to do. In the second example the forcing three-spade bid will invite a raise to four spades, with a doubleton spade. With a singleton, opener will re-bid three no-trump and responder can now bid five clubs. Six clubs might be cold on a hand where opener would pass three spades, if three spades were not forcing. At a total point game where a game is worth two or three part-score contracts, Goren's style may be best. In duplicate, I prefer playing all these bids as non-forcing. Bid four hearts with ♠ A J x x x, ♡ K J x, ◇ A x, ♣ J 10 x, since four hearts is probably the best spot even if partner only has a four-card suit. On the second hand, any bid might turn out right, although my choice is a raise to four clubs, which I consider as forcing. Even at duplicate, I cannot go all the way with Culbertson. If

OPENER	RESPONDER		OPENER	RESPONDER
1 ♡	1 ♠	and	1 ♡	2 ♣
2 ♡	3 ♣		2 ♡	2 ♠

are not forcing sequences, responder is left with impossible problems. Over a two-heart re-bid, what should he bid with ♠ A K x x x, ♡ J x, ◇ J x, ♣ A Q x x, or ♠ K J x x x, ♡ K x, ◇ x x x, ♣ A K x if three clubs is not forcing? Surely "general strength" bids such as four hearts or three no-trump leave something to be desired. Even if three no-trump, for example, happens to be the right spot, it should be played by opener, not responder.

OPENER	RESPONDER
1 ◇	2 ♣
2 ◇	?

If two spades is not forcing, what can responder bid, holding ♠ K Q x x, ♡ x, ◇ J x, ♣ A K Q x x x, or ♠ A K x, ♡ x, ◇ Q x x, ♣ A 10 9 x x x? With the last hand he wants to bid two clubs, two spades, and three diamonds (the latter bid being inferentially forcing) to suggest a minor-suit contract, while allowing partner to play three no-trump with a double stopper in hearts. Whether you agree to play a certain bid forcing or non-forcing, you will get hands that will make you wish you had decided the other way. Nevertheless, it is necessary to adopt some definite rules. I have always been annoyed with the kind of doubletalk where "such and such a bid is not forcing, but partner will not pass." So I suggest the following general rules:

A new suit by responder (who has not previously passed) is forcing on the first round and forcing on subsequent rounds *unless opener could show a preference for the first suit at the two-level*. In other words,

OPENER	RESPONDER
1 ◇	1 ♠
2 ◇	2 ♡

is *not* forcing, but if partner had responded one heart followed by two spades, the latter bid would be forcing. A new suit by either player at the three-level is forcing. Second-round jump bids by responder in a previously bid suit or no-trump are not forcing—with exceptions.

Remember that these are only general rules. Let us look at

a few bidding sequences, and then we shall state our rules in more detail:

OPENER	RESPONDER
1 ◇	1 ♡
2 ♠	3 ♠

The two-spade bid was a force to game. Consequently, three spades is forcing, simply because game has not been reached. Some players have the peculiar idea that if the two-spade bid was a stretch and responder can only raise to three, opener may pass. Playing three spades non-forcing defeats the primary purpose of a game-forcing bid, which is to give up one round of bidding early in order to make subsequent bidding easier. If responder has a hand good enough to raise from two spades to five spades, he should be able to bid just three spades so that more information may be exchanged.

OPENER	RESPONDER
1 ♡	2 ♡
3 ◇	

According to our general rule, a new suit at the three-level is forcing. Furthermore, three diamonds *should* be forcing. Opener would pass two hearts unless he were interested in reaching game. Since responder may have no diamond support, opener must be prepared to play three hearts even when responder has a minimum hand and three-card heart support. Since opener is willing to push the bidding to the three-heart level, even when responder has no fit for diamonds, opener should be equally willing to reach three hearts when responder has a diamond fit (♠ x x, ♡ Q x x, ◇ K x x x, ♣ J x x x). Let's look at this problem from opener's point of view.

♠ A x x, ♡ A K J x, ◇ A Q J x, ♣ 10 x: After a raise to two hearts, he cannot settle for less than game. Yet three no-trump is likely to be the best spot, played preferably by responder, who may have the king of clubs or queen of spades. If opener risks being dropped in a three-diamond bid, he must guess whether to bid three no-trump or four hearts and would probably choose four hearts.

OPENER	RESPONDER
1 ♡	2 ♡
3 ◇	3 ♡
3 ♠	3 NT

is a far more logical sequence when responder has ♠ x x, ♡ Q x x, ◇ K x x x, ♣ J x x x. The three-spade bid would not show a biddable suit, of course, since biddable hearts, diamonds and spades are not shown in that order.

SOUTH	WEST	NORTH	EAST
1 ♡	Pass	2 ♡	Pass
Pass	Double	Pass	2 ♠
3 ◇			

This time three diamonds is not forcing. Opener (South), by passing two hearts, showed that he was not interested in reaching game. True, he forces the bidding to the three-heart level if responder has no diamond fit, but he does not do so willingly, and he does not guarantee that three hearts will be safe. He only bids again because he has been pushed. Since the opener is not interested in reaching game, the only purpose in bidding three diamonds is to suggest this bid as a final contract if responder's heart support is weak. Responder should pass even with *three* diamonds and three hearts, since opener is very likely to have four hearts and five diamonds. With a 4-4-3-2 distribution, he would tend to pass, since he was too weak to re-bid on the second round.

OPENER	RESPONDER
1 ♣	1 ♡
1 ♠	2 ♡
2 NT	3 ◇

According to the general rule, three diamonds is forcing, since it is a new suit at the three level. But common sense tells us that the general rule should not apply. The two-heart bid, while not a complete sign-off, was not a strong bid. With nine or ten points, responder would cheerfully bid three no-trump or four hearts upon being given another chance. The three-diamond bid must show a hand that is too weak to pass! As another general rule, when partner takes a two no-trump bid out to a minor suit at duplicate, it is a warning rather than a constructive bid. Responder may have ♠ K, ♡ Q J x x x x, ◇ 9 8 x x x, ♣ x, or even weaker. Opener will take a preference for three hearts if he can, but should avoid bidding more no-trump. ♠ A J x x, ♡ x, ◇ A Q x, ♣ A J 10 x x would be an obvious pass.

Should the following sequence be forcing?

OPENER	RESPONDER
1 ♠	2 ♡
3 ♣	

This is a difficult question, but most players treat the three-club bid as forcing. Otherwise, they would have to pass the three no-trump level to show a good hand. Once responder bids at the two-level and opener shows extra values, the occasions where you could profitably stop on the dime (at three clubs) and know what you were doing are very rare. By making three clubs absolutely forcing, opener can coax a spade preference or heart re-bid, or get responder to bid three no-trump with diamonds stopped. In other words, a forcing re-bid at the three level is a very useful bid, and the alternative, a jump to four clubs or four diamonds, would crowd the bidding too much. Incidentally, a preference bid of three spades over three clubs guarantees better than a worthless doubleton and is inferentially forcing. If responder has a real "rag," he must re-bid his suit rather than give a preference.

Neither Culbertson nor Goren states a different rule for forcing sequences, depending upon whether the response was at the one-level or two-level—although Goren makes an exception to the new-suit-forcing principle after a no-trump re-bid. Perhaps they feel that the average player would be confused by the distinction and that it is better to state a rule that everyone can remember.

OPENER	RESPONDER
1 ◇	1 ♠
2 ♡	?

Opener has reversed, showing a very strong hand. Usually, responder will bid again, but occasionally he will pass.

OPENER	RESPONDER
1 ◇	2 ♣
2 ♡	

I cannot imagine a hand with which responder would even be tempted to pass. If his two-club bid was based upon six or seven clubs to the K Q J and nothing else, he can at least re-bid his clubs.

OPENER	RESPONDER
1 ♡	1 ♠
2 ◇	?

♠ A K J x x, ♡ Q x x, ◇ J x x, ♣ x x: You would like to be able to bid three hearts as non-forcing. Even if you play three hearts as forcing, you must bid it, since three hearts would be less of an overbid than two hearts would be an underbid.

OPENER	RESPONDER
1 ♡	2 ♣
2 ◇	?

♠ x x, ♡ Q x x, ◇ J x x, ♣ A K J x x: This time most experts would choose a two-heart bid, since the two-club response has already suggested a fair hand. If

OPENER	RESPONDER
1 ♡	2 ♣
2 ◇	2 ♡

is roughly equivalent to

OPENER	RESPONDER
1 ♡	1 ♠
2 ◇	3 ♡

why not save

OPENER	RESPONDER
1 ♡	2 ♣
2 ◇	3 ♡

as a force? That is my suggestion. A jump preference is forcing after a two-level response. And a jump all the way to four hearts is a mild slam suggestion.

No one has attempted to state all the bids that should be forcing, and you could not remember the list if one were made. Many bids are logically or inferentially forcing because one or both partners have shown enough strength so that a good play for game is certain.

OPENER	RESPONDER
1 ♡	2 ◇
2 NT	3 ♡

The three-heart bid is absolutely forcing. With a weak hand and heart support, responder would raise hearts immediately. Therefore, responder must have at least 11 points in support of hearts. Opener has shown a better-than-minimum hand by re-bidding two no-trump, at least 15 points and probably more. Consequently, the hands add up to game. Responder may be giving opener the choice between three no-trump and four hearts, or he may intend to follow up his three-heart bid with a slam try.

OPENER	RESPONDER	or	OPENER	RESPONDER
1 ◇	1 ♠		1 ◇	1 ♠
2 NT	3 ♠		3 ◇	3 ♠

In both cases opener's re-bid was strong but not forcing. However, any bid by responder is considered an acceptance of the invitation to game, and the bidding must continue. This is the orthodox view shared by Culbertson, Goren, and most good players. Occasionally you would like to play three spades, but not often enough to reserve three spades as a sign-off. A three-spade bid gives partner a choice between three no-trump and four spades, and you may even follow up the three-spade bid with a slam try after showing that you have a long suit.

According to my experience, one exception should be made to this acceptance-of-the-invitation rule. A return to a previously-bid minor after a one-level response should be a sign-off, since you seldom want to play five of a minor at duplicate, and when you are interested in a slam you can jump to four clubs or four diamonds.

OPENER	RESPONDER
1 ◇	1 ♠
2 ◇	2 ♡
2 NT	3 ◇

Responder has made a non-forcing two-heart bid. The three-diamond bid completes the picture, denoting relative weakness or unsuitability for play at no-trump. Of course, he cannot be too weak or he could not risk a bid over two diamonds in search of a major-suit fit. Typical hands would be ♠ A 10 x x x, ♡ K J x x x, ◇ Q x, ♣ x, or ♠ K J 10 x, ♡ K Q x x x, ◇ Q x x, ♣ x. With the latter hand, responder had to bid spades on the first round in order to avoid a reverse (since he wanted to show both suits).

OPENER	RESPONDER
1 ◇	2 ♣
2 ◇	2 ♠
2 NT	3 ◇

This time the three-diamond bid is forcing. After two *forcing* bids, responder has shown so much strength that he cannot want to give opener the option of passing. If responder wanted merely to *invite* another bid, he would have to bid either clubs or spades (*but not both*) and raise to three diamonds on the second round.

OPENER	RESPONDER
1 ◇	1 ♠
2 ♣	2 NT
3 ♠	

The three-spade bid is forcing. With a minimum hand, opener would raise to two spades immediately. Logically, three spades must be forcing. Opener shows only a three-card spade support by his failure to raise or force immediately. If responder has a weak four-card suit, he has to bid again because he cannot "stand" a three-spade contract. He can "stand" a two-level contract with a poor trump suit and a poor hand, since there may be no better spot, but with a good hand (combined total of 24 points or more), he cannot afford to risk a minus score by choosing the wrong contract. The delayed raise to three spades gives responder the choice between no-trump and four spades. A typical hand for the opener is ♠ Q x x, ♡ x, ◇ A K x x x, ♣ K Q J x. Just as a take-out of two no-trump into a minor-suit is a warning or sign-off, a major-suit bid over two no-trump is generally constructive and forcing.

OPENER	RESPONDER	OPENER	RESPONDER	OPENER	RESPONDER
1 ♡	1 ♠	1 ♠	2 ◇	1 ◇	1 ♠
2 ◇	4 ◇	4 ◇		2 NT	4 ◇

In all the above sequences, the four-diamond bid is forcing. In the first two cases, three diamonds would be a strong bid and an urge to game. Consequently, the jump past the three no-trump level is forcing. You may argue that it should not show such a terrific hand to pass the three no-trump level; perhaps the hand is so distributional that the four-diamond bidder could not safely pass a three no-trump bid. Nevertheless, when you wish to give partner the option of passing, you must just raise to three. If he bids three no-trump and you cannot "stand" it, you may *then* bid four diamonds or five diamonds. The forcing raise to four makes slam bidding easier than would a raise to five, and it leaves four no-trump as a resting spot if the slam invitation is refused.

As I stated before, you cannot be expected to remember every forcing sequence, but you should try to understand *why* certain bids are inferentially forcing. Let's look at some bids which are not forcing to see why they are not.

SOUTH	WEST	NORTH	EAST
1 ◇	Double	Pass	2 ♠ or 3 ♠

A jump response to a take-out double is not forcing because there is a better forcing bid at your disposal. If you wish to insist upon game, you must cue-bid the opponents' suit. Even a cue bid of the opponents' suit by the "defending" side (the side which does not open the bidding) may not be a game-force if it is followed up by a raise of partner's suit.

SOUTH	WEST	NORTH	EAST
1 ◇	Double	Pass	2 ◇
Pass	2 ♠	Pass	3 ♠

allows the take-out doubler to pass with a minimum. Similarly,

SOUTH	WEST	NORTH	EAST
1 ◇	2 ◇	Pass	2 ♠
Pass	3 ♠		

The raise to three spades is not forcing, but in either of these sequences, the bid of a new suit would be forcing. The cue bid is forcing to game or until the cue-bidder limits his hand by raising his partner's suit.

SOUTH	WEST	NORTH	EAST
1 ◊	Double	Pass	1 ♠ or 2 ♣
Pass	3 ♡		

The three-heart bid is a very strong urge but not quite forcing. The take-out doubler has limited his hand by failing to bid two diamonds at his first opportunity.

OPENER	RESPONDER
Pass	1 ♠
2 NT	3 ♠

The bridge authorities whose systems are based upon rubber bridge say that three spades is forcing. The opener must pass the two no-trump response unless he is interested in reaching game. However, at duplicate, if opener makes a third- or fourth-hand bid with ♠ K J 9 x x x, ♡ A x x x, ◊ Q x, ♣ x, he can hardly afford to let his partner play two no-trump at duplicate merely because he is too weak for game. So a re-bid of the opener's suit should be another sign-off bid.

Culbertson treats all bids by a passed hand as non-forcing. Goren states that a jump response in a new suit is forcing. Again, I prefer Culbertson's view for duplicate. When responder jumps in a major suit, opener should bid again even with a bare opening bid and neutral support for partner's suit. Responder may have passed an excellent playing hand with not quite enough high cards to open. But opener should pass a two-spade response with ♠ x x, ♡ x x x, ◊ K Q J x x, ♣ K x x (I am sure Goren would agree), or even ♠ x x, ♡ Q x x, ◊ K Q J x x, ♣ K Q x. The latter aceless hand is very likely to be a disappointment to partner if he is distributional. The jump response in a minor suit can be used to show either of two hand types provided you decide in advance. Goren would bid three diamonds over a one-spade bid with ♠ A x x x, ♡ x, ◊ A J 10 x x x, ♣ x x. As so played, the three-diamond bid must be absolutely forcing, and it is more descriptive than a direct raise to four spades. The alternative is to use the jump in a minor to show six tricks, which invites opener to bid three no-trump with three top tricks. A typical holding would be a six-card minor to the ace-king-queen.

Following is a summary of forcing bids:

(1) A jump in a new suit by the opening side is forcing to game. An immediate double raise of a major suit or a two no-trump response is also forcing to game unless responder has previously passed. Thereafter, it is not necessary to jump again, since all bids below game are forcing. If the opponents bid, you may make a forcing pass.

(2) A new suit by responder (who has not previously passed) is forcing—except when opener can show a preference for the first suit at the two-level.

(3) A new suit by opener or responder at the three-level is forcing, unless it is preceded by a limit bid or sign-off.

(4) After two forcing bids, a third bid below the level of game is usually inferentially forcing.

(5) A bid is inferentially forcing when both partners have indicated enough strength so that the combined total will be enough for game.

(6) A jump preference or reverse is forcing after a two-level response.

(7) A jump raise or jump preference to the four-level in a minor suit is forcing.

(8) A raise or re-bid of a major suit at the three-level over two no-trump is forcing. Two typical exceptions:

OPENER	RESPONDER	OPENER	RESPONDER
Pass	1 ♠	1 ♠	1 NT
2 NT	3 ♠	2 ♠	2 NT
		3 ♠ or 3 ♡	

(9) A raise or re-bid of a minor suit over two no-trump is weak and not forcing, unless it is preceded by a strong bid.

(10) A jump in a new suit is forcing whether made by the opening or defending side, provided the jumper's partner has made a voluntary bid, with few exceptions.
Examples:

SOUTH	WEST	NORTH	EAST
1 ♡	1 ♠	Pass	Pass
3 ◇			

The three-diamond bid is not forcing because responder has not bid.

SOUTH	WEST	NORTH	EAST
1 ♡	Double	Pass	2 ♣
Pass	3 ♠		

The three-spade bid is not forcing since the two-club bid was not voluntary.

SOUTH	WEST	NORTH	EAST
1 ♠	1 NT	Pass	3 ◇

or

1 ♡	Double	Pass	3 ◇

Neither three-diamond bid is forcing because of special rules which apply to defensive bidding.

(11) A pass is forcing whenever your side has a balance of strength and the opponents are obviously attempting a sacrifice.

Chapter 2

Problems of the Opening Bidder

THE DISAGREEMENT among the experts as to what constitutes a minimum opening bid is partially real and partially illusory. For example, no bridge player worth his salt would open the bidding in first or second position with the following hand: ♠ Q J x, ♡ K x, ◇ Q J x x x, ♣ Q J x. The decision is not even close, but each explains it differently. One expert deducts a point because the hand is aceless. Another refuses to open because he doesn't have two "quick tricks." A third says this hand falls within his "optional bid" classification, but since there are several bad features, he passes. A fourth expert says that he requires 14 points to open. While the four experts use different yardsticks, the result is the same. The last expert, the one who says he needs 14 points to open, would open many 13-point hands such as ♠ x x, ♡ A K J 10 x, ◇ A x x, ♣ x x x. In other words, whatever they may *say*, the difference in actual practice between the various bridge authorities is not as great as it seems.

Now let us consider the real differences. Al Roth and Tobias Stone recommend "heavy" opening bids with a 14-point minimum. It is obvious from their examples of minimum and optional opening bids that they really do require considerably more strength to open than Culbertson or Goren. If Roth and Stone were the only prominent players to suggest heavy openings, you might believe that this was just a peculiarity of the Roth-Stone system, adopted to increase the spread between a normal opening and a psychic opening, so that responder could "catch the psych" more easily.

However, support for the heavy opening bids comes from orthodox quarters. John Crawford recommends a 14-point minimum, and Edgar Kaplan advocates the weak no-trump even when vulnerable so that an opening suit bid will suggest better than a minimum (old-fashioned minimum) hand. When players of their ability and reputation recommend heavy openings, you can be certain that they have many followers. The trend seems to be toward "sounder" opening bids, followed by more forcing sequences later in the bidding. (Again note Roth-Stone.) If all jump bids or new suit bids by responder on any round are to be treated as forcing, perhaps the opening requirements should be raised. However, I believe the whole trend is wrong, and I am not alone in this belief. Many of the best players still favor light opening bids.

Instead of counting noses and comparing reputations, let us look at the problem of setting the opening requirements as though it were a new proposition. First, let us assume that 26 points guarantee a good play for game; anything less is inadequate. Never mind how we count points or find the fit. And for the present, assume that we are discussing rubber bridge. Since a game contract is worth about three part-score contracts, our primary objective must be to reach sound game contracts.

We cannot expect to reach the best contract every time, and we may pass out a few hands when our side has a slight superiority of strength. However, we cannot afford to set our opening-bid requirements so high that game hands will be passed out. Obviously *someone* has to open 13-point hands. If reaching game were the only objective, and if there were no practical difficulties, dealer and second position could require 14 points to open, while third and fourth position would open with 13. Thus dealer would pass with 13 points and jump to game or make an absolutely forcing bid if his partner could open.

A major objection to this style is that it involves trapping. When you pick up 13 points as dealer, either the deal is passed out or game is reached. The only way you could get to a part-score contract would be for the opponents to open the bidding for you. Then what? If your hand is balanced or your suit is weak, it is much more dangerous to enter the bidding at this point than it would have been to open, especially when *both* opponents have bid.

Suppose that you pass originally with the following hand, ♠ x x x, ♡ A K x x, ◇ A Q x, ♣ x x x. Fortunately, partner: rather than an opponent, opens the bidding with one spade. What do you do now? Bid two no-trump? Partner would not raise to three no-trump with ♠ A K Q x x, ♡ Q x x, ◇ x x, ♣ x x x, or ♠ A K Q x x, ♡ x x, ◇ K x x, ♣ x x x, because a jump to two no-trump in this position only purports to show 11 or 12 points. Should you jump all the way to three no-trump and punish partner for opening light? Or miss the heart fit if he has ♠ A Q x x x, ♡ Q J x x, ◇ K x x, ♣ x? The problem of what to do after failing to open with a good hand exists both at rubber bridge and duplicate, but trapping is more costly at duplicate.

Suppose you hold ♠ A K Q x x x x, ♡ x x, ◇ x x, ♣ x x. This is too strong a hand defensively and too weak offensively for a four-spade pre-empt regardless of vulnerability. In order to make ten tricks, partner must turn up with three *top* tricks. Queens and jacks will not help. If partner has something like ♠ x x, ♡ Q J x x, ◇ K Q x x, ♣ Q J x, for example, you would be down two at four spades, and the opponents could not make anything their way. Besides, three no-trump might easily be your best contract. How about an opening three-spade bid? A three bid, particularly in a major, would not guarantee seven solid tricks for no-trump, or even seven playing tricks, unless you were vulnerable. Another possibility is to pass originally and jump to four spades if partner should open the bidding. However, if the opponents have the balance of strength, they may push you too high if they are permitted to open and find their fit. Remember this point! We are often inclined to consider the problem of reaching the best spot by just looking at our own hand and partner's. The opponents are also permitted to bid, and there is a definite advantage in making the first bid. The best way to reach your proper contract, whatever it is, is to open the bidding with one spade.

Thus far, we have not considered how points were figured. When we do, we see additional reasons for light openings. Whenever responder has a good distributional fit for opener's suit, his hand, which contains nine or ten points in high cards and is worth 11 or 12 points as an original bidder, may be worth a

full 13 points in support of opener's hand. If dealer opens his
13-point hand, game is reached. If dealer passes, the deal is
passed out. South: ♠ x x x, ♡ A K x x x, ◇ A x x, ♣ x x;
North: ♠ A x x x, ♡ Q x x x, ◇ x, ♣ A x x x: If South opens,
North will insist upon game; his best response is three hearts.
Some players might open North's hand in third or fourth position, but not I! Incidentally, opener only has 12 points unless the
evaluation factors are considered.

Another example: South: ♠ x, ♡ A Q x x x x, ◇ A x x,
♣ x x x; North: ♠ x x x, ♡ K x x x, ◇ K J x x, ♣ K x. The
bidding was

SOUTH	NORTH
1 ♡	2 ◇
2 ♡	3 ♡
4 ♡	

Opener starts with 12 points, but is able to revalue his hand to
15 points after the raise. Notice something else. The opponents
can probably make about three spades, possibly more, depending
upon their distribution. Apparently East had the stronger of the
two opponents' hands, but he could not afford to experiment at
the two-level after both opponents had bid. Suppose that West
had held the good hand. Over one heart he would double or overcall one spade. In that event, it is difficult to say how the bidding
would have continued. The opponents might have sold out for
four hearts, and if they had bid four spades confidently enough,
you might have sacrificed at five hearts. In any event, you would
not have been stolen blind. Had you passed originally, allowing
West to open and East to raise, it would have been too risky for
you to compete at the three-level, and the opponents would have
bought the bid for some number of spades.

The advantages of light openings are so obvious that you may
wonder why we should not reduce the requirements further still,
to 10 or 11 points. The first limiting factor is safety. Not only
must you be able to make one bid without undue risk of penalty.
You must be prepared to re-bid over an exploratory response
without getting into trouble when responder has a minimum.
Everyone agrees that opener must prepare one re-bid. Those who

recommend a large number of forcing bids are the same ones who recommend "sound" openings.

If opener is obligated to bid three or four times in many sequences when he does not want to, he needs more strength than when he is allowed to pass at his first reasonable opportunity. Two examples should make this point clear.

SOUTH	NORTH
1 ♡	1 ♠
2 ♡	3 ♠
?	

What should you bid with ♠ x, ♡ A Q x x x x, ◇ A x x, ♣ x x x? In my opinion, you should pass, but if you play all jump bids by responder as forcing, you would like to have another queen or jack in order to make your re-bid more comfortable.

SOUTH	NORTH
1 ♣	1 ♠
2 ♣	2 ♡
?	

With ♠ A x, ♡ x x x, ◇ x x x, ♣ A K 10 9 x, you would like to pass, and I believe that you should be able to do so.

It pays, in the long run, to open with 2½ honor count and a six-card major or three honor count and a re-biddable suit. Yet, if you are forced to continue bidding round after round, even in the face of a misfit, you need additional strength. You may argue that responder has a good enough hand to take care of the situation or he would not force. As a practical matter, that is not true. There are only so many bids at one's disposal. If responder has the choice between two bids, one of which is very weak or misleading, and the other is forcing, he will make the forcing bid—not because he wants to, but because it is the lesser of two evils. Or with a mediocre two-suited hand, he has the choice of showing his second suit (which is forcing) or passing. We have the ironical situation where opener would like to pass, but responder, who would also like to permit opener to pass, has forced opener to re-bid!

Safety is not the only factor in deciding upon the minimum requirements for an opening bid. Flexibility is also important. The opener should guarantee a certain amount of general strength which will be of value whoever buys the bid. The more leeway opener has to bid on playing tricks alone, the less leeway responder has in a competitive situation. Remember the statement that it is a definite advantage to make the first bid? The reason for this is that responder can double the opponents or bid a new suit freely, knowing that the opening bid guarantees general strength while the partner of the overcaller is pretty much in the dark.

At the beginning of this discussion, it was stated that we were considering rubber bridge. At rubber bridge, opening bids are keyed to reaching game. At duplicate, part-score hands are just as important as game hands. However, most authorities agree that the opening bid in first or second position should be about the same in duplicate as in rubber bridge. The advantages of light opening bids in duplicate are obvious. You have to enter the bidding at duplicate even when game is remote and the risk is relatively great, and the safest time to do so is right away. On the other hand, there is still the risk of getting too high, and you still need enough general strength so that reasonable aggressiveness on the part of responder will not get you into trouble.

Another reason why the requirements are about the same is laziness. Most bridge players and bridge authorities play both rubber bridge and duplicate. In competitive situations, certain differences of bidding philosophy are necessary because of the difference in scoring, but it is too much trouble to change the whole bidding structure. If the requirements for opening the bidding are changed, the requirements for responses and re-bids must be changed too. The tendency, therefore, is to develop a style of bidding that works well for duplicate or rubber bridge, whichever one plays more, and make as few changes as possible in going from one game to the other.

My recommendation is to open 13-point hands unless you have a good reason not to, and to open certain types of 12-point hands. For each hand type, you should consider how best to describe your hand—whether by an original bid and anticipated re-bid or by subsequent bidding after an original pass.

Consider first the balanced 4-3-3-3 hand with 13 points in high cards. If your hand is aceless, particularly when it contains a preponderance of queens and jacks, you may pass. This is just an application of evaluation factors. ♠ Q J x, ♡ K J x, ◊ Q J x, ♣ Q J x x is not as good as ♠ K x x, ♡ A x x, ◊ x x x, ♣ A Q x x. However, as a general rule, open whenever you have 13 points in high cards. When your hand is balanced, the other hands are likely to be balanced also—which means that no one else will open with less than 12 or 13 points in high cards. When you hold 13 points, the other players hold an average of nine points, making a passed-out deal a strong probability. You should not want the deal to be passed out when you have a decided preponderance of strength. Occasionally you should pass because of an anticipated re-bid problem. For example, with ♠ A Q x, ♡ A Q x, ◊ J x x x, ♣ x x x, a one-diamond bid is undesirable since diamonds are so weak, and a two-club response would force you to overbid considerably. A two no-trump re-bid shows at least 15 points (16 according to Goren). But change the jack of diamonds to the queen, and you should certainly open. Partner may not bid two clubs, and even if he should, it would be less misleading to open and re-bid two no-trump than not to bid at all. Even an opening one-club bid on three small is better than a pass with 14 points.

What would you bid with ♠ A K x x, ♡ x x x, ◊ A Q x, ♣ x x x? If you open the bidding with one spade, you will be forced to raise a two-heart or two-diamond response or to re-bid two diamonds over two clubs. Is that so bad? In the first place, partner may not bid, or he may raise spades or bid no-trump, all of which will cause you no problems. Even if you have to overbid slightly or re-bid a three-card suit, no harm may result. Almost anything you do is better than to pass with 3½ top tricks. Could partner visualize game with ♠ x x, ♡ x x x, ◊ K x x x x x, ♣ A x opposite a passed hand? Similarly, it is better to open and re-bid your suit, if necessary, than it is to pass with the following hands: ♠ x x x, ♡ A K Q x, ◊ A x x, ♣ x x x; ♠ A K J x, ♡ K Q x, ◊ x x x, ♣ x x x.

Normally, you should open with 5-3-3-2 distribution and 12 points in high cards. The fifth card is worth a full point, and, if necessary, the five-card suit may be re-bid. While the suit length is worth a point or more offensively, it does not increase your defensive strength. If your strength is largely in minor honors, a pass is recommended (♠ J x, ♡ K J x, ◇ A x x x x, ♣ Q J x).

A 4-4-3-2 distribution deserves special consideration. While this distribution is supposed to be worth one point (for the four-card "side suit"), this point is of dubious value when partner or the opponents buy the bid. It is also of dubious value at no-trump. I suggest this rule: When the strength of the hand is concentrated in two suits with no wasted values, count one point for the 4-4-3-2 distribution. When the strength is scattered throughout the hand, disregard this point. With ♠ K Q x x, ♡ x x, ◇ x x x, ♣ A K x x you should open one club and re-bid one spade. At either clubs or spades, your hand is worth 13 points. ♠ K x x x, ♡ A x x, ◇ x x, ♣ K Q x x is a borderline hand. Change two small spades to the ten-nine, and it is a good opening bid. With ♠ K x x, ♡ Q x x x, ◇ A x, ♣ K 10 x x you should pass. Unless partner has a heart suit, your hand will be a disappointment to him. At no-trump or spades, for example, it is worth only 12 points. The sequence

OPENER	RESPONDER
1 ♣	1 ♠
1 NT	

should show 13 points *for no-trump*, just as a raise should show at least 13 support points for partner's suit.

Whenever you count as much as two points for distribution (6-3-2-2, 5-4-3-1, etc.) it becomes increasingly important whether or not your strength is top-card strength. ♠ Q J x, ♡ K Q x, ◇ x, ♣ K x x x x x (13 points) is not worth a bid, while ♠ A Q x x x x, ♡ A x x, ◇ x x, ♣ x x (12 points) is a sound opening bid. Make the distribution in the minors 3-1 instead of 2-2 with the latter hand, and a pass would be very bad. Change the long suit to a minor, and the hand is close, but I still prefer an opening bid. Give partner as little as three kings and an ace with a balanced hand, and you are cold for three or four no-trump, but these hands are hard to bid if you pass originally.

OPENER	RESPONDER
	Pass
1 ♠	?

♠ x x, ♡ A Q x x x x, ◇ A x x, ♣ x x. Should you bid three hearts and risk finding partner with a singleton or void in hearts? Or bid two hearts and hope partner will bid again with ♠ A 10 9 x x, ♡ K x, ◇ K x x, ♣ K x x? (He would not bid again, and you will miss a cold three no-trump). Incidentally, what would you do if he should re-bid two spades?

Another example: I saw two fine players bid as follows: South: ♠ A x, ♡ K x x x x x, ◇ A x x, ♣ x x; North: ♠ K Q x x, ♡ x, ◇ K Q x x x, ♣ Q 10 x.

SOUTH	NORTH
Pass	1 ◇
1 ♡	1 ♠
3 ♡	Pass

What a contract! The opponents led the unbid suit, clubs, cashing two tricks, and now declarer needed a 3-3 heart break with the ace on side, and he was not quite that lucky. Perhaps you do not like South's bidding after the original pass, but you have to admit he has a problem. How can he show such a good hand after passing? How can he jump without showing a stronger suit? If South opens the bidding, the bidding should go as follows:

SOUTH	NORTH		SOUTH	NORTH
1 ♡	2 ◇		1 ♡	2 ◇
2 ♡	2 NT	or	2 ♡	2 ♠
Pass			3 ◇	Pass

Even three no-trump is a better contract than three hearts. At least if you are lucky, you can expect to get a top.

You should open 12-point hands only when they contain a good suit, at least 2½ honor count in top strength, and no wasted values. Examples: ♠ x, ♡ A K 10 x x, ◇ K 10 x x, ♣ x x x; ♠ x x x, ♡ A 10 9 x x, ◇ A K x, ♣ x x; ♠ A x x x x x, ♡ A Q x, ◇ x x, ♣ x x; ♠ x x x, ♡ x x, ◇ A J x, ♣ A Q 10 9 x.

There is another type of hand that I believe you should open. It is the hand containing a long, solid suit. As stated a few pages back, the only way to get to three no-trump or a part-score contract in spades (and know what you are doing) is to open one

spade with ♠ A K Q x x x x, ♡ x x, ◇ x x, ♣ x x. You do not
have the general strength and flexibility partner expects, but you
are willing to mislead him because you do not think it will do
him any harm. If he trustingly doubles the opponents at a low
level, you take out to a minimum number of spades. It is slightly
more risky to open this type of hand when your long suit is a
minor, as you may have to pull out at an uncomfortably high
level. However, the risk is worth while with seven solid tricks because partner needs so little strength to make three no-trump.

Once you decide to bid, there is still the problem of what to
bid. In order to reach the proper decision, it is necessary to consider what your re-bid will be. With a minimum opening bid,
you must avoid making a strength-showing re-bid. Any re-bid
which takes you to the three-level, or forces partner to the three-
level if he returns you to your original suit, is a strength-showing
re-bid. But if partner's response is at a higher-than-normal level,
he needs added strength. All other re-bids show or may show a
minimum hand. For example:

OPENER	RESPONDER	OPENER	RESPONDER	OPENER	RESPONDER
1 ◇	1 ♡	1 ◇	1 ♡	1 ◇	1 ♡
1 ♠		1 NT		2 ♣	

OPENER	RESPONDER	OPENER	RESPONDER
1 ◇	1 ♡	1 ◇	1 ♡
2 ◇		2 ♡	

These are all minimum re-bids and may show as little as 13
points. If the re-bid is no-trump, opener should have 13 points
for no-trump; if the re-bid is a raise of partner's suit, opener
should have 13 support points. Examples of re-bids requiring
additional strength:

OPENER	RESPONDER	OPENER	RESPONDER	OPENER	RESPONDER
1 ◇	1 ♠	1 ◇	1 NT	1 ◇	2 ♣
2 ♡		2 ♠		2 ♠	

OPENER	RESPONDER	OPENER	RESPONDER	OPENER	RESPONDER
1 ◇	2 ♣	1 ◇	2 ♣	1 ♡	2 ◇
3 ♣		2 NT		3 ♣	

How much additional strength is required for these bids will be discussed in detail later. Suffice it to say that the weakest of the strong re-bids is a raise of partner's suit to the three-level. In a pinch, you may do this with as little as 14 points, although partner will assume at least 15. The two no-trump re-bid after a two-level response may be made with as little as 15 points. The other re-bids show so much additional strength that you should not consider them with a minimum hand, even on a least-of-evils basis. The re-bid of a higher-ranking suit (higher than the original bid) at the two-level, as in the first three sequences, is called a reverse.

What should you open with ♠ A Q x x, ♡ A K x x x, ◇ x x, ♣ x x? To me, the answer is clear-cut. Bid one spade, because if you bid one heart, you are not strong enough to re-bid two spades over partner's response, *and I think that you should show both suits.* Everyone agrees that you cannot reverse with this hand, but some players bid and re-bid hearts, figuring that spades would not be the spot unless responder can bid them. The argument against bidding one spade is as follows:

OPENER	RESPONDER
1 ♠	1 NT
?	

You must bid two hearts. It would be decidedly weird to pass one no-trump without showing the five-card suit and with no strength in the minors. However, if you bid two hearts and partner returns you to two spades with a tripleton (or even a doubleton), you won't like the contract—and surely you cannot bid any more in an effort to get out of spades. In other words, the disadvantage in bidding spades and hearts is that in some sequences you can hardly stand a preference for spades. But why be a pessimist? Failure to bid spades can also work out badly.

Give partner a mediocre hand (7-11 points) with four or five spades, and a minor-suit overcall will shut your side out of spades (and probably out of the bidding) unless you open one spade originally. If you open one spade, you can risk a two-heart re-bid even if your left-hand opponent overcalls a minor suit and partner passes, but if you open one heart, it is too dangerous to bid again in this sequence. The real point of this example is that in deciding when or what to open, you should consider not one bid, but two. What will you do now and what will you do next time? Either open one spade, with the intention of bidding both suits or open and re-bid hearts—unless subsequent bidding makes this action too dangerous.

What is your opening bid with the following hand? ♠ x, ♡ K Q 9 x, ◇ K x x, ♣ A x x x x: Make up your mind what you would bid over any non-jump response and decide which alternatives are most attractive. Remember that a one-level response is somewhat more probable than a two-level response, and that partner is most likely to bid your shortest suit. Suppose that you open one club. Over one diamond you would re-bid one heart. Obviously a one-heart response would be raised to two hearts. You would either pass or re-bid clubs over a one no-trump response and surely pass a two-club response. But a one-spade response, which is by far the most likely, would create difficulties. Two hearts, a reverse, is not to be considered. One no-trump should not be re-bid with a singleton. By the process of elimination you are forced to re-bid two clubs. If you open one heart, you can re-bid two clubs over a one-spade or one no-trump response, or you would raise a minor-suit response. You do not really want to open one heart and raise a diamond response any more than you want to bid and re-bid clubs over a spade response. However the heart opening bid is preferable, because a spade response or overcall is quite likely, and either bid might prevent you from showing your heart suit.

What would you open with ♠ A K x x, ♡ K x x, ◇ A x x x, ♣ x x? The proper opening bid is one spade. No response will create problems since you are quite willing to raise if partner bids two hearts. A diamond opening bid would be bad since a two-club response would leave you no adequate re-bid. Without changing the distribution, change the hand to ♠ A x x x, ♡ x x x, ◇ K Q J x, ♣ K x. Now one spade would be a very bad bid. The suit is too weak to open except as a last resort, and you don't want to raise a heart response. Aside from the fact that you are not strong enough for a heart raise, partner would never visualize you with a combined total of four points in the majors. The proper opening bid is one diamond. You hope partner will not respond two clubs, but if he does, a two-diamond re-bid is satisfactory. This two-diamond re-bid will permit you to stop under game (you would pass a two no-trump re-bid by responder), while a two no-trump re-bid by you would get you to game automatically if partner has even ten points. With ♠ A Q x x, ♡ K x x, ◇ A x x x, ♣ x x, you open one spade and raise a two-heart response (reluctantly), but with ♠ A Q x x, ♡ x x x, ◇ A x x x, ♣ K x x, bid one diamond and, if necessary, raise a two-club response. The weaker your hand, the more difficult it is to bid, while almost any opening bid will work out fairly well when you have 15 points or more in high cards.

♠ K Q x x, ♡ A J 9 x, ◇ K x, ♣ Q x x: The orthodox bid is one spade. The only embarrassing response would be one no-trump, since you would have to pass rather than gamble on finding a heart fit. Of course, passing the no-trump response risks *missing* a heart fit. Some players tend to open one club so as not to shut out a heart response, but this bid may work out badly in a number of ways. If the opponents buy the bid, you don't want a club lead. If the opponents compete, you don't want a club raise with three or four trumps. Furthermore, the opponents are much more likely to enter the bidding over one club than over one spade. While making it easier for partner to bid, you make it easier for the opponents, too. An opening club bid gives up too much for one possible advantage, finding partner with a heart suit and a weak hand.

The bid I prefer with the above hand is one heart. If you bid one heart, you must never bid spades except to raise partner if he bids them. Over a minor-suit response, bid two no-trump.

Suppose you hold ♠ K x x x, ♡ A Q x x, ◇ x x, ♣ A x x. Spades are too weak to bid. A two-diamond response would create an impossible re-bid after a one-heart opening, since you are too weak to re-bid two no-trump. So one club wins by elimination. Change the heart and spade suits, and one club is still the best bid because you can't, or don't want to, bid both majors.

♠ A K x x, ♡ A Q J x, ◇ K x, ♣ K x x: One club is the favored opening bid again, since an opening one-spade bid would shut out a heart response with five or six points in high cards and a singleton spade. Tend not to open a four-card major, especially spades, with more than 18 points. Also note that with a good hand, you have fewer problems than with a poor one. There is little wrong with a heart opening bid. If partner has a balanced hand without enough strength to respond to *any* bid, one heart will be a better contract than one club.

♠ x x x, ♡ K J x, ◇ K Q x x, ♣ A x x: There is a split of opinion on this type of hand. One club is the safe bid. No response can be embarrassing. If you open one diamond, you have no good re-bid over a two-club response. However, a majority of players would bid one diamond, which is a much more satisfactory bid, unless partner responds two clubs. Even then no calamity may take place. There is a strong chance of opposing bidding when you open a minimum hand. If you are only able to bid once, you are better at diamonds than clubs. If partner leads, you prefer a diamond lead; if he raises you with four trumps to a jack opposite K Q x x, you are all right, but J x x x opposite A x x is not a very satisfactory trump suit.

With a 13- or 14-point hand distributed 4-3-3-3, a club opening is always the *safe* bid. Since you may not have to bid again —perhaps will be unable to bid again—I prefer opening the four-card suit, provided it is fairly strong (K Q 10 x or better). If worse comes to worst, you can re-bid it. A majority of the time either the opponents or partner, by a raise or no-trump response, relieves you of the embarrassment of re-bidding, and you are glad you indicated where your strength lay.

To avoid overstating the strength of your hand and to avoid bidding weak major suits, it is sometimes necessary to bid a three-card minor. Usually this minor is clubs, since a one-diamond opening bid on a weak hand and three-card diamond suit can create a re-bid problem. It is proper to bid one diamond with ♠ A x x x, ♡ K x x x, ◇ A Q x, ♣ Q x, since, if partner bids two clubs, you are strong enough to re-bid two no-trump. With ♠ A x x x, ♡ K Q x x, ◇ K Q x, ♣ x x, you should not open one diamond because you are not strong enough to re-bid two no-trump. Some players might choose a one-spade bid despite the weak suit. I prefer a one-heart bid. The only annoying response is two clubs, and you can then re-bid two diamonds. The odds are better than 10 to 1 that someone will bid over two diamonds. Usually partner is strong enough for another bid; otherwise he would tend to respond one no-trump instead of bidding at the two-level.

♠ J x x x x, ♡ A x x, ◇ K x, ♣ A 10 x, or ♠ Q x x x x, ♡ x, ◇ A x x, ♣ A Q J x: The bid is one club, with the weak five-card spade suit treated like a four-card suit. Surely you don't want to bid and re-bid spades. Incidentally, with four spades and four clubs and 3-2 distribution in the red suits, always bid one club regardless of strength. The only excuse for violating this rule is that clubs are so weak that you choose not to bid them at all (♠ A K Q x, ♡ K x, ◇ K x x, ♣ J x x x). With three four-card suits, bid the suit under the singleton provided it is biddable.

Holding two five-card suits, you normally bid the higher ranking. With ♠ x x, ♡ K Q x x x, ◇ x, ♣ A Q x x x, it is better to bid hearts and risk having clubs shut out by a two-diamond bid than to bid clubs and risk having hearts shut out by a one-spade response. However, when your five-card suits are clubs and spades, you can open clubs without risk of being shut out of spades. A one no-trump response over one club is infrequent, and since it guarantees nine or ten points with a balanced hand, opener can afford to show his five-card spade suit, even with a minimum hand in high cards. The choice of opening bids depends both upon the general strength of the hand and the strength of the suits. ♠ J x x x x, ♡ A, ◇ x x, ♣ A K x x x: Bid one club. The spades are so weak that you only plan to bid them once. ♠ K Q x x x, ♡ A x, ◇ x, ♣ A Q x x x: Bid one club, followed by a spade bid and re-bid unless some startling development changes your plans. ♠ A Q J x x, ♡ K x, ◇ x, ♣ Q 10 x x x: Bid one spade, and if partner responds two hearts or two diamonds, forget the club suit, at least till next round.

With 6-5 distribution, it almost always pays to bid the longer suit first. The playing strength of a 6-5 hand opposite a fit justifies a reverse, if necessary, and it is important to show the long suit first, so that partner can make the best choice. Even here I make an exception when the suits are touching and the hand is an absolute minimum opening bid. Open one heart with ♠ x, ♡ A K x x x, ◇ K x x x x x, ♣ x so as to avoid reversing, but bid one diamond with ♠ x, ♡ A K x x x, ◇ K Q x x x x, ♣ x.

What would you bid with the following hand? ♠ K x, ♡ 10 x x, ◇ A Q J x x, ♣ A K x: You should bid one no-trump.

Admittedly, this is not a perfect no-trump hand, since most of the strength is concentrated in two suits. However, the alternatives are less satisfactory. Do you remember the advice to decide upon two bids before you make the first one? Suppose you were to open one diamond. What would you re-bid over a one-heart or one-spade response? There is no satisfactory re-bid. Two no-trump is a stretch. Besides, all the objections that apply to a one no-trump opening bid apply to a two no-trump re-bid in greater degree. The least of evils is a two-club re-bid. In rubber bridge, the diamond opening and club re-bid may be all right, but this method of bidding is very unsatisfactory for duplicate.

Suppose the best contract is a no-trump part-score. This is not a very wild supposition, since this looks like a no-trump type hand. How do you get to this no-trump part-score unless partner suppresses his major suit and responds one no-trump? Over

OPENER	RESPONDER
1 ◇	1 ♠
2 ♣	

if responder passes, you play two clubs. If he bids two no-trump, you will raise to three no-trump. If he re-bids two hearts, you will jump to three no-trump. Even if he shows a preference for diamonds or re-bids spades, you would re-bid diamonds or raise spades. In other words, by opening one diamond, you make it very difficult to reach a no-trump part-score. While waiting for the perfect no-trump hand, you throw away many excellent contracts. Suppose that you and partner have enough cards to reach three no-trump whatever approach you use. Wouldn't you rather reach three no-trump by bidding

OPENER	RESPONDER
1 NT	3 NT

or even

OPENER	RESPONDER
1 NT	2 ♣
2 NT	3 NT

than by bidding

OPENER	RESPONDER
1 ◇	1 ♠
2 ♣	2 ◇
3 ◇	3 NT

for example? Even the perfectionist, who does not want to reach three no-trump unless it is cold against double dummy defense, must consider the factor of overtricks.

What does opener plan to re-bid after opening one no-trump? This is one case where he does not need to plan ahead. Since he has described his hand pretty well in one bid, he only bids again when asked to do so by responder. The details will be discussed in the next chapter. The requirements for a no-trump opening bid are 4-3-3-3, 4-4-3-2, or 5-3-3-2 distribution with 17 or 18 points, or 16 good points with aces, tenaces, and/or left-over ten spots. Stayman's point requirements (17½ to 20 points, counting an additional half point for each ace or ten) are accurate enough, but I hate to get involved in another point count requiring 27½ points for game. With a borderline hand, bid more with a smattering of aces and tens; bid less without them. A good five-card suit is worth a point provided you have your strength largely in top cards. Following are examples of minimum one no-trump bids: ♠ K Q x, ♡ Q J x, ◇ A Q J x, ♣ J 10 x; ♠ A 10, ♡ 10 x x x, ◇ K Q x x, ♣ A K x; ♠ A Q, ♡ Q 10 x x x, ◇ K x x, ♣ A J x. Maximum one no-trump bids: ♠ A x, ♡ A J 9, ◇ Q J 8 x, ♣ A Q 9 x; ♠ K x, ♡ A Q 10, ◇ A 10 x, ♣ K J x x x; ♠ K Q x, ♡ K J x, ◇ K Q x, ♣ K Q 10 x. The following hands are too strong: ♠ A 10, ♡ A J 10, ◇ Q J 9 x, ♣ A Q 9 x; ♠ K x, ♡ A Q 10, ◇ A 10 x, ♣ K J 10 9 x; ♠ A J x, ♡ K J x, ◇ A J x, ♣ K Q 10 x.

An opening two no-trump bid shows 22-24 points, unless you use an artificial two-club bid as explained in a later chapter, in which case the spread may be reduced to two points, 22-23 or preferably 21-22. To show a no-trump hand with 13-15 points or a skimpy 16, open a suit and re-bid one no-trump. With 19 or 20 points, bid one of a suit and jump to two no-trump over a suit response at the one-level, or bid three no-trump with 21 points. If partner responds one no-trump rather than one of a suit, jump to three no-trump with 20 points and raise to two no-trump with as little as 18 since the one no-trump response guarantees at least six points *in high cards*. Over a two-level response, opener may jump to three no-trump with as little as 18 points.

When partner responds at the two-level after having passed, the requirements for no-trump re-bids are lowered a point for two reasons. There is no danger of reaching a losing slam, and there is greater danger in re-bidding a weak suit.

RESPONDER	OPENER
Pass	1 ♠
2 ◇	?

Bid two no-trump with ♠ A 9 x x x, ♡ K x x, ◇ K x, ♣ A 10 x rather than re-bid spades because, as we shall see later, partner is very unlikely to have three spades, and is much more likely to pass a spade re-bid than would be the case if he had not passed originally. Responder should pass this two no-trump re-bid unless, by counting everything, suit length, ten spots, etc., he can scrape up 11 points.

When partner has already passed, his suit response is not forcing. Since you don't have to re-bid, the requirements for a third- or fourth-hand bid are changed slightly. But only *slightly*. So often I have seen this sort of bidding: A player passes with ♠ x x, ♡ Q 10 x x, ◇ K J 10 x, ♣ A x x and raises his partner's third-hand heart bid to two hearts. Is opener supposed to re-bid three hearts with ♠ x x x, ♡ A J x x x, ◇ A x x, ♣ K x to confirm an opening bid? Or responder bids one no-trump over an opening one-club bid with ♠ K x x x, ♡ K x x x, ◇ K x x, ♣ x x. Why did he bid that way? "You could have passed a heart or spade bid, partner, since I was a 'passed hand.' I can't bid a suit unless I am prepared to play it."

We are not concerned with responder's problems right now, but the point is that when third or fourth hand frequently opens light and fails to re-bid, and when responder tries to make allowances, the result is chaos. In third position it is foolish to open with eleven well-distributed points and a balanced hand. If the opponents buy the bid, they have a good indication where the strength is. Partner will make the wrong decisions and frequently get too high unless he starts making allowances, which is worse. With a balanced hand and distributed strength, third and fourth hand may shade the opening requirements by one point. Fourth hand has more justification for this shading than third hand has, since if fourth hand passes, no one else can bid. Often when the hand is passed out, you discover the opponents have the better hands. Even when you have slightly the better of it and can make one no-trump, two hearts, or three diamonds while the opponents can only make one spade or three clubs, have you lost anything? Not necessarily. Probably if you had opened, you couldn't have stopped at the right spot. It is better to pass the hand out than to get one trick too high with the best cards. Even if you only average forty per cent on passed-out boards, it is better to sacrifice something so that when you open in any position, responder can bid normally.

With concentrated strength, you have much more to gain by opening light in third position. Suppose you hold ♠ A x, ♡ K Q 10 9 x, ◇ x x x, ♣ x x x. Whatever the final contract is, a minor-suit lead by partner might sacrifice a trick. A heart lead is very likely to be the best lead, and it may be the only lead to beat three no-trump. Furthermore, if you open one heart and partner raises to three or four, you may make it. All that he needs is a good distributional fit. You have a much better chance than if you had opened with ♠ Q x, ♡ Q J x x x, ◇ K J x, ♣ Q 10 x, the type of hand with which you should automatically pass. Another advantage in opening light only with concentrated strength is that if partner bids three or four hearts and you go down with ♠ A x, ♡ K Q 10 9 x, ◇ x x x, ♣ x x x, the opponents could probably make at least nine or ten tricks at their own suit. Consequently −50 or −100 is not a bad board. When you get too high with ♠ Q x, ♡ Q J x x x, ◇ K J x, ♣ Q 10 x, there is no salvation.

In first or second position you may have to pass borderline hands because of the lack of a satisfactory re-bid. Open this type of hand in third or fourth position. Any hand with three honor count is an opening bid. Just bid your best suit. Some hands that would be a minimum opening bid in any position are best opened with a major suit in third or fourth position without the intention of re-bidding them. As dealer you would open one club with ♠ K Q x x, ♡ x x, ◇ A x x, ♣ K J x x. After partner has passed, open one spade. You are not anxious to hear a heart bid from either partner or the opponents. A spade bid has considerable pre-emptive value. With as much as 15 points in high cards, bid exactly the same as though you were dealer. When your side has a substantial preponderance of strength, it is unwise to give up the advantages of approach bidding. For that matter, you should not go out of your way to exercise the privilege of passing partner's response, particularly at the one-level. Unless you have opened a sub-minimum hand, you should tend to re-bid even though game is remote. If one heart is all your side can make, you won't buy the bid for one heart. Passing partner's one-level response with a singleton or doubleton is the best way I know to discourage a response on a four-card major.

♠ K J x, ♡ x x x, ◇ Q J x, ♣ A Q 10 x: You open one club in third or fourth position and partner bids one heart. Bid one no-trump. If partner responds one spade, you have a close decision, and a pass is probably justified. Always make another bid with 14 points. If partner knows you won't pass his response with 14 points, he will not be so tempted to respond two no-trump in preference to showing his four-card major. Again, we are not considering responder's problems here, but I *like* my partner to show his four-card major. Too often this sort of thing happens: North: ♠ K Q x x, ♡ K x x, ◇ A x x x, ♣ x x; South: ♠ A x x x, ♡ A x x, ◇ x x x, ♣ K Q J x.

NORTH	SOUTH
Pass	1 ♣
2 NT	3 NT

While four spades is a much better contract than three no-trump, this is not nearly as gruesome an example as others I can remember from actual play where both hands had the same doubleton or a suit was unstopped.

Now let us consider opener's re-bids in more detail. One no-trump re-bid is not necessarily the most discouraging re-bid. An opening bid may be made with ten points in high cards and good distribution. The one no-trump re-bid suggests at least 13 points in high cards or 12 points with a five-card suit. It negates the possibility of a misfit for partner's suit, whatever it is. The no-trump re-bid should not be made with a singleton in partner's suit unless it is the king or queen. Jump re-bids in no-trump have already been discussed. Again responder will assume a doubleton in support of his suit, although the jump re-bid may be based upon a strong minor suit, in which case a fit is not necessary. Jump to two no-trump over a spade response with ♠ x, ♡ Q J x, ◇ A J x, ♣ A K Q J x x.

A reverse bid should show four honor count or 17 points in high cards unless it is based upon 6-5 distribution, or somewhat less than 17 points when based upon 6-4. Usually with 6-4, you should re-bid the six-card suit before showing the four-card suit. In no event should you bid the lower-ranking of touching suits of the same length just to show extra strength. Do not open one diamond with ♠ A Q x, ♡ K Q x x, ◇ A K x x, ♣ x x, or ♠ A x, ♡ K J 10 x x, ◇ A K x x x, ♣ x. A typical hand for a reverse is the following: ♠ A x, ♡ K Q x x, ◇ A J 10 x x, ♣ A x. Open one diamond, intending to re-bid hearts next time. As you will remember from the first chapter, a reverse is not forcing unless partner has responded at the two-level. If partner responds one no-trump to your opening diamond bid, jump to three hearts with ♠ x, ♡ A J x x x, ◇ A Q J x x x, ♣ A. Jump to three hearts even if partner responds two clubs. Though two hearts is forcing, it would not show such a good hand, and you would have problems on later rounds.

♠ A Q x x, ♡ x, ◇ A Q x x x x, ♣ K 10: This is an obvious one-diamond bid. Over a one-heart response, the best re-bid is one spade. For one thing, a diamond re-bid is too discouraging. A spade re-bid does not guarantee any more strength (minimum is the same), but the maximum for a change of suit is higher. If partner now re-bids one no-trump over one spade, complete the picture of your hand by jumping to three diamonds (invitational, but not forcing). Over an original two-club response, it is proper to bid two spades, a slightly shaded reverse. The fact that partner has bid a suit at the two-level for which you have a mild fit justifies this action. With heart and club holdings reversed, you would only re-bid two diamonds.

♠ K Q 10 x, ♡ A J 9 x x x, ◇ K x x, ♣——: You open one heart and re-bid hearts over a club response. But if partner re-bids two diamonds, the hand improves considerably, justifying a two-spade re-bid. This is an exceptional shading of high cards, and it violates the rule of re-bidding a six-card suit before showing a four-card suit. Hands with voids often require unusual treatment. Note how little partner needs for a slam (not to mention game) if his strength is in the right spots.

As already stated, a non-reverse change of suits does not guarantee additional strength. The range covered is about 10 to 18 points in high cards. Even with 19, you may fail to jump to two no-trump with a singleton in partner's suit. Bid one heart followed by a two-diamond re-bid over a spade response with ♠ x, ♡ A x x x x, ◇ A Q x x x, ♣ x x, or ♠ A, ♡ A Q x x, ◇ A Q J x, ♣ Q x x x. Regardless of the general strength, it is better if it can be done without reversing, to show a second biddable suit before re-bidding a five-card suit. The exception occurs when the five-card suit is very strong and the four-card suit is very weak. A six-card suit should be re-bid before showing a four-card suit, unless the six-card suit is a minor and the four-card suit is a major. Even then it is sometimes better to re-bid the minor.

The re-bid of a three-card suit, particularly a minor, is sometimes chosen as the least of evils. I prefer bidding a strong three-card suit to a worthless four-card suit. After opening one spade, re-bid two diamonds rather than two hearts over a two-club response with ♠ A K x x, ♡ x x x x, ◇ A J x, ♣ J x. After opening one diamond with ♠ J x, ♡ x x x, ◇ A K x x x, ♣ A K x, you should re-bid two clubs over a major-suit response. If no-trump is the best spot, it should be played from partner's direction, since you have no tenaces.

OPENER	RESPONDER
1 ◇	1 ♡
?	

♠ K Q x, ♡ x x, ◇ A K x x x, ♣ A 10 x: Bid one spade as the least of evils. Two no-trump is a gross overbid; one no-trump is an underbid. That is why you like to open one no-trump with a hand in this range, although you were prevented from doing so this time by the worthless doubleton in hearts. If partner now makes a non-committal bid, such as one no-trump or two diamonds, bid two no-trump, which will not be as strong an invitation to game as a jump to two no-trump.

A major suit re-bid has little significance other than to show a re-biddable suit when the response was at the two-level. But a major suit re-bid after a one-level response shows a hand either unsuited for play at no-trump or somewhat stronger than a bare minimum.

OPENER	RESPONDER
1 ♡	1 ♠
?	

Bid one no-trump with ♠ Q x, ♡ A Q 10 x x, ◇ K J x, ♣ Q x x. Bid two hearts with ♠ K x, ♡ A Q J 9 x, ◇ A J x, ♣ x x x, or ♠ x, ♡ A Q 10 x x, ◇ A J x, ♣ x x x x. You should pass a one no-trump response with the first two hands but re-bid two hearts with the third.

At rubber bridge, even a minor-suit re-bid may show a better hand than a no-trump re-bid. However, a minor-suit re-bid in duplicate should be used as the most discouraging re-bid available. It denies the ability to re-bid one no-trump. When the bidding is

OPENER	RESPONDER
1 ◇	1 ♠
2 ◇	

opener usually has his strength concentrated in diamonds or a singleton in his partner's suit—or a hand otherwise unsuited for play at no-trump. A typical two-diamond re-bid would be ♠ x, ♡ J x x x, ◇ A K x x x, ♣ A x x, or ♠ x x, ♡ A x x, ◇ A Q J x x x, ♣ x x. With ♠ x x, ♡ K x x, ◇ A K Q x x x, ♣ Q x, you should re-bid one no-trump. Partner may have to pass either a one no-trump or two-diamond re-bid. In duplicate you want to be in no-trump if there is any reasonable play for it. If partner's response had been one heart, you would have raised.

Whenever you have a choice of bids, tend to raise partner's major suit. It is surprising how many problems can arise when this basic rule is broken.

OPENER	RESPONDER
1 ◇	1 ♠
?	

♠ A x x, ♡ x, ◇ A Q J x x x, ♣ x x x: If partner has a weak hand and a weak spade suit, two diamonds will be safer than two spades. However, if such is the case, the opponents can probably make two or three hearts, and they are much more likely to enter the auction over a two-diamond bid than over a two-spade bid. But suppose partner has a weak hand and a fair spade suit, something like ♠ K J x x x, ♡ Q x x, ◇ x x, ♣ Q 10 x. He must pass either a two-diamond or a two-spade re-bid, and in duplicate you should prefer spades. Since neither opponent has bid, partner is likely to have a good hand. If you re-bid two diamonds and partner jumps to three no-trump, you are really in a quandary. It is too dangerous to bid spades now, but four spades may be a vastly superior contract. This is a guess no one should have to make. Or suppose that partner re-bids two no-trump. If your first re-bid had been a spade raise, you would have a comfortable bid at this point, three diamonds. If you had re-bid diamonds, you would not know what to do. A spade raise at this point would be forcing, and you are not sure that you have a game. Another example: ♠ K x x, ♡ A K Q x x, ◇ x x x, ♣ x x:

OPENER	RESPONDER
1 ♡	1 ♠
?	

Raise to two spades. Partner would pass either a two-heart or two-spade re-bid with ♠ J 10 x x x, ♡ x, ◇ K Q x, ♣ J x x x, and a two-spade contract is much better. Or suppose his holding is ♠ A Q 8 x x x, ♡ x, ◇ A x x, ♣ x x x. Over a raise to two spades, he will promptly bid four spades. If you re-bid two hearts, he should only bid two spades because of the apparent misfit.

There is a tendency among rubber-bridge players to raise with three trumps only when they have substantial extra values. That way, a raise is always an encouraging re-bid. If they get to the wrong part-score contract, the loss is negligible. They are willing to sacrifice accuracy in part-score bidding for increased accuracy in game bidding. This philosophy does not pay when the scoring method rewards reaching the best part-score contract just as much as reaching the best game contract. With a worthless doubleton and three of partner's suit to an honor, it usually pays to raise partner rather than to re-bid no-trump for the purpose of discouraging him.

A double raise requires 17-19 support points. Typical minimum raises to three hearts are ♠ A x, ♡ 10 x x x, ◇ A Q J x x, ♣ A x; ♠ x, ♡ J x x x, ◇ A K J 10 x, ♣ A J x; ♠ A x, ♡ Q 10 x x, ◇ A Q 10 x x x, ♣ x. While a double raise normally shows four-card support, good three-card support may be adequate. ♠ K J x, ♡ x, ◇ A K J x x, ♣ K Q 10 x:

OPENER	RESPONDER
1 ◇	1 ♠
?	

The rubber-bridge bid is two clubs. Three spades is the best bid at duplicate. Many players fail to realize that a trump suit split 4-3 is sufficient when the three-card suit will take the first ruff. If partner bids four spades, surely he will have a good play for it. If he has to pass three spades, he would probably pass two clubs, and it is a good gamble that any spade holding will provide an adequate play for nine tricks. Though two clubs might be safer, duplicate puts a small premium on safety. For that matter, responder might pass a two-club re-bid with some hands that justify a four-spade bid over three spades. For example: ♠ Q 10 x x x, ♡ x x x x, ◇ x, ♣ A x x; ♠ A Q x x, ♡ x x x, ◇ x x, ♣ J x x x.

Other examples of raises with three trumps:

OPENER	RESPONDER
1 ◇	1 ♡
?	

Bid three hearts with ♠ x x, ♡ A Q x, ◇ A K J x, ♣ K J x x or ♠ A x, ♡ K Q x, ◇ A J 10 x x, ♣ A x x. The latter hand meets the requirements for a two no-trump re-bid, but when partner responds one heart rather than one spade, the three-heart bid is preferable, since you have top tricks and ruffing support. Partner can still bid three no-trump if he wishes. Change the hand to ♠ K x, ♡ K Q x, ◇ A J 10 x x, ♣ A J x, and a two no-trump re-bid is preferable.

A triple raise of partner's major should be made when all he needs for game is a four-card suit with one honor count in the right spot. That means that you need about 20 support points. Raise a one-heart response to four hearts with ♠ A x, ♡ K x x x, ◇ A Q x x x, ♣ A Q, or ♠ A x, ♡ Q J x x, ◇ A K Q x x x, ♣ x. With enough strength to insist upon game, you must weigh the advantages of a direct raise against a jump re-bid and a raise. The latter sequence is a stronger slam try and guarantees a singleton or void in the fourth suit. Change the heart holding in the last hand to K x x x, and a two-spade bid is better than an immediate raise to four hearts. All partner would need for a slam is ♠ x x x, ♡ A Q x x, ◇ x x x, ♣ x x x.

A jump re-bid of opener's major suit after a one-level response urges responder to bid again with about eight points, depending upon his degree of fit. A jump re-bid after a response at the two-level may be made with a slightly weaker hand provided you have a strong trump suit. ♠ Q x x, ♡ A K Q x x x, ◇ K x x, ♣ x: After a one-spade response, bid just two spades or two hearts. Re-bid two hearts over a two-club response, but over a two-diamond response jump to three hearts. You only need ♠ A x x, ♡ J x, ◇ A Q 10 x x, ♣ x x x for a lay-down slam, and as little as ♠ K x x, ♡ x, ◇ A Q 10 x x, ♣ 10 x x x or ♠ J x x, ♡ x x, ◇ A J 10 x x, ♣ A x x would be enough for game. Failure to jump would result in missing game with these last two dummies. A jump to game shows a better hand either in playing strength or honor count than a jump to three. Logically, a game bid should show more strength than a try for game.

OPENER	RESPONDER
1 ♡	1 ♠
?	

Bid three hearts with ♠ K x, ♡ A K Q x x x, ◇ A x x, ♣ x x, or ♠ K x, ♡ A K Q x x x x, ◇ x x x, ♣ x. Bid four hearts with ♠ K x, ♡ A K Q x x x x, ◇ A x, ♣ x x, or ♠ K x, ♡ A K Q x x x x x, ◇ x x, ♣ x.

You may be forced to underbid if your suit is ragged. ♠ K x, ♡ A K 9 7 x x, ◇ A K Q, ♣ x x: If partner responds one no-trump, jump to four hearts. The no-trump response shows a mild fit. But if partner responds one spade, you should make the underbid of three hearts. A four-heart bid should show an independent suit, at least A K J x x x. You would not want to bid four hearts and go down when partner had ♠ A Q J x x, ♡ x, ♢ x x x, ♣ x x x x. Nor would a three-diamond bid solve your problems. Partner would probably re-bid three no-trump, and you would not know whether to pass or bid four hearts. Besides, if partner should re-bid three spades over your three-diamond bid, a raise to four spades would overstate and wrongly describe your hand. Partner would expect better spade support and a singleton club.

A jump re-bid in a minor suit may be weaker than a jump re-bid in a major. It is usually an invitation to three no-trump, but it denies the ability of opener to re-bid two no-trump, probably because one or both unbid suits are unstopped.

OPENER	RESPONDER
1 ♢	1 ♠
?	

Re-bid three diamonds with ♠ x x, ♡ A x, ♢ A K Q 10 x x, ♣ x x x (minimum); ♠ A Q, ♡ J x, ♢ A K Q x x x, ♣ x x x; ♠ A x, ♡ A Q x, ♢ K J 10 x x x x, ♣ x. With the latter hand, if partner bids three no-trump over your three-diamond bid, you should bid four diamonds rather than gamble by passing. This tells partner that you have a lot of playing tricks but that diamonds are not ready to run for no-trump. With a slightly better hand, you would jump to five diamonds over three no-trump to insure reaching game and suggest a slam.

When partner raises your major suit to the two-level, revalue your hand as explained in the first chapter. Upon revaluation, make a game try with 17-19 points or bid game with 20 points. Don't forget to apply evaluation factors whenever you have a borderline decision. After a single raise, you should not give a thought to bidding again with ♠ K Q J x x, ♡ A K, ♢ J x x x, ♣ J x. The two unguarded jacks are probably worthless, and it is undesirable to have so much strength concentrated in a short suit. Unless partner is very short in diamonds and very long in trumps, there will be too many losers for you to make game. Suppose you hold ♠ A K x x x x, ♡ A Q, ♢ x x x, ♣ x x. Whether you count playing tricks or points, at rubber bridge you would surely bid three spades. I favor a pass at duplicate because of the five quick losers. If partner has the wrong cards (♠ Q J

x x, ♡ K x x x, ◇ x x x, ♣ Q x), even three spades will be too
high. I do not mean to suggest that your bidding philosophy
should be based upon unreasonable pessimism. Partner does not
always have the wrong honor cards and the wrong doubleton.
However, he would raise to game with the suggested hand, and
even the right doubleton would not prevent your losing the first
four tricks. You should expect a certain amount of duplication or
wasted strength. It is just as unrealistic to count on a perfect fit
on every hand as it is to fear the worst. Don't bid again if
partner has to have a singleton in the right suit or a two honor
count for game. Unless 1½ honor count and the right doubleton
in responder's hand will give you a lay-down game, just pass.
Let's apply this test to the last hand (♠ A K x x x x, ♡ A Q,
◇ x x x, ♣ x x). Suppose partner has the queen-jack of spades.
If he has one honor count elsewhere in the hand, say an ace of a
minor, you may still have four or five losers (depending upon
the heart finesse). Even with ♠ Q J x x, ♡ x x x, ◇ x x,
♣ A x x x which is as good a raise and as good a fit as you have
any right to expect, you will still have only a fifty per cent play
for game. At rubber bridge you would want to be in game, but
in duplicate, you should not care whether you are in game or
not in the long run. Suppose partner's doubleton were in some
suit other than diamonds. Then you would have no play for
game. I am aware of the fact that the queen-jack of spades are
duplicated values, but that is what you must expect—either the
queen-jack of spades or a queen and jack in the minors.

Suppose you hold ♠ A K x x x x, ♡ A Q x, ◇ x x, ♣ x x.
Now your hand is somewhat stronger. The opponents are not
likely to take the first five tricks anyway. This is a sound, minimum three-spade bid. Change your distribution to ♠ A K x x
x x, ♡ A Q x, ◇ x x x, ♣ x. Now you have a very fine three-
spade bid. As little as the doubleton ace of diamonds will give
you some sort of play for game, and little values like the jack
of hearts will change a satisfactory contract to an excellent contract. Is there any doubt in your mind that the singleton is worth
an additional point?

Suppose you had the original hand except that your six-
card suit were hearts (♠ A Q, ♡ A K x x x x, ◇ x x x,
♣ x x). Over the raise to two hearts, against good opponents,

bid three hearts! If you pass, the opponents may wake up to the fact that they can make more than you can. Your offensive chances are no better than when your suit is spades, but there is more danger in taking a conservative view. If your six-card suit were a minor, you should undoubtedly bid again. The minor-suit raise invariably contains four or more trumps, increasing your offensive strength and decreasing your defensive strength. You hope partner cannot scrape up a bid, but if he bids three no-trump, he may make it. All he needs is a favorable lead plus the spade finesse.

Another example of the same principle is the following. ♠ A K x x x x x, ♡ K x, ◇ x x, ♣ x x:

OPENER	RESPONDER
1 ♠	2 ♠
?	

Bid three spades. The miracle is that the opponents have not entered the auction yet with at least half of the high-card strength, probably more. Even though you have the spades, it is dangerous to pass with so little defensive strength. A re-bid is not entirely psychic, for if partner has the right cards, four spades will be cold. If he passes, the odds are that the opponents are cold for game and would have reopened over two spades. With ♠ A K x x x x x, ♡ K x x, ◇ x x, ♣ x, you would bid three spades with much more confidence. While partner could have several wasted values, the doubleton ace of hearts is all that you need for game. Many times, you don't care so much how many points partner has as you care where his points are.

Suppose your hand is ♠ A K x x x, ♡ x x, ◇ A K x x, ♣ x x. When partner raises to two spades, you have another bid because of your evaluation factors. If partner has three small diamonds, he will need a maximum in honor strength to give you a good play for game. However, if he has the queen of diamonds or a doubleton diamond, a seven-point raise may be enough. The proper re-bid is three diamonds, showing your second suit. In addition to checking for a diamond fit, partner will discount his queens and jacks in the other two suits after you have shown a two-suiter. With ♠ Q x x x, ♡ A x x x, ◇ x x, ♣ x x x he will jump to game over a three-diamond re-bid, but over a three-club re-bid he would surely sign off at three spades.

♠ K Q x x x, ♡ x x x, ◇ A K Q x, ♣ x:

OPENER   RESPONDER
1 ♠   2 ♠
?

This time a three-diamond bid would accomplish nothing because you don't care whether partner has a diamond fit or not. My unorthodox recommendation is to bid three hearts. A heart fit (either in high cards or distribution) will mean more to you than any other feature of partner's hand, and partner will discount his club strength. Another advantage of the heart bid is that it may stop a heart opening lead or cause the defenders to miscount your hand.

A two no-trump re-bid shows 17-19 points for no-trump, but it is not forcing. This completes the picture of your hand, and responder should attempt to place the contract.

After a minor-suit opening and raise, a re-bid is often for the purpose of showing a concentration of strength in order to reach or stay out of three no-trump. Any re-bid shows an interest in game. It does not pay to re-bid with a balanced hand and less than 17 points in an effort to find a major-suit fit. When responder raises a minor suit, the odds are 10 to 1 against his having a four-card major, and it is best to pass quickly with ♠ K Q x x, ♡ A Q x, ◇ A J x x, ♣ x x, for example, hoping the opponents will reopen. With one more diamond and one less spade, bid two no-trump, gambling that partner has club length or that the opponents will lead a major suit.

When responder bids two no-trump, opener should raise to three no-trump unless he has a singleton or two doubletons or unless he is strong enough for a slam try. A sequence such as

OPENER   RESPONDER
1 ♡   2 NT
3 ♡

shows more than a re-biddable heart suit. It indicates a decided preference on the part of opener for a suit contract. Opener must exercise his judgment whenever he has a six-card suit and no singleton. With a worthless doubleton, he should re-bid his suit. If he has some strength in every suit, he should just raise to three no-trump. Opener should re-bid three hearts with ♠ x x, ♡ A Q x x x x, ♢ A J x, ♣ x x, planning to pass if responder re-bids no trump. With ♠ Q x, ♡ A Q x x x x, ♢ x x x, ♣ A x, or ♠ J 10, ♡ A K J x x x, ♢ Q x x, ♣ K x, opener should raise to three no-trump rather than even suggest a four-heart contract.

After a double raise of a major suit, opener has only two alternatives unless he wants to suggest a slam. He can bid game in his major or three no-trump. Any other bid is a slam try. After a double raise of a minor suit (non-forcing), opener may pass with a bare minimum, try three no-trump with a smattering of strength in every suit (and about 15 points), or bid a second suit in an effort to determine whether three no-trump, five of the minor, or a part score is the best spot, since responder will re-value his hand in the light of his degree of fit for the second suit.

A jump re-bid in a new suit is forcing to game. There are some advantages in playing a jump as a strong urge or forcing for just one round, but they are out-weighed by the convenience of an absolute force. If either player jumps thereafter, except for a very good reason, he loses the major advantage of the game force, which is to give up a round of bidding early in order to save more rounds later. A jump re-bid should be made whenever you have a good unbid major and 21 points.

♠ K Q x x, ♡ A x, ♢ A Q x, ♣ A Q x x:

OPENER	RESPONDER
1 ♣	1 ♡
?	

Bid two spades. Since you have enough strength to bid three no-trump, you might as well look for a spade fit on the way. Even if partner bids three spades, you will bid three no-trump and let him make the choice. Partner will show that you have a genuine spade suit when you fail to raise hearts. Change your queen of diamonds to the jack or ten, and you are slightly too weak for a game force, too strong to bid one spade. Consequently you must bid two no-trump.

A jump re-bid is made whenever you have enough strength to raise partner's bid to game, but because of good controls, prefer to show your distribution so that partner will know where he needs his strength for a slam.

OPENER   RESPONDER
1 ◇   1 ♡
?

♠ x x, ♡ A Q x x, ◇ A K 10 9 x, ♣ A x: Bid four hearts, but with one more club, one less spade, bid three clubs followed by four hearts since ♠ x x x, ♡ K x x x x, ◇ Q J x, ♣ x x would be enough strength opposite the latter hand for a cold slam.

The remaining type of jump re-bid is made with a powerful two-suiter where you should have game unless most of partner's cards are in the wrong places. ♠ x, ♡ A K 10 9 x, ◇ A Q J x x, ♣ K x:

OPENER   RESPONDER
1 ♡   1 ♠
?

This is a minimum three-diamond bid. If partner has ♠ K J 10 x x, ♡ x, ◇ x x x, ♣ J x x x, you are headed for trouble. However he would pass a two-diamond bid with ♠ A x x x x, ♡ x x, ◇ K x x, ♣ x x x, or ♠ Q J x x x, ♡ J x, ◇ K x x x, ♣ x x. Besides, a two-diamond bid would make it more difficult to reach a slam in many cases. With a two-suiter, the jump re-bid is merely a percentage bid with no guarantee of success. It pays to jump because there are so many possibilities.

The same philosophy should control your opening two-bids. You don't need a sure game. Just be sure that there is a better chance of gaining than of losing by forcing partner to bid when he does not want to. The game-forcing two-bid serves two purposes. It keeps the bidding open so that you can choose the best game contract when responder does not have enough strength for a voluntary bid, and it makes slam bidding easier. ♠ A K Q x x, ♡ A Q x x x, ◇ x, ♣ A x is not enough strength for game opposite ♠ x, ♡ x x, ◇ J 10 9 x x x, ♣ J x x x, but the risk of a two-bid is justified, since ♠ J x, ♡ K x x x, ◇ x x x x, ♣ x x x is enough for a cold slam; yet partner could not keep a one-bid open. With a borderline hand, open a two-bid when you have good controls. Bid one with a worthless doubleton or only two aces.

Culbertson introduced the limit two-bid only requiring about eight plus playing tricks and four honor count. When responder bids two no-trump, a re-bid by opener of his original suit permits responder to pass with a hopeless hand. If opener thinks he can make game opposite a blank hand, he must jump to game or bid a new suit. If responder bids anything other than two no-trump, game must be reached, and the bidding proceeds normally. Examples of limit two-bids: ♠ x, ♡ A K Q x x x x, ◇ A x x, ♣ K x; ♠ A x, ♡ A Q 10 x x x x, ◇ A J x, ♣ x; ♠ K Q J 10 x x x, ♡ x, ◇ A Q x, ♣ A x; ♠ A K J 9 x x, ♡ A Q x , ◇ K Q x, ♣ x; ♠ A Q J x x x, ♡ K J x, ◇ —, ♣ A Q x x; ♠ K x, ♡ A K Q J x x x x, ◇ —, ♣ K x x. To bid two spades on the following hands defeats the purpose of the limit two-bid since no matter what partner bids, you must keep signing off. ♠ A K Q x x x x, ♡ K x, ◇ J x x, ♣ A, or ♠ A K Q x x x x, ♡ A K, ◇ x x, ♣ x x: Partner must be able to bid safely to the five-level with a doubleton in your suit and two well-distributed honor count.

You were reminded to consider your first two-bids (including a possible pass if partner made a non-forcing response) before opening the bidding. When it comes time to re-bid, it often pays to look ahead another round. ♠ K x x x, ♡ K Q x, ◇ A J 10 x, ♣ x x:

OPENER	RESPONDER
1 ◇	1 ♡
?	

Should you bid two hearts or one spade? You should bid two hearts since you must show the good trump support, and you are too weak to bid one spade now and show heart support later. Besides, if you bid diamonds and spades followed by a heart raise, particularly if hearts are not re-bid, partner may figure you for a singleton club. With a minimum hand, it is important to raise partner's suit right away. ♠ A x x x, ♡ K Q x, ◇ A Q x x x, ♣ x: This time you should bid one spade, since you want to suggest a singleton club and extra strength. However, this sort of bidding is wrong:

OPENER	RESPONDER
1 ◇	1 ♠
2 ♡	

Opener's hand: ♠ K x x x, ♡ A J x x, ◇ A K x x x, ♣ —.
Admittedly there is no completely satisfactory re-bid. Three
hearts is a stretch; three spades is an underbid; and four spades
does not show where the strength lies. Yet you cannot compromise by bidding two hearts. Two spades is an encouraging bid,
a reverse, but what if partner passes? What a horrible contract
two hearts will be! And if partner thinks along the same lines
I do, you will never be able to convince him that you have four
spades. Whenever partner bids a major suit, you must either
raise immediately with four trumps or must make a forcing bid.

There is a tendency among the top American players to make
a jump to game almost a slam try in many sequences. Thus,
after a spade opening bid and a two-heart response, they would
bid three hearts rather than four hearts with ♠ A K Q x x,
♡ x x x x, ◇ K Q x, ♣ x, or ♠ A K x x x, ♡ K x x x, ◇ K Q,
♣ x x. Responder is always supposed to bid four hearts over
three hearts with any hand, even ♠ x x, ♡ A Q 10 x x x,
◇ J 10 x, ♣ x x. The argument is that once responder has bid
at the two-level and gets a raise, he will never want to stop short
of game. The fact that he stretched to bid at all is no excuse for
passing. If the experts had all learned to play duplicate before
they learned rubber bridge, I do not think bridge would have
developed this way. At first, raises were given on a playing-trick
basis, but since responder hardly ever stopped at the three-level
(rubber-bridge players don't like to "hang" one trick short of
game), the necessity of jumping to insure reaching game soon
ceased to exist. In order for the jump to serve some useful
purpose, it was reserved to show lots of strength to spare, something like the three no-trump response to an opening bid. As
I intimated, I think that opener should raise to game with
either of the above hands, and responder should pass with
♠ x x, ♡ A Q 10 x x x, ◇ J 10 x, ♣ x x, whether opener
raises to three or four. After all, opener would raise to three
hearts with ♠ A K J x x, ♡ K J x, ◇ x x x, ♣ Q x.

Few rules in bridge are absolute. I do not advocate raises

on playing tricks alone. There are a few freak hands justifying a deliberate underbid. ♠ K J x x x x x, ♡ K Q 10 x, ◇ —, ♣ K x:

OPENER	RESPONDER
1 ♠	2 ♡
?	

When your hand is so distributional, it is inconceivable that a raise to three hearts will close the bidding. A four-heart bid is dangerous because you are aceless, and you don't know who has the diamonds. If you bid four hearts, partner will try for seven but stop at six over your sign-off with ♠ A Q, ♡ J 9 x x x, ◇ A K x x x, ♣ x. Can you blame him for thinking he will have a play for six? If the opponents had been bidding clubs, you would have all the more reason for caution. If they had been bidding diamonds, you could bid four hearts since, if partner has diamond strength, he will know it must be duplicated by your singleton or void.

♠ 9 x x x x, ♡ A K, ◇ x, ♣ K Q J 10 x:

NORTH	EAST	SOUTH	WEST
Pass	Pass	1 ♣	1 ♡
1 ♠	2 ◇	?	

Even though partner has passed originally, you should bid three spades rather than make a "playing trick" raise to four. Over four spades, a good partner would bid six with ♠ A Q 10 x, ♡ x x, ◇ x x x x, ♣ A x x because he knows he has three key cards and no wasted values. (Note that if opener has the king of spades, as he should, six spades would be a lay-down.) Furthermore, it is unlikely that responder would pass a raise to three spades unless he has a very poor trump suit and secondary values, in which case three spades could be high enough.

An unfortunate tendency I have observed among duplicate players is their failure to raise a minor-suit response with a good hand. They realize that minor-suit contracts are to be avoided whenever possible at duplicate, but they go a step further by never supporting a minor suit when there is another possible bid. Ironically, the best way to get out of a minor suit may be to raise it. Suppose responder has something like six or seven diamonds to the king-queen-jack and an ace on the side. You open a major and re-bid your major over his two-diamond bid. With a worthless doubleton in your suit or a singleton, he will bid three diamonds, because he figures his hand may be worth very little to you, and your top strength will be enough for him to make his bid. But if you raise his diamonds, he will bid three no-trump, gambling that you hold the ace of diamonds.

Another example: Opener has ♠ A K 10 x x, ♡ x x, ◇ A Q x, ♣ Q x x. Responder has ♠ x, ♡ K x x, ◇ K 10 x x x x, ♣ K x x. If opener raises the two-diamond response as he should, responder will bid three no-trump. If opener re-bids his suit, responder will pass. Incidentally, opener should raise a two-club bid also, although a re-bid of two diamonds is permissible. Suppose responder passes the diamond raise. Then he probably has something like ♠ x, ♡ K x, ◇ K J 10 x x x x, ♣ x x x, and three diamonds will be an excellent contract. Even five diamonds may be the right contract, for all opener can tell. Instead of trying to mastermind the hand, he should raise, because the raise is his proper bid. Sometimes it is important to show a rebiddable major suit, but more often it pays to show a fit. So far all the experts would agree. I believe a diamond raise is correct even without the queen of clubs. At this point, I have lost a few supporters. But let's be practical about this thing. If with ♠ A K 10 x x, ♡ x x, ◇ A Q x, ♣ x x x, you re-bid two spades over partner's two-diamond bid, will you pass if he re-bids two no-trump or raises to three spades? No, your top tricks and diamond fit will persuade you to go to game. What is the purpose of bidding two spades to show a minimum hand if you are going to take partner to game over any game try anyway? Of course, partner is more likely to pass a two-spade re-bid than a raise to three diamonds, but if he passes two spades, you won't like his spade support and you probably won't like the contract. What if partner expects more? Even if he bids a slam in diamonds, your hand should not be too great a disappointment, since there are no wasted values.

We have not discussed all of opener's problems yet, but they will be more easily understood after considering some of responder's problems, since responder has the major burden of directing the progress of the bidding.

Chapter 3

Problems of the Responder

THE RESPONDER has the primary responsibility for guiding the bidding. He knows that approximately 26 points are required for game in a major suit or no-trump. When responder has 6-10 points, he plans to make only one constructive bid, leaving the initiative to opener. With 11-12 points responder should plan to make two constructive bids so as to invite game, while allowing opener with a minimum hand to stop at a part score. With 13 or more points, responder should see that game is reached. Of course, if proper bidding were as simple as just outlined, anyone who could count points would be a top-notch player. There are still problems in reaching the *proper* game contract, stopping at the right part-score contract if game cannot be bid, avoiding trouble on misfit hands, and deciding which cards will be useful and which will not. Sometimes it is necessary to distort the picture of your distribution in order to avoid giving a false impression as to your general strength and vice versa. Sometimes you must make a bid which is not the best possible so far as enabling the partnership to reach or stay out of game, but it is a bid which, if passed, will provide an excellent part-score contract.

Some bids are more encouraging than others within the same range. When responder has just enough strength for one bid, he must pick the best bid. When he has enough strength to bid more than once, he must plan ahead to determine what *sequence* of bids will best describe his hand. This topic will be treated in detail later in this chapter. Incidentally, don't take too literally the comments about "only enough strength for one bid." After

OPENER	RESPONDER
1 ♣	1 ♡
1 ♠	?

you don't need a very good hand to raise to two spades. This is just a chance-giving bid. Or with no support for spades, you must take a preference for clubs, or you could bid one no-trump with very little strength beyond that required for a minimum response. It might be more accurate to characterize these calls not as bids but as refusals to pass. Let us now consider the requirements for various first-round responses.

A one no-trump response shows 6-10 points with no biddable major suit that could be shown at the one-level. There should never be a void or a singleton in an unbid suit. Only on rare occasions should you bid one no-trump with a singleton in partner's suit or a worthless doubleton in a side suit. In duplicate, a one no-trump response should show a hand reasonably suited for play at no-trump. If you were to bid one no-trump with ♠ x x, ♡ —, ◇ J 10 x x x x, ♣ K Q J x x, or even ♠ x x, ♡ x x, ◇ x x x, ♣ K Q J x x x, you would almost surely get into trouble if partner should pass. A one no-trump response over one club shows 9-10 points, since you don't want to force partner to show his second suit at the two-level (or shut out his second suit) with a weaker hand. With 6-8 points, a balanced hand, and no biddable major suit, bid one diamond even with a three-card suit.

A two no-trump response shows 13-15 points and is forcing to game. The distribution must be 4-3-3-3, 4-4-3-2, or 5-3-3-2, and tenaces are desirable. According to the orthodox view, a two no-trump response denies possession of a biddable four-card major which could be shown at the one-level. However, I believe that with tenaces and a hand otherwise well suited for no-trump, you should bid two no-trump despite possession of a four-card major. Bid two no-trump over one club with ♠ Q 10 x x, ♡ K J x, ◇ A J x, ♣ K 10 x, or ♠ A J x, ♡ K x x x, ◇ Q 10 x x, ♣ K 10. If *opener* has a somewhat unbalanced hand, including a four-card major, he can re-bid his minor suit (even with a four-card suit, for example, ♠ K x x x, ♡ K Q x x, ◇ x, ♣ A x x x) and responder must bid his four-card major if he has one. It is better for opener to re-bid his minor suit than to bid his major since, if responder has no major suit to show, and if three no-trump is reached anyway, the opening leader will have no clue which suit to lead (or not to lead). Suppose opener has ♠ K x x x, ♡ A x x, ◇ K x, ♣ A x x x. He would raise to three no-trump because his hand is balanced; the odds are against his partner's having four spades, and even if he should have four spades, three no-trump might be a superior contract. After opening with one diamond, opener should re-bid three diamonds over a two no-trump response with ♠ K J x x, ♡ x x, ◇ A Q x x x, ♣ A x, or ♠ K Q x x, ♡ x x, ◇ A K Q x, ♣ x x x but raise to three no-trump with ♠ K Q x x, ♡ Q x, ◇ A K x x, ♣ x x x.

A new suit may be bid at the one-level with as little as five points and a good major suit. Respond one spade over a club or diamond opening with ♠ A 10 9 x x, ♡ x x x, ◇ x x x, ♣ x x, or ♠ K x x x x x, ♡ x x x, ◇ x, ♣ x x x, but pass a heart opening bid. There is no point in risking a bid on subminimum values when you are already in a good spot and have both majors (consequently there is less danger in letting the opponents enter the bidding cheaply). There is no upper limit for the one-over-one response, although with good hands (17 points or sometimes less), the subsequent bidding is usually handled best after an immediate jump response.

To bid a new suit at the two-level, somewhat more strength is required. With ten points or less, prefer bidding a four-card suit at the one-level to a five-card suit at the two-level. Also prefer a one no-trump response unless the hand contains a worthless doubleton or singleton. The two-level response normally shows a minimum of eleven points counting distribution, but exceptions should be made for hands unsuited for play at no-trump.

OPENER	RESPONDER
1 ♠	?

♠ x x, ♡ x x, ◇ A J x x x x, ♣ x x x: Pass. One no-trump is a bad bid with only five points in high cards and no strength in three suits. Add the queen of hearts and you would respond one no-trump. Change the diamond suit to K Q J 10 x x and you should bid two diamonds followed by three diamonds. This sequence is constructive or at least ambiguous at rubber bridge, but it should be used as a sign-off at duplicate.

OPENER   RESPONDER
  1 ♡   ?

♠ x x, ♡ x x, ◊ A Q x x x, ♣ Q x x x: Bid two diamonds! The standard response with this hand is one no-trump. However, a no-trump response is undesirable with a worthless doubleton, particularly a worthless doubleton in spades. A no-trump response in duplicate is passed more often than at rubber bridge; consequently you should be prepared to play one no-trump if partner passes. Change the queen of clubs to the jack, and I still like a two-diamond bid. Admittedly this is somewhat unusual and misleading, but no harm is likely to result. In addition to avoiding a no-trump contract played from the wrong direction, you make it more dangerous for the opponents to enter the bidding in spades. When you pass your partner's two heart re-bid, they will figure you for a better hand with a misfit for hearts.

Just as it pays to deliberately overbid sometimes to shut out the opponents, I approve of a gambling pass over one spade with eight or nine points and a misfit.

OPENER   RESPONDER
  1 ♠   ?

♠ x, ♡ K 10 9 x, ◊ Q J x x, ♣ Q 10 9 x: Rather than respond one no-trump with a singleton, make a fast pass. Don't count your points, hum a tune, re-count your points, and finally pass. Pass as though you had a jack-high hand so as to invite a re-opening bid. Perhaps a no-trump response would get partner too high if he should re-bid spades. But it is greed rather than cowardice that induces you to pass. If the bidding is reopened, you should have a lucrative double. The bidding is more likely to be reopened if your opponents are good players than if they are poor players.

If you don't know your opponents, it might be a good idea to ask them a bridge problem before the auction starts, so that if you have a close decision in the bidding or play, you'll know the caliber of opposition you have to face. More revealing than the opponents' answer to the problem is their attitude. If they are courteous and seem interested, they must be novices. If they snarl, "No time for foolishness; let's play the boards," you can set your trap. Another type of hand in which a gambling pass is justified is the following: Partner opens the bidding with one spade and you hold ♠ x, ♡ K Q 10 x x, ◇ Q 10 x, ♣ x x x x. Two hearts is probably your best contract, but your best chance to play two hearts is to pass partner's spade bid and to bid two hearts if your left-hand opponent reopens the bidding with a minor suit. If you bid one no-trump right away, partner will probably pass or bid two spades.

Do you remember the method of counting support points as explained in the first chapter? Count one point for each doubleton outside of trumps, three points for each singleton, and four points for each void. Usually you should deduct a point for possession of only three trumps, but not always. For example, after

OPENER	RESPONDER
1 ♠	2 ◇
2 ♠	?

♠ K x x, ♡ x x, ◇ A Q J x x, ♣ x x x is probably as good a hand as ♠ K x x x, ♡ x x, ◇ A Q J x, ♣ x x x. However, if opener re-bids two hearts rather than two spades, the second hand is worth an additional point. The recommended method of counting support points is almost an exact copy of Goren's method except for failure to promote certain trump holdings. Consequently the points you compute this way will usually be one point less than in Goren's method.

Since you know there is a slight undervaluation, be liberal in awarding yourself an additional point when the evaluation factors are favorable. Give partner an immediate single raise of his major suit with six to ten points. Whenever you hold five trumps or more, shade the raise to five points, not because the hand is better, but because your combined defensive strength is worse, and you want to make it hard for the opponents to enter the bidding. Holding eleven or twelve points, make a temporary bid followed by a raise. If your temporary bid was at the two-level and partner bids a new suit, just show a preference unless you have twelve points and four trumps.

For example:

OPENER   RESPONDER
1 ♡   ?

♠ A x x, ♡ K x x x, ◇ x x, ♣ K x x x: You are too strong to bid two hearts, too weak for a game-forcing raise to three. So you must bid two clubs or one spade. Assume that you make the more orthodox bid of two clubs. If partner re-bids two hearts, raise to three. If he re-bids two diamonds, bid just two hearts, since your two-club bid suggests 11 points and a three-heart bid would be forcing. You would bid the same way with ♠ A x x, ♡ K x x, ◇ x x, ♣ K J x x x, but with ♠ A x x, ♡ K J x, ◇ x x, ♣ K J x x x, or ♠ A x x, ♡ K x x x, ◇ x x, ♣ K J x x, you may stretch slightly and bid three hearts over a two-diamond re-bid.

Let us return to the original hand (♠ A x x, ♡ K x x x, ◇ x x, ♣ K x x x). Assume that you respond one spade. If partner re-bids two clubs, two diamonds, or two hearts, you should bid three hearts (which is not forcing). A return to two hearts over a minor suit re-bid is a weak bid which does not even guarantee three-card heart support (♠ A x x x x, ♡ Q x, ◇ x x, ♣ J x x x). But if partner re-bids one no-trump over your one-spade bid, you should bid just two hearts. Partner will know that you had heart support for an unre-bid suit all along. With a weak hand, you would raise to two hearts immediately. The reason for only bidding two hearts is that a no-trump re-bid is not as encouraging as a suit re-bid so far as a heart contract is concerned. A raise to three hearts (still not forcing) should show a maximum temporary bid.

Perhaps you think there is an inconsistency in my bidding suggestions. You merely showed a preference after a two-level response with 11 points since a two-level response had already suggested 11 points. Yet I recommend a two-club bid over one heart with ♠ x x, ♡ x x x, ◇ x x, ♣ K Q J 10 x x, or ♠ x x, ♡ J x, ◇ x x x, ♣ A Q 10 x x x, for example. Whenever you make a two-level response on this type of hand, you must refuse to give a preference. Suppose partner re-bids two diamonds. With the first hand, re-bid three clubs. With the second hand, you should pass. With one more spade and one less diamond in the second example hand, a one-no-trump response would be preferable to two clubs in order to avoid the impossible problem created by a two-diamond re-bid. Besides, a worthless doubleton in diamonds is not as dangerous for no-trump as a worthless doubleton in spades, because partner is more likely to have diamond strength than spade strength, and the opponents are more likely to lead spades than diamonds. If partner had re-bid two spades over two clubs, you could not pass, but again you should avoid a preference bid of three hearts. Re-bid three clubs with either hand.

Culbertson has always emphasized that a preference is no stronger than a pass. This is a good rule for beginners and mediocre players to prevent them from dropping their partners in hopeless contracts just because they have no more values.

OPENER	RESPONDER
1 ♡	1 ♠
2 ◇	?

♠ K J 9 x x, ♡ x x, ◇ x x, ♣ J 10 x x: Theoretically a return to two hearts shows no extra strength. But the fact is that partner *can* bid again if you give him another chance, and you have no reason to believe that hearts are better than diamonds, even at duplicate. Undertricks count the same at a major- or minor-suit contract. When you have one more of partner's first suit than of his second suit, you should almost invariably return him to his first suit. With the same number of both suits, you should show a preference for the first suit as a general rule, but refuse to show a preference with a particularly bad hand or when you suspect that you are already too high. On rare occasions you may show a preference for the suit which you do not prefer in order to give partner another chance.

OPENER	RESPONDER
1 ◇	1 ♠
2 ♣	?

♠ A J x x, ♡ x x, ◊ Q 10 x, ♣ Q x x x: A raise to three clubs is too strong a bid since partner would try three no-trump with many hands that would provide no reasonable play for game. So you bid two-diamonds, hoping partner can scrape up another bid.

Suppose that you have 11 or 12 points in support of partner's major suit, which means that you must make a temporary bid followed by a raise. How do you choose your temporary bid? The tendency is to bid your longest side suit. However, you should bid the suit where a fitting honor in partner's hand would do the most good. Opener may bid game with little or no extra strength after a temporary bid and raise provided he has a good fit for responder's suit.

OPENER	RESPONDER
1 ♠	2 ◊
2 ♠	3 ♠
?	

♠ A K 10 9 x, ♡ K x x, ◊ Q x x, ♣ x x: Neither a pass nor a four-spade bid could be severely criticized, but if responder had bid clubs or even hearts, opener should surely pass, since the queen of diamonds would be a very dubious value. A typical hand for responder is ♠ Q J x, ♡ Q x, ◊ A J 10 x x, ♣ x x x. Suppose responder has ♠ Q x x x, ♡ A x, ◊ 10 x x x, ♣ A x x. In that case, he has misbid his hand! He should have bid two clubs rather than two diamonds. Notice that there is an adequate play for game if the minor-suit holdings are reversed.

One requirement for a raise which has not been mentioned is adequate trump support. Q x x or J 10 x is supposed to be minimum support for an unre-bid suit. You are not supposed to raise partner's second suit without four trumps. Thus

OPENER	RESPONDER
1 ♣	1 ♡
1 ♠	2 ♠

the two-spade bid "guarantees" four trumps. However most rules should be broken on occasion. An orthodox exception is with three-card trump support and a singleton.

OPENER	RESPONDER
1 ♠	?

♠ x x x, ♡ x, ◇ A x x x x, ♣ K x x x: This is a standard raise to two spades. Another exception is after an opponent's bid.

NORTH	EAST	SOUTH	WEST
1 ♠	2 ♡	?	

♠ x x x, ♡ A x, ◇ K Q x x x, ♣ x x x: Surely you can't bid three diamonds, so a raise to two spades is the only bid left. The tendency among the top players, at least those on the West Coast, is to bid two spades with this hand whether there is an intervening bid or not. When you bid two diamonds and partner re-bids two spades, a raise to three is too encouraging while a pass risks loss of game. Opener cannot be expected to bid three spades over two diamonds with a ragged suit and a fair hand, for example, ♠ A J x x x x, ♡ x x x, ◇ A x, ♣ A x, but he would re-bid three spades over a raise to two. Similarly you should raise a heart opening bid with ♠ x x, ♡ x x x, ◇ A J x x, ♣ Q J x x rather than bid one no-trump with a worthless doubleton, especially in spades. In other words, trump support is just one factor to be considered in choosing the best bid.

OPENER	RESPONDER
1 ♣	1 ♡
1 ♠	?

♠ K Q x, ♡ A x x x x, ◇ x x, ♣ x x x: You must find another bid with this hand since the spade bid covers a wide range of strength. A club preference would be particularly bad at duplicate and a little weird at rubber bridge. A two-heart re-bid, after opener shows two suits, is an extremely bad bid. Opener would pass with ♠ A J x x, ♡ x, ◇ J 10 x, ♣ A Q x x x. What is wrong with a raise to two spades? Nothing! Even though partner has four spades and a minimum hand, he will have an excellent play for eight or nine tricks. Any good player would raise to two spades since K Q x is pretty good support, and a no-trump re-bid is out of the question with a worthless doubleton in the unbid suit. Give responder one more diamond and one less club and a no-trump bid is not quite so bad, but it is still greatly inferior to a spade raise.

Change the hand to ♠ K x x, ♡ A x x x x, ◊ x x x, ♣ K x.
A weak player does not even consider a raise because he figures
a combined holding of seven trumps and thinks no farther. He
doesn't know that 4-3 trump holdings are playable, so he chooses
no-trump, despite his lack of a stopper in the unbid suit. A
strong player realizes that two spades should be safe enough,
but he is afraid that his partner may jump to four spades without
further investigation. This hand presents a close problem, but
my preference is for a spade raise.

Perhaps I should state that a raise of a secondary suit may
be proper with good three-card support and drop the subject.
But I can remember a controversial hand where I believe that a
raise on three small is the proper bid!

OPENER	RESPONDER
1 ♣	1 ◊
1 ♠	?

♠ x x x, ♡ x x, ◊ A Q x x x, ♣ A x x: Again, a two-diamond
bid would be very dangerous after partner has shown two suits.
A jump to three clubs would be a gross overbid. A cheery two-
club preference is the recommended bid at rubber bridge, but
we are concerned with duplicate. Consider a raise to two spades.
It shows the right amount of encouragement (slightly more than
a return to two clubs). But the important consideration is that
partner may have a minimum hand. If he would pass either a
two-spade or two-club bid, you should prefer that he play spades.
Despite the poor support, he should have a play for eight or
nine tricks. If partner bids again, he should not bid more spades
with a weak four-card suit since you *do not guarantee* four
trumps.

OPENER	RESPONDER
1 ♣	1 ◊
1 ♠	?

♠ K Q x, ♡ x x, ◊ A K J x x, ♣ x x x: Three spades is
by far the best bid. This is a very strong urge to game, and
opener needs a good excuse to pass. If he bids three no-trump,
you will pass, of course. But unless partner has a double heart
stopper, four spades is probably the proper contract.

An immediate double raise of a major suit shows strong trump support and 13-16 supporting points. The maximum varies somewhat with controls and honor count. For example, ♠ K x x x, ♡ x x, ◊ A K J x, ♣ A x x is much too strong for a double raise of partner's spade bid. However, when your hand falls within the proper range, prefer the double raise to any other bid. Examples of proper double raises of a spade opening bid: ♠ Q x x x, ♡ K x, ◊ A J x, ♣ Q J x x; ♠ A x x x, ♡ x, ◊ A Q x x, ♣ x x x x; ♠ K Q x x x, ♡ x, ◊ A 10 9 x, ♣ x x x; ♠ A Q x, ♡ x x, ◊ A x x x, ♣ K x x x. A triple raise shows lots of offensive strength, little defensive strength: Over one heart, bid four hearts with the following hands: ♠ x, ♡ K Q x x x, ◊ Q J x x, ♣ J 10 x; ♠ A J 9 x x, ♡ Q 10 x x x, ◊ x, ♣ J x; ♠ x x x, ♡ K Q 10 x, ◊ J 10 9 x x x, ♣ —. Note that it is impossible to be scientific with this type of hand. Partner needs very little for game if his strength is in the right spots. Furthermore, if partner cannot make game, the opponents can surely make a nine- or ten-trick contract if they are allowed to find it.

When partner opens in third or fourth position, he knows that you don't have an opening bid, and he is permitted to pass any bid you make. Consequently, a raise to four is stronger than a raise to three, which is merely invitational. Since partner can pass any bid, you cannot afford to make a temporary bid followed by a raise since you might be left in your temporary bid. For that reason, a suit take-out denies four-card support for partner's major suit or even good three-card support. Whenever you have trump support, you simply raise to the full extent of your hand.

OPENER	RESPONDER
	Pass
1 ♡	?

♠ A x, ♡ 10 x x x, ◊ A Q x x, ♣ x x x; ♠ Q x x x, ♡ K Q x, ◊ x, ♣ A x x x x; ♠ x x x, ♡ Q x x x x, ◊ —, ♣ K J 10 x x: Bid three hearts with all of these example hands. With the second hand, you would have bid four if partner had opened one spade. The last hand is the type with which you would bid four hearts if you had not already passed. Now that you and both opponents have passed, there is no need for a pre-empt, so you just bid three hearts. It is true that partner needs very little for game (♠ x x, ♡ A K x x, ◇ x x x x, ♣ Q x x), but there is almost no danger of his passing when your hand is so distributional and the opponents are quiet. If his hand were as weak as that, the opponents would be cold for four spades, and surely they would have entered the bidding. The danger of missing game is less than the danger of reaching an unmakable slam if you bid four hearts and partner has a good hand with duplicated strength in diamonds.

OPENER	RESPONDER
	Pass
1 ♡	?

Bid four hearts with the following hands: ♠ x, ♡ K J x x, ◇ A Q x x x x, ♣ x x; ♠ x x, ♡ K x x x x, ◇ A J x x x, ♣ x; ♠ x x, ♡ K x x x, ◇ K x x, ♣ A Q x x.

While a two-level response is often passed by a third- or fourth-hand bidder, a suit response at the one-level is seldom passed. Consequently, responder should bid one heart or one spade over a minor-suit opening just as though he had not passed originally.

A raise of a minor suit shows the same point range (6-10) as does a major-suit raise. Unless the opponents overcall, it should never be given with less than four trumps or with 4-3-3-3 distribution. Also the raise denies possession of a biddable four-card major. Occasionally you may gamble by raising a one-diamond bid with a weak four-card heart suit on the theory that partner probably does not have hearts (he normally opens one heart with biddable hearts and diamonds) and two diamonds is more pre-emptive than a one-heart bid. A double raise is not forcing, but it invites partner to bid three no-trump with about 15 points. Typical double raises of one diamond are ♠ x x, ♡ K x x, ◇ K J x x x, ♣ K x x and ♠ x, ♡ A x x, ◇ Q J x x x x, ♣ J x x.

When one bid describes your hand perfectly, prefer the one bid to two bids. At one time, it was fashionable in some circles never to open the bidding with one no-trump and never to respond two no-trump to a suit opening bid

OPENER	RESPONDER
1 ♠	?

♠ Q x x, ♡ K x x, ◇ A Q x x, ♣ K x x. Suppose that you respond two diamonds and partner re-bids two hearts. Now you can't bid less than three no-trump. Partner would pass your three no-trump bid with ♠ K J 10 x x, ♡ A Q x x, ◇ K x, ♣ x x. For all he knows, you may have a double club stopper or a long diamond suit which the king will solidify. If responder bids two no-trump on the first round, the bidding will be very easy.

OPENER	RESPONDER
1 ♠	2 NT
3 ♡	3 ♠
4 ♠	

After responder describes his hand by bidding two no-trump, he should normally show the three-card support when his partner bids a new suit—unless he is very strong in the unbid suits, for example: ♠ J x x, ♡ K x x, ◇ K Q 10, ♣ K Q 9 8. After bidding two no-trump and three spades, responder should pass opener's re-bid, even if it is four hearts. To re-bid hearts, opener must have five, but he might have only four spades (♠ K J 10 x, ♡ A Q x x x, ◇ K x x, ♣ x).

OPENER	RESPONDER
1 ♠	?

♠ K x x x, ♡ x x, ◇ A Q x x, ♣ K x x: This is a perfect minimum three-spade bid. Perhaps no harm will result from a two-diamond bid, but you can't tell for sure. If nothing worse happens, you may help the defenders to choose the best opening lead. Add a little more strength (♠ K x x x, ♡ x x, ◇ A K J x, ♣ K x x) and the two-diamond bid may create bidding difficulties. When opener re-bids two spades, you can only raise to four. He is supposed to pass with ♠ A x x x x x, ♡ K Q x, ◇ x, ♣ A x x, or ♠ Q J x x x x, ♡ A K x, ◇ x x, ♣ A x, since another bid on his part would constitute the bridge crime of trapping. However, over a three-spade response, he would make a mild slam try and the rest would be easy.

Let's get back to the single raise. Six to ten points is a rather wide range to be covered by a so-called limit bid. If opener makes a re-bid under game, responder is supposed to take aggressive action with eight points or more. However, at this stage, an intelligent use of evaluation factors is vital. When opener re-bids his suit,

OPENER	RESPONDER
1 ♡	2 ♡
3 ♡	

practically any eight points are enough to bid game. Even then, it pays to be conservative when most of your strength is in queens and jacks (♠ J 10 x, ♡ Q x x x, ◇ Q x, ♣ Q J x x), but for the most part, you must simply hope that your values fit partner's hand. If you bid again, you don't necessarily have to bid four hearts. Bid three no-trump with ♠ K x x, ♡ Q x x, ◇ K x x, ♣ Q x x x, or ♠ Q 10 x, ♡ K x x, ◇ A x x x, ♣ x x x. Bid three spades with ♠ Q J x x x, ♡ A J x, ◇ x x x, ♣ J x in order to give partner a chance to bid three no-trump.

When partner bids a new suit, for example

OPENER	RESPONDER
1 ♡	2 ♡
3 ◇	

he does not necessarily deny a five-card suit, but you must take the possibility of a four-card suit into consideration. The bullish features of your hand will be four-card, or longer, trump support, a fit for partner's second suit, and top strength. The bearish features will be skimpy trump support, a bad fit for partner's second suit (a worthless tripleton is the worst possible fit, while a singleton or doubleton and lots of trumps is a good fit), and scattered queens and jacks in the unbid suits.

Suppose the bidding in each of the following examples is

OPENER	RESPONDER
1 ♡	2 ♡
3 ◇	?

(a) ♠ A x, ♡ K Q x x, ◇ x x x, ♣ x x x x: Bid four hearts. Your diamond fit is the worst possible, but everything else about the hand is good.

(b) ♠ x x x, ♡ K 10 9 x, ◇ Q J, ♣ x x x x: Bid four hearts again. You should have passed like a flash if partner had re-bid three hearts, but your hand is pretty good in support of a heart-diamond two-suiter.

(c) ♠ A x x, ♡ Q x x x x, ◇ x x, ♣ x x x: This hand also rates a four-heart bid. When partner bids two suits, it is better to have a side ace than a side king-queen which might be opposite partner's singleton. You also like a doubleton in partner's second suit with five trumps. This is a better hand than ♠ A x x, ♡ Q x x x, ◇ x x, ♣ x x x x even though both count the same.

(d) ♠ A x x, ♡ K J x, ◇ J x, ♣ x x x x x: Bid four hearts despite the three-card trump holding. There is too much strength for a return to three hearts, too little in the black suits to be enthusiastic about a no-trump contract.

(e) ♠ K x x, ♡ Q x x, ◇ K J x x, ♣ x x x: Bid three no-trump. Partner may not like three no-trump, but you should suggest the spot, since your king of spades is more valuable at a no-trump contract than at a suit contract. Even though you have fewer points in the unbid suits than in the previous hand, your diamond holding suggests that you can run more tricks when you once get in. Partner may have ♠ A, ♡ A K x x, ◇ A Q x x, ♣ x x x x, for example. Change the spades in the responding hand to the queen-jack instead of the king, and a conservative return to three hearts is best. The hand is that close. If opener is unable to pass three no-trump, he will not find this hand as useful at hearts—nor, for that matter, is it quite as good for no-trump.

(f) ♠ K J 10 x, ♡ Q 10 x, ◇ x x x x, ♣ Q x: Bid three hearts. Most of your strength will be useless.

(g) ♠ x x, ♡ J 10 x, ◇ K J x x x, ♣ x x x: Much as you would like to pass, you simply are not allowed to. Return to three hearts. Four diamonds is a forward-going bid which would be justified if the jack of hearts were exchanged for the king.

(h) ♠ x x x x, ♡ Q 10 x x, ◇ K x, ♣ A x x: Bid four clubs. Partner will not be interested in a third suit, especially a minor, when he has already shown two suits, one of which has been supported by you. Since he cannot be interested, you would not bother to show him a club *suit*. So the four-club bid must mean that you have a maximum raise and a particularly good fit and would bid four diamonds or four hearts except that you want to show the ace of clubs on the way in case partner should have one of the following hands: ♠ x, ♡ A K J x x, ◇ A Q J x, ♣ K J x, or ♠ —, ♡ A J x x x, ◇ A Q x x x, ♣ K Q x.

When opener re-bids two no-trump after a raise, responder may pass, and any bid he makes may be passed by opener. After a heart raise and a two no-trump re-bid, responder should

pass with ♠ x x x, ♡ K x x, ◇ x x, ♣ Q J x x x,
bid three no-trump with ♠ J 10 x, ♡ K x x, ◇ x x, ♣ Q J 9 x x,
bid three hearts with ♠ x x, ♡ J x x x, ◇ K J x x, ♣ x x x, or
♠ x, ♡ K x x, ◇ K x x x x, ♣ x x x x.

He should bid four hearts with ♠ x x x x, ♡ K x x x, ◇ A x x, ♣ x x, and he should also bid four hearts, not three diamonds, with ♠ x, ♡ K J x, ◇ K J x x x, ♣ x x x x, since a three-diamond bid would show a weak hand, such as ♠ x, ♡ Q x x, ◇ Q J x x x x, ♣ x x x.

When you as responder have just enough strength for one bid, consider the following factors: In all the following examples, partner has opened one heart.

(*a*) ♠ Q 10 x, ♡ Q x x, ◇ Q J x x, ♣ x x x: Bid one no-trump. Your heart support is adequate for a raise to two; but with secondary honors and no ruffing values, your hand should produce seven tricks at no-trump more easily than eight tricks at hearts. Besides, a raise to two hearts is more encouraging than a one no-trump response and is more apt to coax a re-bid. You should not want to encourage partner with this hand. Prefer a no-trump response with 4-3-3-3 distribution and less than nine points, particularly when your strength is mostly in queens and jacks. Also bid one no-trump with ♠ Q 10 x, ♡ Q x x x, ◇ Q J x, ♣ x x x despite the four-card heart support.

(*b*) ♠ A x x, ♡ Q x x, ◇ K x x x, ♣ x x x: This time you want to offer a little encouragement, since your hand is near the top of the 6-10 point range. Bid two hearts, and if partner bids three hearts, you may then bid three no-trump.

(c) ♠ A x x x x, ♡ K x x, ◇ x, ♣ x x x x: One spade looks like the natural bid, but it is not best. If partner should re-bid one no-trump, you would have to return him to hearts, and the combination of bids would promise a better hand. Or if partner re-bids two hearts, you would overbid by raising to three and risk missing game by passing. Always plan to show adequate trump support for partner's major suit. If you are too weak to show it later, you must show it right away.

(d) ♠ A x x x, ♡ Q 10 x, ◇ x x x, ♣ x x x: Bid one spade for the same reason that you bid one no-trump without a biddable spade suit. With this hand you don't want to pass the seven-trick level voluntarily.

Already I have expressed my dislike of a no-trump response with a doubleton, particularly a worthless doubleton. The worst doubleton is in spades unless partner has bid spades.

OPENER   RESPONDER
1 ♡   ?

♠ x x, ♡ 10 x x, ◇ K J 10 x, ♣ A x x x: A two-heart response is considerably better than a one no-trump response. A doubleton king or queen is not too bad for no-trump, but a doubleton ace is undesirable. With ♠ K x, ♡ 10 x x, ◇ K x x x, ♣ J x x x, respond one no-trump, but with ♠ A x, ♡ 10 x x, ◇ K x x x, ♣ x x x x, bid two hearts.

OPENER   RESPONDER
1 ♡   ?

♠ A x x, ♡ Q x x, ◇ A x x, ♣ x x x x: This is a deceptive hand, in a way. It is a very good hand if partner has a long heart suit, but just a mediocre hand if he has balanced distribution. Obviously it is too strong for a one no-trump response. The orthodox bid is two hearts, but you may miss a cold three no-trump contract if partner has ♠ x x, ♡ A K x x x x, ◇ x x x, ♣ A x, or even ♠ x x, ♡ A K x x x x, ◇ K x, ♣ x x x. The best response is one spade. If partner re-bids one no-trump, you pass, having probably stopped the most dangerous lead. If he re-bids two hearts, you bid two no-trump. If partner then bids three hearts, intending to sign off, you bid three no-trump! You must have a good play for three no-trump opposite a six-card heart suit with your heart fit and controls.

OPENER   RESPONDER
  1 ♡   ?

♠ K J 10 x, ♡ x x, ◇ x x, ♣ K Q 10 x x: Whether playing duplicate or rubber bridge, you are too weak for two forward-going bids. At rubber bridge many players would bid two clubs, hoping for a raise or two no-trump re-bid with about 16 points. A two-club bid is slightly better than one spade if your only concern is getting to game. But over two clubs, partner may bid two hearts because he has no better bid, while he would have re-bid one no-trump over a spade response. The probability of reaching a better part-score contract and the lessened inducement for reaching skimpy game contracts dictate a choice of one spade at duplicate. There is another danger in responding two clubs. What if opener re-bids two diamonds? A preference bid of two hearts shows a much better hand and much better hearts. A two no-trump re-bid would be quite a stretch. A reverse bid of two spades would be worse. Of course a two-diamond re-bid over one spade would also present a problem. However, the two-diamond bid is not quite so likely. Opener would re-bid one no-trump over one spade with ♠ Q x, ♡ A Q x x, ◇ A Q x x, ♣ x x x, but he is forced to re-bid diamonds over two clubs. If he bids two diamonds over one spade anyway, a return to two hearts will not be quite so misleading. He will hope for better heart support, but he will not expect a better hand.

OPENER   RESPONDER
  1 ♡   ?

♠ K Q J x, ♡ x x, ◇ x x, ♣ K Q x x x: If you intend to show both suits, bid clubs first. The problem is whether you should show both suits. If partner's strength is in the red suits, this hand will not help him much. I recommend a one-spade response with the intention of re-bidding as follows: Raise a one no-trump re-bid to two no-trump. Bid three clubs over a club re-bid or a raise to two spades. (If the bidding is

OPENER	RESPONDER
1 ♡	1 ♠
2 ♡	3 ♣

responder guarantees five spades; he should not bid both suits with four of each; and if he has five clubs and four spades, he should bid clubs first if he intends to bid both suits. However, when opener raises the spade bid instead of re-bidding his own suit, responder may bid a new suit with only four spades. He may not have intended to bid both suits unless his spades were raised.) Bid two no-trump over a re-bid of two diamonds. *Pass* a re-bid of two hearts. This last decision appears rather conservative, but if the hands fit badly, even two hearts may be too high.

OPENER	RESPONDER
1 ♣	?

♠ K J x x, ♡ Q 10 x x x, ◇ A x, ♣ x x: Bid one spade. You are strong enough to bid both suits so long as you don't reverse. A one-heart response would force you to pass a two-club or one no-trump re-bid.

OPENER	RESPONDER
1 ♣	?

♠ K J x x, ♡ Q 10 9 x, ◇ K x, ♣ x x x: Bid one heart. If partner re-bids one no-trump or two clubs, for example, you must pass. Since you have only enough strength for one bid (except that you would raise if partner should re-bid one spade), prefer the heart bid which will not shut out a spade re-bid by partner. A one-spade response would force partner to re-bid one no-trump with ♠ A x, ♡ A x x x, ◇ x x x, ♣ A J x x, and the heart fit would not be discovered.

OPENER	RESPONDER
1 ♣	?

♠ K J x x, ♡ Q 10 9 x, ◇ K x, ♣ Q 10 x: This time you are strong enough to bid both spades and hearts, but to do so would give partner an erroneous impression as to your distribution. He would expect you to have at least nine cards in the majors to bid both suits. The proper bid is one heart again.

Unless partner bids spades, you intend to re-bid some number of no-trump.

OPENER	RESPONDER
1 ♣	?

♠ K J x x, ♡ 10 9 x x, ◇ K x, ♣ x x x: Don't bid one heart! If you want partner to raise your suit with three trumps to an honor and a doubleton, you can't afford to bid such ratty suits. Besides, when you have this bad a hand, there is a reasonable possibility that the opponents will buy the bid, and you surely don't want a heart lead. A one-diamond response has some merit in that partner is extremely unlikely to raise you, and it leaves the way open to finding a fit in either major. The trouble is that sometimes the opponents overcall and partner passes. Then you are forced to bid one of the majors later yourself—perhaps not with this weak a hand, but with one of similar distribution—which gives a very different impression of your distribution and hand-type from what you have. On the other hand, the opponents are not likely to get too exuberant in the majors when you have four of each; if they have a suit, it is probably diamonds. So one diamond is probably a good bid at duplicate, although you would prefer one spade at rubber bridge.

OPENER	RESPONDER
1 ♣	?

♠ J x x x, ♡ Q x x, ◇ K x x x, ♣ A x: Bid one diamond rather than one spade, since your spades are too weak to bid. If partner had opened one diamond, you wouldn't want to shut out the spade suit, so you would be forced to bid one heart or one spade. I prefer a one-heart bid. If partner re-bids one spade, you can be pretty sure that the hand should be played in spades, while if you bid one spade and partner raises, you won't know how strong partner's spade support is. If partner re-bids one no-trump over your one-heart bid, you can pass comfortably, having probably stopped the most dangerous opening lead. Even if partner raises hearts, you can re-bid no-trump with reasonable safety, and if worst comes to worst and partner takes you to four hearts, you should have a good play for it. However, this is the weakest hand you can afford to bid that way. Normally you need 11 points to bid a three-card spade suit over one heart or a three-card heart suit over one diamond; in other words, you need enough strength for two bids so that you can rescue yourself if partner raises. The purpose of such a bid is to stop the lead of what is often your weak point against an eventual notrump contract. When partner opens the bidding, his least likely side suit is the one just above it in rank, and it is this suit which an expert defender tends to lead if he has a close decision.

OPENER	RESPONDER
1 ♣	?

♠ x x, ♡ Q x x x, ◊ K J x x, ♣ Q x x: Bid one diamond. Unless partner can bid hearts, you are not interested.

OPENER	RESPONDER
1 ♣	?

♠ x x, ♡ K J x x, ◊ K J x x, ♣ x x x: I do not believe in carrying this idea of letting partner bid the suits too far. This is a normal one-heart response. There is nothing to be gained by responding one diamond unless your partner plays the hands better than you. The diamond response may lose when two hearts is the best contract despite three-card support. It loses heavily when your left-hand opponent overcalls one spade and causes your side to miss a 4-4 heart fit, because neither you nor your partner is strong enough to bid hearts at the two-level. I also prefer a one-heart response to a one-diamond response with ♠ Q x x, ♡ K Q J x, ◊ 9 x x x x, ♣ x and other hands of a similar nature.

In choosing your opening bid, you were urged to consider what you would re-bid over any minimum response. This principle of anticipation should be kept in mind by all the players at all times.

OPENER	RESPONDER
1 ◊	?

♠ x x, ♡ K Q J 10 x x x, ◊ x x, ♣ x x: Suppose that you respond one heart, and partner re-bids one spade. What next? Three hearts would be a terrific overbid, guaranteeing more honor strength and asking for a raise with any excuse. A two-heart re-bid would be passed by partner with four top tricks and a singleton or void in hearts. If you had looked ahead, you would have foreseen this dilemma and would have avoided it by responding three hearts the first time. This bid shows a good solid suit, six playing tricks, and little defensive strength. Besides, at the time you first responded, you didn't know that your left-hand opponent would pass or that partner's second suit was spades. The three-heart bid has a good chance of pre-empting the opponents out of their best contract if they have the balance of strength. An immediate four-heart bid shows the same type of hand with seven playing tricks instead of six. Tend not to pre-empt with a suit as good as A K Q x x x x. When you have two top tricks, the need for a pre-empt is less, and three no-trump may be the best contract. Another reason for not pre-empting is that opener will assume a trump loser and not so much as a king outside the trump suit after a pre-empt; consequently, you might miss a slam.

Over one diamond bid four hearts with ♠ x x, ♡ K Q J 10 x x x. ♢ x, ♣ Q J x; or ♠ x, ♡ A Q J x x x x, ♢ Q x x, ♣ x x.
Bid one heart followed by four hearts with ♠ Q x, ♡ A K Q x x x x, ♢ x x x, ♣ x; or ♠ K Q J, ♡ K Q J 10 x x, ♢ x x x, ♣ x.
Bid two hearts with ♠ x x, ♡ A K J 10 x x x, ♢ A x, ♣ x x; or ♠ A x x, ♡ A K Q J x x, ♢ Q x, ♣ x x.

Let us look to the later rounds of bidding to see how responder, primarily, guides the bidding.

OPENER	RESPONDER
1 ♣	1 ♡
1 ♠	?

♠ K x, ♡ K J x x x, ♢ Q x x, ♣ J x x: Bid one no-trump. A no-trump re-bid at this point shows about 7-11 points and at least three small cards or a stopper in the unbid suit. With only seven points, you should have something like K J x or Q 10 x x of diamonds. A two no-trump re-bid shows a good 11 points up to a poor 13. Opener may pass the second round jump to two no-trump with ♠ K Q x x, ♡ x, ◇ 10 x x x, ♣ A Q 10 x; or ♠ A K 10 x, ♡ x x, ◇ x x x x, ♣ A J 9 x. A non-jump two no-trump re-bid by responder such as the following

OPENER	RESPONDER
1 ♡	1 ♠
2 ◇	2 NT

shows about the same range except that responder may have as little as ten points. Very often it is hard for responder to evaluate his hand accurately.

OPENER	RESPONDER
1 ♡	2 ◇
2 ♡	?

♠ K x x, ♡ x, ◇ K Q x x x x, ♣ K x x: If opener has a diamond fit, responder's hand is worth 13 points or more. If opener has a singleton diamond and most of his strength in hearts, even two no-trump may be too high. With this type of hand, responder should bid two no-trump, which opener will carry to three with about 14 points, being influenced somewhat by his degree of diamond fit.

OPENER	RESPONDER
1 ♡	2 ♣
2 ♡	?

♠ K x x, ♡ x x, ◇ Q 10 x, ♣ K Q x x x: In the long run, it pays to pass rather than stretch to two no-trump. Ten points in high cards with a worthless doubleton in hearts are not quite enough. If partner had re-bid two diamonds rather than two hearts, you would bid two no-trump. For one thing, while a two-diamond re-bid does not guarantee more strength than a two-heart re-bid, the maximum is higher. Another consideration is that two diamonds is not likely to be a good contract, and if you bid, two no-trump is your only choice. Many players would respond one no-trump with this hand instead of two clubs, but I think that is being slightly too conservative. To put it another way, I think that a one no-trump response should not cover such a wide range of strength.

OPENER	RESPONDER
1 ♣	1 ♡
1 ♠	?

♠ Q x x x, ♡ K x x x, ◇ x, ♣ J x x x: Bid two spades. The raise shows 8-11 points in support of spades. With ♠ K x x x, ♡ K J x x x, ◇ K x x, ♣ x, bid three spades, showing 12 or 13 points in support of spades. Why bid only three with 13 supporting points? The answer to this particular hand could be given in terms of evaluation factors. These are bad points with no aces. Besides, a singleton in partner's suit is not an unmitigated blessing; it is certainly not worth three points. However, unless you have a very good fit, you need 14 points to raise to four. There are many times when the point-count requirement for bids doesn't mesh with the requirement of 26 points for game. In this sequence quite a bit of duplication is probable. Also, opener's spade suit may be very weak. Support points are based upon the assumption that opener has a good suit, the kind that would make him open the bidding. Over this three-spade bid, opener tends to bid again if he has a good spade suit and a heart fit, even with a minimum hand. With ♠ A Q 10 x, ♡ A x, ◇ x x, ♣ Q 9 x x x, or ♠ A J 10 x, ♡ Q x, ◇ x x x, ♣ A Q x x, opener would not have a particularly good play for game opposite ♠ K x x x, ♡ K J x x x, ◇ K x x, ♣ x, and if opener held ♠ A J 10 x, ♡ Q x, ◇ x x x, ♣ K Q J x, the play for game would be almost non-existent.

OPENER	RESPONDER
1 ♣	1 ♡
1 ♠	?

♠ x x, ♡ A Q 10 x x, ◇ x x x, ♣ J x x: You should bid two clubs, although a pass or no-trump re-bid might work out all right. You certainly should not re-bid two hearts. With this weak a hand, you need another heart for a heart re-bid. You could re-bid two hearts with ♠ x x, ♡ A Q J x x, ◇ x x x, ♣ K x x, although you would prefer a no-trump re-bid with your king in diamonds instead of clubs.

OPENER	RESPONDER
1 ♡	1 ♠
2 ◇	?

♠ K J 5 4 3, ♡ J x, ◇ x x, ♣ K x x x: Bid two hearts. Again a spade re-bid is much too dangerous. While two hearts may not be a good spot, two spades is likely to be a horrible contract. Change your five-four of spades to the ten-nine, and a spade re-bid would be permissible. Then you would be in a playable contract if partner should have a singleton spade, as is quite probable when he has bid two suits.

OPENER	RESPONDER
1 ♡	1 ♠
2 ♡	?

♠ A Q 7 x x x, ♡ x, ◇ x x x, ♣ A x x: Bid just two spades. The heart bid and re-bid suggest the probability of a misfit. Had partner opened another suit or re-bid anything else, a jump to three spades would be justified. Even then, you'd feel much prouder of your hand with the ten-nine of spades instead of such small ones.

OPENER	RESPONDER
1 ♡	1 ♠
2 ◇	?

♠ A K x x x, ♡ x x x, ◇ —, ♣ Q J x x x: This time you should bid three hearts. What is wrong with three clubs? Partner would probably bid three no-trump, and you surely wouldn't leave him there. You would bid four hearts. But that gives you no chance to stop short of game. Even worse, this sequence is a slam invitation. You would bid spades, clubs, and raise hearts with ♠ A K x x x, ♡ K x x, ◇ x, ♣ A J x x, so you obviously can't bid the example hand the same way.

OPENER	RESPONDER
1 ♡	1 ♠
2 ♡	?

♠ A K x x x, ♡ x x x, ◇ A J x x, ♣ x: Bid four hearts. A three-diamond bid could lead to complications. If you bid three diamonds followed by four hearts, partner will figure you for a singleton club—which you have—but he will also picture you with a stronger hand. You can see that a slam is remote and there must be an excellent play for four hearts, so why beat around the bush?

In all the following example hands, the bidding has been

OPENER	RESPONDER
1 ◇	1 ♠
2 ♣	?

(a) ♠ Q J 9 x x, ♡ Q x x, ◇ x, ♣ K x x x: Pass! I might as well admit that not many good players share my views on this type of hand. Of course game is possible, but I think the odds are greatly against it. A two-spade bid is likely to result in an inferior contract. If you can make eight tricks at spades, you can probably make ten tricks at clubs. A raise to three clubs is too encouraging. Partner almost always bids three no-trump with a heart stopper in this sequence, even with 13 or 14 points. For all he knows, you may have a pretty good hand with nothing else to bid (♠ K Q x x, ♡ x x, ◇ x x x, ♣ A K x x). If you do raise to three clubs, you should take partner to four clubs rather than let him suffer in three no-trump if he bids three no-trump. But with secondary strength and the likelihood of a misfit, I can't see the future in inviting five clubs. Even four clubs may be too high.

(b) ♠ x x x x x x, ♡ A x, ◇ K x x, ♣ Q x: Bid two diamonds. This is a pretty good hand for partner, and it is tempting to bid two spades as a sort of compromise (too strong for two diamonds, too weak for three diamonds). But I have found that it does not pay to compromise in a suit where none of your strength lies. When this hand came up in a tournament, opener's hand was ♠ x, ♡ K x x, ◇ A Q x x x, ♣ A K x x. Over two spades, opener usually elected to pass; a two no-trump re-bid seemed slightly too aggressive in view of the probable misfit. Whenever responder bid two diamonds, opener could justifiably bid two no-trump, which responder gladly raised to three no-trump. One possible matching hand does not prove anything conclusive, but I think you are bucking the odds to re-bid spades when all your strength is elsewhere.

(c) ♠ A J x x, ♡ x x, ◇ Q 10 x, ♣ Q x x x: Again, in my opinion, three clubs is an unjustifiable stretch. If you bid three clubs, you are likely to reach a 23-point three no-trump contract.

Simply bid two diamonds, hoping that partner can bid again. Suppose that partner makes the unlikely re-bid of two spades over your two-diamond preference. He cannot have four spades in this sequence, and he may have only two—such as the king-queen doubleton. He wants to take care of the possibility that you have a fairly weak five-card spade suit (like A 10 x x x), which you would not re-bid after he has shown two suits. The two-spade bid in this sequence guarantees poor spades and a good hand—good enough so that if your spades are weak, you will be safe at three diamonds. Partner's two-spade bid is very tentative, and if your spades are weak *you cannot pass*. Obviously you are not interested in a spade contract with the example hand, nor are you interested in no-trump. So you should jump to four clubs.

(d) ♠ x x x x x, ♡ K J 10, ◇ K Q x x, ♣ x: This time the temptation is to bid two no-trump because of the powerful heart stopper. Again, however, the correct bid is two diamonds, since game is not particularly likely unless partner can bid again. He needs 16 or 17 points to have a good play for three no-trump or five diamonds unless the hands fit perfectly. With ♠ A x, ♡ A x, ◇ J 10 x x x, ♣ A Q 10 x, for example, he should make the mild game try of three diamonds over your preference. As you will note, a preference bid, particularly a minor-suit preference, covers a fairly wide range, just as a first-round raise or no-trump response. Obviously, with the same type of hand, responder would have jumped if opener's suit had been a major. Remember that when no major-suit fit has been found, minor-suit raises and jump preferences are primarily invitations to three no-trump. If responder bid three diamonds with ♠ x x x x x, ♡ K J 10, ◇ K Q x x, ♣ x, then he would not know whether to pass his partner's three no-trump re-bid or not. If he bids only two diamonds and still gets to three no-trump, he knows that there will be a good play for it.

We agreed earlier that when responder bids and re-bids a minor suit, such a re-bid is not constructive, but is in the nature of a sign-off bid. Suppose opener bids the majors, responder bids and re-bids diamonds, and opener then bids three no-trump. What should responder do with ♠ x x, ♡ x, ◇ A Q 10 x x x x, ♣ 10 x x? His hand will be almost worthless for no-trump if

his partner has a singleton diamond; and it will be pretty dangerous for no-trump if his partner has a worthless doubleton in
diamonds. But responder should pass, confident that opener has
the king of diamonds. Opener would have no right to bid three
no-trump over the sign-off without a diamond fit. Suppose that
responder has ♠ x x, ♡ x, ◇ A K Q 10 x x x, ♣ 10 x x. Again
opener bids and re-bids either major (or both). This time responder should bid three clubs in an attempt to force his partner
to bid three no-trump. With seven solid tricks, responder cannot afford to sign off in diamonds.

OPENER	RESPONDER
1 ♠	2 ◇
2 ♠	?

♠ x x, ♡ J x, ◇ A K Q 10 x x, ♣ x x x. If responder had
passed originally, he could have jumped to three diamonds to
show six tricks for no trump. As it is, he simply has to guess
what to do. I usually re-bid two no-trump with this type of hand,
hoping my suit will break and that the opponents will not run
too many tricks before I get in. Why do we have to distort the
bidding like this? In order to save a minor-suit bid and re-bid
for weak hands, which occur more frequently than the solid-suit
hands.

OPENER	RESPONDER
1 ♠	2 ♣
2 ♡	3 ♣
4 ♣	?

♠ x x x, ♡ K x, ◇ x x x x, ♣ Q 10 x x: Bid five clubs.
When you only bid three clubs over two hearts, you showed a
minimum raise, but partner was still interested in game. Your
excellent heart fit makes a raise to game mandatory. Partner's
hand: ♠ A Q, ♡ A 9 x x, ◇ x, ♣ A J 9 x x x.

OPENER	RESPONDER
1 ♠	2 ◇
2 ♠	2 NT
3 ♡	?

♠ K, ♡ Q x x, ◇ A x x x x, ♣ A x x x: Bid four spades. Partner's bidding shows 6-4 distribution in the majors, and you must go all the way to game with your minor-suit aces and fitting honors in the majors.

OPENER	RESPONDER
1 ♣	1 ♠
2 ♣	2 NT
3 ◇	?

♠ A Q x x, ♡ J x x, ◇ A x x, ♣ 10 9 x: Bid four clubs. This is an easy problem. Partner's three-diamond bid must be forcing. Perhaps he has 6-4 distribution in the minors, and perhaps he is just trying to warn you away from three no-trump unless you have a heart stopper; in fact you probably should have a double heart stopper or a single stopper with a high honor in clubs in order to bid three no-trump. If partner had a solid club suit, he would gamble on your ability to stop hearts.

OPENER	RESPONDER
1 ♣	1 ◇
1 NT	3 ♣
3 ◇	?

♠ x x, ♡ x, ◇ K Q J x x, ♣ K Q x x x: Bid just four clubs. If partner can then bid four spades, you will bid six clubs. Is four clubs forcing? I do not believe so, but you have no assurance that you should be in game anyway since this is duplicate. If three no-trump will not make, any plus score your way will be a good board, even plus 150, so there is no point in reaching a close or doubtful game. While four clubs is not forcing, it is inconceivable that opener will pass with three aces when you have shown a distributional hand. When I held this hand, my partner did the inconceivable and passed with three aces. Plus 170, and it was still a good board! More than half the teams were in three no-trump, going down.

OPENER	RESPONDER
1 ♡	1 ♠
1 NT	?

♠ 10 x x x x x, ♡ x x, ◊ A x x, ♣ x x: Bid two spades. Partner has limited his hand with the one no-trump re-bid and is bound to pass your two-spade bid. You don't feel very sure of making two spades, but you are almost certain that partner will go down in one no-trump, possibly two or three tricks.

OPENER	RESPONDER
1 ♡	1 ♠
1 NT	?

♠ J x x x x, ♡ x, ◊ K J x x x, ♣ x x: Bid two diamonds. Again partner can take no aggressive action. He must pass or bid two spades. On rare occasions he may raise to three diamonds or jump to three spades (♠ K 10 9, ♡ A J 9 x, ◊ A Q x, ♣ J 9 x), but he must not re-bid no-trump.

OPENER	RESPONDER
1 ♡	1 ♠
1 NT	?

♠ A Q x x x x, ♡ x x, ◊ K 10 x, ♣ x x: At rubber bridge you might bid two spades. The fact that you bid at all is somewhat encouraging, and partner would bid again with a maximum. But two spades is a complete sign-off at duplicate, so you must bid three spades. Partner will pass with 13 points, or 14 points including a worthless doubleton in spades.

OPENER	RESPONDER
1 ♡	1 ♠
1 NT	?

♠ A Q x x x x, ♡ x x, ◊ A 10 x, ♣ Q x: Bid three no-trump since you have supporting honors in the unbid suits. Suppose your hand were ♠ A Q 10 x x x, ♡ x x, ◊ A J x, ♣ 10 x. Now you don't know whether four spades or three no-trump is the right spot. You are too strong to bid three spades, since you surely wish to reach game. The solution is to bid three diamonds. Partner should bid three spades or even raise diamonds in preference to bidding three no-trump without a double stopper in clubs. He needs a *good* spade fit, not a poor one, to bid three no-trump with K x x of clubs.

OPENER	RESPONDER
1 ◇	1 ♠
2 ♣	?

Opener has shown about 13-16 points in support of spades. In rubber bridge you would scrape up another bid with 10 points, especially if the raise is reversed for better-than-minimum hands. In duplicate, you don't want to reach skimpy game contracts, so *after revaluing your hand*, you should normally pass unless you have 11 points or more. ♠ A Q x x x, ♡ x x, ◇ K x x, ♣ x x x; ♠ K Q x x x, ♡ x, ◇ Q J x x, ♣ x x x: Bid three spades with these hands despite the ten points because of the five-card suit, which is really worth more than a point, and the fact that your high cards are all favorably located. You would surely pass with the second hand if your singleton were in diamonds, and you would probably pass if your club and diamond holdings were exchanged. ♠ A Q x x, ♡ J x, ◇ K x x x, ♣ x x x: Bid three diamonds, giving partner the option of passing, bidding three no-trump, or three or four spades. ♠ Q x x x, ♡ K x x, ◇ J x x, ♣ A J x: Bid two no-trump, intending to pass almost any bid partner makes, including three diamonds. ♠ K 10 x x x, ♡ A x, ◇ K x, ♣ A x x x: Bid three clubs (100 per cent forcing) to find out what kind of raise partner has. If he can jump to four spades, you may have a good play for six.

OPENER	RESPONDER
1 ◇	1 ♠
3 ♠	?

If partner's hand were always distributed 4-4-3-2, you could bid game with eight points and pass with less. But frequently partner's hand is unbalanced, and the important thing is to have a good trump suit and strength in your suit and his. You should bid four spades with K Q x x x of spades even with no other values. Bid four spades with ♠ K x x x, ♡ x x, ◇ K x x, ♣ x x x x, but pass if either king is in another suit. You should pass with ♠ Q x x x, ♡ Q x, ◇ x x x, ♣ K J x x, since your strength is poorly placed. With another jack, you would bid three no-trump.

OPENER	RESPONDER
1 ♠	2 ♡
3 ♡	?

Most of the time you bid again automatically. ♠ x x, ♡ K Q x x x x, ◇ K x x, ♣ x x is a borderline hand. Give yourself a singleton spade or the queen-jack of diamonds in place of the king, and it is a clear-cut pass.

OPENER	RESPONDER
1 ♠	2 ◇
3 ◇	?

You would pass with ♠ x x, ♡ x x, ◇ K Q J 10 x x, ♣ x x x, or ♠ A x, ♡ x x x x, ◇ K J 10 x x, ♣ x x. With a normal two-diamond bid (11 points or more), you usually take a shot at three no-trump unless you have support for partner's major suit.

OPENER	RESPONDER
1 ♡	1 ♠
2 ◇	3 ♠
3 NT	?

♠ A J 9 x x x, ♡ J x x, ◇ A Q x, ♣ x: In the first place, note that we would have bid four spades rather than three spades if partner had re-bid one no-trump. However, when he bids suits of his own, there is a strong possibility of a misfit, and we bid more conservatively. Partner could have passed three spades. Three no-trump might be the right contract, but it is very unlikely. If partner has 4-4-3-2 distribution, he would have re-bid one no-trump instead of two diamonds. If partner has nine cards in the red suits, and something like K Q x of clubs, then he must fit spades very badly, and the opponents can run the club suit before the spades are established. There are two schools of thought as to what the correct bid is at this point. Many players prefer a four-diamond bid, which is a very flexible bid. Opener can bid four hearts over four diamonds if he has a five-card heart suit. However, I feel that a four-heart bid by opener over four diamonds shows a *good* five-card suit—strong enough to play opposite a doubleton honor in support. Consequently, opener would not bid four hearts with A x x x x, for example. For that reason, I prefer a four-heart bid by *responder* over three no-trump. Responder cannot have four hearts in this bidding sequence, and opener cannot pass the four-heart bid with a four-card suit (unless it is A K Q x). He must return to four spades despite his singleton! Since responder's spades are not particularly good, and since opener probably has five diamonds if he only has four hearts (although 1-4-4-4 distribution is possible), responder should "run out" of four spades to five diamonds, despite his six-card suit.

The reason that you could afford to raise an unre-bid suit at the four level with J x x was that your strong efforts to arrive at four spades denied good heart support and showed partner a place to go if his hearts were weak. There are other occasions where you may make a bid which partner cannot pass unless he has what you need.

NORTH	EAST	SOUTH	WEST
1 ◇	Pass	1 NT	2 ♡
Pass	Pass	?	

♠ A Q x, ♡ K x, ◇ x x x x, ♣ x x x x: Bid two spades! Partner knows you don't have a biddable spade suit because you responded one no-trump. He absolutely must not pass unless he has four spades. You hope that he has something like ♠ K 10 x x, ♡ x x x, ◇ A K x x, ♣ A x. If partner does not have four spades, he must bid *something*, two no-trump or three diamonds, for example.

OPENER	RESPONDER
1 ◇	1 NT
2 ♡	?

♠ A K x, ♡ J 10 x, ◇ x x x, ♣ x x x x: Bid two spades. This time the spade bid obviously shows a concentration of strength. After the two-spade bid, partner will not be afraid of a three no-trump contract with ♠ x, ♡ A K Q x, ◇ A K x x x, ♣ Q 10 x, but he will bid four diamonds with ♠ Q 10 x, ♡ A K Q x, ◇ A K x x x, ♣ x, enabling you to reach five diamonds. Responder could not bid three clubs over two hearts to show a concentration of strength in clubs; at least such a three-club bid would be ambiguous, since a one no-trump response does not deny a biddable club suit.

OPENER	RESPONDER
1 ♣	1 ♡
1 ♠	1 NT
2 ♡	?

♠ Q x x, ♡ K J x x, ◇ K x x x, ♣ J x: You know that partner has only three hearts from his failure to raise immediately. So which is better, to play two hearts with a 4-3 trump holding or two spades with a 4-3 trump holding? Hearts will definitely be better. In the first place, you have a sure diamond stopper if you are declarer and diamonds are led originally. If the opening lead is not a diamond, you have additional time. Even with J 10 x x of diamonds, you should prefer hearts to spades because you can take the diamond ruffs with partner's three-card holding while preserving your four-card trump length intact. In choosing between two trump suits split 4-3, tend to choose the one where the three-card trump holding will take the ruffs. If your hand were ♠ x x, ♡ A Q J x, ◇ J 10 x x, ♣ Q x x, you should bid three hearts. Partner's series of bids shows better than a minimum hand as well as a shortage of diamonds. Your strong trump holding and absence of duplication in diamonds warrant another bid.

OPENER	RESPONDER
1 ◇	1 ♡
1 NT	3 ♣
3 ♡	?

♠ A, ♡ 10 9 x x x, ◇ A x, ♣ A 9 x x x: Bid three no-trump! Your hearts are too weak to bid four hearts by yourself. It is conceivable that partner has only a doubleton honor in hearts with no spade stopper. You have already shown by your three-club bid that you have some doubts about three no-trump being the right contract, and if partner has something like ♠ Q x x, ♡ A Q x, ◇ K x x x x, ♣ K x, he will surely continue to four hearts. On the other hand, if partner has weak hearts and good club support, three no-trump is probably a better contract. (♠ K x x, ♡ J x x, ◇ K Q J x, ♣ K J x, or ♠ 10 9 x, ♡ A x, ◇ K Q 10 x x, ♣ K Q x.)

OPENER	RESPONDER
1 ♠	2 ◇
2 ♡	?

♠ Q x, ♡ K x x, ◇ A K 10 x x x x, ♣ x: This is the type of hand one finds in the *Bridge World* problems. I am sure that the experts would choose at least four different bids, but a majority would bid four diamonds. There is no clear-cut answer, but we can learn a lot by analyzing the advantages and disadvantages of various alternatives. Four diamonds is, of course, the most natural bid, which is an advantage in itself. Perhaps partner can solve all our problems by bidding six diamonds with ♠ A J x x x, ♡ A Q x x, ◇ Q, ♣ A x x. What are the disadvantages? First, is four diamonds forcing? To be practical, you must decide whether *partner* will consider four diamonds forcing, not whether you think so. According to the Goren school of players, four diamonds is forcing because it is a jump by responder—as simple as that. While I have a lingering doubt that it should be forcing, I am tired of bucking the tide, so I will concede this point. The biggest danger in bidding four diamonds is that partner will raise to five. This is duplicate, remember? There is probably a good play for four hearts. Suppose you bid four hearts. Everything will be fine if opener has five hearts or even A Q x x, but if he has a weak four-card suit, he may lose control of the hand. Four spades might be the right spot if partner has five spades and four hearts. How can you find out? You could bid three clubs, which is forcing. Partner will probably re-bid spades at this point with a good five-card suit. A club raise is very unlikely, since partner would open one club with a singleton diamond and 4-4-4-1 distribution. While I cannot quite put my finger on it, I know there must be something wrong with a bid as unnatural as three clubs. A more orthodox solution is a raise to three hearts. If partner bids again, he would bid three spades with five good spades and four mediocre hearts. Of course three hearts might be passed when you were cold for four hearts or five diamonds. What is my recommendation? For a change, I have none.

OPENER	RESPONDER
1 ♠	2 ♣
2 ♡	?

♠ x x, ♡ K, ◇ A x x, ♣ A J 9 8 x x x: This is another tough one, but I believe there is a clear-cut answer. Bid three diamonds. If partner now bids three no-trump, then three no-trump is probably the best contract and it will be played from the right direction. If partner bids four clubs, you should gamble on six clubs. But suppose he bids three hearts. Now partner probably has five of each major. This will not leave him many cards in the minors. Either he has a misfit for clubs or the opponents have too many diamonds between them for you to try three no-trump with a single stopper. So you bid just four clubs despite your good hand. However, the tale is not over, and justice triumphs in the end. Partner has ♠ A x x x x, ♡ A Q J x x, ◇ x x, ♣ Q, and realizing that his major suit aces and queen of clubs constitute much better support for a club contract than you are able to count on, he raises to five clubs.

OPENER	RESPONDER
1 ◇	1 ♡
2 NT	?

♠ Q 10 x x, ♡ K x x x, ◇ K x x, ♣ x x: Bid three no-trump. It is possible that partner has four spades, but you cannot afford to investigate. Three diamonds is non-forcing, and three spades would be extremely dangerous, since partner would take a preference for four hearts with three-card support, figuring you for five hearts and four spades—consequently a somewhat distributional hand. When you responded one heart on this hand, you had decided not to bid spades except to raise partner if he should bid them. Don't let the two no-trump re-bid change your mind.

OPENER	RESPONDER
1 ◇	1 ♡
2 NT	?

♠ x x, ♡ K 10 x x x x, ◇ K x x, ♣ J x: Bid three hearts to give partner a choice between three no-trump and four hearts.

If partner has a long diamond suit and poor hearts, four hearts could be a very bad contract. On the other hand, four hearts might be vastly superior to three no-trump. This hand illustrates why three hearts should be forcing in this sequence.

OPENER	RESPONDER
1 ◊	1 ♠
3 ◊	?

♠ A J 10 x x, ♡ Q x, ◊ x x x, ♣ K x x x: Bid three no-trump. This hand might be captioned "First Things First." A re-bid of three spades would be forcing, but it is unlikely to get you anywhere. Partner is unlikely to have good spade support, and he may be forced to pass the three no-trump level or play three no-trump from the wrong direction. I do not mean to imply that you are certain that three no-trump will make, but you have enough general strength to make it a good gamble. Perhaps a better hand to illustrate the principle would be ♠ Q J 10 9 x, ♡ A x x, ◊ J x, ♣ Q 10 x.

OPENER	RESPONDER
1 ◊	1 ♡
2 ◊ or 1 NT	?

♠ K Q x, ♡ A Q 10 x x, ◊ Q 10 x x, ♣ x: Whether partner's re-bid was one no-trump or two diamonds, you should bid two spades. The only way that you can accurately describe your hand is by bidding hearts, spades, and diamonds in that order, which you should be able to accomplish without passing the three no-trump level unless partner shows a preference for hearts. In that case you can afford to pass the three no-trump level since four hearts is a satisfactory stopping place. It would be a pity to reach three no-trump if partner should hold ♠ A x x, ♡ J x, ◊ A J 9 x x, ♣ A x x, for example. With a club lead, he might go down at three no-trump by taking the wrong finesse when six diamonds would be cold. On the other hand, if partner has quite a bit of his strength in clubs, you can still get to three no-trump.

A sequence such as

OPENER	RESPONDER
1 ♠	2 ◇
2 ♠	3 ♣

should guarantee at least 11 points in high cards in the respond-ing hand, preferably more. This sequence is forcing, and opener usually closes his eyes and bids three no-trump if he has a stopper in the unbid suit. Responder may have a genuine two-suiter (♠ x, ♡ x x, ◇ K Q x x x, ♣ A Q 10 x x) or he may have a good balanced hand in which he is fishing for a three no-trump re-bid by opener if he has hearts stopped (♠ Q x, ♡ x x x, ◇ K Q x x x, ♣ A K x). With the latter hand, if opener bids three diamonds over three clubs, responder should bid just three spades to give opener another chance to bid three no-trump. Besides, a jump to four spades at this stage would be a mild slam try, showing a singleton heart among other things.

Let's return to opener's problems for a moment. While opener usually bids three no-trump with a heart stopper in this sequence,

OPENER	RESPONDER
1 ♠	2 ◇
2 ♠	3 ♣
?	

he may be able to exercise his judgment. Suppose he holds ♠ A K 10 x x x, ♡ A x x, ◇ x, ♣ x x x. With no fitting cards in responder's suits and only the ace in hearts (for no-trump, it would be better to have the king of hearts and a jack in one of the minors), the proper bid is three spades.

♠ A K 10 x x, ♡ A x x, ◇ x x, ♣ x x x: Things are getting worse! Probably three hearts is the best bid. This suggests a mis-fit, and if responder bids three no-trump or four diamonds, you may pass. If he has the queen of hearts, three no-trump should be played from his direction. However, if partner bids four clubs, you must raise to five with the three top tricks in the majors and no real misfit.

♠ A K x x x x, ♡ x, ◇ K x x, ♣ K x x: Thank goodness! A decent hand for a change! Over three clubs you would bid four diamonds. Suppose partner then bids five clubs. You should raise to six clubs. The worst hand he can have is ♠ x, ♡ x x, ◇ A Q 10 x x, ♣ A Q J x x. In fact, I doubt that responder would be justified in bidding so much with this hand, since he needs a perfect fit, including a singleton heart. Weaken the hand to any extent and he certainly should have bid five diamonds rather than five clubs.

Most of the bids discussed so far were voluntary bids. The problem was to choose the best bid available to describe your holding, but you had the alternative of passing. An embarrassing situation arises when you are forced to bid; yet no bid is satisfactory. We touched upon the problem in the last paragraphs.

OPENER	RESPONDER
1 ♡	1 ♠
3 ♣	?

♠ J 9 x x x, ♡ x x, ◇ x x x, ♣ A 10 x: A re-bid of three spades would show a much better suit; a three no-trump bid would show a diamond stopper. A raise to four clubs would at least *suggest* better club support, and it would pass the three no-trump level. Bid three hearts as the least of evils. Three hearts is the cheapest of your alternatives; it allows opener to show spade support at the three-level (he might be afraid to show it at the four-level if he only has three spades); it permits him to bid three no-trump himself or four hearts. In a forcing situation such as this, a preference bid at the three-level is the most noncommital bid available. Even so, you would prefer a three no-trump bid with Q x x of diamonds or a three-spade bid with Q 10 9 x x or J 10 9 x x of spades. You don't *like* to show a preference with two small cards.

OPENER	RESPONDER
1 ◇	1 ♡
2 ♠	?

♠ J x, ♡ Q x x x x, ◇ x, ♣ K x x x x: Bid three clubs. This bid does not promise additional values unless you follow up with a voluntary raise. Surely a two no-trump re-bid would be misleading as to your distribution.

After an opening two-bid, it is extremely important to locate a satisfactory trump suit right away—or to confirm partner's suit if you have adequate support. I believe that it almost always pays to raise partner's suit immediately with adequate trump support (and enough strength for a positive response). When partner bids two spades, raise to three spades with ♠ K 10 x, ♡ x x, ◇ A J 10 x x, ♣ Q x x rather than bid diamonds. A single raise of an opening two-bid is *not* a limit bid. Conversely, you should avoid an immediate raise without adequate trump support; however, in support of an opening two-bid, Q x is adequate trump support while x x x is not. If the bidding is

OPENER	RESPONDER
2 ♠	3 ◇
3 ♡	4 ♠

opener can visualize a fair responding hand lacking adequate trump support—something like ♠ x x x, ♡ x, ◇ A K J x x, ♣ x x x x, or ♠ x x x, ♡ Q x, ◇ A Q 10 x x, ♣ x x x. The hand cannot be much better, or responder would bid just three spades over three hearts and take stronger action later over the game level.

I hear so much about the "trick and a half" requirement for a positive response that I wonder where it originated. I do not know of any good players who would refuse to raise an opening two-spade bid with ♠ K Q 10 x, ♡ x x, ◇ x x x x, ♣ x x x, or ♠ Q x x, ♡ x x, ◇ A x x x, ♣ x x x x. In fact, many would raise with ♠ Q x, ♡ x x x, ◇ A x x x x, ♣ x x x. Provided your strength is not all in minor honors, six or seven points are enough for a raise or new suit bid at the two-level, and not much more is required for a three-level response. A three no-trump response normally shows 1½ honor count or eight points, and is usually considered forcing (if so, it may show a much stronger hand). In the old days, if responder had too much strength for a three no-trump response and no biddable suit, he could bid four no-trump as a natural bid. The theory was that opener was "captain" of the hand and responder would always give rather than request information. However, the tendency now is to consider a four no-trump bid by responder as Blackwood unless no-trump has been bid previously.

When the opening bid is one no-trump, a suit response must be a definite sign-off at duplicate. It simply means, "This hand will play better in my suit than in no-trump, and game is either unlikely or impossible." In rubber bridge, responder usually passes one no-trump with a bad hand on the theory that nothing horrible can happen until one no-trump is doubled. But in duplicate, you can't afford to wait for a double to rescue partner when you hold ♠ x, ♡ 9 x x x x, ◇ J 10 x x, ♣ x x x, for example. You are likely to be down three tricks at one no-trump, while two hearts should not be down more than one; in fact you might make two hearts. The opponents cannot double your sign-off for penalties very safely. You would bid the same way with a better hand, which might take eight or nine tricks but was not quite strong enough for a game try.

You could get by, after a fashion, playing all suit responses as sign-offs. You would have to bid three diamonds or three clubs with ♠ A Q x x, ♡ x x, ◇ K x x x x, ♣ x x, or ♠ K x x x, ♡ K x x x, ◇ x x, ♣ A x x, to ask partner to bid a four-card major. This is a clumsy system at best, and it gives you no opportunity to play a major-suit part-score contract when the suit is split 4-4. Also there is no way to *invite* game except to bid two no-trump. You could not try for game in a major without committing yourself to game.

The Stayman convention is almost a necessity. The basic idea is to have an artificial response, two clubs, to show an interest in game and to demand a re-bid. Opener must re-bid two hearts or two spades with a biddable major suit. Lacking a biddable major (Q x x x or better), he shows a minimum or average no-trump opening by re-bidding two diamonds or a maximum by bidding two no-trump. With both majors, he bids two spades. Some players bid three clubs to show both majors. This is all right provided opener has a maximum, but it is not a good idea with a minimum. While the primary purpose of the Stayman convention is to find a major-suit fit, the two-club bid does not guarantee a four-card major. If so used, it would be too much help to the opening leader. Since responder may bid two clubs with eight points and no major suit, a three-club bid on 16 or 17 points, just to show both majors, might get the partnership overboard.

The two no-trump re-bid commits the partnership to game unless responder re-bids clubs, showing that he has a poor hand

and a long club suit. Over the two no-trump re-bid, responder may bid three hearts or three spades, guaranteeing at least a five-card suit, and offering the choice between game in the major and no-trump; or responder may continue the bidding past the game level with a good hand. Responder never has the occasion to bid a four-card major suit when the Stayman convention is used, the idea being to make opener bid the four-card major so that responder can raise.

OPENER	RESPONDER	or	OPENER	RESPONDER
1 NT	2 ♣		1 NT	2 ♣
2 ◇	2 ♠		2 ♡	2 ♠

Stayman says that the two-spade bid is forcing. Opener cannot pass till the two no-level has been reached. And since the two-spade bid is forcing, it is possible that it is an artificial bid of some sort; consequently, opener is not supposed to raise straight to four spades. I prefer to play two spades as natural and non-forcing. Of course two spades cannot be a sign-off. Responder must have some interest in game or he would bid two spades right away instead of bidding two clubs first. Still, opener should be able to pass with an absolute minimum hand and poor spade support. Normally he will bid two no-trump or three spades, depending upon whether his strength is in fillers or top cards. Occasionally he will bid four spades even after a two-diamond re-bid. ♠ K Q x, ♡ A 10, ◇ A Q J 9, ♣ 10 9 x x and ♠ x x x x, ♡ A K x, ◇ K Q 10 x, ♣ A J are minimum hands for no-trump (or at least not maximum) but are maximum no-trump openings in support of a spade contract. The treatment I suggest is called "non-forcing Stayman."

When responder has a hand good enough to insist upon game, he must jump or bid a new suit at the three-level.

OPENER	RESPONDER
1 NT	2 ♣
2 ♡	?

Bid three spades with ♠ K Q x x x, ♡ x x x, ◇ A x x, ♣ x x. Raise to four hearts with ♠ x x, ♡ K x x x, ◇ A J 10 x x, ♣ x x. A raise to three hearts would give opener the option of passing.

OPENER	RESPONDER
1 NT	2 ♣
2 ♠	?

♠ A x, ♡ K 10 x x x, ◇ x x x x, ♣ x x: Bid two no-trump. You are not strong enough to bid three hearts, which would force the bidding to game. If opener is strong enough to bid again, and if he has the type of hand with which he would like to support hearts, he should mark time with a minor-suit bid to permit you to bid three hearts with a heart suit. Of course, with *four* hearts, he could bid hearts himself.

OPENER	RESPONDER
1 NT	2 ♣
2 ♠	3 ◇

What does the three-diamond bid mean? At this stage opener cannot tell; it may be an artificial marking-time bid. Opener should not raise to four diamonds but should re-bid as follows: With a biddable heart suit, he should bid three hearts. While a two-heart re-bid by opener would deny a spade suit, a two-spade re-bid does not deny a heart suit. Lacking a biddable heart suit, opener should re-bid spades with good spades—a five-card suit or a good four-card suit (with any three honors or two of the top three honors). Otherwise he must re-bid three no-trump. This re-bid to show a good suit is a very useful bid. Suppose responder has ♠ Q x x, ♡ K x x x, ◇ x, ♣ A x x x x. He bids two clubs and opener re-bids two spades. Responder must re-bid three diamonds at this stage since a three-club bid would just show a long club suit and a poor hand. Over three diamonds, if opener re-bids three hearts, responder will raise to four hearts. He will also raise if opener re-bids spades. Q x x is adequate trump support opposite A K x x or K J 10 x, but not adequate opposite K x x x. Another example:

OPENER	RESPONDER
1 NT	2 ♣
2 ♡	?

♠ A x, ♡ J x x x, ◇ K x x, ♣ Q J x x. You have plenty of strength for game if you find the right spot. If partner has a good heart suit, four hearts is probably a better contract than three no-trump. If he has a weak heart suit with his strength elsewhere, three no-trump will be a better contract. Suppose opener has ♠ K Q x, ♡ K x x x, ◇ A Q x, ♣ K 10 x. At four hearts he may lose three trump tricks, and the ace of clubs. With a more favorable heart break, four hearts is makable, but four no-trump would also be cold. Bid three diamonds over two hearts and pass if partner re-bids three no-trump; raise a heart re-bid to four.

Another use for the marking-time three diamond bid:

OPENER	RESPONDER
1 NT	2 ♣
2 ◇	?

♠ K x x x x, ♡ K x x x x, ◇ —, ♣ J 10 x: There should be a good play for game in a major, particularly if played from opener's direction. Over a three-diamond bid, opener should bid his stronger three-card (or unbiddable four-card) major. He has already denied possession of a biddable major suit.

Don't get the impression that a three-diamond bid is always artificial. Much depends upon the follow-up.

OPENER	RESPONDER
1 NT	2 ♣
2 ◇	3 ◇
3 ♠	3 NT
?	

♠ A x x, ♡ A x, ◇ K J x x x, ♣ K Q x: Bid six diamonds. You bid three spades because you did not know what partner had in mind, and he could have been looking for your stronger major. When he did not raise your spade bid, it looked as though three diamonds was a mild slam try and really showed a diamond suit. This is one submitted by Al Roth to the *Bridge World* magazine. Mr. Roth's recommendation was an immediate six-diamond bid over three diamonds. Apparently he never bids three diamonds in this sequence without a diamond suit. A majority of experts chose to bid three spades, which is a more flexible call.

The convention I have just explained in some detail is the original Stayman convention as recommended in Sam Stayman's first book on the Stayman system. I suggested a modification or so, but nothing basic in the way of a change. Many tournament players, including Stayman himself, now prefer a rather drastic modification, which is that opener must not re-bid two no-trump over two clubs. This may not appear to be a drastic modification, but it permits a very different sort of use of the convention. When opener is permitted to re-bid two no-trump, responder cannot afford to "monkey around" with a bad hand, and a two-club response guarantees at least 7 points, probably more. If he should bid two clubs with ♠ K x x x, ♡ J x x x, ◇ J x x x, ♣ x, he would hope to improve the contract if opener should re-bid two spades, two hearts, or two diamonds. Two diamonds might not be a very good contract, but responder would gamble on using Stayman if he could be sure that the re-bid would not be two no-trump. Once the bars are lowered and responder is permitted to bid Stayman on bad hands, all sorts of adjustments have to be made. Even then, two clubs, followed by a major-suit bid, shows some interest in game, although it may be very mild. Opener may pass such a major-suit re-bid unless responder jumps; opener may re-bid two no-trump or raise to three. To show a maximum, most players make a marking-time, new-suit bid rather than raising directly to game in a major, or jumping to three no-trump.

OPENER	RESPONDER
1 NT	2 ♣
2 ◇	2 ♡
?	

♠ Q x x, ♡ A x, ◇ K Q x x x, ♣ A Q x: Two spades is the recommended bid. It will pay off if you find partner with a rather weak two-suiter in the majors. If partner had re-bid two spades over two diamonds, this hand would be slightly too strong for a mere raise to three spades. How you show the additional strength in this situation is pretty much a matter of style.

After a two no-trump opening bid, any response commits the partnership to game. For that reason, it does opener little good to show a maximum or minimum on his first re-bid. If responder makes a slam try, opener can bid or refuse to bid to reflect his general strength. It is more useful, for slam purposes, to show distribution over a three-club response. Naturally, opener bids a four-card major if he has one. Lacking one, he should bid three diamonds with four or more diamonds or three no-trump to deny a biddable diamond suit—consequently, four or more clubs.

Remember that any response to a two no-trump bid is forcing. Experience has shown that no response can profitably be used as a sign-off. Suppose responder has ♠ J 10 x x, ♡ K x x x x, ◇ Q x, ♣ x x, or ♠ x x, ♡ K J 10 x x x, ◇ x x, ♣ x x x.

OPENER	RESPONDER
2 NT	3 ♣
3 NT	?

Obviously responder has no satisfactory bid. It would be rather odd not to mention the heart suit at all. Yet, three no-trump may be the best contract. The obvious solution is to respond three hearts on the first round, intending to pass a three no-trump or four-heart re-bid. Or with the first hand, you hope partner will bid three spades so that you can raise to four. In other words, you can't afford to bid Stayman over a two no-trump opening bid with a five-card major, particularly when it is hearts. Since any bid over two no-trump is forcing, and since there is no need to pre-empt when partner has so strong a hand, a jump to four of a major is a mild slam try. With a poor hand, just bid three of your major, and if partner re-bids three no-trump, re-bid your major if you don't like no-trump.

Some players like to use transfer bids over no-trump openings. If responder is using the Texas convention, he would respond four diamonds with ♠ x x, ♡ Q J x x x x x, ◇ A x, ♣ x x, forcing opener to re-bid four hearts (the suit immediately higher in rank). Having the opening lead come up to the opening no-trump hand may easily be worth a trick. Similarly, a four-heart response demands a four-spade re-bid by opener. While responder usually passes opener's forced re-bid, he is not obligated to do so. With ♠ K Q x x x x, ♡ x x, ◇ A K x x, ♣ x, he would bid four hearts over an opening no-trump bid and raise the four-spade re-bid to five spades or six spades.

Oswald Jacoby has suggested a transfer bid, which he calls the Jacoby Transfer Bid, to be used at the two-level. A two-club response is still Stayman, to be used for finding a 4-4 major-suit fit. But a two-diamond response demands a two-heart re-bid; a two-heart response demands a two-spade re-bid; and a two-spade response may be used to demand a three-club re-bid. Aside from placing the contract with the strong hand for low-level contracts, it is useful to describe two-suiters, and it also may be used to show the 2½-spade response type of hand. With ♠ x, ♡ A 10 9 x x x, ◇ 10 x, ♣ K 10 x x x, respond two diamonds (showing hearts and forcing partner to bid them), and bid three clubs on the next round. How else could you show both suits without reaching a higher level or risking being dropped on your first response? Also the following two sequences can be given more distinct meanings:

OPENER	RESPONDER		OPENER	RESPONDER
1 NT	2 ♣	and	1 NT	2 ♡
2 ◇	2 ♠		2 ♠	3 ♠

Both sequences show an interest in reaching four spades while giving opener the option of stopping short. The first should be used on a semi-balanced hand where no-trump is still well within the realm of possibilities, while the second sequence would show a hand that will definitely play in spades. In other words, if opener cannot raise spades to four, he should not take a fling at three no-trump to show a full 18 points, counting his scattered jacks and tens.

Chapter 4

When the Opponents Enter the Bidding

WHEN YOU or your partner opens the bidding and the opponents compete, several new problems arise. Should you double? Should you pass to let partner double? How is your offensive bidding affected? The opponents may have stuck their necks out for one reason or another. Your first thought should be to chop them off. If you can't double, consider giving partner a chance to double, provided that you have already shown some strength by a previous bid. Some of the toughest problems are along this line, whether to make another bid with additional values or to pass the bid around to partner, hoping that he can double, or at least take some action.

Let us consider what responder needs to double an overcall. The first requirement is one-and-a-half honor count, preferably more. Don't double a one-spade overcall with ♠ K J 10 9 x x, ♡ x x, ◇ x x, ♣ x x x. Someone, either partner or opponent, will surely run out. You can't help partner if he re-bids his suit. If partner doubles a rescue bid by the opponents, you have no defensive tricks to contribute and nowhere to go. With this type of hand, your only hope is that partner will reopen the bidding with a double, in which case you will pass for penalties.

In addition to the honor-count requirement, a double at the one-level requires pretty good trump strength. Responder should double a one-heart overcall with the following hands if his partner has opened the bidding with one diamond: (a) ♠ A x, ♡ Q J 10 8 x, ◇ x x, ♣ x x x x; (b) ♠ J x x x, ♡ K J 8 x, ◇ x x, ♣ A Q x; (c) ♠ Q x x, ♡ K Q 9 7, ◇ x x x, ♣ K x x; (d) ♠ K x x, ♡ Q 8 x x, ◇ x, ♣ A J x x x; (e) ♠ A Q,

♡ J 9 x x x, ◇ x x, ♣ K x x x. Hand *a* is the absolute minimum in honor count. Some players would not double with hands *b*, *c* and *d*. They save their doubles for better hands so that opener can leave the double in with ♠ Q J x, ♡ x, ◇ K Q J x x, ♣ K J x x. Everyone agrees that low-level doubles are tentative, and that opener must pull with good distribution or poor defense, but the problem is one of degree. I prefer fairly light doubles. They come up much more often than strong doubles. A minimum double opposite a minimum leave-in may not work out well, but usually one hand has a little strength to spare. The skimpiest doubles often produce the biggest sets.

A double at the two-level doesn't require as much trump strength. Three or four small trumps are enough with a good hand and a singleton in partner's suit. With four of partner's suit, you should almost never double—not unless your trumps are so solid that you can pull the opponents' trumps.

SOUTH	WEST	NORTH	EAST
1 ♡	2 ◇	?	

(*a*) ♠ A x x x, ♡ K x, ◇ Q J x x, ♣ x x x: typical double.

(*b*) ♠ K x x, ♡ x, ◇ A 9 x x, ♣ J x x x x: minimum double.

(*c*) ♠ A x, ♡ A x, ◇ 9 8 x x, ♣ Q x x x x: typical double.

(*d*) ♠ K J x x x, ♡ x, ◇ Q 10 x x, ♣ A x x.

(*e*) ♠ A Q x x, ♡ x, ◇ x x x, ♣ K J x x x.

(*f*) ♠ A x x x, ♡ x x, ◇ 9 x x, ♣ A Q J x.

Many players fail to double with hands *d*, *e*, and *f*. Hand *d* might make four spades, but there is no guarantee that game will be reached or made. The set of two diamonds may be big enough anyway. Hands *e* and *f* are not very ideal doubles, but there is no reasonable alternative. If you bid two spades and partner bids three hearts, what then? Remember, the double is only tentative.

All the doubles made so far were on hands where responder had no reason to expect game. With a good hand (♠ A Q x, ♡ J x x, ◇ K J x x, ♣ K x x), after partner opens one heart and opponent overcalls two diamonds, vulnerability enters the picture. When the vulnerability is unfavorable, it is too dangerous to double, since game seems certain, and you can't expect to beat the opponents four tricks even if partner leaves the double in. Since you seldom have a good enough hand to try for a four-trick set, partner will assume that you are doubtful about making game whenever you make a penalty double with unfavorable vulnerability. With equal vulnerability you should double with the above hand. With a close decision, try for game with a fit or length in partner's suit; double with a misfit. Consequently, when the bidding is

SOUTH	WEST	NORTH	EAST
1 ◇	2 ♣	2 NT	

responder invariably has three or more diamonds.

♠ A K x, ♡ J x x, ◇ x x x, ♣ A J 10 x:

SOUTH	WEST	NORTH	EAST
1 ♡	2 ◇	?	

The normal bid is three clubs in order to get to game. With favorable vulnerability, a double is a good gamble. If partner passes, you will probably obtain a two-trick set. If he takes the double out, you are almost certain of game. At least, he won't have three small diamonds.

Opener should pull the double at the one level slightly more frequently than a double at the two level. However, the difference is not great, since responder needs a better hand to double at the one level. As a general rule, do not pull the doubled contract, regardless of your strength or weakness if you have three of the opponents' suit or a doubleton honor. With 5-3-3-2 distribution (worthless doubleton in the opponents' suit), leave the double in unless your hand is an absolute minimum and your five-card suit is strong. In other words, with a close decision, pass when you don't have a good rescue bid. With a singleton in the opponent's suit, you need about three plus honor counts to let the double stand. With 6-4-2-1, 5-5-2-1, et cetera, or a void, the double should seldom be allowed to stand, regardless of strength.

SOUTH	WEST	NORTH	EAST
1 ◇	1 ♠	Double	Pass
?			

(a) ♠ K x, ♡ K x, ◇ A Q 10 x, ♣ 10 9 x x x: pass.
(b) ♠ x x x, ♡ x, ◇ K Q J x x, ♣ K Q J x: pass.

(c) ♠ Q, ♡ A 10 x, ◇ K J 9 x x, ♣ K J x x: pass (queen of spades is a very important card).

(d) ♠ x x, ♡ x, ◇ A K J x x, ♣ K Q 10 x x: bid two clubs.

(e) ♠ x, ♡ A Q x, ◇ A Q x x x x, ♣ K x x: pass.

(f) ♠ x x, ♡ K J 10 x x, ◇ A K 10 x x x, ♣ —: bid two hearts.

(g) ♠ x, ♡ x x x, ◇ A K Q x x x x, ♣ K x: bid three diamonds.

(h) ♠ —, ♡ A Q x, ◇ K Q x x x, ♣ A Q J x x: bid three clubs.

(i) ♠ x, ♡ Q x, ◇ A K Q 10 x x, ♣ A J x x: bid three no-trump, or three diamonds unless the opponents are vulnerable and you are not, in which case you should pass.

(j) ♠ x x, ♡ K x, ◇ A K Q J x x, ♣ A 10 x: with this last hand, you should bid three no-trump if you are vulnerable and pass otherwise. While you need a three-trick set whether both sides are vulnerable or neither side is vulnerable, there is a stronger probability that the overcall was weak if the opponents are not vulnerable.

The following hand illustrates an important point: ♠ x, ♡ J x x x, ◇ A K J x, ♣ Q x x x (both sides vulnerable):

SOUTH	WEST	NORTH	EAST
Pass	Pass	1 ◇	1 ♠
Double	Pass	?	

Bid one no-trump! Normally, a one no-trump re-bid is to be avoided with a singleton, but this is an unusual case. One no-trump must be a very weak bid, and it best describes your hand. With a mediocre balanced hand and two spades, you would pass and gamble for a one-trick set. A one no-trump bid in this situation strongly suggests 4-4-4-1 or 5-4-3-1 distribution. A two-club re-bid should show a two-suiter, not a three-suiter, and partner would never venture a two-heart bid with ♠ 9 8 7 x, ♡ A Q 9 x, ◇ Q x, ♣ A x x. Over one no-trump he should surely bid two hearts, since one no-trump could hardly be the right spot. At worst, he expects to find three hearts and a singleton spade in the south hand.

SOUTH	WEST	NORTH	EAST
1 ♠	2 ◇	Double	Pass
?			

(a) ♠ K x x x x x, ♡ K Q x, ◇ x, ♣ A x x: bid two spades.

(b) ♠ K Q J 10 x, ♡ A x, ◇ x x, ♣ Q 10 9 x: bid two spades.

(c) ♠ K x x x x, ♡ A J 10 x, ◇ x, ♣ A x x: bid two hearts.

(d) ♠ K 10 x x x, ♡ A x x, ◇ x, ♣ A J 10 x: pass (No safe rescue).

(e) ♠ K Q x x x, ♡ A K J x x, ◇ x, ♣ K x: bid two hearts.

(f) ♠ K Q x x x, ♡ A K J x x, ◇ x, ♣ A x: bid three hearts.

(g) ♠ K Q 10 9 x x, ♡ A x, ◇ x, ♣ A J 10 8: bid three spades.

(h) ♠ K Q 10 x, ♡ A 8 x x, ◇ Q x x, ♣ x x: pass.

Presumably, hand *h* was opened in third or fourth position. The point is that this is a clear-cut pass. You should beat two diamonds easily, while it is doubtful that you could make a plus score anywhere else.

Responder needs general strength, preferably two-honor count, to double an overcall when his partner has opened with a one-bid. When the opening bid is a two-bid (strong), a penalty double denies general strength. Otherwise, opener could never pass the double for fear of missing a slam. If partner opens the bidding with two spades and your right-hand opponent bids three clubs, you should be delighted to double with ♠ x x, ♡ x x x, ◇ x x x, ♣ K J 10 9 x, or ♠ x x x, ♡ J x x, ◇ x x x, ♣ Q J 8 x. However, you should not double with ♠ x x, ♡ A J x, ◇ K x x x, ♣ Q 9 x x, or ♠ J x, ♡ K x x x, ◇ K x x, ♣ A 8 x x. The double with a poor hand and concentrated strength is the only kind that makes sense if your double is for penalties. Opener must be able to pass the double with ♠ A K Q x x x, ♡ A x, ◇ A Q J x, ♣ x, without fear of missing a cold grand slam.

After a no-trump opening bid, responder can double an overcall with considerably poorer hands than he would double after a suit opening bid. One reason is that opener promises about an ace more in high cards than a suit-bid guarantees. Another reason for the lighter double is that responder can assume three trumps in opener's hand, and there can be no unpleasant surprises in the form of ruffing values in the dummy. In fact, dummy may have no entries, which will force declarer to keep leading away from whatever strength he has. Responder should double a two-heart overcall with as little as ♠ K x x, ♡ K 10 x, ◇ x x x, ♣ x x x x, or ♠ A x x x, ♡ x x x, ◇ K x x x, ♣ x x.

Opener needs about a king over a minimum to double if the opponents bid his second suit at the one-level, but he needs very little, if any, extra strength to double at the two-level.

SOUTH	WEST	NORTH	EAST
1 ◇	Pass	1 ♡	1 ♠
?			

(a) ♠ K Q x x, ♡ x x, ◇ A K x x, ♣ K x x: double.
(b) ♠ K Q 7 4, ♡ x x, ◇ A Q x x, ♣ K x x: pass.
(c) ♠ K Q 10 8, ♡ x x, ◇ A Q x x, ♣ K x x: double.

SOUTH	WEST	NORTH	EAST
1 ◇	Pass	1 ♡	2 ♣
?			

(a) ♠ x x, ♡ Q 10 x, ◇ A K x x, ♣ K 10 8 x: double.
(b) ♠ A K x, ♡ A x, ◇ K Q 8 7 x, ♣ x x x: double.

Since partner may have a poor hand and nowhere to run, these doubles can turn out badly. However, the risk is worth while. If partner has about eight points and two trumps, a set should result—sometimes a good one.

(a) ♠ A Q 9 x x, ♡ K x, ◇ A x x x, ♣ Q x (both vulnerable)

SOUTH	WEST	NORTH	EAST
1 ♠	Pass	2 ♣	2 ♡
?			

(b) ♠ Q 10 x, ♡ K x x, ◇ K x x, ♣ A K x x (both vulnerable)

SOUTH	WEST	NORTH	EAST
1 ♣	Pass	1 ♡	2 ◇
?			

(c) ♠ A x, ♡ K Q 8 7 x, ◇ x x x, ♣ A Q x (vulnerability immaterial)

SOUTH	WEST	NORTH	EAST
1 ♡	Pass	1 ♠	2 ◇
?			

In all three cases you should pass! Get rid of the idea that a pass in this situation shows a bare minimum. It is an opportunity-giving bid, especially when the opponents are vulnerable. Perhaps partner is eagerly awaiting a chance to double. More likely than that the opponent has hit partner's second suit in the possibility that you cannot make game, but partner can make a speculative double, hoping for a 200-point penalty. Under these circumstances, he can double very light, or, if unable to double, can bid again on rather meager values. Why? Because normal expectancy is to find you with a queen or jack over minimum, and you won't leave the double in if short in the opponents' suit and long in his. More tricks develop for the defenders than one would expect when declarer has a good hand and a barren dummy.

Both vulnerable:

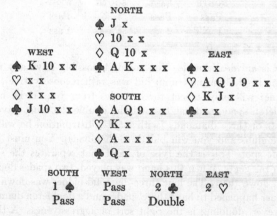

```
                    NORTH
                    ♠ J x
                    ♡ 10 x x
       WEST         ◇ Q 10 x         EAST
    ♠ K 10 x x      ♣ A K x x x      ♠ x x
    ♡ x x                            ♡ A Q J 9 x x
    ◇ x x x          SOUTH           ◇ K J x
    ♣ J 10 x x      ♠ A Q 9 x x      ♣ x x
                    ♡ K x
                    ◇ A x x x
                    ♣ Q x
```

SOUTH	WEST	NORTH	EAST
1 ♠	Pass	2 ♣	2 ♡
Pass	Pass	Double	

Even with the king of spades off-side for the defenders, a one-trick set is certain. If declarer misplays, he may be down two.

♠ K x x, ♡ A x x x x, ◇ x x, ♣ 10 x x (both vulnerable):

SOUTH	WEST	NORTH	EAST
1 ♣	Pass	1 ♡	2 ◇
Pass	Pass	?	

At rubber bridge you would surely pass. Game is out of the question, and a heart re-bid is fraught with danger. At duplicate, you would risk a two-heart bid, running to two spades if doubled.

♠ J x x x, ♡ A J x x, ◇ x x x, ♣ x x:

SOUTH	WEST	NORTH	EAST
1 ♣	Pass	1 ♡	2 ◊
Pass	Pass	?	

This time, obviously, you have no bid. Compare the last two hands with opener's hand *b*. By his passing two diamonds around to you this time instead of bidding two hearts, you will probably be plus instead of minus. The ideal hand for you to have in this bidding sequence is ♠ A x x, ♡ A 10 x x, ◊ 10 9 x x, ♣ x x. Two diamonds, doubled, should be down two or three tricks while you can't come close to making game.

♠ A x x, ♡ x x, ◊ A x x x x, ♣ Q x x (neither side vulnerable):

NORTH	EAST	SOUTH	WEST
Pass	Pass	1 ♡	Pass
1 NT	2 ♠	Pass	Pass
?			

This is an ideal double. You couldn't possibly have any more strength (the one no-trump bid was rather conservative), and partner will only expect three spades from you. If he has a singleton spade and can't stand the double, he must have six hearts or three diamonds (with 1-5-3-4 distribution he will bid three clubs and you will bid three diamonds). You must have a safe spot. This is the type of hand that separates the sheep from the goats. When this hand was played, two spades doubled went down three. The lone three-diamond bidder was down one. Opener happened to have three spades and a doubleton diamond. However, doubling is the right sort of aggressiveness. A three-diamond bid is just as risky at duplicate (minus fifty was a bottom), and it doesn't have nearly as much to gain.

A frequently misbid sequence is one in which opener bids one no-trump, responder bids two clubs (Stayman), and the next hand doubles or overcalls. Opener has a tendency to disregard the overcall and continue bidding. ♠ K Q x x, ♡ A x x, ◊ A Q x, ♣ Q 10 x:

SOUTH	WEST	NORTH	EAST
1 NT	Pass	2 ♣	2 ◊
?			

Most players would bid two spades. Didn't their partner ask for a major? A few players would double two diamonds, especially with favorable vulnerability. Neither bid is proper if one has a good partner. Why not pass? This is a typical no-trump bid. Since opener has described his hand accurately in one bid, he should leave the decision to responder, who may have a very sound double. On the other hand, a double by opener should show a better-than-normal hand in defense against diamonds—with a four-card diamond suit or A Q 10, for example. When responder bid two clubs, he was asking opener for a major suit, but at the time he bid two clubs, he did not know that East was going to enter the bidding. When an overcall comes in, the priorities change. The most important thing is to give the partnership the best chance to penalize the opponents. If opener is not justified in doubling because he has just a normal defensive hand, he should give his partner the opportunity to double. If responder cannot double, he can still look for the major-suit fit. Suppose the bidding continues:

SOUTH	WEST	NORTH	EAST
1 NT	Pass	2 ♣	2 ◊
Pass	Pass	?	

If North has a hand strong enough to insist upon game, he can bid three diamonds to demand that opener show his major if he has one. Even if responder bids two no-trump, opener should show his major at the three-level, if he is strong enough to bid again. On a few occasions, the loss of a round of bidding may hurt, but more often the partnership interests are served by a pass on opener's part—unless he only has two of the overcaller's suit. In that case, his defense against the overcall would be poorer than normal, and even if responder were able to double, the penalty might be inadequate. The combined chances that responder would be unable to double, causing a round of bidding to be lost, or that if he should double, the double would turn sour, justify opener in disregarding the overcall and making his normal bid. With ♠ A Q x x, ♡ K x x, ◊ K x, ♣ A 10 9 x, he should bid two spades rather than pass two diamonds.

Suppose that, instead of overcalling, East doubles two clubs. This sort of double is often made with K J 10 x x of clubs and nothing else in order to call for a club lead against the eventual contract. If North and South have seven clubs between them, and 25 or 26 points in high cards, they can surely take eight tricks at clubs. After a no-trump opening bid and a two-club overcall, responder would double with ♠ A J x x, ♡ K x, ◇ x x x, ♣ J x x x if the vulnerability were equal. He should be just as willing to play two clubs redoubled if he gets the chance. With three clubs, opener should tend to pass the double around to responder. With four clubs, *opener* should redouble so that responder can pass with three clubs. When you use Stayman, the opponents can get in a cheap bid or double for a lead, but you should make them pay for the privilege whenever you can.

When responder cannot double an overcall, he normally makes the same bid he would have made without the overcall, if that is possible. He needs very little additional strength for his "free bid" if it is the call he was planning to make anyway. The problems arise when the opponents' bidding prevents him from making his intended bid. Should he respond at a higher level, pass, or bid something else? The tendency among the text-writers has been to make all free bids strong, on the theory that if opener cannot bid again, only an unimportant part-score will be lost. When responder does make a free bid, he wants to get to game unless opener has a bare minimum. However, in duplicate, part-scores are important; furthermore, I doubt that the American style of bidding is right even for rubber bridge. There is too big a chance of being stolen blind by aggressive opponents.

Suppose partner deals and bids one heart. You hold ♠ J x x, ♡ A x x, ◇ J x x x x, ♣ x x, or ♠ Q x x, ♡ K x x x, ◇ x x x, ♣ J x x. You are afraid to pass one heart for fear partner has almost a two-bid. Yet, if you bid two hearts, he will often jump to four hearts and be down one. In rubber bridge, you would bid one no-trump to give partner a chance while giving him the least amount of encouragement. In duplicate, you bid two hearts despite some misgivings because of the pre-emptive value of a raise, and because you figure that hearts will be better than no-trump if partner has a minimum hand and has to pass. If the opponents overcall two clubs, you gladly pass. Partner still has a chance, provided for him by the opponents, and you don't run the risk of encouraging him unduly. However, if you held ♠ Q 10 x, ♡ A x x, ◊ J x x x x, ♣ x x, or ♠ x x, ♡ K x x x, ◊ K x x x, ♣ x x x, you should have been willing and anxious to give partner his raise, and you should still give it despite the overcall.

If you require something like ♠ A x x, ♡ K x x, ◊ A x x x, ♣ x x x, or ♠ x x, ♡ K Q x x, ◊ A x x x, ♣ x x x for a free raise, you will sell out to the opponents too often when your side could make a part-score. Either that, or opener is forced to re-open the bidding on a minimum at a considerable risk. I would rather raise partner with ♠ x x, ♡ K x x x, ◊ K x x x, ♣ x x x than pass and have him bid again on a minimum, *hoping* I had this sort of hand, and taking a dive when I did not. Besides, a fairly light free raise gives you the best chance to play the hand at a low level. If you were to pass a hand like this, and if partner should bid again, wouldn't you feel obligated to raise? If two hearts is your proper spot, the only way to get there is for you to bid it right away.

How did the theory that free bids should show a strong hand (at least 10 points) ever get started? Was it just a brain-storm? Most players outside the United States would say yes, and I am inclined to agree. Nevertheless, there is a problem. Suppose partner opens with one spade and the next hand over-calls two hearts. You hold ♠ Q 10 x x, ♡ x x x, ◊ x, ♣ A Q 10 x x, or ♠ A x x x, ♡ x x, ◊ K J 10 x, ♣ Q x x. If the overcall had not come in, you would have bid two clubs or two diamonds, followed by a raise in spades. Now you cannot bid that way. If you bid three of your minor, and if partner re-bids his spades, you must guess what to do, and your inclination would be to raise to game. After all, partner could not jump to four spades with K J x x x of spades, even with 14 or 15 points. Since the overcall often deprives you of your temporary bid, one solution to the problem is to pass with a normal raise and only raise when you have enough strength to make a temporary bid followed by a raise. This is the "American" way. A much simpler solution to the problem is to raise to two with a normal raise, and raise to three whenever you are strong enough for a temporary bid, followed by a raise. After an overcall, make the raise to three non-forcing! After an overcall, raise partner's one-spade bid to three spades with the following hands:

(a) ♠ K x x x, ♡ A x, ◇ K x x x, ♣ J x x
(b) ♠ K Q x, ♡ x x, ◇ A Q x x x, ♣ x x x
(c) ♠ Q x x x x, ♡ x, ◇ K x x, ♣ K J x x

Since a raise to three spades is not forcing, a four-spade bid shows a better hand than three spades. The triple raise may be made on the type of hand you would have bid three spades on without the overcall, or it may be made on a somewhat distributional hand. Raise just as though partner had opened in third or fourth position. Bid four spades with (a) ♠ K Q x x, ♡ A x, ◇ K J x x, ♣ x x x, or (b) ♠ K x x x x, ♡ x, ◇ A J 10 x x, ♣ x x.

The same rule should apply for free bids as for raises. If you wanted to make a bid, and if the opponents' bidding does not prevent you from making it, go ahead and bid.

SOUTH	WEST	NORTH	EAST
1 ◇	1 ♡	?	

Pass with ♠ K x x x, ♡ Q x x, ◇ J x x, ♣ x x x, but bid one spade with ♠ K Q x x, ♡ x x x, ◇ x x x, ♣ Q 10 x, or ♠ K x x x, ♡ x x x, ◇ x x, ♣ A x x x. In this case, there is no reason that I can think of for requiring 10 or 11 points for a bid. Not even the problem in connection with free raises applies to this situation. Suppose opener has ♠ A x x x, ♡ x x, ◇ A K J x, ♣ J x x. Is it better for him to re-open the bidding and risk a big set, or is it better for responder to make his normal response? Some way, North-South should reach two spades. More often than not, when the strength is so evenly divided, East will raise the one-heart overcall to two hearts. South would then have to pass for sure if North has refused to bid one spade on the first round, and it will be much more dangerous for North to bid at the two-level than it would have been at the one-level. Even if opener does not have a good fit, it is better in the long run for North-South to be playing one no-trump or two of opener's suit, when responder has about seven points, than it is to sell out to the overcall.

While free suit responses and free raises should be made with as little as seven points, the free no-trump response should be slightly stronger. Probably eight points should be the minimum. You don't want to play one no-trump with only half the combined strength when the opponents have a good suit and the opening lead. Besides, the same problem exists as in the case of free raises.

♠ Q 10 x, ♡ K x x x, ◇ A x x, ♣ Q x x:

SOUTH	WEST	NORTH	EAST
1 ◇	1 ♠	?	

Without the overcall, you would have bid one heart, followed by a two no-trump bid on the next round. After the one-spade bid, you are forced to bid just one no-trump—unless you want to adopt a solution analogous to the one for raising, that is, make two no-trump non-forcing.

When you have a distributional hand, you are willing to get to the three-level opposite a minimum. If the cards are so unfavorably placed that you can't make your bid, then surely the opponents could make something their way. However, a non-forcing two no-trump bid with the last hand would be too risky, because you have defensive strength. Since you may have to make a free one no-trump response with as much as eleven points, the minimum should be eight in order to limit the spread. An eight-point response should contain a double stopper, something like ♠ Q 10 x x, ♡ K x, ◇ K x x x, ♣ x x x. An eleven-point hand with a good double stopper is too strong for a free one no-trump response.

SOUTH	WEST	NORTH	EAST
1 ◇	1 ♡	?	

♠ J 9 x, ♡ K J x x, ◇ Q 10 x x, ♣ A x: Make the unorthodox bid of two clubs. If partner re-bids diamonds, bid two no-trump. If he re-bids anything else, he shows better than a minimum opening.

All authorities agree that you need a good hand to skip a level of bidding. When partner opens the bidding with one club and the next hand bids one heart, you can almost disregard the heart bid so far as deciding whether or not to bid one spade, but you need a very strong hand to bid two diamonds since, without the overcall, your bid would have been one diamond.

Similarly, if partner opens the bidding with one spade and you were planning to bid two diamonds, you shouldn't let a two-club overcall stop you. Whether or not to bid three diamonds over a two-heart overcall is another problem. If you only had to consider the risk of your own bid—that is, whether or not two diamonds or three diamonds would be safe—you could be reasonably aggressive. However, your bid is forcing, and when partner bids again, he expects you to bid again unless game has been reached. Experience has shown that it is very difficult to stop under game after a response at a higher level. Furthermore, opener will not know what to do if he has to worry about being dropped in his re-bid. On rare occasions, responder is justified in making a skip-level response and passing opener's re-bid, but responder should usually be prepared to carry the bidding to game if he bids at all. For that reason, Goren sets the requirements at 12 points. The requirements may be shaded slightly when responder has a good suit, but he should look for another bid with less than 12 points. For example: ♠ x x x, ♡ J x, ◇ A K x x x, ♣ K x x:

SOUTH	WEST	NORTH	EAST
1 ♠	2 ♡	?	

Rather than bid three diamonds, bid two spades.

Sometimes you are forced to make a free single raise with as much as eleven points and poor trump support. Opener will not re-bid with 15 points; you hope that he has either more points so that he can bid again, or fewer points so that game cannot be made. Incidentally, when opener re-bids over a free raise, responder needs at least nine points to bid game, since his range is approximately one point higher, and opener should take that into account in re-bidding. Sometimes a free raise with two-card support is justified on a least-of-evils basis. After a two-heart overcall, raise partner to two spades with ♠ K 10, ♡ x x, ◇ A x x, ♣ Q J x x x x, or ♠ A x, ♡ K x, ◇ x x x x, ♣ K x x x x. He should have a good play for eight or nine tricks at spades, whatever his spade suit may be, and there is no reasonable alternative. If you bid three clubs and partner bids three no-trump with a minimum hand, there will be no play for the contract. If he bids three spades, you won't know whether or not to bid four spades. Even three spades might be too high.

SOUTH	WEST	NORTH	EAST
1 ◇	1 ♠	?	

With ♠ x x, ♡ A K x x x, ◇ Q x x, ♣ x x x, bid two diamonds. A two-heart bid would be an unjustifiable stretch. Change a small heart to the jack, and a two-heart bid is probably the least of evils. If partner should then raise to three hearts or re-bid two no-trump, you should pass. One overbid is enough. With ♠ Q x x, ♡ A K x x x, ◇ x x x, ♣ x x, a one no-trump response is best. This is not a good hand for a no-trump bid, but the alternatives are all inferior.

SOUTH	WEST	NORTH	EAST
1 ◇	2 ♣	?	

♠ A Q J x, ♡ 10 x x x x, ◇ Q x x, ♣ x: Two diamonds is your best bid. If you bid two hearts and partner re-bids two no-trump, for example, you can't leave him there, while a return to three diamonds would show a much better hand, and should be forcing.

Although opener expects another bid after a skip-level response, he should relieve the pressure on responder whenever he can.

SOUTH	WEST	NORTH	EAST
1 ◇	1 ♠	2 ♡	Pass
?			

South should jump to four hearts with ♠ A x, ♡ K 10 x, ◇ A K 10 x x, ♣ x x x, or bid three no-trump with ♠ K Q x, ♡ K x, ◇ A K x x x, ♣ 10 x x. When opener has 19 points or more, he should cue bid after a skip-level response, since a jump to three no-trump or four of partner's suit doesn't show a particularly good hand.

Responder has to take some risks to avoid being shut out of the bidding altogether. If he never bids, opener won't know whether he has nine points or no points. On the other hand, opener has already shown his opening strength, and it is not nearly so important that he re-bid, particularly when his hand is balanced.

SOUTH	WEST	NORTH	EAST
1 ♡	Pass	1 ♠	2 ♣

♠ K x x, ♡ A K J x x, ◇ Q x, ♣ Q x x: Pass if the opponents are vulnerable, not because you are afraid to bid two spades, but because you may do better defending. Your hand is just as good defensively against a club contract as it is offensively in support of a spade contract. Even if partner has to pass the two-club bid, you may beat it 200, or you may be unable to make two spades. However, with ♠ x, ♡ A K x x x, ◇ K J x x x, ♣ x x, or ♠ x x, ♡ A K Q x x x, ◇ K x x, ♣ x x, you should bid two diamonds or two hearts because these are offensive-type hands. Partner cannot make an intelligent decision without this distributional information. You should raise partner's spade bid with four trumps or three trumps and a singleton whether you have additional strength or not. In other words, your free bids should be motivated by distribution more than by general strength.

A free bid at a higher level than normal requires at least a 16-point hand, counting distribution.

SOUTH	WEST	NORTH	EAST
1 ◇	Pass	1 ♠	2 ♡

Bid three diamonds with ♠ K x, ♡ x x, ◇ A K Q x x x, ♣ Q x x; bid three clubs with ♠ x, ♡ x x, ◇ A Q x x x, ♣ A K 10 x x. Partner may expect a better hand for the three-club bid than the latter, but a pass would be more misleading than a three-club bid. Besides, this hand will make a lot of clubs or diamonds if the responding hand fits. Responder will assume a minimum of 14 points for any free bid, 15 points for a free one no-trump bid, and 16 points for a skip-level free bid. Notice how the requirements of increased strength compare with those of the responder:

SOUTH	WEST	NORTH	EAST
1 ◇	Pass	1 ♡	1 ♠
1 NT	Pass	?	

Bid three no-trump with ♠ x x, ♡ K Q J x x, ◇ A x x, ♣ x x x, and bid two no-trump rather than two hearts with ♠ x x, ♡ K Q 9 8 x, ◇ A x, ♣ x x x x.

SOUTH	WEST	NORTH	EAST
1 ◊	Pass	1 ♠	2 ♡
3 ♣	Pass	?	

Bid six clubs with ♠ A x x x x x, ♡ x, ◊ K x, ♣ K J x x.

SOUTH	WEST	NORTH	EAST
1 ◊	2 ♣	2 ♡	Pass
?			

♠ A Q x x, ♡ x x, ◊ K Q x x, ♣ Q x x. Bid two spades. This is a frequently misunderstood sequence. When you opened the bidding, you planned to bid one spade over a one-heart response. Since partner has bid two hearts, you bid two spades. This is not a reverse. You are one level higher, but that is partner's responsibility, not yours.

A free bid shows additional strength or distribution, but don't confuse a free bid with a competitive bid. Any bid after partner has made a limit bid is competitive, and may show *less* than normal values. Thus, a bid following two passes is competitive, since partner's pass limits his hand. A suit re-bid after a raise from partner is a competitive bid when made over an opponent's bid. Example of competitive bids:

(a)	SOUTH	WEST	NORTH	EAST
	1 ♡	Pass	2 ♡	2 ♠
	Pass	Pass	3 ♡	

(b)	SOUTH	WEST	NORTH	EAST
	1 ◊	Pass	1 ♠	2 ♡
	Pass	Pass	2 ♠	

(c)	SOUTH	WEST	NORTH	EAST
	1 ♡	Pass	2 ♡	2 ♠
	3 ♡			

In example *a*, opener must pass. If he were interested in game, he should not have passed the two-spade bid. In example *b*, opener probably will pass, but it is permissible for him to raise to three spades (not four spades). His second-round pass could have been made with a strong balanced hand, hoping that responder could double the overcall, or he might have passed because he lacked adequate trump support for spades till they were re-bid. The last sequence causes the most problems. What does opener bid if he was planning to re-bid three hearts without the overcall; that is, if he was interested in, but not sure of, game? He has three choices: If he has a skimpy three-heart bid, he bids three hearts anyway. Responder will bid game with an absolute maximum raise and no wasted cards (consequently, not even a competitive bid should be made without *some* extra values). If opener feels that his chances for game are good, he may stretch to bid game by himself or he may bid a new suit. In the following examples, the bidding is the same:

SOUTH	WEST	NORTH	EAST
1 ♡	Pass	2 ♡	2 ♠
?			

(a) ♠ K x, ♡ A J x x x, ◇ A J x, ♣ x x x: Pass. This is too close to a minimum for you to bid again. If you pass, partner will re-open very optimistically, knowing that no misunderstandings can arise; you are bound to pass if he bids three hearts.

(b) ♠ K x, ♡ A J x x x, ◇ A J x, ♣ Q x x, or ♠ x x, ♡ K x x x x, ◇ A Q 10 9, ♣ A x: Bid three hearts with these hands. It would be a mistake to bid three diamonds with the latter, since partner would think you were interested in game.

(c) ♠ x, ♡ A Q x x x x, ◇ A x x, ♣ K J 10, or ♠ x x, ♡ K Q x x x, ◇ A Q 10 9, ♣ A x: These hands warrant a three-diamond bid. Even a four-heart bid on the first one could be the winning bid.

Let's look at this problem from responder's point of view:

(a) ♠ Q x, ♡ K J x x, ◇ K x x x, ♣ x x x
(b) ♠ x x, ♡ K x x x x, ◇ K x x, ♣ K x x
(c) ♠ x x x, ♡ Q 9 x x, ◇ x, ♣ A x x x x.

If the bidding were

SOUTH	WEST	NORTH	EAST
1 ♡	Pass	2 ♡	2 ♠
Pass	Pass	?	

you would bid three hearts with all three. In fact, you would bid three hearts with quite a bit less. If the bidding were

SOUTH	WEST	NORTH	EAST
1 ♡	Pass	2 ♡	2 ♠
3 ◇	Pass	?	

you would again bid four hearts with all three hands. However, if the bidding were

SOUTH	WEST	NORTH	EAST
1 ♡	Pass	2 ♡	2 ♠
3 ♡	Pass	?	

you should pass with hand *a* or bid game with the other two hands.

Two other situations in which all bids are "competitive" rather than free are when partner opens one no-trump or an opponent overcalls one no-trump.

SOUTH	WEST	NORTH	EAST
1 ♡	1 NT	?	

If you should hold as much as nine points, or eight points with a good lead, you would double. Failure to double (or jump with a freak) denies nine points, and a new suit bid is not forcing. You should bid two spades with ♠ Q J 9 x x x, ♡ x x, ◇ Q x x x, ♣ x.

Similarly, when partner opens the bidding with one no-trump, you must not sell out to an overcall if you think you can make anything your way. You may bid when you expect to be down one if you think you have no defense against the opponents' bid.

SOUTH	WEST	NORTH	EAST
1 NT	2 ♡	?	

Bid two spades with ♠ J 10 9 x x, ♡ x x, ◇ Q 10 9 x, ♣ x x. Bid three clubs with ♠ x x, ♡ x, ◇ 10 9 x x x, ♣ K 9 x x x x. A raise to two no-trump can be strictly competitive (♠ x x, ♡ x x, ◇ K Q x x x, ♣ J x x x). Consequently, with a maximum raise to two no-trump, go all the way to three no-trump. Obviously, you do not need a stopper in the opponents' suit to raise no-trump, since partner probably has the stopper. Unless you have a long suit, tend to double the overcall rather than raise no-trump, provided you have at least three of the suit. Since the no-trump bidder has told his story, he should normally let the responding hand do all the bidding and doubling. However, after a two-heart overcall and a three-club bid by responder, opener would be entitled to gamble on three no-trump with ♠ A K J, ♡ K J x, ◇ x x x x, ♣ A Q x, or ♠ A x x, ♡ K x x, ◇ A Q x, ♣ A x x x.

Since an overcall deprives responder of the opportunity to use Stayman (three clubs is *not* Stayman), how can he find a major-suit fit or give opener the choice between game and partscore in a major? With enough strength for game, he can cue bid the opponents' suit if he is interested in opener's re-bid. However, if he has a hand that should play in spades, the question being how many spades, responder should make a non-forcing jump to three spades. The reason for making a jump nonforcing is the same as for making a jump raise of partner's major non-forcing. When the opponents steal your temporary bid, you need some way to tell partner that you have a two-and-a-half spade bid. The alternative to a non-forcing jump is to use forcing or semi-forcing free bids, which would tie your hands in the close competitive situations.

In the Roth-Stone system, when the opening bid is overcalled, and responder and the other defender passes, opener may reopen the bidding with no extra values. In any other system I know, opener needs something over a minimum opening bid. The fact that the bidding threatens to die so low does not mean the opponents have no cards. Fourth hand may be trapping with a strong hand and a singleton or void in his partner's suit. Or the overcaller may have a powerful two-suiter, and he hopes that someone would give him another chance to bid. Besides, your bid ought to show some additional strength, or partner will not know what to do when the bidding continues.

SOUTH	WEST	NORTH	EAST
1 ♠	2 ◇	Pass	Pass
?			

(a) ♠ K Q x x x, ♡ A Q x, ◇ x x, ♣ K x x: pass.
(b) ♠ K Q 10 9 x, ♡ A Q x, ◇ x x, ♣ K x x: bid two spades.
(c) ♠ K Q x x x, ♡ A Q x, ◇ x x, ♣ K Q x: double.

(d) ♠ A 10 x x x, ♡ K x x x, ◇ x, ♣ A Q x: pass.

(e) ♠ A J 9 x x, ♡ K 10 9 x, ◇ 10, ♣ A Q x: double.

(f) ♠ A J 10 x, ♡ K 10 x x x, ◇ x x, ♣ A x: bid two hearts.

The above hands are examples of minimum bids or maximum passes. Almost any hand with a six-card suit is worth a re-bid. With a hand such as e, a double is much more flexible than a two-heart bid, since partner has the option of passing for penalties or bidding three clubs. With ♠ Q J 10 9 x, ♡ A Q 10 x, ◇ x, ♣ K x x, you should bid two hearts. Any bid is risky, but a double is much too risky; partner is too likely to make a penalty pass.

Holding a good, semi-balanced hand, opener should reopen with a double. Responder might be able to pass for penalties, and, if not, a double, followed by a re-bid shows a better hand than a simple re-bid. When the decision is close, tend to double, provided you have good support for the unbid major.

SOUTH	WEST	NORTH	EAST
1 ♠	2 ◇	Pass	Pass
?			

(a) ♠ A K Q x x x, ♡ K x x, ◇ x, ♣ A x x: double, planning to bid spades unless partner passes for penalties.

(b) ♠ A K x x x x, ♡ K x, ◇ A x, ♣ A x x: double, hoping partner can pass, but intending to re-bid spades otherwise.

(c) ♠ A Q 10 x x x, ♡ x x, ◇ A, ♣ K Q J x: bid three spades.

(d) ♠ K Q 9 x x, ♡ A J 10 x x, ◇ A, ♣ K x: bid two hearts.

(e) ♠ K Q 9 x x, ♡ A J 10 x x, ◇ A, ♣ A x: bid three hearts.

(f) ♠ K Q J x x x, ♡ K Q 10 9 x, ◇ A, ♣ x: bid four hearts.

(g) ♠ A K Q 10 x x, ♡ A x, ◇ K x, ♣ J x x: bid two no-trump.

(h) ♠ A 10 x x x, ♡ K x, ◇ A Q x, ♣ A Q x: bid two no-trump.

(i) ♠ K Q x x x, ♡ A Q J x, ◇ —, ♣ A Q x x: bid three diamonds.

Once responder has limited his hand by passing, he should bid strongly when he almost had a bid the first time—unless opener's re-bid clearly shows that game is out of the question.

SOUTH	WEST	NORTH	EAST
1 ♠	2 ◇	Pass	Pass
2 ♠	Pass	?	

(a) ♠ J 9 x x x, ♡ K x, ◇ x x x, ♣ x x x: Pass, although this is
a close decision. You have so little defensive strength that a
raise to three might serve well as a pre-empt.

(b) ♠ x x x, ♡ A J x x x, ◇ x x x, ♣ Q x: Bid three spades.
A free raise on the previous round could not have been criticized. You must show you have some values.

(c) ♠ 10 x, ♡ Q x x x, ◇ K J x, ♣ K x x x: Bid two no-trump.
Now consider the same hands with the following bidding situation:

SOUTH	WEST	NORTH	EAST
1 ♠	2 ◇	Pass	Pass
Double	Pass	?	

With hand a, you should jump to three spades, with hand b,
jump to three hearts, and if partner re-bids spades, raise him to
four spades. Hand c is very close between bidding two no-trump,
three no-trump or passing for penalties. I prefer a penalty if the
opponents are vulnerable.

SOUTH	WEST	NORTH	EAST
1 ♠	2 ◇	Pass	Pass
3 ♠	Pass	?	

(a) ♠ x x x, ♡ Q 10 x, ◇ Q x x, ♣ J x x x: Pass. The queen of
diamonds must be a worthless card, and the queen of hearts is
of doubtful value when partner does not double. Club strength
would be more valuable.

(b) ♠ x x, ♡ A x x x, ◇ x x x, ♣ J 10 x x.

(c) ♠ x x x, ♡ K x x x, ◇ x x x, ♣ Q x x.

Both of these hands (b and c) rate a raise to four spades.
You may argue that you should pass, since you would not have
kept the bidding open for partner in the first place if West had
not bid. However, that is a form of negative thinking. Is your
objective in bridge to avoid bottoms at all cost? You would have
passed, not because game was impossible: but because, as a
matter of probabilities, you would have more to lose in the long
run by bidding than by passing. Once you know that partner has
a good spade suit and a good hand, your smattering of strength
in the right places should solidify his hand considerably. What

does he need for his three-spade bid? Something like ♠ A Q J x x x, ♡ x x, ◊ A, ♣ K Q x x, or ♠ A K J x x x x, ♡ A, ◊ x x, ♣ K x x.

SOUTH	WEST	NORTH	EAST
1 ♠	2 ◊	Pass	Pass
3 ♡	?		

(a) ♠ x x x, ♡ K x, ◊ x x x, ♣ x x x x x: Bid four spades. Your king of hearts is worth as much as an ace in the minors. It is worth several times as much as the queen-jack of both minors. You don't need much to take partner to game in a sequence like this if your strength is in the right spot.

(b) ♠ x, ♡ K x x x, ◊ A x x, ♣ x x x x x: Bid four diamonds followed by five hearts.

(c) ♠ x x x, ♡ Q 10 x, ◊ Q x x, ♣ J x x x: Bid three spades. Your hand is not entirely hopeless, and if partner gambles on four spades, he may make it (♠ A K x x x x, ♡ A K x x x, ◊ x, ♣ x). However, with two worthless doubletons and a very bad hand, you would refuse to take a preference.

SOUTH	WEST	NORTH	EAST
1 ♠	2 ◊	Pass	Pass
2 ♡	Pass	?	

(a) ♠ Q x, ♡ Q x, ◊ x x x x, ♣ A x x x x: bid two spades, hoping partner can bid again.

(b) ♠ 10 x, ♡ x x, ◊ K J x x, ♣ Q x x x x: pass, so that partner will not get another chance to bid. You don't know that spades will be better than hearts anyway.

(c) ♠ x x, ♡ A Q x x, ◊ x x x x, ♣ x x x: raise to three hearts.

(d) ♠ K x, ♡ A Q x x, ◊ x x x, ♣ x x x x: bid four hearts.

SOUTH	WEST	NORTH	EAST
1 ♠	2 ◊	Pass	Pass
3 ◊	Pass	?	

(a) ♠ J 10 x, ♡ x x x, ◊ x x x, ♣ K x x x: bid four spades. A return to three spades would show a hopeless hand.

(b) ♠ Q x, ♡ J 10 x x x, ◊ x x x x, ♣ J x: bid four hearts.

(c) ♠ x, ♡ K x x x x, ◊ x x x, ♣ K x x x: bid five hearts.

Since partner did not open with a two-bid, you can't expect him to bid game over a minimum bid by you. So accept your responsibility and make a strong bid yourself with as much as 4 points in *usable* values (outside the opponents' suit).

SOUTH	WEST	NORTH	EAST
1 ♠	2 ◇	Pass	Pass
2 NT	Pass	?	

(a) ♠ J x x x, ♡ x x, ◇ x x, ♣ Q x x x x: bid three spades.
(b) ♠ x x, ♡ x x x, ◇ x x x, ♣ A Q x x x: bid three no-trump.

After a take-out double, responder should not rescue. The odds against a penalty pass are so great that the possibility simply is not worth worrying about. An immediate suit take-out shows a concentration of strength and a hand too weak to redouble or to pass and await developments. Since a suit take-out is a limit bid, it is not forcing. The suit itself must be pretty good—the kind you would overcall if the opponents had opened.

SOUTH	WEST	NORTH	EAST
1 ◇	Double	?	

(a) ♠ K Q x x, ♡ Q J x x, ◇ x x x, ♣ x x: pass.
(b) ♠ 9 8 x x x, ♡ x x x x, ◇ x, ♣ x x x: pass.
(c) ♠ x x x, ♡ Q J x x x, ◇ x, ♣ x x x x: bid one heart.
(d) ♠ x x, ♡ A Q J x x, ◇ x x, ♣ Q x x x: bid one heart.
(e) ♠ K J 10 x x, ♡ x, ◇ K x x x x, ♣ x x: bid one spade.
(f) ♠ K Q 10 x, ♡ x x, ◇ Q x x, ♣ 10 x x x: bid one spade.
(g) ♠ x x x, ♡ x x, ◇ Q x x, ♣ Q J 10 9 x: bid two clubs.
(h) ♠ x x x, ♡ x x x, ◇ J x, ♣ A K Q x x: bid two clubs.

With a fair hand and a good suit, something like ♠ A Q J x x x, ♡ x x, ◇ Q x, ♣ x x x, or ♠ K Q J x x, ♡ A x, ◇ x x x x, ♣ x x, or ♠ x x, ♡ K x x, ◇ x x, ♣ A K 10 8 x x, pass, and plan to enter the bidding later. Thus

SOUTH	WEST	NORTH	EAST
1 ◇	Double	Pass	1 ♡
Pass	2 ♡	2 ♠	

or

SOUTH	WEST	NORTH	EAST
1 ◇	Double	Pass	1 ♠
Pass	2 ♠	3 ♣	

shows a pretty good hand. Unless you are strong enough to bid at a higher level, you must put in your bid right away. The reason for not redoubling is that any new suit bid after a redouble is forcing. You wouldn't mind redoubling if you were sure you could show your suit at a low level, but you are not strong enough to redouble and risk having to make your next bid, (which is forcing), at a high level. A one no-trump bid by responder over the double shows a balanced hand with a smattering of strength—probably 7 to 9 points—and a fair fit for opener's suit. With a hand of this type, it is a good idea for responder to show his strength at a safe level so that opener will know how high to push and when to double. A two no-trump response over the double is often used as a crude form of psych. With a hand good enough to try for three no-trump, why not redouble? A legitimate use for the bid is to show minor-suit strength and little defense against the majors.

SOUTH	WEST	NORTH	EAST
1 ◇	Double	?	

Bid two no-trump with ♠ K x, ♡ Q x, ◇ K x x x x x, ♣ Q x x, or ♠ x x x, ♡ K x, ◇ x x x, ♣ A Q J x x.

As for raises over a take-out double, you should stretch a bit if your hand is distributional.

SOUTH	WEST	NORTH	EAST
1 ◇	Double	?	

(a) ♠ x x, ♡ x x x, ◇ K J x x, ♣ J x x x: bid two diamonds.
(b) ♠ x, ♡ x x x, ◇ Q x x x x, ♣ K x x x: bid three diamonds.

SOUTH	WEST	NORTH	EAST
1 ♡	Double	?	

Bid two hearts with ♠ x x, ♡ K x x, ◇ K x x x, ♣ J x x x, or three hearts with ♠ x x, ♡ K Q x x, ◇ K x x x x, ♣ x x.

With general strength, redouble. The redouble guarantees 11 points (occasionally 10) unless it is based upon good trump support. When partner bids one heart and the next hand doubles, raise to two hearts with a typical minimum or average raise. With a maximum single raise because of distribution, raise to three hearts. With a maximum single raise because of high cards, pass or redouble, followed by a raise to two hearts.

SOUTH	WEST	NORTH	EAST
1 ♡	Double	?	

(a) ♠ K x x, ♡ Q x x, ◊ A x x x x, ♣ x x: Pass, followed by a raise to two hearts.

(b) ♠ K x x, ♡ K x x, ◊ A x x x x, ♣ x x: Redouble, followed by a raise to two hearts.

(c) ♠ A x, ♡ K Q x x, ◊ Q x x x, ♣ J x x: Redouble, followed by a raise to three hearts. (Not forcing, but almost.)

(d) ♠ K x x, ♡ Q x x x, ◊ A Q x x, ♣ x x: Redouble, followed by a raise to three hearts.

(e) ♠ x, ♡ K x x x x, ◊ K J x x x, ♣ x x: Bid four hearts.

(f) ♠ A x, ♡ K Q x x x, ◊ K x, ♣ x x x x: Redouble, followed by a raise to four hearts.

(g) ♠ K x x, ♡ Q x x x, ◊ A Q x x, ♣ K x: Redouble, followed by a raise to four hearts.

Usually, with nine or ten points in high cards, you can redouble and give a single raise. The opponents will not have enough cards to crowd the bidding. But when they do, you must pass.

SOUTH	WEST	NORTH	EAST
1 ♡	Double	Redouble	1 ♠
Pass	2 ♠	?	

(a) ♠ A x, ♡ K x x x, ◊ Q x x x, ♣ x x x

(b) ♠ Q x, ♡ A x x, ◊ A x x, ♣ x x x x x

With either hand, you should pass. The redouble has already created a forcing situation. If partner doubles, bid three hearts with hand a; pass with hand b. If partner has something like ♠ K x, ♡ A Q x x x, ◊ K x x, ♣ x x x, or ♠ x x, ♡ K Q x x x, ◊ K 10 9 x, ♣ A x, he will bid two no-trump or three diamonds, and you will take him back to hearts at the three-level, which he will pass. If you had bid three hearts directly over the two-spade bid, he would have bid game since there was nothing "wrong" with his hand. Incidentally, many players prefer a first-round pass to a redouble with hand a.

SOUTH	WEST	NORTH	EAST
1 ♡	Double	?	

♠ K Q x x, ♡ x x, ◊ J x, ♣ A J x x x: You should redouble. If the opponents bid clubs or spades, you can double. If they bid diamonds, you hope partner can double after hearing your redouble. This is a hand in which you may require partner's co-operation in the bidding. But suppose you held ♠ K Q x x, ♡ x, ◊ Q J x x, ♣ A x x x. This is a standard book redouble. You want partner to keep quiet so that you can double anything that is bid. But I doubt the wisdom of a redouble with this type of hand. It is very unlikely that opener will find a re-bid if you pass. Even if you redouble, he will still bid if his hand is very distributional or very weak—that is, if he would be afraid to let a double stand. The point in passing is that many players have the dangerous habit of raising their partner's response after a take-out double whenever they have four-card support, even with a minimum double. A redouble will warn West to keep quiet. If you pass, you may get to double two spades, or three of a minor. Even when your evil plot does not work, nothing is lost. You are prepared to double any bid that comes around to you, and you do not need partner's co-operation.

After a redouble by responder, opener should double the opponents' bid if he can or pass, to enable his partner to double unless opener is too weak or distributional to leave the double in.

SOUTH	WEST	NORTH	EAST
1 ♡	Double	Redouble	2 ♣
?			

(a) ♠ x x, ♡ A K x x x, ◊ Q 10 x x, ♣ K x: pass.
(b) ♠ x x, ♡ A K Q x x x, ◊ Q x x, ♣ x x: bid two hearts.
(c) ♠ K x, ♡ K J 10 x x, ◊ K Q x x x, ♣ x: bid two diamonds.
(d) ♠ x x, ♡ A K 10 x x, ◊ x x, ♣ K 10 x x: double.
(e) ♠ x, ♡ K J 10 x x, ◊ K Q x x x, ♣ K x: bid two diamonds.

In the last example, you are strong enough to leave in a double of two clubs, but there is no assurance that partner can double, and you anticipate a two-spade bid anyway. If the bidding were

SOUTH	WEST	NORTH	EAST
1 ♡	Double	Redouble	2 ♣
Pass	2 ♠	Double	Pass
?			

you would hate to leave the double in. Partner might have ♠ A J x x, ♡ x x, ◇ A x x x, ♣ Q x x, and the combined diamond length (which he would not know about) would kill the defense. However, after warning partner of your two-suiter, you can trust his decision. If he doubles spades despite your two-diamond bid, he should know what he is doing.

When responder bids and the next hand doubles, opener should redouble with 17 points in high cards, just as responder normally redoubles with 11. Like responder, he can shade the redouble with good trump support. If opener has a normal single raise for his partner, he makes it. With a maximum single raise because of distribution, he gives a double raise. With a maximum raise with top cards, he redoubles.

SOUTH	WEST	NORTH	EAST
1 ◇	Pass	1 ♡	Double
?			

(a) ♠ A x, ♡ K Q x, ◇ K J x x x, ♣ J x x: bid two hearts.

(b) ♠ A x x, ♡ K x x x, ◇ A Q 10 x x, ♣ x: bid three hearts.

(c) ♠ A x x, ♡ K J 10, ◇ A K x x x, ♣ x x: redouble, followed by a single raise.

(d) ♠ A Q x, ♡ A x x, ◇ A Q J x x, ♣ x x: bid like hand *c* (this is the maximum).

(e) ♠ A x x, ♡ K x x x, ◇ A K Q x x, ♣ x: redouble, followed by three hearts.

(f) ♠ x x, ♡ Q x x x, ◇ A K J x, ♣ A K J: redouble, followed by three hearts.

(g) ♠ x, ♡ A K J x, ◇ A Q J x x, ♣ K x x: redouble, followed by four hearts.

(h) ♠ x, ♡ A Q x x, ◇ A Q J x x x, ♣ x x: bid four hearts.

Without trump support or 17 points, opener should tend to pass with a balanced hand, just as he would pass an overcall. The opponents may already be in trouble, and a bid would merely rescue them.

The toughest decisions in bridge are what to do in competitive situations—pass, bid, or double? Duplicate calls for close decisions. You can't always afford to "play safe" and take a sure profit or refrain from doubling because you only expect to set the opponents one trick. On the other hand, there are contracts which you should not double even when you are quite confident of setting them. Suppose the opponents reach six no-trump, and you are on lead with the ace-king of diamonds. Surely a majority of pairs will not reach six no-trump, and any plus score your way will be a top board or pretty close. If you double, an opponent may run out to seven of a suit with partner on lead. You should not double when the opponents are in the only contract they can't make. Just as you would refuse to double a two-club overall with ♠ x x, ♡ x x, ◇ x x x, ♣ K Q J 10 x x, it would be very unsophisticated, to say the least, to double a three-diamond overcall with ♠ x x, ♡ K x x, ◇ Q J 10 x x, ♣ K x x, if partner had opened with a weak two-heart bid. The opponents must be cold for at least nine tricks in spades. If you pass, there may be no more bidding. Your left-hand opponent would be afraid to bid spades without a diamond fit because it might sound like a constructive bid. If you double, he can bid three spades as a rescue.

When the opponents attempt to sacrifice against your game contract, you know that it is necessary to defeat them two, three, or four tricks, depending upon the vulnerability, to compensate for the loss of game. Occasionally, you double because you believe you can beat them the necessary two, three, or four tricks. Usually, you double because you don't believe you can bid and make any more, and the penalty is the best score available. When the opponents take your part-score contract away from you, you must double if you think you could have made your bid and the opponents cannot make theirs. If the opponents are not vulnerable, plus 100 may not be much better than plus 50, but you should double anyway when you think they are too high and hope for a two-trick set. If they are in exactly the right contract, the double will not lose much.

SOUTH	WEST	NORTH	EAST
1 ♡	Pass	2 ♡	2 ♠
Pass	Pass	3 ♡	Pass
Pass	3 ♠	Pass	Pass
?			

♠ x x, ♡ A J x x x, ◇ K Q x x, ♣ K x: If you are vulner-able, you should not even consider a four-heart bid. Good oppo-nents would double four hearts automatically on the theory that if four hearts can be made, few teams would bid it, and the double would have little to lose. Not vulnerable, you would only bid four hearts if you were confident that you would be down just one, and that the opponents could make three spades. If you should be wrong on either point, you would get a poor board. Nevertheless, three hearts is probably cold if partner can bid it. Whether or not the opponents can make three spades depends upon their distribution. West cannot have a good hand or he would have raised to three spades on the previous round in order to give his partner a chance to bid game. Consequently, a double of three spades might be your best action. This is a very close decision.

Of course, you can lurk in the bushes occasionally with good distribution to entice a double on the "he-must-be-weak-or-he-would-have-bid-more" type of reasoning.

SOUTH	WEST	NORTH	EAST
1 ♡	1 ♠	2 ♡	2 ♠
?			

♠ x, ♡ K Q J x x x x, ◇ x, ♣ A Q J x: Bid just three hearts. Almost surely someone will find another bid; in fact, there may be lots more bidding. The best chance to buy the bid for four or even five hearts is to make it appear that you are sacrificing. Perhaps you think that bright opponents should not be so easily fooled, but they cannot tell what you are doing. Usually, when the bidding goes like that, you are taking a deliberate sacrifice, and it will cost them points not to double.

♠ x x x, ♡ A K Q x x x, ◇ K Q x x, ♣ —:

SOUTH	WEST	NORTH	EAST
1 ♡	1 ♠	2 ◇	4 ♠
?			

Six diamonds looks like an excellent contract, since partner is almost bound to have the ace of diamonds and a singleton or void in spades. However, the opponents may not sell out to six diamonds unless they are misled. Bid five hearts, hoping for an attempted five-spade sacrifice. Then a six-diamond bid may sound like a shot in the dark, and the opponents would be less likely to bid six spades. Even if you buy the bid for five hearts, you may do better than you would defending against six spades. Another thought: Suppose the bidding to be

SOUTH	WEST	NORTH	EAST
1 ♡	1 ♠	2 ◇	4 ♠
5 ♡	Pass	Pass	5 ♠
?			

You might pass. Partner, not knowing about the diamond fit, will almost surely double. Then when you pull to six diamonds, the opponents may think you have a very distributional hand and no defense against spades. Even though you don't mislead them to the point of doubling your "sacrifice," they are very unlikely to bid six spades after this sequence.

Determining how many tricks you can take offensively or defensively is not easy. Tend to bid higher offensively with top strength, unbalanced hand patterns, and no strength in the opponents' suit or suits. With queens and jacks, balanced hands, and strength in the opponents' suits, tend to double or refuse to sacrifice. With just a normal hand, accurately described by the previous bidding, pass the decision around to partner, unless the opponents are obviously too high and you feel that any further bid by partner will result in a minus score. In other words, don't try to make all the decisions.

NORTH	EAST	SOUTH	WEST
Pass	Pass	1 ♠	2 ♡
3 ♠	4 ♡	?	

(a) ♠ K Q x x x, ♡ x x x, ◇ K Q x, ♣ K x: Bid four spades. Partner is short in hearts, and the hands must fit well.

(b) ♠ K Q x x x, ♡ x x x, ◇ K Q x, ♣ J x: Pass. You might be able to make four spades if partner's hand fits well enough, and you don't know whether you can beat four hearts.

(c) ♠ K Q 10 x, ♡ Q x, x ◇ x x x, ♣ A 10 x, or

(d) ♠ K x x x x, ♡ Q J x, ◇ Q x x, ♣ A x: Double.

You have no guarantee that a double will turn out best. However, four spades looks very doubtful, and you have good defensive strength against four hearts. Failure to double would be quite a gamble.

Now let us look at the problem from the point of view of the player last to speak. If the four-heart bid is passed around to responder, he should bid four spades with ♠ J 9 x x x, ♡ x, ◇ A J 10 x, ♣ K x x, or double with ♠ J 10 x x, ♡ K x, ◇ A J x x, ♣ Q x x. With either hand, he would pass if his partner had doubled four hearts.

The most common use of the redouble is after a take-out double. However, there are other important uses for it. When made in fourth position (after two passes), it is a request for a rescue, particularly when made at a low level. When you think you can make one heart doubled, for instance, you are content to pass rather than risk having either opponent run out. It is very unlikely that you could successfully double all run-outs at such a low level, and plus 160 should be good enough for a top. However, a redouble directly over a double has an entirely different meaning. If the double was a penalty double, it tells partner *not* to run; if it was a take-out double, the redouble shows a strong hand, urging partner to enter the auction on meager values, either by bidding or doubling. If the bidding were

SOUTH	WEST	NORTH	EAST
1 ◇	Pass	Pass	2 ♣
?			

you would double with ♠ A Q x x, ♡ K J x, ◇ A K J x x, ♣ x to show your general strength, enabling partner to make a penalty pass with nothing but four clubs to the queen-jack, or to bid one of the majors with a four-card suit. Similarly, if East had doubled instead of bidding two clubs, you should redouble. You wouldn't redouble to ask for a rescue; why scream before you are hurt? The redouble simply tells partner that your side may have the balance of strength despite his original pass.

SOUTH	WEST	NORTH	EAST
1 ♠	Pass	2 ♠	Double
?			

♠ A J x x x, ♡ x x, ◊ A Q x, ♣ K Q x: A redouble is your only correct bid. Consider your various alternatives. If you bid three spades immediately, disregarding the double, partner will figure you for a long spade suit and very little defensive strength—something like ♠ A Q x x x x x, ♡ A x, ◊ x x, ♣ x x. In other words, an immediate three-spade bid would be in the nature of a pre-empt. If you pass, the most likely development is a three-heart bid by West, followed by two passes. What would you do then? A three-spade bid at this point would be strictly competitive, since your failure to redouble shows that you have no interest in game. Possibly partner could have doubled three hearts if you had shown a good defensive hand by redoubling. But if the bidding goes: redouble by you; three hearts by West; pass; pass; three spades, partner will know that you are still interested in reaching game. My inclination would be to double if the opponents bid three of either minor, or even three hearts if the opponents are vulnerable, but that is simply a matter of judgment. After the redouble partner will tend to let the bid go around to you with a balanced hand or a close decision, but if his hand is unbalanced enough, he will still insist upon a spade contract.

SOUTH	WEST	NORTH	EAST
1 ◊	4 ♡	4 ♠	Double
?			

♠ A J 8 x, ♡ x x x, ◊ K Q x x, ♣ K x: You should make a confirmatory redouble. Partner's spade suit cannot be very good, and he may try another spot if you pass. The whole hand:

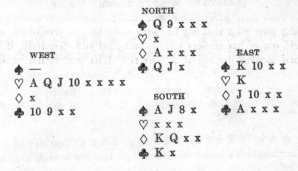

```
                    NORTH
                    ♠ Q 9 x x x
                    ♡ x
    WEST            ◊ A x x x          EAST
    ♠ —             ♣ Q J x            ♠ K 10 x x
    ♡ A Q J 10 x x x x                 ♡ K
    ◊ x             SOUTH              ◊ J 10 x x
    ♣ 10 9 x x      ♠ A J 8 x          ♣ A x x x
                    ♡ x x x
                    ◊ K Q x x
                    ♣ K x
```

You may argue that West will run out if you redouble. Perhaps. While he probably will not pay any attention to your redouble, almost surely responder would run to five diamonds without the redouble. His trump suit gives him something to worry about.

Next, let us discuss the complex problems that pre-emptive overcalls create. How much are you entitled to shade your bidding after a pre-empt or jump bid by the opponents? You need a strong single raise to bid at the three-level and good distributional support to bid at the four-level.

SOUTH	WEST	NORTH	EAST
1 ♡	3 ♣	?	

(a) ♠ K x x, ♡ K x x x, ◇ x x x, ♣ J x x: pass.

(b) ♠ K x, ♡ K x x x, ◇ J 10 x x, ♣ x x x: bid three hearts.

(c) ♠ A x, ♡ K J x x, ◇ Q x x x, ♣ x x x: bid three hearts.

(d) ♠ A x, ♡ K Q x x, ◇ Q x x x, ♣ x x x: bid four hearts—this is your gamble to take. Partner needs very little more than a minimum, and he would not know but what you were stretching if you just bid three hearts. If West had overcalled four clubs, you would need a hand as good as hand *c* to bid four hearts. Holding hand *b*, you should pass, intending to bid four hearts if partner doubles the four-club bid.

A double by either player after a pre-emptive overcall is sort of an optional double, often without strength in the opponents' suit. The double by responder, in particular, merely shows he had some strength somewhere and doesn't know what else to do.

SOUTH	WEST	NORTH	EAST
1 ♡	3 ♠	?	

♠ x x x, ♡ x x, ◇ A J x x, ♣ K 10 x x: You should double. Opener would probably pull to four hearts with ♠ x, ♡ A K Q 10 x x, ◇ K Q x, ♣ Q x x.

SOUTH	WEST	NORTH	EAST
1 ♣	Pass	1 ♡	3 ♠
?			

♠ A x, ♡ K x x x, ◇ A x x, ♣ K x x x: You should pass. Four hearts is a sucker bid, since if partner has a weak hand and a four-card suit, the hearts will surely be stacked, and you could easily take a three-trick set. If you pass, and partner doubles three spades, showing he has some cards, you have a close decision and could not be severely criticized whatever you do. With ♠ A x, ♡ K x x x, ◇ A x, ♣ K 10 x x x, you should definitely pull to four hearts when partner doubles three spades, but not before. The important thing with this type of hand is to get a plus score and not to be stolen blind. Your doubles should not be too close, since if you can't make game, it doesn't matter much whether you are plus 50 or plus 100. As we said before, doubles after a pre-empt are used primarily to show general strength, even when they are technically for penalties.

SOUTH	WEST	NORTH	EAST
1 ♡	4 ♣	Pass	Pass
?			

♠ x x, ♡ A x x x x, ◇ A x x, ♣ K Q J: Pass! Surely you can't make much of anything, so you should accept your plus score rather than stir up more bidding. If you double, partner would bid four hearts with ♠ K x x x, ♡ K x x x, ◇ x x x x, ♣ x

SOUTH	WEST	NORTH	EAST
1 ♣	Pass	1 ♡	3 ♠
Pass	Pass	?	

♠ Q J 10, ♡ Q 10 x x, ◇ K x x x, ♣ J x: Again, you should pass, since a double might get you a heart raise with ♠ A x, ♡ K x x x, ◇ A x x, ♣ K x x x.

Just as a double after the *opponents* have pre-empted is very tentative, a double after *partner* has pre-empted is an absolute command for him to pass.

SOUTH	WEST	NORTH	EAST
4 ♡	4 ♠	Double	Pass
?			

Pass, whatever your hand is. For all you know, partner may have three tricks in spades, and two aces on the side.

SOUTH	WEST	NORTH	EAST
1 ♡	Double	4 ♡	4 ♠
?			

Even though you are pretty sure that you can defeat four spades, you should pass unless you think you could make four hearts. Even then, you should not double too close, since partner may have anywhere from a trick and a half down to no defensive strength. If you pass, he should almost always pass. All bidding accuracy is tossed to the winds if you must double on a hunch just to keep partner from bidding five hearts. When you do double, it means you can set four spades all by yourself. Partner must pass, whatever his hand is.

Chapter 5

Defensive Bidding

WHEN ONE SIDE has opened the bidding, the other side's chances of bidding and making game are decreased considerably. There is less (in total points) to be gained by entering the bidding, and the risk of serious loss is greater. Sound opening bids must often be passed if the opponents open first. That is, one should pass *balanced* hands with opening strength. Good distribution or concentrated strength justifies a bid with less than opening values. There are six positive actions available to defenders.[1] The four strong actions are the cue bid, take-out double, no-trump overcall, and jump overcall—all of which guarantee an opening bid, or better. The simple (non-jump) overcall is a limit bid showing a minimum opening bid or worse, and the pre-emptive overcall[2] shows little defensive strength. For pre-emptive overcalls. Culbertson's rule of two and three applies with modifications. When not vulnerable against vulnerable opponents, you may overbid four tricks. With equal vulnerability, you may overbid three tricks. With unfavorable vulnerability, you should not pre-empt by more than a trick and a half. Thus you must only require something like the right queen in partner's

---

[1] In this chapter, "defenders" merely refers to the side which does not open the bidding, irrespective of who finally plays the hand.

[2] Pre-emptive overcalls are double or triple jump bids in a new suit, or jump bids in the opponents' suit. Thus,

SOUTH	WEST
1 ♡	3 ♡

shows ♠ x, ♡ Q J 10 9 7 x x, ◇ K J x, ♣ x x. Single jump overcalls are not pre-emptive bids unless you have so announced.

hand for a one-trick set. For all practical purposes, don't pre-empt with unfavorable vulnerability.

In duplicate you can't afford a three-trick set when the vulnerability is equal. The reason it is permissible to overbid by three tricks is that if you evaluate your winners conservatively, one key card in partner's hand will hold the set to two tricks. The tacit assumption is that the opponents can make game. Pre-empts should have a sliding scale of winners, depending upon defensive strength. Over one club, bid just one heart or two hearts with ♠ Q x x, ♡ A K Q 10 x x x, ◇ Q x, ♣ x, unless the vulnerability is unfavorable, in which case you may bid three hearts. Under other vulnerability conditions, it is too strong for three hearts—partner would pass with ♠ K J x, ♡ J x, ◇ K 10 x x, ♣ J 9 x x, or considerably more—and is too weak for four hearts. In the long run, it does not pay to pre-empt with so much defensive strength. But with ♠ x, ♡ K Q J 10 x x x, ◇ Q 10 x x, ♣ x, a bid of four hearts is justified. Partner needs nothing but the king-jack of diamonds to hold the set to one trick while giving you no defense against four spades.

Pre-empts are much more desirable with 7-4-1-1 or 7-3-2-1 distribution than with 7-2-2-2. A four-heart bid, whether an overcall or opening bid, with ♠ x x, ♡ A K Q x x x x, ◇ x x, ♣ J x, is very unsound, in my opinion. The top hearts offer some defense, and nothing but top tricks in partner's hand will be of value to you. Very frequently when a pre-empt is made on this type of hand, you go down two or three tricks for a bad board while partner has so many queens and jacks that the opponents could not have made anything. When your suit is spades, you should be more reluctant to pre-empt than with any other suit, since you can outbid the opponents at their own level. Similarly, with spade strength or length, even Q x x, you should avoid a pre-empt. The opponents are not so dangerous when you have spade strength, and you don't want to shut partner out of a spade bid. Nor should you pre-empt with a two suiter. A pre-empt is not designed to locate the best spot.

Culbertson's rule of two and three is not a very helpful guide for simple overcalls at match points. The question is not how much you might lose, but how often you expect to get caught. Pre-empts invite a double, so you must be prepared for the consequences. But for simple overcalls, especially at the one-level, the risk of loss is not the controlling factor. The opponents do not double frequently enough to worry you. The major restraint is that the overcall must serve a constructive purpose. Why overcall if you don't want the suit led, and if you don't want partner to compete for a part-score or sacrifice? So it is fear of partner—or, more accurately, the fact that you want his co-operation in the auction—that prevents you from bidding on nothing. With favorable vulnerability, you may overcall with slightly poorer hands than under other circumstances in order to suggest a sacrifice. However, normally, the difference between neither side vulnerable and favorable vulnerability is considered only in making the final decision whether to take a deliberate sacrifice over the opponents' game bid. It might seem that neither side vulnerable and both sides vulnerable would have much in common, since the opponents must obtain a three-trick set to compensate them for the loss of game. But the typical low-level double is made on about ten points and a misfit. Game is sufficiently remote so as not to enter into the doubler's calculations.

With unfavorable vulnerability, overcalls should be made even more cautiously than at rubber bridge. Responder will double with a mediocre hand in an effort to get a one-trick set. If it turns out that his partner has extra values sufficient for game, he can probably beat you two tricks and get a top that way.

Of course, one must not be over-awed by the risks. Overcalls have lead-directing and pre-emptive value. For example, after

OPENER	YOU	RESPONDER	PARTNER
1 ♣	1 ♠	2 ♡	Pass

it is very difficult for the opponents to stop at a sound part-score contract. Opener must bid again, and he expects responder to bid again. Responder has a tendency to count on opener for a queen more than minimum. Sometimes there is no extra queen. Responder is faced with a dilemma. If he bids, he may get too high. If he passes, he may get shut out altogether. When responder takes a conservative course and passes or raises opener's suit, a raise by partner completes the dirty work you started.

SOUTH	WEST	NORTH	EAST
1 ♣	1 ♠	2 ♣	2 ♠
3 ♣	Pass	Pass	Pass

NORTH
♠ J
♡ K Q x x
◇ x x x x
♣ K x x x

WEST
♠ Q 10 9 x x x
♡ x x
◇ A x
♣ x x x

EAST
♠ K x x
♡ J 10 x
◇ K J 10 x x
♣ Q x

SOUTH
♠ A x x
♡ A x x x
◇ Q x
♣ A J 10 x

North and South not only fail to reach game; they don't even find the heart suit. Because of the disruptive effect, it pays to overcall a minor suit with one spade on poorer hands than you would bid on under other circumstances.

Enough of generalities. Just what are the requirements for an overcall? An overcall should show concentrated strength in an offensive-type hand. Over one diamond, bid one heart with

(a) ♠ x x, ♡ K J 10 x x, ◇ x x, ♣ K J 10 x
(b) ♠ x x x, ♡ A Q J x x x, ◇ x, ♣ x x x
(c) ♠ x x, ♡ A Q J x, ◇ x x x, ♣ K Q 10 x

but pass with

(d) ♠ Q x, ♡ K 8 x x x, ◇ Q x, ♣ K J x x
(e) ♠ K x x, ♡ Q x x x x x, ◇ x, ♣ K J x

Hand c is a borderline, vulnerable overcall at duplicate. If you wish to compete, now is the safest time. If the suit were spades, the additional pre-emptive value of the overcall would change it from a borderline decision to a compulsory bid. Hands d and e are not good overcalls for a number of reasons. First, the fact that so many high trumps are out increases the probability of an immediate double. Second, partner may bid too much in a competitive situation, since hands with scattered strength are better than normal defensively, worse than normal offensively.

Third, if the opponents buy the bid in no-trump, for example, it may work out badly for partner to lead a worthless doubleton in hearts rather than to make his natural lead without the over-call. When you overcall with a weak trump suit, your general strength and distribution should be good enough to give you a good chance of buying the bid.

♠ A Q J x, ♡ x, ◇ Q 10 x x x, ♣ x x x: Not vulnerable, overcall one club or one heart with one spade. Over one dia-mond, it is better to pass. Length in the opponent's suit in-creases the danger of a penalty double. Responder will double with a singleton diamond when he would not double otherwise.

♠ 10 x x x x x, ♡ x x, ◇ A x, ♣ A Q x:

SOUTH	WEST	NORTH	EAST
1 ♡	Pass	2 ♡	?

You should pass regardless of vulnerability. If opener passes, partner will strain a G-string to reopen the bidding unless he is short in spades. The danger of a spade overcall is that it will induce partner to lead a spade against a heart contract. With ♠ K Q J x x, ♡ x x, ◇ J 10 9 x, ♣ x x, you might risk a non-vulnerable overcall because you want a spade lead very much.

♠ K x x, ♡ Q x x, ◇ A Q 10 x x, ♣ A x:

SOUTH	WEST
1 ♣	?

Not vulnerable, a no-trump overcall is probably best. Vulnerable, you should pass. Two diamonds is a poor bid because you do not have concentrated strength. If partner is short in diamonds, two diamonds might be down a couple of tricks, while the opponents could not make anything their way. The two-diamond bid has too little to gain to justify the risk. Also, tend not to overcall a minor suit with support for an unbid major. This statement will be explained later in connection with reopening bids.

♠ x x x, ♡ x, ◇ A Q 10 9 x, ♣ K J 10 x: Over one spade, this is a sound overcall under any conditions of vulnerability. The risk of being shut out is no less than taking a dive. This is not a flexible hand where you can await developments. If you bid, the time is now. Furthermore, the two-diamond bid will prevent partner from reopening the bidding later with two hearts or three hearts.

Remember the statement that overcalls are limit bids? If one of a suit is opened, these are maximum overcalls of one spade:

♠ A Q 10 x x, ♥ x, ♦ K 10 x x x, ♣ A x

♠ K Q J x x, ♥ A J x, ♦ K x x x, ♣ x

♠ A K x x x, ♥ K x, ♦ K x, ♣ Q 10 x x

♠ Q 10 x x x x, ♥ A x, ♦ A x, ♣ K x x

♠ A Q x x x x, ♥ —, ♦ x, ♣ A J x x x x

Don't overcall if two-honor count and a doubleton trump in partner's hand will produce game. Exception: with a very distributional two-suited hand, you may overcall with the intention of showing both suits unless partner raises the first one. Usually, everyone will be distributional, and there will be another opportunity to bid.

After West overcalls, if the next hand passes, East should raise with about the same type of hand with which he would raise an opening bid. This gives West a chance to bid more with a freak or a maximum, but the main purpose is not constructive, but pre-emptive. When responder bids a new suit (forcing), a single raise by East does very little good and may do harm by slowing up the bidding. In this case, the raise should not be made on a balanced hand with good defensive strength. Raise only with a distributional hand or when the strength of your hand is primarily in partner's suit and the unbid suit. However, if you are considering a sacrifice, raise early. Then if partner passes the opponents' game bid, it shows that he has good defense or is afraid the sacrifice will be too costly. The point is, with ♠ K x x x, ♥ x, ♦ A x x x, ♣ x x x x, when partner overcalls one spade, don't pass until the opponents get to four hearts and then bid four spades. Bid two spades or three spades and pass if partner elects to defend.

The single raise of a one-level overcall, when responder passes or raises opener's suit, shows about 8 to 12 points, counting distribution. With a distributional hand in the upper ranges, stretch and jump to three as a pre-empt. A one no-trump bid is fairly constructive, showing 9 to 12 points. Two no-trump shows 13 or 14 points but is not forcing. After

SOUTH	WEST	NORTH	EAST
1 ♡	1 ♠	Pass	?

bid two spades with the following hands: ♠ Q x x x, ♡ x x, ◊ A x x, ♣ J x x x; ♠ Q 10 x, ♡ A x x, ◊ A x x, ♣ x x x x; ♠ K x, ♡ x x x, ◊ A K x x, ♣ Q x x x. With the following hand raise only to two spades, but if partner had overcalled one heart and you had a similar hand with heart support, you would raise to three hearts in an effort to shut out the spade suit: ♠ K x x x x, ♡ x, ◊ K x x x, ♣ Q x x.

Bid three spades with ♠ K Q x, ♡ x x x x, ◊ A Q J x, ♣ x x; ♠ J x x x, ♡ x, ◊ A J x x, ♣ K 10 x x; ♠ Q 10 x x x, ♡ —, ◊ Q J x x x, ♣ x x x.

Bid one no-trump with ♠ K J x, ♡ Q 10 x, ◊ A x x, ♣ Q x x x; ♠ J 10 x, ♡ K J x, ◊ x x x, ♣ K 10 9 x (this last hand is a slight overbid in order to avoid an opening lead through your king-jack).

Notice that the raises to four were made on somewhat distributional hands. What would you do with ♠ K J x, ♡ A x, ◊ K J x x, ♣ K x x x, or ♠ Q 10 x x, ♡ K x x, ◊ A J x x, ♣ A x? These hands should be enough for game opposite most overcalls, but why punish partner for overcalling with ♠ A Q 10 x x x, ♡ x x, ◊ x x x, ♣ x x, or ♠ A K J x x, ♡ x x x, ◊ x x, ♣ x x x? Such overcalls are normal enough at duplicate and probably at rubber bridge. You can't investigate your legitimate game chances without getting too high occasionally; you can scarcely stop short of three spades, but by not bidding four you will save lots of points. How do you show a semi-balanced hand with fourteen or fifteen points and good trump support? By cue-bidding the opponents' suit, then raising to the three-level. A cue bid by a defender followed by a raise of his partner's suit is always a limit bid. West: ♠ A J 10 x x, ♡ x x x, ◊ Q x x, ♣ Q x; East: ♠ Q 9 x x, ♡ x x, ◊ A K x, ♣ K J 10 x:

SOUTH	WEST	NORTH	EAST
1 ♡	1 ♠	Pass	2 ♡
Pass	2 ♠	Pass	3 ♠
Pass	4 ♠		

Despite the shabby trump suit and dubious overcall, West visualizes the value of his minor-suit queens. Without the queen of diamonds, he would pass since he can't tell how well the hands fit. Notice that a cue bid *followed by a raise to game* is a different bid. West: ♠ A Q 10 x x, ♡ x x x, ◇ K x, ♣ K x x; East: ♠ K x x x, ♡ —, ◇ A Q x x x x, ♣ Q J 10:

SOUTH	WEST	NORTH	EAST
1 ♡	1 ♠	Pass	2 ♡
Pass	2 ♠	Pass	4 ♠
Pass	6 ♠		

The bid of a new suit by the partner of the overcaller is definitely not a strong bid, and it does not guarantee support for the overcaller's suit. When you bid a minor suit, the inference is that you don't have support for partner's major. However, you do show a good suit.

♠ x x, ♡ x x x, ◇ K Q 10 9 x x, ♣ J x x:

SOUTH	WEST	NORTH	EAST
1 ♡	1 ♠	Pass	?

Bid two diamonds. You wouldn't mind if your bid were followed by three passes, but it is likely that your side will not buy the bid, and you also want to indicate a good lead. Change the jack of clubs to the ace, and you would still bid two diamonds. Change the hand again to ♠ Q x, ♡ x x x, ◇ K Q 10 9 x x, ♣ A x x, and you do not expect to defend. A two-diamond bid might well be followed by three passes. It is a close question whether to bid two diamonds or two spades.

The last example illustrates the fact that a new suit bid is not encouraging and should not be made with a weak suit. True, you will miss some good contracts, but in the long run you profit by staying out of trouble. Some risk is justified in an attempt to find a major suit.

♠ A Q J x x, ♡ x x, ◇ x x x, ♣ K x x:

SOUTH	WEST	NORTH	EAST
1 ♡	2 ♣	Pass	?

Bid two spades. This is a pretty good spade suit. Change the spades to A Q 8 x x, and you should bid three clubs, not two spades. The odds are against partner's having a good spade fit, especially since he tends to pass rather than bid with K x x of an unbid major.

Culbertson players use a single jump overcall to show a strong hand—at least 3½ honor count with a six-card suit. Such a hand can also be shown by a take-out double followed by the suit bid. Admittedly, the jump overcall has advantages over a take-out double. It makes a penalty double by partner impossible when you hold a freak. The jump overcall is also better when you have a strong two-suiter, since the best[3] way to show two suits is to start bidding them right away. However, many players consider it wasteful to use two bids for almost the same purpose. The Four Aces used all jump overcalls as pre-emptive bids, based on playing tricks alone. Many of the present top players use jump overcalls as weak and pre-emptive when not vulnerable, strong when vulnerable. Goren suggests using a jump overcall to show one more trick than a sound overcall. Since he would overcall one spade with ♠ Q J 10 x x, ♡ x, ◇ x x x, ♣ A J 10 x, he bids two spades with ♠ Q J 10 x x x, ♡ x, ◇ x x, ♣ A J 10 x. Jacoby uses the jump overcall to show an offensive hand (for example, 6-4-2-1 distribution) with a wide range of strength where partner raises with trump support. Not knowing "whose hand it is," he may be pre-empting or he may be putting his partner in a sound game contract.

The practice on the West Coast and the one I favor is to show an intermediate hand, about three-honor count with a good six-card major. The honor-count requirement may be shaded slightly with an offensive-type hand. The bid as thus used is partially pre-emptive, partially constructive. Thus a double followed by a major-suit bid shows a stronger hand, in honor count anyway, than the jump overcall. The single jump in a minor shows a slightly better hand and is an invitation to three no-trump if partner has about a trick and a half, including a stopper in the opponents' suit.

SOUTH	WEST	NORTH	EAST
1 ◇	?		

[3] Or next-to-best. See the suggestion on page 183.

♠ K Q 10 x x x, ♡ A x, ◇ x x, ♣ K J x: bid two spades.

♠ K Q 10 x x x, ♡ A x, ◇ x x, ♣ A Q x: double.

♠ x, ♡ Q J 10 9 x x, ◇ A x, ♣ K Q 10 x: bid two hearts.

♠ x x, ♡ A J 8 x x x, ◇ A Q x, ♣ K x: bid two hearts.

♠ x x, ♡ A J x, ◇ x x, ♣ A K Q x x x: bid three clubs.

♠ A x, ♡ x x x, ◇ x, ♣ A K J x x x x: bid three clubs.

Partner bids or raises as much as he can. A single raise limits his hand and may be pre-emptive, so the overcaller uses his judgment whether to pass or bid game. The jump overcall often avoids problems for East on the first round. For example: West: ♠ A Q J x x x, ♡ x, ◇ K J 10 x, ♣ x x; East: ♠ K, ♡ x x x x, ◇ A x x x, ♣ K J x x:

SOUTH	WEST	NORTH	EAST
1 ♡	2 ♠	Pass	4 ♠

Note that without the jump overcall, the bidding would probably be

SOUTH	WEST	NORTH	EAST
1 ♡	1 ♠	Pass	Pass
Pass			

East's pass after a one-spade overcall would be quite normal at both rubber bridge and duplicate. He cannot tell how strong the spade suit is. Since game looks remote, the best chance for a good score from his point of view is to pass quickly and hope that opener sticks his neck out with another bid.

A one no-trump overcall shows at least one stopper in the opponent's suit and 16-19 points. When not vulnerable, you may count a good five-card suit for a point in order to get your 16. The no-trump overcall shows *approximately* the same type of hand as an opening no-trump bid, but with these differences: The range is slightly greater. The opening bidder bids a suit with 19 points. If his partner responds showing at least five or six points, opener jumps to two no-trump. But it is too dangerous to make a take-out double, which may force partner to bid at the two-level on nothing, and re-bid two no-trump with 19 points. So a take-out double followed by a two no-trump bid shows 20 or 21 points. Another difference between a no-trump overcall and an opening bid is that the overcall may be made with a worthless doubleton in an unbid suit, the kind of hand one would prefer to *open* with a minor suit. The biggest difference of all is that one should not overcall one no-trump on every hand that meets these qualifications. When the opponents are vulnerable, a no-trump overcall should not be made with too much strength in the opponent's suit, especially when the suit is a major. It is better to pass and let the opponents get into trouble. Over a one-diamond bid, bid one no-trump with ♠ K Q x, ♡ x x, ◇ A J 10, ♣ A Q J x x, or ♠ A x x x, ♡ K x x, ◇ K Q x, ♣ A Q x, or ♠ x x, ♡ K x, ◇ A Q 10, ♣ A K 10 x x x. With ♠ K 10 x x, ♡ A J x x, ◇ A x x, ♣ A x, you should double. Support for *both* majors makes a no-trump overcall a bad percentage bid, since it would shut partner out if he should have four or five points with a four-card major. However, even with the last hand, you should overcall one heart or one spade with one no-trump if you bid at all. Now the odds are that a double would evoke a minor-suit response, and you are not strong enough to bid two no-trump. If the opponents are vulnerable you should pass a major-suit opening bid.

Responder can use Stayman over a no-trump overcall. However, if the one no-trump overcall is doubled, any bid by responder is natural, even two clubs or a bid of the opponents' suit. The only strong bid responder can make is a redouble or a jump. It pays to reserve all the other bids for rescue. Suppose the bidding is

SOUTH	WEST	NORTH	EAST
1 ♠	1 NT	Pass	?

East has ♠ x, ♡ x x x, ◇ Q J x x x x, ♣ A x x. He has enough points for three no-trump, but if opener only has a single spade stopper and a so-so fit in diamonds, he will not be able to make his contract with a spade lead. A three-diamond bid in this spot should not be forcing, only invitational. Over East's three-diamond bid West would bid three no-trump with ♠ K Q 10, ♡ A x x, ◇ K x x, ♣ K J x x, or ♠ K x x, ♡ A Q x, ◇ A K x x, ♣ J x x, but he would pass with ♠ A 10 x, ♡ A K x x, ◇ K x x, ♣ K x x, or raise diamonds with ♠ A x x, ♡ A K x, ◇ K x x, ♣ K Q x x. Since three diamonds is not forcing, East should bravely raise no-trump himself if his suit is ready to run, assuming one high honor in West's hand, or if he has a helping jack or better in the opponent's suit. For example: ♠ x x, ♡ x x, ◇ K Q x x x x, ♣ K x x, or ♠ J x, ♡ x x, ◇ Q J x x x x, ♣ A x x.

A double of an opening no-trump bid is a penalty double. West needs about as good a hand as the opener and a good suit to lead. East may take the double out with a long suit and a poor hand. Normally he should leave the double in with as little as five points, although with strength concentrated in one suit he may pull the double rather than gamble on partner's leading the suit. Over

SOUTH	WEST	NORTH	EAST
1 NT	Double	Pass	?

bid two spades with ♠ Q 10 x x x, ♡ x, ◇ J x x x, ♣ x x x, or ♠ K J 10 x x, ♡ x x, ◇ x x, ♣ J 10 x x, but pass with ♠ K 10 x x x, ♡ J x, ◇ x x x x, ♣ J x. However, with no five-card suit or longer, East must pass, regardless of strength.

		NORTH	
		♠ 9 x x x	
		♡ 10 x x	
WEST		◇ 10 x	EAST
♠ K Q J x		♣ K 10 x x	♠ x x
♡ x x			♡ Q J x x
◇ K Q J x x		SOUTH	◇ x x x
♣ A x		♠ A 10 x	♣ J x x x
		♡ A K 9 x	
		◇ A x x	
		♣ Q x x	

SOUTH	WEST	NORTH	EAST
1 NT	Double	Pass	2 ♡
Pass	Pass	Pass	

There is no excuse for East's cowardice. A rescue on a four-card suit is simply jumping from the frying pan into the fire. Nor is there any reason for him to feel so pessimistic about his chances of beating one no-trump. Even when he has less strength his partner could have more. Tournaments are not won by consistently settling for a minus score in situations such as this.

Experts do not all use the take-out double alike. Everyone would agree that ♠ K Q x x, ♡ A J x x, ◇ x, ♣ A 10 x x is an excellent take-out double of an opening one-diamond bid. Most players would double an opening bid of one club. A few would double one heart or one spade. In other words, everyone doubles with a good hand and support for all the unbid suits. With length in opener's suit or poor support for one suit and no satisfactory re-bid to get out of trouble, there is a parting of the ways. One person believes the take-out double is risky and misleading; another says, "Why be pessimistic? Maybe partner will bid one of my good suits. Anyway, I've got to show I have some stuff."

Or, suppose you pick up the following hand: ♠ A J 10 x x x, ♡ x, ◇ K Q 10 x x, ♣ A. What do you do over an opening club bid? Most top players would bid one spade (unless they saved a two-spade bid for this type of hand), expecting more bidding, in which case they would rely upon their judgment to tell them what to do. A double followed by a spade bid would give the correct impression of strength but would put all your eggs in one basket by not seeking a diamond fit. There is also the danger that partner will jump to four hearts, which would certainly leave you guessing. If you like to double with this type of hand, you must train your partner not to make preemptive responses without a very solid suit. For a long time I doubled with this type of hand and hoped for the best. This style of bidding now seems wild and incomprehensible, a sure sign that I am getting old.

Another problem: Everyone agrees that a take-out double implies major-suit support, but how strong is the implication? And how good does the support have to be? I almost *guarantee* four-card support for *an* unbid major (not both majors necessarily). Many good players are willing to double with only three-card support. A few are willing to double with no support—just a good hand. The advantages of requiring four-card support are many and obvious.

SOUTH	WEST	NORTH	EAST
1 ♡	Double	2 ♡	?

♠ A Q x, ♡ x, ◇ K J x x x, ♣ 10 x x x. East can and should bid three spades. Notice that a three-diamond or four-diamond bid would not enable the partnership to reach the best spot if West had ♠ K J x x, ♡ x x, ◇ A 10 x, ♣ A Q x x.

♠ K J x x x, ♡ 8 x x x, ◇ x x, ♣ x x:

SOUTH	WEST	NORTH	EAST
1 ◇	Double	Pass	1 ♠
Pass	2 ♣	Pass	?

You can bid two hearts, since you are sure that partner would not double without a four-card major. If you were not sure, you could not risk another bid.

When the opening bid is a minor, the defenders have plenty of bidding room in which to maneuver. However, a one-spade opening bid really creates problems. West: ♠ x x, ♡ A Q x x, ◇ A J x, ♣ K Q x x; East: ♠ x x x, ♡ K 8 x x, ◇ K Q x x, ♣ x x: West doubles the opening spade bid, and what should East do? Most players would bid two hearts. I recommend a three-heart bid! This is the rock-bottom minimum for such a bid. You have to be pretty sure of heart support to risk it, but if you require ten or eleven points in high cards for a jump bid, West will really have a problem, since your two-heart bid covers such a wide range. West does not know what to raise to three hearts with, and East will not know what he needs to bid four hearts. Since East is almost positive that a take-out double of one spade shows heart support, he should evaluate his hand as though he were supporting his partner's heart bid. With ten or eleven support points (not counting minor honors in spades, but promoting for "good" points), he should "raise" to three hearts, or with twelve points or more bid four hearts. When East bids just two hearts, West needs a powerhouse to raise, and East may then bid game with as little as ♠ x x x, ♡ K x x x x, ◇ J x x, ♣ x x. The three-heart bid is definitely not forcing or even close. West needs something like ♠ x x, ♡ A J x x, ◇ A J x, ♣ K Q x x to bid four hearts, since East has already counted on a little better than a minimum double. For that matter, West needs a better hand to double one spade than he needs to double any other suit, since the response must necessarily be at the two-level. Note that this adjustment is only necessary over a spade bid. After

SOUTH	WEST	NORTH	EAST
1 ♡	Double	Pass	?

bid just one spade with ♠ K x x x, ♡ x x x, ◇ K Q x x, ♣ x x, since partner can safely raise to two spades with ♠ A Q x x, ♡ x x, ◇ A J x, ♣ K Q x x.

The main point of this discussion was to show the many advantages of requiring four-card support for an unbid major when you make a take-out double. The disadvantages are that when a bid is made too rigid, you can't use it on hands where you would like to, and must pick an inferior alternative. It is permissible to make a take-out double with only three-card support, provided it is good three-card support and you have a singleton or void in the opponents' suit, or when you have better than four-honor count. Double one heart with ♠ K J x, ♡ x, ◇ A Q x x, ♣ K x x x x, or ♠ K Q x, ♡ x x, ◇ A K x x x, ♣ A J x. By requiring additional high-card strength or a singleton in the opponents' suit, a safety factor is automatically introduced. If partner bids a three-card suit at a low level for which you have only three-card support, there will probably be more bidding, and neither of you will re-bid the suit. You can't get hurt badly at the one-level. Partner will not jump or bid freely with a three-card suit unless he is short in the opponents' suit, since a 4-3 trump holding is unsatisfactory when the four-card holding must take the first ruff. Since you must have a singleton, the probability of the opponents' having a combined holding of ten or eleven cards in their suit is not great; and if they do, they will probably keep bidding. In all the time I have jumped or bid freely at a high level on a three-card major, I have never hit my partner with only three. It does not pay to become inhibited because of some remote possibility of disaster.

Still another problem in connection with the inference of four-card support is as follows: Suppose East bids a major suit in response to the take-out double and West now bids a new suit. East now knows that West does not have four-card support. But does he have any support? If the bidding is

SOUTH	WEST	NORTH	EAST
1 ◇	Double	Pass	1 ♠
Pass	2 ♣	Pass	?

East can't even safely assume three-card spade support. West may have ♠ A x, ♡ A x x x, ◇ x, ♣ K Q J x x x. Therefore East should not re-bid his suit unless it is fairly strong.

SOUTH	WEST	NORTH	EAST
1 ◇	Double	Pass	1 ♠
Pass	2 ♡	Pass	?

Again, East cannot count on even three-card spade support, since the double may have been based on 3½ or 4 honor-count and a strong heart suit. However, when the opening bid was a major, for example

SOUTH	WEST	NORTH	EAST
1 ♡	Double	Pass	1 ♠
Pass	2 ◇	Pass	?

East may re-bid a five-card spade suit on the assumption that the doubler had a good hand and good three-card spade support. Sometimes the doubler must raise with three trumps, since it is the best bid available, but he should try hard to find some other bid.

After a take-out double and a minimum response, opener can bid a minor suit without showing extra values. He is just trying to find a better spot. It is proper to double a one-diamond bid with ♠ J 9 x x, ♡ K x, ◇ x, ♣ A K J x x x, and bid two clubs if partner responds one heart. An immediate two-club bid might result in shutting out a good spade fit. However, a take-out double followed by a raise of partner's suit, or a re-bid of a major suit over a minimum response, shows substantial extra values.

SOUTH	WEST	NORTH	EAST
1 ◇	Double	Pass	1 ♠ or 2 ♣
Pass	2 ♡		

shows at least ♠ K x, ♡ A Q J x x, ◇ A x, ♣ Q x x x, or ♠ A x, ♡ A K x x x x, ◇ x x, ♣ Q J x. A jump after the double is very strong but not forcing. West would bid three hearts with ♠ A x, ♡ A K J 9 x x, ◇ x, ♣ K Q 10 x, and East would raise to four hearts with ♠ K x x x, ♡ x x x, ◇ x x x, ♣ x x x.

When East makes a minimum response, West needs almost as much for a single raise as he would need for a double raise if West had opened the bidding and East had responded. After

SOUTH	WEST	NORTH	EAST
1 ◇	Double	Pass	1 ♠

whether opener bids or not, West needs something like this to raise to two spades: ♠ K x x x, ♡ A x x, ◇ x x, ♣ A K x x (minimum), or ♠ A x x x, ♡ A Q x, ◇ x x, ♣ A K x x. If West raises just because he has four trumps, East will not know what to do.

West: ♠ A x x x, ♡ Q x, ◇ A J x x, ♣ K x x; East: ♠ K Q 9 x, ♡ x x x, ◇ x x x x, ♣ Q x:

SOUTH	WEST	NORTH	EAST
1 ♡	Double	Pass	1 ♠
2 ♡	Pass	Pass	2 ♠

East is no coward. He will not sell out with his substantial values. Suppose that West decides to raise rather than risk selling out to two hearts (forgetting that he has a partner). Then East should bid three spades. He cannot tell that his partner has a minimum double. West's two-spade bid would be proper with ♠ A x x x, ♡ x, ◇ A Q x, ♣ A J 10 x x, or ♠ A x x x, ♡ x x, ◇ A Q x, ♣ A K x x. Another reason why West should not raise with a minimum double is that responder may be trapping. The four hands could be:

```
                   NORTH
               ♠ K Q 10 x
               ♡ x
               ◇ K 10 x x
    WEST       ♣ Q 10 x x        EAST
♠ A x x x                    ♠ J x x
♡ Q x                        ♡ J x x x
◇ A J x x         SOUTH       ◇ x x x
♣ K x x        ♠ x x          ♣ J x x
               ♡ A K 10 x x x
               ◇ Q x
               ♣ A x x
```

In responding to the take-out double, forget about the penalty pass unless you have a sequence in trumps. A pass calls for a trump lead since a one-bid cannot be set badly if declarer is allowed to make his little trumps. You might get a good board occasionally by passing with five or six trumps to the king-ten, and an otherwise good hand when the opponents are vulnerable, but it is a bad gamble. Partner may have a singleton or void with a freak hand. It is surprising how often you will get an opportunity to double at a higher level. A one no-trump response shows six to ten points. With six points you should have a double stopper in the opponents' suit. With nine or ten points, no stopper is necessary, although it is desirable to have at least a partial stopper. A two no-trump response is not forcing, but shows 11 or 12 points, possibly 10 points with a strong holding in the opponents' suit.

SOUTH	WEST	NORTH	EAST
1 ♠	Double	Pass	?

Bid two no-trump with ♠ K x x, ♡ K J x, ◇ x x x, ♣ A x x x, or ♠ Q 10 8 x, ♡ x x, ◇ A x x x, ♣ A x x. Over

SOUTH	WEST	NORTH	EAST
1 ◇	Double	Pass	?

bid three no-trump with ♠ K x, ♡ A x x, ◇ A J 9 x, ♣ J x x x, or ♠ 10 x, ♡ Q x, ◇ K J x, ♣ K Q J x x x.

With a normal hand (4-9 points), East bids his best suit with the following qualifications: He tends to bid a major suit in preference to a minor suit that is one card longer. In fact, a minor-suit response almost denies a four-card major suit. Occasionally, when East predicts that he will want to bid again later, he anticipates the subsequent bidding and makes his first bid so that his second bid will be easier.

SOUTH	WEST	NORTH	EAST
1 ♡	Double	Pass	?

Bid one spade with ♠ Q 9 x x, ♡ A x x, ◇ x, ♣ J x x x x, or ♠ K 10 x, ♡ x x, ◇ Q x x x, ♣ J x x x. But bid two diamonds with ♠ 9 x x x, ♡ x, ◇ Q J x x x, ♣ K x x. Partner should be short in hearts for his double. If the opponents have ten hearts between them, there will almost surely be a heart re-bid. Then you plan to bid two spades, which partner may interpret to show a three-card suit. That doesn't matter; you want to give partner the impression that your diamonds are much better than your spades. Besides, it would be too risky to bid one spade now and three diamonds over a heart re-bid later. Similarly,

SOUTH	WEST	NORTH	EAST
1 ♣	Double	Pass	?

bid one spade with ♠ K 10 x x, ♡ Q x x x x, ◇ x, ♣ x x x. There will probably be more bidding, and you can then show the heart suit without reversing.

As for free bids, East should strain to bid rather than get shut out. At the one-level, he should bid one spade with as good as ♠ K Q x x, ♡ x x x, ◇ x x x, ♣ x x x, or ♠ K x x x x, ♡ x x, ◇ x x x, ♣ J x x. A minor-suit free-bid at the two- or three-level should show a pretty good suit. Bid two clubs freely with ♠ x, ♡ x x x, ◇ x x x, ♣ A x x x x x, or ♠ K x, ♡ x x x, ◇ x x x, ♣ Q J 8 7 x. Even at the two- or three-level, a major suit should be bid with a mediocre hand.

SOUTH	WEST	NORTH	EAST
1 ◇	Double	2 ◇	?

♠ K Q x x, ♡ x x x, ◇ x x x, ♣ x x x: Pass. ♠ K Q x x, ♡ Q x x, ◇ x x x, ♣ x x x, bid two spades. With ♠ K x, ♡ J x x x x, ◇ x, ♣ x x x x x, bid two hearts. With ♠ K x, ♡ A J 10 x x, ◇ x x, ♣ J 10 x x, bid three hearts.

SOUTH	WEST	NORTH	EAST
1 ◇	Double	3 ◇	?

Bid three spades with ♠ 10 x x x x, ♡ A x, ◇ x x, ♣ Q x x x, or ♠ K Q x x x, ♡ x, ◇ x x x x, ♣ 10 x x. At rubber bridge, you might pass some of these hands. Then if partner were able to double again, you would jump to game. But that method of bidding makes it impossible to play three hearts or three spades, which may be just the right spot. Since the free bid at duplicate does not show a great deal, West should not raise or double for penalties too optimistically.

With a very poor hand, East may break the rules occasionally, but whatever he does, he must not pass (unless responder has bid) or bid one no-trump.

SOUTH	WEST	NORTH	EAST
1 ♠	Double	Pass	?

♠ J 10 9 x, ♡ 9 x x x, ◇ x x, ♣ J x x: The orthodox response is two hearts. The responsibility is not on East. He has merely been told to bid his best suit. But psychologically, two clubs is a better response, since West is less likely to fit clubs than hearts and is therefore less likely to raise. Suppose you bid two hearts. Partner would raise to three hearts with ♠ x x, ♡ A K x x x, ◇ A Q x x, ♣ A x. Over two clubs, he will just bid two hearts. Of course, if the two-club bid is doubled, you gladly return to two hearts, since the double will warn partner not to raise. The reason a two-club bid is not very risky, even when vulnerable, is that one of the three hands is bound to have a bid. The bidding will almost never stop at two clubs. Even if North has a five-card club suit, he may be afraid to let you play undoubled for fear he has game.

East does not need a particularly strong hand to jump the bid. As we have seen, over

SOUTH	WEST	NORTH	EAST
1 ♠	Double	Pass	?

he can bid three hearts with as little as ♠ x x x, ♡ K x x x, ◇ K Q x x, ♣ x x. But over any other bid, a jump should show a somewhat better hand.

SOUTH	WEST	NORTH	EAST
1 ◇	Double	Pass	?

♠ A Q 10 x, ♡ x x, ◇ x x x, ♣ K x x x, or ♠ K x x x x, ♡ A x x, ◇ J x, ♣ J 10 x, or ♠ Q x x x x x, ♡ x, ◇ x x x, ♣ A x x, or ♠ x x, ♡ x x, ◇ x x x, ♣ A Q J x x x: These are all minimum jump bids, especially the second one.

The jump bid is not forcing, but the doubler should bid again except with a bare minimum to give his partner a chance. ♠ K x x x, ♡ A x x, ◇ x x, ♣ A J 10 x: After doubling one diamond and receiving a two-heart response, you should pass, but you would raise a two-spade response to three spades. East should pass the raise to three spades with ♠ A Q 10 x, ♡ K x x, ◇ J x x, ♣ x x x, or ♠ A Q J x x x, ♡ x x, ◇ x x x, ♣ x x, or bid four spades with ♠ A J 10 x, ♡ K x, ◇ x x x x,

♣ Q x x, or ♠ Q x x x x, ♡ x, ◇ A x x, ♣ K x x x.
♠ K x x x, ♡ A x x, ◇ x x, ♣ A J 10 x was a minimum raise
to three spades. The maximum is not much stronger. Raise to
four spades with ♠ K x x x, ♡ A x x, ◇ x x, ♣ A Q J x.
Or, if East had bid two hearts, raise him to three hearts. There
is no reasonable alternative to the raise with three trumps.

Whenever East has enough strength to insist upon reaching
game, but is not sure of the spot, he must bid the opponents'
suit, which is his only forcing bid. Over

SOUTH	WEST	NORTH	EAST
1 ◇	Double	Pass	?

bid two diamonds with ♠ x, ♡ A Q 10 x, ◇ A x x x, ♣ Q 10
x x, or ♠ A J 9 x x, ♡ K x, ◇ x x x, ♣ K J x, or ♠ J x x x,
♡ A x x x, ◇ A x x, ♣ K x. For example, West: ♠ K x x x x,
♡ K Q x, ◇ K x, ♣ K x x; East: ♠ x x, ♡ A x, ◇ x x x,
♣ A Q 10 x x x:

SOUTH	WEST	NORTH	EAST
1 ◇	Double	Pass	2 ◇
Pass	2 ♠	Pass	3 ♣
Pass	3 NT		

You may wonder how the cue bid solved any problems.
Couldn't the bidding have gone as follows?

SOUTH	WEST	NORTH	EAST
1 ◇	Double	Pass	3 ♣
Pass	3 NT		

No, the doubler would have no right to bid three no-trump over
a three-club bid if the partnership is bidding correctly. Responder could bid three clubs with ♠ Q x, ♡ x x, ◇ x x x,
♣ A Q 10 x x x, or ♠ x, ♡ x x x, ◇ x x x, ♣ A Q J x x x.
West should pass a three-club bid, since he cannot expect to take
nine tricks before the opponents get in to run their diamond
suit. But with an additional ace, responder cue bids to insist
upon game.

However, the cue bid is not quite forcing to game. Any time
a defender cue bids and later raises his partner's suit, the bidding may stop. Thus,

SOUTH	WEST	NORTH	EAST
1 ◇	2 ◇	Pass	2 ♡
Pass	3 ♡	Pass	?

Pass with ♠ x x x, ♡ J x x x, ◇ Q x x, ♣ x x x. Partner probably has something like this:
♠ A K x x, ♡ A K x x, ◇ x, ♣ A Q x x.

Similarly,

SOUTH	WEST	NORTH	EAST
1 ◇	Double	Pass	?

Bid two diamonds with ♠ J 10 x x, ♡ K x x x, ◇ x x, ♣ A J 9 (minimum). Partner should have a four-card major. When he bids it, raise him to three. Then, if he has a minimum take-out double, he can pass. Notice how much better the cue bid works than bidding either suit. Whether you bid hearts or spades, and whether you jump or not, you risk being dropped in the wrong suit. Perhaps you bid spades and partner passes, while if you had guessed to bid hearts, partner would have raised and you would have reached game. With ♠ Q 10 x x, ♡ K 10 x x, ◇ x x, ♣ A J x, you would bid as suggested. But with ♠ A 10 x x, ♡ K 10 x x, ◇ x x, ♣ A J x, when partner bids his major suit, you must raise him straight to game. The cue bid may also be used to show a mild slam interest.

SOUTH	WEST	NORTH	EAST
1 ◇	Double	Pass	?

♠ K Q x x x x x, ♡ A x x, ◇ x, ♣ Q x: You know what your spot is, in all probability. It is four spades. But you would bid four spades without the ace of hearts. So you bid two diamonds, followed by a jump to four spades over partner's probable heart re-bid to show you are not just pre-empting. You could bid two spades over two hearts without fear of being dropped after the cue bid, but the cue bid followed by the jump best describes the hand.

Suppose East makes a minimum response and gets a single raise. What should he have to bid again? Very little! As a rule of thumb, pretend you have responded to partner's opening bid and he has given you a double raise. Disregard minor honors in

the opponents' suit. If you would have passed this bid with
what you have left, or if you would not have responded at all,
you should pass. If you would have gone to game, bid once
more. With a very little additional strength, bid game yourself.

SOUTH	WEST	NORTH	EAST
1 ◊	Double	Pass	1 ♠
Pass	2 ♣	Pass	?

♠ K Q x x, ♡ x x, ◊ x x x, ♣ J 10 9 x: This is a borderline hand. If partner had opened the bidding with one club or one
heart, you would have bid one spade. Then when he raised to
three spades, you would have a close decision whether to bid
or pass. Give yourself the jack of hearts, and you should definitely bid three spades.

♠ J x x x x, ♡ x, ◊ x x x, ♣ K J x x: bid three spades.
♠ Q x x x, ♡ x x x, ◊ K J x, ♣ J x x: pass.
♠ K x x x, ♡ 10 x x, ◊ K J x, ♣ J x x: bid two no-trump.
♠ K x x x x, ♡ x, ◊ x x x, ♣ K J x x: bid four spades.
♠ A Q x x, ♡ x x x, ◊ x x x, ♣ K x x: bid four spades.
♠ A x x x, ♡ K x x x, ◊ x x x, ♣ J x: bid three hearts.
♠ 10 x x x x x, ♡ x, ◊ x x x x, ♣ A x: bid four spades.

When partner raises to three, bid game with any excuse
(♠ x x x x, ♡ A x x, ◊ x x x, ♣ x x x). From these examples
it can be seen how important it is that the take-out doubler
refrain from raising with a minimum hand.

When responder redoubles, East may pass without a clear-
cut bid. The pass is *not* for penalties. A redouble often means
the opponents are going to try to double any bid that comes
along, and it is very important to find the right spot. So East
bids more in an effort to guide the bidding to the right suit than
to indicate whether he has one point or five. If a heart bid is
doubled, he should bid one spade with four spades. Failure to
bid one spade virtually denies four spades. Except for this
special case, East should usually have a five-card suit to bid,
although an important consideration is what suits partner would
be shut out of by a bid, and whether East is willing to shut out
the suit. For example, after

SOUTH	WEST	NORTH	EAST
1 ♡	Double	Redouble	?

Responder should pass with ♠ x x, ♡ J x x x x, ◇ x x x, ♣ x x x, or ♠ x, ♡ Q x x x, ◇ 9 x x x x, ♣ J 10 x. He should not bid two diamonds with the latter hand, since he does not want to shut out a rescue to two clubs. But with ♠ x x, ♡ J x x x x, ◇ Q 10 9 x x, ♣ x, East does not mind shutting out a two-club bid, so he should bid two diamonds. He would be restless and uneasy till he got his diamond bid in anyway. Now, if by any chance, West has ♠ A x x x, ♡ x, ◇ A K x x x, ♣ Q x x, he can raise to three or four diamonds as a pre-empt, knowing that there will be a good distributional fit.

Occasionally, responder will redouble rather light, or someone will psych, so East will have a fair hand. If he has a one-suit hand, he can jump as though there were no redouble. He should bid two spades with ♠ K J 10 x x, ♡ A x, ◇ x x x x, ♣ x x. But suppose East has ♠ A x x x, ♡ Q x x x, ◇ x x x, ♣ K x. There is some danger in bidding one spade since West may pass, even with a normal raise, having been intimidated by the redouble. So East should pass. Then when West rescues himself, as he must do, East raises.

The immediate cue bid is the strongest action a defender can take. Over one diamond, bid two diamonds with ♠ K Q J x, ♡ A Q J x, ◇ x, ♣ A Q x x, or ♠ A K x x, ♡ A K x x x, ◇ —, ♣ A x x x. The classical reason given for the cue bid is to prevent a penalty pass by partner. But the penalty pass is made so seldom that it is not worth while to alter the bidding to take care of that remote possibility. The main reason is to take advance protection against a pre-empt. If the bidding were

SOUTH	WEST	NORTH	EAST
1 ◇	Double	4 ◇	

nothing you could do would induce partner to bid five clubs with ♠ x x x, ♡ x x x, ◇ x x, ♣ K 10 x x x. But after

SOUTH	WEST	NORTH	EAST
1 ◇	2 ◇	4 ◇	Pass
Pass	Double	Pass	?

he should bid five clubs with equal or unfavorable vulnerability. However, he should wait for you to double before bidding five clubs. You would also have bid two diamonds with ♠ A K Q x x x, ♡ A Q x x, ◇ x, ♣ A x, for example, and over four diamonds you would bid four spades instead of doubling. Aside from the fact that he might shut out your suit, partner should pass rather than bid "freely" with so little. The free five-club bid should at least show something like the king six-long, so that you could safely bid six clubs with hand No. 2.

The immediate cue bid may also be used to show a completely different type of hand. Over an opening diamond bid, bid two diamonds with ♠ A, ♡ A Q J 9 x, ◇ x, ♣ K Q 10 9 x x, or ♠ —, ♡ A Q J x x x, ◇ x, ♣ A K x x x x. Partner will surely bid spades, but you repeat your diamond cue bid to ask for a choice of the remaining suits. This illustrates a good reason why partner should not jump on the first round over your cue bid. With ♠ A Q x x x, ♡ x x x, ◇ x x x, ♣ Q x, he should not bid six spades. He must bid spades at a minimum level, intending to bid at least six if spades are raised. Incidentally, the cue-bidder guarantees another bid. If a hand is strong enough for a cue bid, it would be illogical to pass the response.

The repeated cue bid to show a powerful two-suiter is old stuff. Experts have used it for quite a while. But I have a suggestion for a less powerful two-suiter. Make a take-out double followed by a cue bid. In this case the cue-bidder has limited his hand and does not guarantee a re-bid.

West: ♠ A x, ♡ x, ◇ K Q x x x, ♣ A K x x x.
East: ♠ J 10 x x, ♡ x x x, ◇ A x, ♣ Q x x x:

SOUTH	WEST	NORTH	EAST
1 ♡	Double	Pass	1 ♠
Pass	2 ♡	Pass	4 ♣
Pass	5 ♣		

East realizes his hand is very fine in support of a diamond-club two-suiter, so he jumps. West has shown that he does not have a strong enough hand to insist upon game, and he would surely pass a three-club bid. Bidding the opponents' suit following a take-out double is supposed to show an honest suit. But the times when the opponents psych and you are too strong for a

trap-pass are quite rare. The recommended delayed cue-bid to
show a 4 honor-count, 5-5 hand is a much more useful bid.
However, you can eat your cake and have it too.

West: ♠ K x, ♡ A K J 10 x x x, ◇ A x x, ♣ x.
East: ♠ Q x x x x, ♡ x, ◇ J x x, ♣ Q x x x:

NORTH	EAST	SOUTH	WEST
Pass	Pass	1 ♡	Double
Pass	1 ♠	Pass	2 ♡
Pass	3 ♣	Pass	3 ♡
Pass	Pass	Pass	

Culbertson says the two-heart bid shows a heart suit but is forcing. If West wants to play two hearts, he must pass the one-heart
bid and hope to reopen with hearts later. For example, with
♠ K x, ♡ A Q J 9 x x, ◇ x, ♣ Q 10 x x, the bidding might
well go

NORTH	EAST	SOUTH	WEST
Pass	Pass	1 ♡	Pass
2 ◇	Pass	Pass	2 ♡

With the first hand, the heart suit is so strong that West sus-
pects a psych and should be willing to bid to the three-level in
an effort to show his hand. While in my example, I had East-
West reach three hearts, a shrewd East might pass the two-heart
bid! How can he do that? He knows that *this time* his partner
has hearts for the heart bid rather than a two-suiter. If West
had a minor-suit hand, North-South would have ten or eleven
hearts between them. With ten or eleven hearts, they would be
bidding more hearts themselves.

The delayed cue bid may be used for still a third purpose:
West: ♠ A Q x x, ♡ —, ◇ K Q x x, ♣ K J x x x; East:
♠ K J x x x, ♡ x x x, ◇ J x, ♣ A x x:

SOUTH	WEST	NORTH	EAST
1 ♡	Double	Pass	2 ♠
Pass	3 ♡	Pass	4 ♣
Pass	4 ♠	Pass	6 ♠

In this last example, West visualizes a slam after the two-spade
bid if his partner's strength is all outside of hearts. So he cue

bids hearts. At this point East does not know what West has, and must assume that he wants a choice of the unbid suits. But the four-spade bid completes the story. West had spade support all along, so the cue bid must have been a slam invitation.

There are only so many bids at one's disposal. A book for beginners or average players must assign one meaning and a limited range to a particular bid. Part of the process of improving one's game is to find different, inconsistent meanings for the same bid so as to be able to show more hand-types with the limited bids available. An example you are probably acquainted with is in the Blackwood responses. Five clubs shows no aces or four aces. The Roth-Stone and Bulldog players make use of a two-way opening bid. They open one diamond with ♠ K Q x x, ♡ A x, ◇ K Q x x, ♣ x x x, or ♠ x x, ♡ J x x, ◇ K 10 x x, ♣ x x x x, figuring that the bidding should soon make it apparent whether the bid was normal or lead-directing. In the last example hand when you bid hearts, partner should be able to tell whether you have seven or none. Similarly, if the bidding is

SOUTH	WEST	NORTH	EAST
1 ♡	Pass	1 NT	Pass
2 ♡	Double		

partner should be able to tell whether you have four or five hearts and are doubling for penalties or one heart (or possibly two hearts) and are doubling for take-out—just so long as you don't make "indifferent" doubles with three hearts. My prediction as to future changes in bridge is that more and more uses will be found for the same bidding sequences.

Action After Pre-emptive Bids

THERE IS no more effective defense against an opening pre-empt than the slow pass. With less than an opening bid, pass fast. With a minimum opener up to about 3½ honor-count (depending upon distribution), hesitate and then pass. Partner bids accordingly.

Unfortunately, too many players use this system whether intentionally or not. The theory of the ethics of the situation is this: You may hesitate any time you have a problem. When you

were planning to bid one heart and you hear a three-spade bid
on your right, it may take a moment to decide whether to bid
four hearts, double, or pass. This delay cannot be avoided. You
are not a machine, and it takes a measurable period of time to
think. But your partner is not supposed to take advantage of
the information given by your slow pass (if you decide to pass)
either in the auction or in the defense. That is very difficult to
do—or not to do. If he has a close decision, he has the alternative of "bending over backward," putting himself at a disadvantage (after all, he might have guessed right) or of making
the bid he might not have made otherwise. When the situation
arises, it is extremely difficult to be completely objective in
deciding what you would have done. Even though you do not
allow partner's hesitation to influence you, the opponents may
take advantage of it. The solution to this problem is always to
hesitate fifteen seconds over any pre-emptive bid, whatever your
hand is. That gives you ample time for a decision. Then whether
you bid or pass, no one (including the opponents) can draw
any inferences from your hesitation.

Some players like the Fishbein convention over three-bids
and weak two-bids. The cheapest suit bid is for take-out, and
a double is for penalties. This is only used by West (left of the
opener). A double by the person to the right of the bidder is
always optional. One's views are influenced by the type of three-
bids used against him. Pre-empts are not as widely used on the
West Coast as in the East, and they are usually based on a
fairly strong trump suit. Consequently, the Fishbein convention
is not popular. Over a three-spade bid it is not often that you
get ♠ —, ♡ K Q x x, ◇ A Q x x, ♣ A Q x x x, or ♠ A Q
10 8, ♡ x x, ◇ A K x, ♣ x x x x. These are ideal Fishbein
hands. In the first case, you definitely want your partner to bid.
In the second case you want to double for penalties. Not playing
Fishbein, you must pass. But for every ideal hand you get, you
will have several indifferent hands. ♠ K x, ♡ Q J x x, ◇ A K x,
♣ K J x x, or ♠ x, ♡ A K x, ◇ Q J x x x, ♣ A J x x. With
these hands you would rather double to show a good hand and
leave the decision whether to pass or bid up to partner. Just
as over a one-bid, a double suggests a major-suit contract. With
a balanced hand, partner tends to leave the double in, regard-

less of strength (as he would over a no-trump double). It is better to pass and defend than run out to a four-card suit which may not be playable. If he has a close decision whether to pass or bid, he tends to pass if his suit is a minor, or bid if his suit is a major.

SOUTH	WEST	NORTH	EAST
3 ♡	Double	Pass	?

♠ x x x, ♡ Q x x, ◊ J x x, ♣ x x x x, pass: With ♠ K x, ♡ A x x, ◊ K x x, ♣ 10 x x x x, pass, although you might gamble on three no-trump if you are vulnerable and the opponents are not. With ♠ K J x x x, ♡ x x x, ◊ x x x, ♣ x x, bid three spades. With ♠ x x x, ♡ x x x, ◊ K J x x x, ♣ x x, pass. With ♠ K J x x x, ♡ x x x, ◊ K x x, ♣ x x, bid four spades. With ♠ x x, ♡ x x x, ◊ K J x x x x, ♣ x x, bid four diamonds. With ♠ x x, ♡ K x, ◊ K Q x x x x, ♣ x x x, bid three no-trump. With ♠ K x, ♡ x x, ◊ K Q x x x x, ♣ x x x, bid five diamonds.

In fourth position, you should reopen with a double with about one honor-count less than in second position. This is dangerous, of course, since responder may be trapping. But partner is in a better position for a penalty pass if he has trump strength, and your strength will be over the strong hand. Anyway, it is a calculated risk. There are other bids you can make over a three-bid besides a double. You overcall on the assumption that responder and partner have approximately equal shares of the outstanding strength, being influenced somewhat by the solidity of your suit. Perhaps it is best to count on partner for a little less than half the outstanding strength to make your bid, because if you find him with just his half so that you could barely make your bid, he will probably raise you to game, which puts you too high again. It is better to pass three hearts for plus 50 or plus 100 than to bid three spades (which you can make) and have partner raise you to game for down one.

Over three hearts with ♠ K Q x x x, ♡ x x x, ◊ A K x, ♣ Q x, pass.

With ♠ K Q J 10 x, ♡ x x x, ◊ A K x, ♣ Q x, bid three spades.

With ♠ A Q J x x x x, ♡ x, ◇ A Q x, ♣ K x, bid four spades.

With ♠ A x, ♡ K x, ◇ Q x x x, ♣ A K Q x x, bid three no-trump.

With ♠ x x, ♡ A Q x, ◇ K x, ♣ A K J 10 x x, bid three no-trump. The requirements for an overcall in fourth position are reduced to about the same extent as in the case of a double.

Action Over a Four-Bid

THE DOUBLE of a minor suit is optional. A double of four spades is primarily for penalties. A double of four hearts should show spade support. At least, it should not be based entirely upon heart strength. As for doubles of four-bids, there are two conflicting considerations. You can't wait for ideal penalty hands or ideal take-out hands for a double. The double must simply be made on general strength to prevent the opponents from stealing you blind. Consequently, the double of a bid at the four-level is generally considered a penalty double, since it is too risky to force or strongly invite partner to bid at the five-level. On the other hand, the double is usually based upon general strength, since the pre-empter's trump suit should be strong. So East tends to pull the double with a strong suit. For that reason, when you do have very good trumps and not much offensive strength, it does not pay to double. Over four hearts, pass with ♠ x x, ♡ K J 10 9, ◇ A K x x, ♣ K x x, since there is a strong possibility of a four-spade bid by partner if you double. When you want to insist upon a bid over four spades, or when you want a choice of minors over four hearts, bid four no-trump as a powerful demand bid.

SOUTH	WEST	NORTH	EAST
4 ♠	?		

♠ —, ♡ A K J 10 x x, ◇ A J x x, ♣ A x x: You should bid four no-trump. If partner bids five of a minor, *then* bid five hearts. But he may be able to jump to six of a minor over the four no-trump bid with nothing but a six-card suit to the king-queen, while he would have to pass an immediate five-heart bid. Suppose that partner has ♠ x x x, ♡ x, ◇ K Q x x, ♣ K x x x x. Over your four no-trump bid, he would bid five no-trump for a choice in the minors. (Five spades would ask for *any* suit at the six-level.) Forget the big hand for a moment, but suppose after the same bidding (four spades, four no-trump) responder elected to double four no-trump. With ♠ x x x, ♡ Q 9 x x, ◇ x, ♣ K Q x x x, you (East) would pass. Since partner's four no-trump bid is artificial and he probably is void in spades, he must pull the double. (In the improbable event you want to play four no-trump you should redouble.) If he bids five clubs or five hearts, you raise to six. If he bids five diamonds, you bid five spades to demand a choice between the other two suits.

One more hand will illustrate what ingenuity can do in a "wild guess" situation.

SOUTH	WEST	NORTH	EAST
1 ◇	Double	4 ◇	?

♠ —, ♡ A J x x x, ◇ A x, ♣ J 9 8 x x x: There is no denying that some guessing must be done. But assuming that you are willing to take a chance on a slam, the proper bidding sequence will help you find the best trump suit. Bid five diamonds. Partner will probably bid five spades, his best suit. Now you bid six clubs. When you show no interest in spades, the five-diamond bid must be based upon a club-heart hand, and partner can either pass or bid six hearts.

Reopening Bids

THE MOST difficult phase of defensive bidding is in reopening the bidding. This subject is treated lightly in most bridge books because reopening bids are usually too risky on a total point basis. When both opponents have bid, it does not pay to enter the bidding just to compete for a part-score when a big set may result. Besides, the "rules" for reopening are very flexible and not easy to state in terms of honor tricks or point count. Let us consider the easiest situation first—where opener's suit bid is passed by responder. East should reopen with a double with ten points and fair support for all unbid suits.

SOUTH	WEST	NORTH	EAST
1 ♡	Pass	Pass	?

Double with ♠ K J x, ♡ x x, ◇ Q x x, ♣ A x x x x, or ♠ Q J x x, ♡ x, ◇ A J x x, ♣ J x x x. While a second-position double is almost never passed for penalties, the fourth-hand double is frequently passed for penalties, since the trump strength will be behind the declarer. The fact that West is likely to pass for penalties has two important effects upon the bidding. East should not double on a hand poorly suited for defense. And if opener redoubles. West's pass is still for penalties!

Long ago, Culbertson said if the bidding was

SOUTH	WEST	NORTH	EAST
1 ♡	Double	Redouble	?

East must bid with weakness, since if he passes, it is for penalties. Otherwise, responder could make a psychic redouble and get out of trouble unless East's pass showed the kind of hand he would pass without the redouble. But Culbertson changed the rule, allowing East to pass with a poor hand, purportedly because psychic redoubles went out of fashion. But a more convincing reason would be that East did not have a hand suitable for a penalty pass more than one time out of fifty (remember, he needs solid trumps), and it did not pay to reserve the penalty pass for such a remote possibility. On the other hand, when the bidding is

SOUTH	WEST	NORTH	EAST
1 ♡	Pass	Pass	Double

West probably leaves the double in one time out of every five. Now, a penalty pass is not just a remote possibility. So the pass should have its normal meaning even when opener redoubles. The rule should be as follows:

Whenever a penalty pass would not be improbable, the pass is for penalties even over a redouble. Another case where this is likely to occur is after an optional double of an opening preempt.

SOUTH	WEST	NORTH	EAST
3 ♡	Double	Redouble	Pass

or

SOUTH	WEST	NORTH	EAST
1 NT	Double	Redouble	Pass

In both cases East's pass is a penalty pass. That does not mean that he has two natural trump tricks or guarantees a set. He would pass a double of three hearts or one no-trump without the redouble, holding ♠ x x x, ♡ J x x x, ◇ J x x, ♣ x x x, and he should also pass over a redouble. West may have to guess what to do, but he should also pass and hope for the best if he has no long suit.

Let us consider the reopening situation once again. After

SOUTH	WEST	NORTH	EAST
1 ♡	Pass	Pass	?

East should not double with a void. West would be very likely to pass for penalties, overestimating the combined defensive strength, and underestimating the combined offensive strength. With 5-4-4-0 distribution, East should reopen with a cue bid. West should then jump the bidding if he has enough strength outside the opponents' suit to justify a jump over a take-out double. If he fails to jump, East will pass with less than 14 points in high cards, and even if he gives a single raise, it will only show about this much strength: ♠ K Q x x, ♡ —, ◇ A Q x x, ♣ K x x x. *Note this is a specialized use of the bid; the general rule that the cue-bidder obligates himself to bid again does not apply.*

Other examples of action over

SOUTH	WEST	NORTH	EAST
1 ♡	Pass	Pass	?

With ♠ K Q J x x x, ♡ x, ◇ x x x, ♣ x x x, bid one spade. With ♠ K J 10 x, ♡ x x x, ◇ x, ♣ A Q x x x, bid one spade. With ♠ Q x x, ♡ x x x, ◇ A K x x x, ♣ x x, bid two diamonds. Aside from being slightly light for a double, if the opponents buy the bid, you want to indicate a diamond lead. ♠ x x, ♡ Q x x x, ◇ A K J x x, ♣ x x. Pass, probably. The opponents may have a better spot in spades. Partner cannot have enough hearts to be trapping, and he did not overcall one spade. This is not a clear-cut decision. With ♠ Q x x, ♡ x, ◇ A K x x x, ♣ Q x x x, you should pass after an opening spade bid has been passed around to you. It is very probable that either partner or the opponents will bid hearts if given another chance.

All bridge authorities agree that a reopening no-trump bid in fourth position can be shaded considerably. Some advocate a no-trump bid with as little as ten points. The problem is how to cover the entire range satisfactorily. If you can bid one no-trump with ten points, what do you do with 15? Bid two no-trump? or double and then bid two no-trump? And what with 18 points, etc.? Over

SOUTH	WEST	NORTH	EAST
1 ♡	Pass	Pass	?

I would like to be able to bid one no-trump with ♠ K x x, ♡ K 10 x, ◇ A 10 x, ♣ 10 9 x x, but a double may work out all right. In order for partner to have some idea what I am doing I prefer a range of 12-16 points for a one no-trump bid. With 17 or 18, double, followed by a two no-trump bid. With 19 or 20, bid two no-trump immediately. With more—but who ever has more than 20 points when the opponents open? These are very wide ranges as it is. Also, it is risky to bid two no-trump virtually by oneself on 17 points when partner may have nothing. But it is better to sacrifice some bidding accuracy to be able to bid one no-trump on the weaker hands (12-14) which come up frequently. Naturally, West must key his responses to the lighter bids. He raises to three no-trump with 12 points. (24 points are enough for three no-trump when 12 are in each hand and when almost all the outstanding cards are in one hand so that you know where they are.) With 10 or 11, he bids two no-trump or uses Stayman.

SOUTH	WEST	NORTH	EAST
1 ♠	Pass	2 ♠	Pass
Pass	?		

SOUTH	WEST	NORTH	EAST
1 ◇	Pass	1 ♡	Pass
2 ♡	Pass	Pass	?

SOUTH	WEST	NORTH	EAST
1 ♡	Pass	1 NT	Pass
2 ♡	Pass	Pass	?

Here the reopening problems are more difficult, as the opponents have stopped at two of a suit. Ordinarily, when the bidding stops at this level, the opponents will have about 18 to 22 points between them in high cards. That leaves 18 to 22 points for your side. Very likely the opponents can make their bid, and there is a bid at the two- or three-level you could make, also. Or perhaps you would be down one if the cards were favorably placed for the opponents (who can make two or three), but it will be too close for them to double. A great deal depends upon the distribution and the particular high cards held. Even when you have a playable trump suit, it is not wise to bid when many of your points are intermediate honors in the opponents' suit or suits.

SOUTH	WEST	NORTH	EAST
1 ♡	Pass	1 NT	Pass
2 ◇	Pass	Pass	?

Bid two spades or double with ♠ K Q 10 x, ♡ x x, ◇ x x x, ♣ A J x x, but pass with ♠ J 7 x x x, ♡ K x, ◇ Q J x, ♣ K J x. Incidentally, just as you figure the opponents for a maximum of 22 points in high cards when they stop at the two-level, you figure them for a maximum of six spades when neither has bid spades. So if you have a four-card spade suit, you can count on partner for at least three-card support, probably four. This is only a general rule. The precise bidding sequence alters the probabilities. In the last example, spade support is certain. Suppose the bidding by the opponents is one heart, two hearts. Responder might have a four- or five-card spade suit but only enough strength for one bid (♠ K J x x x, ♡ K x x x, ◇ x x, ♣ x x). Or opener may have a weak four-card spade suit while responder has three. In other words, when the opponents have the heart suit, they do not have to investigate a spade fit. However, your side is still very likely to have a total of eight spades. When the bidding is

SOUTH	WEST	NORTH	EAST
1 ♣	Pass	2 ♣	Pass
Pass	?		

it is very unlikely that responder has a four-card major suit, but opener may have one which he is not strong enough to show, or would not care to show anyway, since he does not expect to find a fit for it. If you reopen over this sequence, it is usually safer to double than to bid a four-card major or even a weak five-card major.

Let's examine some typical reopening situations:

SOUTH	WEST	NORTH	EAST
1 ◇	Pass	1 ♡	Pass
2 ♡	Pass	Pass	?

♠ 9 x x x x, ♡ x x, ◇ A x x, ♣ K x x: This is an automatic reopening bid of two spades. You haven't many high cards, but partner must have some, and you can't afford to sell out so cheaply. Notice the bullish features of this hand. You have a five-card suit, which is always a help. Your high cards are "good cards"—an ace which is always valuable, and the king in an unbid suit. Since you operate on the premise that your side has about half the high cards (because of the opponents' bidding), the important factor is how good a suit you have, and how well the cards are placed. Change the hand to ♠ 9 x x x x, ♡ Q x, ◇ K x x, ♣ A x x, and it is probably best to pass, your weak suit being the deciding factor. The king of diamonds could be a worthless card, and possession of the queen of hearts decreases the probability of finding partner with the queen of spades or clubs. The more strength you have in the opponents' suit in intermediate honors, the more reason to pass and defend. If your spade suit were improved a bit (♠ J 10 9 x x, ♡ Q x, ◇ K x x, ♣ A x x), you could bid. Now, even if you catch partner with just Q x of spades, you won't automatically take a dive. One very important thing about this sort of bidding is for partner to realize that you are bidding on his values. He must not get enthusiastic and raise or double just because he has a good hand. For example, West ♠ K Q x x, ♡ A x x, ◇ x x x, ♣ K x x; East: ♠ A J 10 x, ♡ J x, ◇ A x x, ♣ x x x x:

SOUTH	WEST	NORTH	EAST
1 ◇	Pass	1 ♡	Pass
2 ♡	Pass	Pass	2 ♠
Pass	Pass	3 ♡	Pass
Pass	?		

West's hand looks pretty good. The best feature is that his high cards are well placed. However, as a compensating disadvantage, he has no ruffing power. He has very little to gain by bidding or doubling. If, as is probable, the opponents have been pushed one trick too high, he will get a very good board, and if the opponents make three hearts, the board should be about average. Heads we win, tails we tie. Those are good odds. Why do anything to risk that advantage? With a doubleton diamond or club, West would be entitled to raise. Except for the high cards being well placed, West has nothing East has not already counted on. He expected spade support and the high cards from the bidding. For partner of the reopener to raise, he must have values that cannot be located by inference—that is good distribution.

If pushed, he will go to the three-level with ♠ K x x x, ♡ x x, ◇ x x, ♣ A x x x x. With as good a hand as ♠ A x x x, ♡ x x x, ◇ x, ♣ A J 10 x x, or ♠ K 10 x x x, ♡ x, ◇ A J x, ♣ Q J x x x, a raise should be given without being pushed. Requirements: high cards well placed and a singleton. Game with a combined holding of 20 points is probable! Notice how well placed West's values are, especially in the first example. There will be an excellent play for *five* spades opposite as little as ♠ K Q x x x, ♡ x, ◇ x x x, ♣ Q x x x. In deciding whether or not to accept the invitation, East does not count his points. The less he has, the more his partner has, as a usual thing. Again, he looks at how well placed his cards are, the strength or weakness of his trump suit, and distributional values. If the bidding is

SOUTH	WEST	NORTH	EAST
1 ◇	Pass	1 ♡	Pass
2 ♡	Pass	Pass	2 ♠
3 ♡	?		

West should bid four spades with ♠ A x x x, ♡ x x x, ◇ x, ♣ A J 10 x x, since a raise to three could not be interpreted as a game try. But whenever the decision is close, tend to be conservative, remembering that many pairs your direction may never even enter the bidding.

Another point: Don't be consistent at all costs. If the opponents stop at a part-score, then go to game over the reopening bid; don't double "just because you pushed them there." If they do not make their bid, you should have a good board anyway (remember they would have stopped at the two-level without your bidding). If they make game, it may be that other pairs will reach game by a less circuitous route and you will have an average board anyway. You always feel bad to give the opponents an average board when you could have got a top by passing, but you feel much worse when you get yourself a bottom.

So far, the reopening bid was always two spades. There are other ways to reopen the bidding. At rubber bridge

SOUTH	WEST	NORTH	EAST
1 ♡	Pass	2 ♡	Pass
Pass	Double		

is supposed to be a penalty double. It would be far more useful in duplicate to use this bid for take-out—that is, if you were forced to choose between two irreconcilable alternatives. It is not often that responder will raise opener's suit when you were trapping over one heart. Such a bid normally shows a hand like this: ♠ K x x x, ♡ x, ◇ K x x x, ♣ K J x x, or ♠ K J x, ♡ x x, ◇ A J x x, ♣ Q 10 x x. The first type of hand is a very safe one for reopening. Partner is almost certain to have at least a four-card suit fit and a fair hand. The second type hand is more dangerous. You hope to find partner with ♠ Q x x x x, ♡ x x, ◇ K x x, ♣ J x x, or ♠ Q x x, ♡ x x x, ◇ Q x, ♣ K J x x x. But sometimes you catch him with no good suit and most of his high-card strength in the opponents' suit. He must bid two spades with ♠ 9 x x x, ♡ K J x, ◇ x x x, ♣ A x x, and he may take a two-trick set or he may be doubled if trumps are split 4-2. So the latter is a dubious reopening double when vulnerable.

In the example so far, the reopener (or potential reopener) was in the last position. There had already been two passes. If he chose to pass, the auction would be closed. A similar situation arises after a sign-off bid.

SOUTH	WEST	NORTH	EAST
1 ♡	Pass	1 NT	Pass
2 ♡	?		

West can be pretty sure that responder has no more bids.[4] West can bid at this point, or he can pass and let his partner reopen. If West's hand is fairly balanced, he should pass and leave the decision to his partner. It is particularly important that a bid in this position show distribution or a concentration of high cards. You don't bid to show general high-card strength since partner knows about your high cards from the opponents' bidding. With ♠ K J 10 x x x, ♡ x x, ◇ x x x, ♣ x x, bid two spades. With ♠ x x, ♡ x x, ◇ K Q 10 9 x x, ♣ K x x, bid three diamonds. With ♠ Q 10 x x, ♡ x, ◇ K J x x, ♣ K x x x, double. Double with ♠ A x, ♡ Q 10 8 x x, ◇ A K x x, ♣ x x. Notice the last example! A double in this position may be either for take-out or penalties. A good partner can tell from looking at his own hand. With a singleton or void in hearts, he knows the double was for penalties. He must pass, relying upon your judgment. When he has three or more hearts, he knows the double was for take-out. With two hearts, he may have to guess. There will be clues. If East has a long spade suit and a poor hand, the double was probably for penalties (since West must be short in spades with a good hand). Whatever West does, he must be careful not to double just to show strength without regard for his bidding in the opponents' suit. The take-out double must be made with a maximum of two cards in the opponents' suit. To double with ♠ J x x x, ♡ K x x, ◇ A Q x, ♣ A J x, just asks for trouble. The opponents may have nine hearts between them, in which case East will surely pass for penalties with something like ♠ K Q x x x, ♡ x, ◇ x x x, ♣ x x x x. If West passes, East should bid two spades by himself!

Another case where one can bid directly over a sign-off is after a suit response to one no-trump (assuming that it is not forcing).

SOUTH	WEST	NORTH	EAST
1 NT	Pass	2 ◇	?

[4] Don't confuse this situation with

SOUTH	WEST	NORTH	EAST
1 ♡	Pass	1 ♠	Pass
2 ♡	Double		

Responder's strength is unlimited, and a double cannot be a reopening double. It must be for penalties.

You may bid two hearts with ♠ x x, ♡ K Q 10 x x, ◇ x x, ♣ Q J 10 x, because you have concentrated strength, and the bidding indicates that your side holds half the deck with partner's distributed strength over the no-trump bidder. Or you would double with ♠ K x x x, ♡ Q x x x, ◇ x, ♣ A x x x. *Warning:* A double of two clubs (Stayman) is either lead-directing or for penalties. It may be made with ♠ x x, ♡ x x, ◇ Q x x x, ♣ K J 10 x x.

It is possible to make a delayed take-out double to show a concentration of strength in the remaining suits. ♠ x, ♡ A Q x x, ◇ K J x, ♣ K x x x x. Over an opening one-diamond bid, you must either pass (best) or bid one heart since a take-out double is too dangerous with only a singleton spade and no rescue suit. So the bidding continues:

SOUTH	WEST	NORTH	EAST
1 ◇	Pass	1 ♠	Pass
2 ♣	?		

Now you may double to show a good hand in hearts and clubs. There is some danger involved, but this bid can turn out well in a number of ways. Perhaps responder was going to pass two spades, and partner would have been forced to pass because of poor distribution (and a reopening bid at the *three*-level is rather dangerous under any conditions). But now you compete successfully for a part-score or push the opponents too high. Or perhaps partner has ♠ x x, ♡ K x x x x x, ◇ x, ♣ Q 10 x x, and he takes a sacrifice of five hearts over four spades. But there is a third possibility. Partner has five spades to the Q 10 9 and about five or six points on the side, so he passes for a big penalty.

A reopening bid in no-trump under "impossible" conditions (where previous bidding shows you couldn't want to play a no-trump contract) is a sort of minor-suit take-out double

SOUTH	WEST	NORTH	EAST
1 ♠	Pass	2 ♠	Pass
Pass	2 NT		

♠ x x, ♡ x x, ◇ K J 10 x, ♣ A Q x x x: When made other than in reopening position, this bid shows a better or more distributional hand. Thus

EAST	SOUTH	WEST	NORTH
Pass	1 ♠	Pass	2 ♠
2 NT			

♠ A x, ♡ x, ◇ K Q x x x, ♣ Q 10 x x x: The same thing is
true at higher levels. With ♠ K Q x x, ♡ —, ◇ A J x x x,
♣ 10 x x x, after

EAST	SOUTH	WEST	NORTH
Pass	1 ♡	Pass	4 ♡
?			

you would double, but with ♠ x, ♡ x, ◇ K Q x x x, ♣ A
10 9 x x x, you would bid four no-trump. At the risk of overstating my hand slightly—I would make the same bids even if I
had not passed originally.

Perhaps after this explanation of reopening bidding, it will
make some sense when I recommend passing an opponent's one-
diamond bid with ♠ K J x, ♡ Q x x, ◇ x x, ♣ A Q J 9 x.
You need not be afraid of being shut out of the bidding with a
good partner. If the bidding continues

SOUTH	WEST	NORTH	EAST
1 ◇	Pass	1 ♡	Pass
2 ♡	Pass	Pass	?

partner will bid two spades with ♠ Q 10 x x x, ♡ K x,
◇ x x x x, ♣ K x. With less strength (take away a king) it
wouldn't matter much whether he reopened or not, since you
couldn't buy the bid anyway. Occasionally, you will miss a good
club contract, but more often by passing, you will avoid shutting
partner out of a good major contract. And when you do bid two
clubs, partner will not be tempted to bid a ratty five-card major.
This is the basic consideration. Tend not to overcall a minor
when you have good major support, especially when you have
support for both majors. Since you have a good defensive
hand, you pass. With the same distribution and a poorer hand
(♠ J x x, ♡ x x x, ◇ x x, ♣ A K J x x) there is more to be
gained by a club overcall, since it may shut the opponents out
of a major suit. With this hand, you are not so complacent about
passing, because the odds are that the opponents have the best

cards. The following example hands should make clear the considerations which influence your decision whether to take immediate or delayed action. In each case the opening bid was one heart by South, and you are West.

With ♠ K J 9 x, ♡ K Q x x, ◇ A x x, ♣ Q x, you should pass. If responder bids one no-trump and opener passes, you will reopen with a double, which would be primarily for penalties. If responder bids two clubs or two diamonds, the opponents are apt to get too high, but you will pass throughout the remainder of the auction, since partner must have a very weak hand. It is unlikely that responder will bid two hearts, but if he does (and opener passes), you may double or pass or bid two spades. My inclination would be to bid two spades and double if the opponents bid again. And if responder passes, partner will probably reopen. If partner bids one spade, raise to three. If he bids two of a minor, gamble on three no-trump.

You would also pass the one-heart bid with ♠ K x x, ♡ Q 10 x, ◇ A Q J 9 x, ♣ Q x. The worst development is a one-spade or one no-trump response and a two-heart re-bid by opener. You would have to pass and hope that partner will be able to take some action or that defending against two hearts is the best spot for you. If responder bids two hearts and opener passes, you would double. Partner will probably have two hearts and will play you for a good defensive hand, but not particularly good hearts. It is unlikely that responder would raise hearts if you had a genuine trap pass. With about five or six points and no good suit, he will pass, and you must hope to defend well.

With ♠ x, ♡ x x x, ◇ K Q J x x, ♣ Q J 9 x you should overcall the heart bid with two diamonds if you are not vulnerable. With so little defensive strength, you can't afford a wait-and-see policy.

When both opponents have bid, you should tend to stay out of the bidding with a balanced hand, but bid with a distributional hand. For example,

SOUTH	WEST	NORTH	EAST
1 ♠	Pass	2 ♠	?

With ♠ x x, ♡ K Q x x, ◇ A x x, ♣ K Q x x, it is best to pass. It is dangerous to force partner to bid at the three-level and risk a two-trick set when the opponents have no game. But with ♠ x, ♡ K Q x x, ◇ A x x x, ♣ K J x x, you may double, since this is a better hand offensively and worth the risk. You might be cold for four hearts, even though partner could not quite reopen over two spades if you and opener should pass. However, if the bidding were

SOUTH	WEST	NORTH	EAST
1 ♡	Pass	2 ♡	?

you would double with ♠ K Q x x, ♡ x x, ◇ A x x, ♣ K J x x, since, with the spade suit, again you have a little more to gain by aggressiveness. Partner would not reopen with ♠ J x x x, ♡ K x x, ◇ J 10 x, ♣ Q x x. Over an opening one-heart bid you double with ♠ K Q x x, ♡ x x, ◇ x, ♣ A K J 10 x x since if partner bids two diamonds, you can bid three clubs without too much risk. But when the bidding is

SOUTH	WEST	NORTH	EAST
1 ♡	Pass	2 ♡	?

a double is too risky, since you surely can't go to four clubs by yourself. But rather than bid three clubs and shut out the spades, you should bid two spades! If partner raises, you will go to game. If either opponent doubles, trust him and run out to three clubs. The two-spade bid may appear rather wild, but partner is extremely likely to have spade length, and a three-club bid could not possibly entice a spade bid out of partner. Nor are you strong enough to bid three clubs followed by three spades, even if the opponents give you another chance.

SOUTH	WEST	NORTH	EAST
1 ♡	Pass	2 ◇	?

You pass with ♠ A J x x, ♡ x x, ◇ K x x, ♣ A Q x x. Surely partner has little or nothing. The double risks a big set with little to gain. It also places the cards for the opponents if they continue to bid. If the bidding continues:

SOUTH	WEST	NORTH	EAST
1 ♡	Pass	2 ◇	Pass
2 ♡	Pass	Pass	?

Now, you can double. And partner may be able to pass for penalties. But with ♠ A J x x, ♡ x, ◇ x x x, ♣ A Q x x x, you should double at your first opportunity. With an offensive-type hand such as this, it is important to get into the bidding. If you pass, the opponents may bid and make four hearts against you when you are cold for four spades.

The problem of reopening the bidding does not plague the defenders alone. Here are a couple of hands where the opening bidder should not risk a bid between two bidding opponents, but when the opponents stop bidding, responder should protect. The hands are considered in this chapter rather than the last, since the balance-of-power concept has been discussed so as to give you a better background.

```
                        NORTH
                        ♠ J 10 x x x
                        ♡ 10 x x x
        WEST            ◇ Q x              EAST
        ♠ —             ♣ x x              ♠ Q x x
        ♡ A J 9 x x                        ♡ K Q x
        ◇ 10 x x        SOUTH              ◇ A x x x
        ♣ K Q x x x     ♠ A K x x x        ♣ 10 x x
                        ♡ x
                        ◇ K J 9 x
                        ♣ A J x
```

The actual bidding:

SOUTH	WEST	NORTH	EAST
1 ♠	2 ♡	Pass	2 NT
Pass	3 ♣	Pass	3 ♡
Pass	Pass	Pass	?

North should have bid three spades, and South probably would have bid four. A poor player would visualize neither the offensive nor defensive strength of the North hand and would feel that South was the under-bidder. Actually, any bid over two no-trump by South would be very dangerous, while a three-spade bid by North would be quite safe!

♠ x, ♡ K x x x, ◇ K x x x x, ♣ J x x:

SOUTH	WEST	NORTH	EAST
1 ♣	1 ♠	Pass	2 ♠
Pass	Pass	?	

A pass would be very cowardly. But what are the alternatives? A three-club, three-diamond or three-heart bid would put all your eggs in one basket. The problem is to find an adequate trump suit. Two no-trump is, in my opinion, the only correct bid. A good partner will realize from his own spade holding and your failure to bid one no-trump that the bid is completely impossible, even if this bid has never been discussed between you before. When I made this bid, it merely had the effect of pushing the opponents to three spades, down one. But if partner had a hand like this: ♠ x x x, ♡ A Q x x, ◇ A x, ♣ A Q 10 x, he should jump to four hearts over two no-trump!

When you have a choice of reopening bids, try to make the one which is most flexible.

SOUTH	WEST	NORTH	EAST
1 ♠	2 ◇	Pass	Pass
2 ♠	?		

♠ A, ♡ x x x, ◇ A J 10 8 x, ♣ A Q x x: Don't bid three clubs. Double! Any action involves some risk, but the double gives partner the most alternatives. With ♠ x x x, ♡ Q 9 x x x, ◇ K x, ♣ J x x, he can bid three hearts—which he would never do over a three-club bid. Partner can tell from his own spade holding that the double is based on a short spade holding, a pretty good hand, and fair support for the unbid suits. He will also know your heart support is not particularly good or you would have doubled the first round. But when the double really pays off is when partner has ♠ J 9 x x x, ♡ A x x, ◇ x x, ♣ x x x, or ♠ Q 9 x x, ♡ J x x x, ◇ K x, ♣ J 10 x and passes for penalties.

EAST	SOUTH	WEST	NORTH
Pass	1 ♠	Pass	2 ♠
?			

♠ x x, ♡ x, ◇ A J 9 x x, ♣ A 9 x x x: You should bid **two** no-trump for a choice in the minors. You can't risk a double since it would surely evoke a three-heart response. But suppose the opponents were bidding hearts instead of spades. Now you could double, and bid two no-trump if partner should bid two spades. However, partner may not bid two spades. With ♠ Q x x x x, ♡ K Q 10 x, ◇ K x, ♣ J 10, he will pass for penalties. Similarly,

EAST	SOUTH	WEST	NORTH
Pass	1 ♡	Pass	1 ♠
?			

With ♠ x x x, ♡ x, ◇ A Q x x, ♣ A 10 x x x, you should double to show the other two suits and good defensive strength (considering your original pass). But with ♠ x, ♡ x, ◇ A J 10 x x x, ♣ J 9 x x x, you should either bid two diamonds, or, if you want to make partner choose the minor and suggest a sacrifice at the same time, bid one no-trump. In a sequence where a no-trump bid or double would both serve the same purpose, double with defensive strength and bid no-trump with distribution. This is logical, since the double makes it *possible* for partner to pass for penalties.

The following is a rather unusual but logical suggestion. ♠ A x x, ♡ A x x x, ◇ x, ♣ A x x x x:

SOUTH	WEST	NORTH	EAST
1 ◇	Pass	Pass	Double
Pass	2 ♠	3 ◇	?

You should double! Partner did not overcall one spade, and he did not hit your best suit. Game is not at all certain. Furthermore, the bidding and partner's diamond holding will surely indicate that you are not loaded with diamonds. The double can only mean that you are doubtful about game and have very good defense, and partner will make his decision accordingly. You can't just pass, since your reopening double could have been made with a much poorer hand. Suppose partner has ♠ K 10 x x x, ♡ J x, ◇ K x x, ♣ K x x. If you pass, it is too close for him to double. But he certainly has the values to leave your double in!

Sacrifice Bidding

IN A TRUE competitive situation where both sides are pushing, and neither knows for sure whose hand it is, the same factors must be considered by the defenders as by the opening side, like strength in the right spots, etc. But suppose you know you cannot make a certain contract and the problem is whether to bid it anyway as a sacrifice. If the final decision is yours, you only sacrifice when you are pretty sure the opponents can make their bid, and when you are pretty sure you won't go down too many tricks, considering the relative vulnerability. It is a bad percentage bid to sacrifice when you are doubtful as to either factor. Again, this is a judgment situation, and there is no substitute for experience. But the important thing is not to be a lone-wolf sacrificer. Whenever you are contemplating a sacrifice, try to get the idea across to your partner early to see what he has to say about it. If partner overcalls one spade, don't pass till the opponents reach game and then bid four spades. Either bid four spades at once, so they can't be sure you are sacrificing, or raise to two or three, and let partner make the decision. There is nothing more infuriating than to have one's partner take a sacrifice all by himself when you sit with enough defense to beat the opponents a trick or two. Whenever you pre-empt, you show that you haven't much defense, and if the opponents bid further, partner should be the one to make the final decision. For the pre-empter to bid again is a flagrant abuse of partnership confidence. Sometimes you have a close decision just how much of a pre-empt to make. But once you have made your decision, stick to it at all costs. Under no circumstances should you bid again.

Let us consider two very bad bids. It happens that both pre-empts were opening bids, but the principle is the same as with pre-emptive overcalls. Not vulnerable against vulnerable opponents, South opened four diamonds in third position with ♠ x, ♡ x, ◇ K Q J x x x x, ♣ Q x x x. West bid four spades, North bid five diamonds, and East bid six spades. South then decided to take the sacrifice at seven diamonds, arguing afterwards that North should not raise unless he was willing to suggest a sacrifice against a slam. How ridiculous! The four hands were as follows:

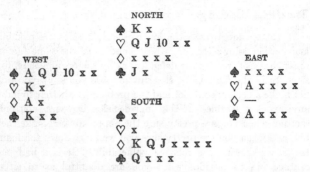

```
                        NORTH
                        ♠ K x
                        ♡ Q J 10 x x
        WEST            ◇ x x x x           EAST
    ♠ A Q J 10 x x      ♣ J x               ♠ x x x x
    ♡ K x                                   ♡ A x x x x
    ◇ A x               SOUTH               ◇ —
    ♣ K x x             ♠ x                 ♣ A x x
                        ♡ x
                        ◇ K Q J x x x x
                        ♣ Q x x
```

It looked to North as though he would have a chance of beating five spades (and with a slight change in distribution so as to give East-West a heart loser, he could). North was only sacrificing against four spades, not six spades. South's bid was very bad indeed. He took control of the bidding after he had already shown his hand. For all he knew, his partner might have two sure tricks. Suppose the bidding had gone

NORTH	EAST	SOUTH	WEST
Pass	Pass	4 ◇	4 ♠
5 ◇	5 ♠	Pass	6 ♠
Pass	Pass	?	

Now, a seven-diamond bid would not be quite so bad, since North's failure to double indicates that he isn't sure of beating the slam. (And with the actual North hand, he couldn't be sure.) However, South should still pass because he holds the queen of clubs. North must have some defensive strength or he would bid seven diamonds himself.

In the next example, South opened three diamonds, again not vulnerable, against vulnerable opponents. West overcalled three hearts (not Fishbein). North held ♠ 9 x, ♡ Q J 10 x, ◇ K x x x, ♣ K 9 x. There are some people of the ostrich school who refuse to face realities. They would pass, intending to sacrifice only if the opponents should get to game. But is there any real possibility that the bidding will die at three hearts? Not with a probable nine spades between them and one or both opponents short in diamonds, plus a substantial smattering of high cards. I would bet ten to one that if North passes, East will bid three spades and West will raise to four. But what if North bids four diamonds? Will East then bid four spades? Probably not. It depends upon how strong his suit is. For all he knows, you may be loaded in spades. The bidding actually went

SOUTH	WEST	NORTH	EAST
3 ◇	3 ♡	4 ◇	4 ♡
5 ◇	Double		

The four hands were as follows:

```
                    NORTH
                 ♠ 9 x
                 ♡ Q J 10 x
      WEST       ◇ K x x x        EAST
   ♠ Q x x       ♣ K 9 x       ♠ A K 10 x x x
   ♡ A K x x x x                ♡ x x
   ◇ x             SOUTH        ◇ x
   ♣ A x x       ♠ J x          ♣ J x x x
                 ♡ x
                 ◇ A Q 10 9 x x x
                 ♣ Q 10 x
```

South's five-diamond bid was very bad. North would have been quite willing to defend against four hearts, not that he could be sure of beating it, but he could be pretty sure of a good board because the opponents must be in the wrong spot. Another reason that South's bid was bad is that North might have this type of hand: ♠ A K x x, ♡ x x x, ◇ x x, ♣ A x x x, with which he would try to push the opponents to the four-level in order to have a cinch double. The point is that you must hope your pre-empt has done its dirty work in crowding the bidding and let well enough alone. When the partner of the pre-empter is about 60 per cent sure of defeating a contract it is nice to know that he does not have to double to keep his partner quiet. Or if he is 100 per cent sure of defeating the contract, but figures there is a better spot for the opponents, he can still pass rather than weigh the probability of the opponents running out if he doubles, against his partner's sacrificing if he passes.

Whenever you can predict with near certainty that you will have to go to a certain level eventually, it is wise to do so immediately. For example: Opponents vulnerable,

SOUTH	WEST	NORTH	EAST
1 ♣	1 ♡	2 ♡	Double
2 ♠	?		

♠ x, ♡ K J 8 x x x, ◇ Q x x x x, ♣ x: With this hand, I believe the best bid is five hearts. Then you are through bidding. No matter what happens after that, you pass. Whatever the opponents now bid will be a shot in the dark. Neither can tell what his partner would have bid without your five-heart bid. Is West's bid at this point a stretch? Or did he want to bid more? As for the argument that you shouldn't drive the opponents to a slam with so little defense, whatever they bid will have less likelihood of being right than if they had had a chance to get more information. And partner may be loaded distributionally if not in high cards. If not, he can take the save since your five-heart bid shows almost no defense.

There is an art in knowing when to sacrifice against slam bids and who should take the save. Whenever the opponents have made a slam try, you should stay out of the bidding altogether with two probable tricks on defense. When you do bid, you make it possible for partner to sacrifice if he has absolutely no defense. With slim defensive possibilities, he raises immediately to give you the option of taking the save. With one sure defensive trick or more, he should keep quiet. The assumption is that the vulnerability and playing strength are such that the sacrifice will be less costly than a slam if the slam is makable. After

SOUTH	WEST	NORTH	EAST
1 ♡	Pass	3 ◇	?

Bid three spades with equal or favorable vulnerability holding ♠ K J 9 x x x x, ♡ x x, ◇ x x x, ♣ x, but pass with ♠ K Q 10 x x x, ♡ Q x, ◇ K x, ♣ J x x. If the bidding continues

SOUTH	WEST	NORTH	EAST
1 ♡	Pass	3 ◇	3 ♠
Pass or 4 ◇	?		

partner should bid four spades with ♠ Q x x, ♡ x x x, ◇ x, ♣ K x x x x x, or six spades with ♠ Q x x x, ♡ x x x, ◇ x, ♣ J x x x x x, or pass with ♠ A x x, ♡ x x, ◇ Q x x, ♣ Q x x x x. The three-spade bid runs a risk of being doubled for a penalty greater than the value of game when the opponents have no slam, but it will be very difficult for them to know when to double. Human nature is such that neither opponent will want to double three spades and announce, in effect, that he believes at this stage there is no slam.

Penalty Doubles

EXAMPLES of reopening or take-out doubles have been given in which you hoped your partner could pass for penalties. But let us now consider some clear-cut penalty doubles. Obviously, you don't double the opponents every time you think you can beat them. Just as in rubber bridge, there should be a slight safety margin so that the double won't enable the opponents to make their contract by placing the cards for them. You should not double when the opponents are in the only contract they can't make. Nor should you double a forcing bid unless you are sure the opponents are on their way to another contract and you want to indicate a lead. Suppose you or your partner attempts a deliberate sacrifice of five diamonds against a four-spade bid. The opponents now bid five spades. You should not double, because the double can only lose. If the opponents have been pushed too high, you will get an excellent board without the double. If they make their bid, they get no more for bidding five than for bidding four. The only way you can get a bad board is to double and not set them.

A double of three no-trump calls for the lead of the doubler's suit if he has bid, or his partner's suit if he has bid, or in the event neither has bid, it calls for the lead of dummy's suit or one of his suits. However, these rules should not be followed blindly.

SOUTH	WEST	NORTH	EAST
1 ◇	Pass	1 ♡	1 ♠
2 ♠	Pass	3 ◇	Pass
3 ♠	Pass	3 NT	Pass
Pass	Double		

The double definitely calls for a *club* lead. The simplest way to ask for a spade lead would be to double three spades. If the double does not call for a spade lead, why does it ask for clubs rather than diamonds? Because declarer showed a jump preference for diamonds. Also, consider the negative implications of partner's failure to raise your suit at a low level. Thus

SOUTH	WEST	NORTH	EAST
1 ◇	1 ♠	3 ◇	Pass
3 NT	Pass	Pass	Double

calls for a spade lead. But

SOUTH	WEST	NORTH	EAST
1 ◇	1 ♠	2 ♣	Pass
2 NT	Pass	3 NT	Double

the doubler's strength should be largely in clubs. Partner must use his judgment.

The double of a slam, bid under competitive conditions, has no meaning other than to tell partner not to bid any more, either expecting to make something, or as a sacrifice. The double has its normal meaning. But a double of a voluntarily bid slam asks for an unusual lead. Some players follow a complicated set of rules which lead to an automatic answer. They can listen to the bidding and tell what suit to lead without looking at their hand. I consider this system too inflexible. It is better to call for an unusual lead, a lead partner probably would not have made without the double, then let partner use his common sense. If the bidding is

SOUTH	WEST	NORTH	EAST
1 ♣	Pass	1 ♠	Pass
3 ♠	Pass	6 ♠	Pass
Pass	Double		

the double probably calls for a club lead. But if you hold ♠ x x, ♡ J 9 x x x x x, ◇ Q 10 x, ♣ x, you should lead a heart, figuring partner for a void. Partner is unlikely to double with several clubs headed by the ace-king or ace-queen. If he has a short club suit with top tricks, he will probably get them anyway. Nor could partner have doubled with just the ace of clubs, since he would have no way of figuring you for a singleton. The hand:

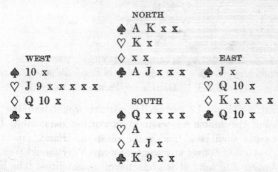

```
                        NORTH
                        ♠ A K x x
                        ♡ K Q x
        WEST            ♢ x x            EAST
        ♠ 10 x          ♣ A J 10 x      ♠ Q x
        ♡ J 9 x x x x                   ♡ —
        ♢ Q 10 x                        ♢ K x x x x
        ♣ x             SOUTH           ♣ Q 9 x x x x
                        ♠ J 9 x x x
                        ♡ A 10 x
                        ♢ A J x
                        ♣ K x
```

You may argue that it is not necessary for partner to double. You would have led a heart without the double, hoping he could ruff. But that is an unsound idea. If partner can ruff something, he asks for an unusual lead. If he does not double, you make a normal, aggressive lead—in this case, a diamond. Without the double, the hands might just as easily be as follows:

```
                        NORTH
                        ♠ A K x x
                        ♡ K x
        WEST            ♢ x x            EAST
        ♠ 10 x          ♣ A J x x x      ♠ J x
        ♡ J 9 x x x x                   ♡ Q 10 x
        ♢ Q 10 x                        ♢ K x x x x
        ♣ x             SOUTH           ♣ Q 10 x
                        ♠ Q x x x x
                        ♡ A
                        ♢ A J x
                        ♣ K 9 x x
```

Now a heart lead, or anything but a diamond, gives them the contract. You can't afford to waste the time on a heart lead unless you know it is going to work. You should only double slams that are bid voluntarily to increase your chance of setting them. That doesn't mean you have to have a sure thing. If you can get partner to lead a suit you can ruff, you don't worry about where the other trick will come from. The double of no-trump slams should be motivated by the same factors. If you have bid a suit, and the opponents get to six or seven no-trump, will partner try for a brilliancy? No, he will almost surely lead your suit rather than try a shot in the dark. If you *don't* want your suit led, you should double. In other words, the rules for slam doubles apply, not the rules for doubles of three no-trump. When you double three no-trump, you want to find a way to take five or more tricks. Your objective in doubling six or seven no-trump should be more modest. A double of seven no-trump (after you have overcalled) is the easiest. The opponents must have bid it with an ace missing. Partner should lead the unbid suit he is longest in.

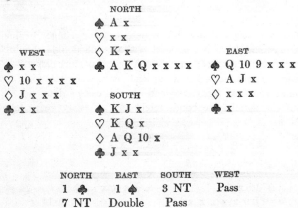

	NORTH	
	♠ A x	
	♡ x x	
WEST	◇ K x	EAST
♠ x x	♣ A K Q x x x x	♠ Q 10 9 x x x
♡ 10 x x x x		♡ A J x
◇ J x x x	SOUTH	◇ x x x
♣ x x	♠ K J x	♣ x
	♡ K Q x	
	◇ A Q 10 x	
	♣ J x x	

NORTH	EAST	SOUTH	WEST
1 ♣	1 ♠	3 NT	Pass
7 NT	Double	Pass	

East could not be certain his partner would lead the right suit, but the double was certainly a worth-while gamble. If the opponents should bid and make seven no-trump, missing an ace, you would not get any points anyway. Why should West lead his *longest* side suit? It is a matter of probabilities. The longer your suit, the fewer tricks the opponents can probably make in it. So if you lead your longest suit, it may not be fatal, even if partner's ace is elsewhere. They may only have eleven or twelve tricks. But if you lead your shortest suit (probably a long suit for the opponents), and partner does not have the ace of that, your chances are very slim.

```
                      NORTH
                    ♠ x
                    ♡ Q 9 x
      WEST          ◇ A Q J x x         EAST
  ♠ x x x x         ♣ Q J x x       ♠ A J 10 x x
  ♡ 10 x x x x                      ♡ K J x
  ◇ x x x x                         ◇ x
  ♣ —                SOUTH          ♣ 10 9 x x
                    ♠ K Q x
                    ♡ A x
                    ◇ K 10 x
                    ♣ A K x x
```

NORTH	EAST	SOUTH	WEST
1 ◇	1 ♠	3 ♣	3 ♠
4 ♣	Pass	4 NT	Pass
5 ◇	Pass	6 NT	Pass
Pass	Double		

The double tells West *not* to lead a spade, and a heart lead is
the most reasonable alternative. If East had a diamond trick, he
would probably get it even without a diamond lead.

Most people know they can double a Blackwood response to
call for a lead. They often forget the negative implications of
failing to double.

```
                      NORTH
                    ♠ K J 10 x
                    ♡ A K 10 x x x
      WEST          ◇ x                EAST
  ♠ x               ♣ Q x          ♠ x x
  ♡ Q                               ♡ J x x x
  ◇ K 10 x x                        ◇ A J x x x x x
  ♣ J 10 x x x x     SOUTH          ♣ —
                    ♠ A Q x x x x
                    ♡ x x
                    ◇ Q
                    ♣ A K x x
```

NORTH	EAST	SOUTH	WEST
1 ♡	Pass	1 ♠	Pass
3 ♠	Pass	4 NT	Pass
5 ◇	Double	6 ♠	

East should have been tickled to death to get a chance to *pass* over five diamonds. But he went out of his way to ask for the lead he did not want or should not have wanted.

Suppose the player who is eventually on lead has doubled a Blackwood response. If his partner doubles the final contract, the double probably calls for the lead of the suit that is doubled.

```
                        NORTH
                        ♠ Q x
                        ♡ A x x
      WEST              ◇ K Q J x x           EAST
  ♠ x x                 ♣ x x x           ♠ x x x
  ♡ K J x x x                             ♡ Q 10 x
  ◇ x x                 SOUTH             ◇ A x x x
  ♣ K 10 x x            ♠ A K J 10 x x     ♣ J x x
                        ♡ x x
                        ◇ 10 x
                        ♣ A Q x
```

SOUTH	WEST	NORTH	EAST
1 ♠	Pass	2 ◇	Pass
3 ♠	Pass	4 NT	Pass
5 ♡	Double	6 ♣	Double

West's double of five hearts must be based upon the king. East risks a double to get the heart lead. Without the double, West might lead something else. Note here, as elsewhere, that there is no "definite rule." If West held four or five diamonds, he would lead a diamond, figuring the double was based upon a void.

It is safer to indicate a void by a cue bid if you can afford it. East: ♠ K Q x x x x, ♡ x x, ◇ —, ♣ J 9 x x x.

SOUTH	WEST	NORTH	EAST
1 ♡	Pass	3 ♡	3 ♠
4 ◇	4 ♠	5 ♣	5 ◇

It is true that you could keep quiet till the opponents reached a slam, then double for a diamond lead. But you could not double anything short of seven with much assurance. It is safer to let partner know now about the diamond void so that he can bid accordingly. He may still bid six spades if he has no defense, since you deny a probable side winner (otherwise you would wait and double six hearts). Or even if you elect to defend, you have indicated a lead without risking a double. If the opponents believe your cue bid, they may stop short of slam, of course. That is why it does not pay to cue-bid with good defensive prospects.

Inferential Doubles

THE MOST lucrative doubles are obtained by the opening side when the defenders overcall at a low level. When the opponents voluntarily bid game without interference, they usually come close to making it. But sometimes their suits break badly and all their finesses are off. If you can predict these bad breaks, and if the opponents have reached game by weak bidding, you should double. For example:

SOUTH	WEST	NORTH	EAST
1 ♣	Pass	1 ♦	Pass
1 ♠	Pass	2 ♠	Pass
2 NT	Pass	3 ♠	Pass
4 ♠	Pass	Pass	?

With ♠ x, ♡ x x x, ◇ K J 9 x x, ♣ Q J 10 x, you should double. In fact, this is an ideal, clear-cut double. Neither opponent has strength to spare. South could not bid three no-trump over two spades, nor could North jump to four spades over two no-trump. The trumps are obviously distributed 4-4-4-1. A 4-1 trump break is usually a nuisance to declarer. In the second place, if declarer is naive, he may think *you* have the spades and plan his play accordingly. Besides all that, you have dummy's diamond suit and declarer's club suit all bottled up. If declarer has a finesse in hearts, it will lose, too. Probably four spades will be set badly with any defense, but another advantage in the double is that it strongly suggests a diamond lead (dummy's suit). Without the double, partner might lead the unbid suit, hearts, into declarer's tenace.

SOUTH	WEST	NORTH	EAST
1 ♠	Pass	2 ◇	Pass
2 ♡	Pass	2 ♠	Pass
3 ♠	Pass	4 ♠	Double

♠ x x, ♡ x, ◇ A Q 10 x, ♣ J x x x x x: This is not quite as good a double as the last hand, but you seldom get that good a double. Again, the opponents took three rounds to get to game, and there should not be any strength to spare. This time the opponents have no apparent trump weakness, but partner should have heart strength behind declarer while you have dummy's suit well taken care of. Besides, you want to direct the defense by asking for a diamond lead. A club lead might cost a trick.

SOUTH	WEST	NORTH	EAST
1 ♡	Pass	2 ◇	Pass
2 ♡	Pass	4 ♡	?

♠ x x x, ♡ x, ◇ A Q 10 x, ♣ J 10 9 x x. This time a double would be much too dangerous. The bidding was not weak, and each opponent may have strength to spare. A singleton trump is nothing to get excited about unless you know the opponents have a weak trump holding. From this bidding, they could easily have a combined trump holding of nine with no losers.

SOUTH	WEST	NORTH	EAST
1 ♠	Pass	2 ♡	Pass
2 ♠	Pass	4 ♠	?

♠ A x x, ♡ —, ◇ J 10 9 x x, ♣ x x x x x: This time the double is a calculated risk. A double of *strong* bidding *commands* an unusual lead just as a slam double does. The set is automatic if partner has one early entry.

SOUTH	WEST	NORTH	EAST
1 ◇	Pass	1 ♠	Pass
1 NT	Pass	2 NT	Pass
3 NT	Pass	Pass	?

♠ K J 9 8, ♡ x x, ◇ x x, ♣ A x x x x: You should double. This is an ideal double of three no-trump. Three no-trump was reached by weak bidding (it would be dangerous to double if responder had jumped to three no-trump) and you don't have too many high cards. Partner will win a trick or two, maybe more, and with a spade lead, you are confident of a set. The most foolish double is one where you have balanced distribution and lots of high cards. By showing where all the cards are, you make it easy for the opponent to squeeze or endplay you if he cannot just finesse. Presumably, the opponents have good distribution for their bidding. And partner cannot co-operate in the defense because he will have nothing. Your chances are decreased considerably by having all the honors in one hand.

SOUTH	WEST	NORTH	EAST
1 NT	Pass	3 NT	?

♠ x x, ♡ A Q J 10 x, ◇ A x x, ♣ x x x: With a good partner, you should double. He will realize your double is not on general strength (because a general strength double is a sucker double) but on a long suit which will run immediately, or with only one loser and an outside entry. Without the double, he would lead the queen of spades from ♠ Q J 10 x, ♡ x x, ◇ J x x, ♣ x x x x. But with the double, he knows your suit is probably hearts (his short suit), and he will lead a heart. Or, if he had ♠ J x x x, ♡ x x, ◇ Q x, ♣ x x x x x, he would lead a heart rather than a diamond, since it is unlikely that you would double with a suit missing the queen.

When the opponents are heading for trouble, you should keep quiet.

SOUTH	WEST	NORTH	EAST
1 ♣	1 ♠	2 ♡	?

♠ K x, ♡ Q 10 9 x x, ◇ A x, ♣ Q J x x: Opener must have a light opening bid; partner must have a skimpy overcall; responder is stretching. There aren't enough cards in the deck for anyone to have extra values. If you bid two no-trump, there will surely be three quick passes. If you pass, opener must re-bid, and you should have a very lucrative double.

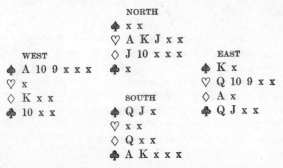

```
                       NORTH
                       ♠ x x
                       ♡ A K J x x
          WEST         ◇ J 10 x x x      EAST
  ♠ A 10 9 x x x       ♣ x               ♠ K x
  ♡ x                                    ♡ Q 10 9 x x
  ◇ K x x              SOUTH             ◇ A x
  ♣ 10 x x             ♠ Q J x           ♣ Q J x x
                       ♡ x x
                       ◇ Q x x
                       ♣ A K x x x
```

SOUTH	WEST	NORTH	EAST
1 ♣	1 ♠	2 ♡	Pass
2 NT	Pass	3 ◇	Pass
3 NT	Pass	Pass	Double
Pass	Pass	4 ◇	Double
Pass	Pass		

You could not double two hearts, since it would be an impossible double (impossible because it is illogical to double a forcing bid), but even if the double were interpreted as a business double, the final contract would be three diamonds doubled instead of four diamonds doubled. The pass of three diamonds was also correct for the same reason; there was bound to be more bidding.

SOUTH	WEST	NORTH	EAST
1 ♣	1 ♠	2 ♡	?

♠ K x x, ♡ K J 9 x, ◇ Q x x x x, ♣ x. This time you are not drooling so much over your prospects; but unless responder has a club fit, the opponents are heading for trouble again. Even with a club fit they may get too high, since hearts and clubs apparently are not distributed well for them. Again, if you bid two spades there may be three passes. Or opener may pass to show a minimum and three clubs will be the final contract. But so long as the bidding continues, each opponent may hope to find his partner with a queen to spare. The bidding will proceed on momentum alone.

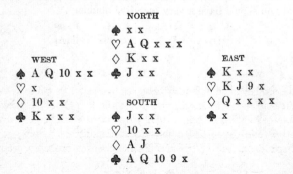

NORTH
♠ x x
♡ A Q x x x
◇ K x x
♣ J x x

WEST
♠ A Q 10 x x
♡ x
◇ 10 x x
♣ K x x x

EAST
♠ K x x
♡ K J 9 x
◇ Q x x x x
♣ x

SOUTH
♠ J x x
♡ 10 x x
◇ A J
♣ A Q 10 9 x

Wrong:

SOUTH	WEST	NORTH	EAST
1 ♣	1 ♠	2 ♡	2 ♠
Pass	Pass	Pass	

Right:

SOUTH	WEST	NORTH	EAST
1 ♣	1 ♠	2 ♡	Pass
3 ♡	Pass	4 ♡	Double

You would even double if responder elected to pass three hearts. You know that if he expected to make just three hearts with normal breaks, he will not even make three hearts this time.

In the following example, the opponents are vulnerable. Whether or not you are vulnerable is immaterial.

SOUTH	WEST	NORTH	EAST
1 ◊	Pass	1 NT	Pass
Pass	?		

♠ A Q x, ♡ K x, ◊ A 10 9 8 x, ♣ K Q x. You should pass again! If you double, partner will certainly pull with the weak hand he has. So it is better to pass and try for a 200 score. Partner's hand: ♠ 10 x x x, ♡ J x x x, ◊ —, ♣ J 9 x x x.

While there are a few occasions where you are too strong to double, it does not pay to go to extremes in passing because you are afraid partner will run from a double. Even if his faith in your judgment is limited, he will usually pass because he knows a run-out will be disastrous for sure.

WEST	NORTH	EAST	SOUTH
Pass	Pass	Pass	1 ♡
1 ♠	Pass	2 ♠	Pass
Pass	3 ◊	Double	Pass
?			

♠ A J 9 x x, ♡ 10 x x x, ◊ —, ♣ K x x x (both sides vulnerable). You should definitely pass. An overcall does not guarantee much defensive strength, and you have two probable tricks—more than partner has a right to expect. Your hand is much better than if you had a six-card spade suit or the king-queen of spades instead of the ace. Responder was probably groping in the dark and hit your partner's hand rather than his partner's. Your partner may easily have five diamonds. Besides, you would have passed the three-diamond bid if partner had passed. You simply don't have enough to bid again. Now that partner says that he can defeat three diamonds and asks you to pass and defend, why frustrate him? It is an odd system where you pass when partner has nothing to say, but whenever he says "Let's defend; I think we can beat them," you say, "No, now that you have doubled, I believe I'll bid."

Another case:

SOUTH	WEST	NORTH	EAST
1 ♡	Pass	1 ♠	Pass
1 NT	Pass	Pass	2 ♣
2 ♡	Double	Pass	?

♠ K x x, ♡ A x, ◇ x x, ♣ J 10 9 x x x: Pass! In the first place, you have a good defensive hand—much better than if all your strength were concentrated in clubs. However, the decisive consideration is that partner will not make a close double after a reopening bid. Partner must have been trapping on the first two rounds. A rescue simply means that you don't think partner knows what he is doing. Don't argue that you don't have the top clubs and that partner's lead may cost a trick. He may not lead clubs; a club lead may not cost a trick; and you have a good enough hand to set the contract, even with a bad lead. Furthermore, you have no reason to think you can make three clubs.

Chapter 6

Slam Bidding

WHEN SHOULD you bid a slam at duplicate? Culbertson says you should bid slam only when you have virtually a sure thing. Why risk a bottom when you can get a good board without bidding the slam? I cannot accept the premise upon which his advice is based. You cannot expect to get a good board or even an average board if you don't bid makable slams that are easy to reach. But, assuming that everyone else subscribes to the theory that slams should not be bid unless they are a sure thing, what should *you* do? Bid a slam whenever you will have better than an even play for it. You should welcome the opportunity to place a bet with favorable odds, unless you have a winning score and cannot afford to gamble. I am reminded of the advice Hal Simms gave his teammates. Under no conditions were they to risk bidding a grand slam. Simms thought his team was good enough to spot any team 500 or 750 points, or whatever the difference was in those days between a little slam and a grand slam. If you are good enough to beat any other team without bidding slams (unless you know they will be a lay-down), that settles the matter. But I don't know anyone that good.

What odds do you need? Three to two in your favor? Six to five? There is no point in trying to cut it that close because you can't tell what your prospects will be to any such degree of accuracy during the bidding. What you need is a workable rule. Whenever you will have an even chance *at best* for a slam, don't bid it. Whenever you will have an even chance *at worst* for a slam, bid it. For example, ♠ A K x x x x, ♡ A K J 10, ◇ A K, ♣ x:

OPENER   RESPONDER

2 ♠   4 ♠

?

Partner's four-spade bid shows good trump support, no aces, kings, singletons, or voids. Nevertheless, six spades will be a laydown if he has the queen of hearts or a doubleton heart. Even if he has three or four little hearts, you will still have a finesse for six spades, so you should bid it. Change your hand to ♠ A K x x x x, ♡ A Q 10 x, ◇ A K, ♣ x, and you should not even try for a slam. The most you can hope for is a finesse for six, and if partner has three small hearts, the odds will be very unsatisfactory. With A Q J x of hearts you may toss a mental coin. Theoretically, you should pass because you have less than an even chance. The opening lead might be ruffed, and there are a few distributions where even the heart finesse would not guarantee success. From a practical point of view, these remote possibilities are outweighed by the chance that a club will not be led, allowing the losing club to be discarded on dummy's queen of diamonds.

So much for the question of whether to bid a slam or not. *Which* slam to bid is a more complicated problem. Should you bid a super-safe six clubs or a more venturesome six no-trump or seven clubs? Several factors should be taken into consideration, but the most important is what you expect others to do. If the slam is hard to reach, or the field is weak, choose the safest slam. If you can get a 70 per cent board by bidding six clubs, you need better than 2 to 1 odds to justify a higher bid. Suppose that you and partner hold a combined total of 32 or 33 points in high cards, each with 4-4-3-2 distribution. With 32 points, if you bid a slam at all it should be in your 4-4 suit fit. With 33 points, you should still choose the suit contract because the play for six no-trump will be skimpy and not everyone will bid it even if it is makable. With 34 or 35 points, bid six no-trump. Most teams will bid six no-trump, and the odds favor their making it.

When you and your partner have such good hands that everyone will bid at least a little slam, you need the same odds for bidding seven that you normally need for bidding six. Bid a grand slam if it might be a lay-down and will require a finesse at worst.

As a general rule, when you have a good major-suit fit, don't bid six no-trump unless an ace is missing! Usually there is a much better play for an overtrick in the major. Remember that it is better to bid six spades and make seven than to bid six no-trump and make six. Another general rule is to play grand slams in the safest suit. So few teams will bid a grand slam that there is little to gain by trying for the theoretical maximum.

With no knowledge of slam conventions, anyone who has the ability to visualize the probability of slams will get along fairly well. Whatever conventions are at your disposal, visualization is the necessary first step. It should be easy for experienced players to determine whether their hands "add up" to a slam when both hands are balanced. As the hands become more distributional, both the visualization and mechanics of slam bidding become more complicated. With balanced hands, when either partner has bid no-trump, the problem is little more than addition. Thirty-four points almost always provide an excellent play for six no-trump, while 37 points virtually guarantee seven no-trump. With the honors well placed and all the aces, one point less is sufficient. For slam purposes, a five-card suit is worth a point, and a six-card suit is worth two or three points, but tens, except in your long suit, are generally disregarded.

OPENER	RESPONDER
1 NT	?

♠ A Q x, ♡ K J x x, ◇ A K 10 x, ♣ x x: You should simply bid six no-trump. It is true that seven may be a lay-down (♠ K x x, ♡ A Q, ◇ Q J x x x, ♣ A 10 x) or that there may be no play for six (♠ K J x, ♡ A Q 10, ◇ Q J x, ♣ Q J 10 x). But there is no means yet devised for taking care of these remote possibilities. You bid three no-trump on 26 points without any money-back guarantee. This six no-trump contract will have considerably better odds in your favor. Can you ask for more?

OPENER	RESPONDER
1 ♣	1 ♡
2 NT	?

♠ K x x, ♡ Q J 9 x, ◇ A K 10 x, ♣ x x: This time you may or may not be in the slam zone. You have a combined maximum of 32 or 33 points. Your strength is well placed (for example, your jack is in hearts, where it will be of value; not in spades, where it might be duplicated by partner's A Q x, and even the ten of diamonds could be an important card), so a combined total of 33 points should be ample. You raise to four no-trump, telling partner to pass if he has a minimum or to bid six no-trump with a maximum. If he hedges by bidding five no-trump, bid six, because you have a "good" 13 points.

Now, give yourself the jack of spades extra. This card might be completely worthless, or it might not. At least when you have it, partner cannot have it, and his values must be elsewhere. A six no-trump bid could not be severely criticized, but a five no-trump bid is best. If partner has stretched a bit, or had to count his ten spots to get nineteen points, he will pass. However, if your extra jack had been the jack of *clubs*, you would bid six no-trump.

This is a good place to discuss when four no-trump bids are Blackwood and when they are not. It is the practice of all the top players to consider an immediate raise of a voluntary no-trump bid as natural. It means, "*Pass* unless you have a maximum holding for your bidding." Examples:

OPENER	RESPONDER	OPENER	RESPONDER
1 ◇	2 NT	1 ♣	2 ◇
4 NT		3 NT	4 NT

Similarly, a direct raise to five no-trump, though less frequently used, asks partner to bid six (though not necessarily six no-trump) unless he has already overbid slightly. There is less agreement among the experts when the raise is delayed. For example:

OPENER	RESPONDER
1 NT	3 ♡
4 ♡	4 NT

There is an excellent reason for considering a four no-trump bid in this spot as natural, also, and most of the experts play it that way. The general rule is as follows: A four no-trump bid is natural whenever either partner has bid no-trump except as a minimum response to a forcing bid. Examples:

OPENER	RESPONDER
1 ♠	2 ◇
2 NT	4 NT

Though the two-diamond bid is forcing, two no-trump is not a minimum response, since it guarantees a king over a minimum opening. Therefore four no-trump is a natural bid.

OPENER	RESPONDER	OPENER	RESPONDER
2 ♠	3 ◇	1 ♡	2 ♠
3 ♠	3 NT	2 NT	3 ♡
4 NT		3 NT	4 NT

In both the latter sequences, the four no-trump bid is Blackwood.

When the partner of the no-trump bidder picks up a hand such as ♠ x, ♡ K Q x x x x, ◇ K Q 10 x x, ♣ x, and wants to find out about aces, he must use Gerber. Four clubs asks for aces and five clubs asks for kings. That leaves four no-trump as a possible final contract.

Gerber may also be used over a no-trump response or re-bid.

OPENER	RESPONDER
1 ♡	2 NT
?	

♠ x, ♡ A K Q x x x, ◇ K Q 10 x x, ♣ x.

OPENER	RESPONDER
1 ◇	1 ♡
2 NT	

♠ x, ♡ K J 10 x x x x x, ◇ K x, ♣ K x: Bid four clubs in both cases, since it is reasonable to assume that the only losers will be aces.

Thus far we have only had to add points to see if we were in the slam zone. The possession of long suits creates problems. The fifth card of a suit is not only good for one extra trick; it increases the probability that the fourth card will be good too. Suppose that dummy holds Q x x x and declarer holds A K x of the same suit. A majority of the time, the suit will not break 3-3, and the suit will only yield three tricks. Now, add another card to dummy's suit, and it will probably be good for five tricks, not four. So, valuing a five-card suit as one additional point may seem unduly conservative, since roughly three points are equivalent to one trick. On the other hand, wherever we have one less point, that means that the opponents have one more point.

When the partnership holds 33 points in high cards, the opponents can have only an ace and a king. When we have to count a five-card suit for a point to get 33, that means that the opponents have 8 points, or conceivably two aces. Counting a five-card suit as one point is a compromise figure. If partner has a good fit for your suit and good controls, the five-card suit will be worth much more than one point. If he holds K x opposite your Q x x x x, your five-card length is worth absolutely nothing for slam purposes (at no-trump) since he will not be able to establish the suit without losing two tricks. It is important that you show weak five- or six-card suits on borderline hands in order that partner can make an intelligent decision. ♠ A K Q x x, ♡ K x x, ◇ Q x, ♣ x x x, partner opens one no-trump. You can assume that spades break. Your fifth spade is worth a full point, and you raise immediately to four no-trump. A spade bid would merely confuse the issue. ♠ K x x x x, ♡ A x, ◇ K Q x, ♣ Q x x. This time it is important to bid three spades. Now, whether partner bids three no-trump or four spades, you bid four no-trump, a natural bid. With an excellent spade fit and good controls, partner might even bid a slam with 17 points. With a spade holding such as A x, he will pass automatically, whatever his general strength may be. ♠ Q J x x, ♡ A x, ◇ A K x, ♣ A K J x; ♠ A x x, ♡ K x x, ◇ Q 10 x x x, ♣ x x: With most good pairs, the bidding would be

OPENER	RESPONDER
2 NT	4 NT
Pass	

If responder bids three diamonds, followed by four no-trump, opener will bid six diamonds.

OPENER	RESPONDER
1 ◇	1 ♠
2 NT	?

♠ A 10 x x x x, ♡ A x, ◇ K x, ♣ x x x: You should bid three spades. If partner re-bids three no-trump, you should pass; but if he raises to four spades, you can then bid four no-trump or even five no-trump. The advantage in re-bidding three spades is that it shows partner what kind of hand he needs for a slam. Twenty points will not be enough if he has a worthless doubleton in spades (that is why you would pass a three no-trump re-bid), but the right 19 points (♠ K Q x, ♡ K x x, ◇ A Q J x, ♣ A x x) would be enough for a cold, but unreachable, *grand* slam.

When you have enough strength for six no-trump but not for a seven-bid, be careful not to bid a suit along the way. If you do bid a suit and partner encourages you by raising, bid six of your suit or just five no-trump. A sequence such as

OPENER	RESPONDER
1 NT	3 ♠
4 ♠	6 NT

invites partner to bid seven. When you want to invite a grand slam but have no long suit, bid two clubs (Stayman) followed by six no-trump unless partner re-bids two no-trump, showing a maximum. The main idea is to be consistent. Suppose partner opens one no-trump and you have 17 points. You simply bid six no-trump. With only 16 points, the play for six no-trump may be skimpy, so you should bid Stayman in an attempt to find a 4-4 suit fit. But if you fail to find it, don't turn optimistic and bid six no-trump unless partner re-bids two no-trump, showing a maximum. Just bid five no-trump to show that you bid Stayman because you were uncertain of six no-trump, not because you were interested in reaching seven.

A no-trump bid somewhere along the line is often an aid in reaching a sound suit slam. Particularly when you have a minor-suit fit, you may want to choose the minor suit as trumps only if you reach a slam; if you stop short of a slam, you prefer no-trump. For example:

OPENER	RESPONDER
1 ◇	1 ♠
2 NT	?

♠ A Q 10 x x, ♡ x, ◇ K x x x, ♣ x x x: Bid four diamonds. If opener has a good diamond suit and good controls (♠ K x, ♡ A 10 x, ◇ A Q x x x, ♣ A J x) he will bid six diamonds. With ♠ K x, ♡ K J 10, ◇ A Q J x, ♣ K Q 10 x, he will sign off at four no-trump and hope to make it.

♠ A 10 9 x, ♡ K J, ◇ 10 x x, ♣ K x x x:

OPENER	RESPONDER
1 ♣	1 ♠
3 NT	?

Bid four clubs. Now, even though partner signs off at four no-trump, raise to five no-trump. You are strong enough to bid six clubs yourself, except that you must allow some leeway for a weak or short club suit. Occasionally four no-trump may be used as a sign-off after a slam try, even though no-trump has not previously been bid.

OPENER	RESPONDER
1 ♠	2 ◇
4 ◇	?

♠ x, ♡ A Q x, ◇ J 10 x x x, ♣ Q J x x: Too little of your strength is in spades and diamonds for you to accept the slam try. But since this is duplicate, you should bid four no-trump rather than five diamonds. Opener should pass the four no-trump bid with ♠ A K J x x, ♡ x, ◇ K Q x x, ♣ A x x, although if he is very distributional (♠ A Q J x x, ♡ x x x, ◇ A K x x x, ♣ —), he will bid five diamonds anyway. Note, however, that a four no-trump bid in this sequence is considered Blackwood by most players. Don't try bidding no-trump at the four-level for the first time as a natural bid unless you have discussed it with your partner.

It is a bad habit to use two different bids for the same purpose. After an opening two no-trump bid, any response commits the partnership to game. Furthermore, there is no necessity for responder to pre-empt, no matter how weak his hand is. With six spades to the jack, he should simply bid three spades followed by four spades if opener re-bids three no-trump. A jump to four spades should be a mild slam try, telling opener to bid six if he has a maximum with his strength mostly in aces and kings. Note that a jump to four spades is not as strong as bidding three spades followed by four no-trump or five spades, etc.

There are other bidding sequences where an "unnecessary" jump should show extra values. North: ♠ A x, ♡ A Q 10 x x x x, ◇ K x x, ♣ x; South· ♠ K J x, ♡ K x x, ◇ A x x x, ♣ A x x:

NORTH	SOUTH
1 ♡	2 NT
4 ♡	6 ♡

If opener were not interested in bidding more than four hearts, he should re-bid three hearts, since responder cannot pass. Naturally, responder accepts the invitation with a maximum two no-trump response and excellent controls. Note that if responder had passed originally, opener should jump to game over the two no-trump response, even when he is not interested in a slam, since under these circumstances, the re-bid at the three-level would not be forcing.

OPENER	RESPONDER
1 ♠	2 ◇
2 NT	?

♠ K x x x, ♡ x x x x, ◇ A J 10 x, ♣ x: Bid just three spades, which is forcing. A jump to four spades should show something like ♠ K Q x x, ♡ x x, ◇ A J x x x x, ♣ x.

Attempts have been made with varying degrees of success to use point count in bidding slams with unbalanced hands. However, I find that another means of evaluation is much more practical. Controls and degree of fit have an important influence which we shall consider in great detail, but generally it requires 1½ more honor-count to make a slam than it does to make game. When you have one more honor-count than enough to bid game, you should consider a slam and suggest your slam interest. Then, if partner has one-half honor-count over a minimum, he will accept your invitation. Admittedly, this is a gross oversimplification of the problem. You may refuse to make a slam try with considerable extra strength when you lack controls. Or, with freak hands you may care less about amount of strength than location of strength. The invitation may be accepted with less than one-half honor-count additional if there are favorable features equivalent to the extra honor strength. Nevertheless, I think the extra honor-count rule is a pretty good starting point. Let's see how it works:

OPENER	RESPONDER
1 ♡	1

♠ A x, ♡ K J x x, ◇ A K x x x, ♣ x x: Without the ace of spades, you would still insist upon reaching four hearts. With the extra honor-count you must make a slam try of some sort. Of course, a slam try does not have to be made above the game level. The proper bid is three diamonds to be followed by four hearts, leaving the initiative with opener. Change the club holding to K x. With 1½ honor-count additional and excellent controls, it is responder's duty to see that a slam is reached. With ♠ A Q, ♡ K J x x, ◇ A K x x x, ♣ x x, responder has the extra 1½ honor-count, but is lacking a crucial control. He will bid in such a way as to demand a slam, even if opener has no extra strength, provided he has a club control.

OPENER	RESPONDER
1 ♠	3 ♠
?	

♠ A J 10 x x, ♡ K x, ◇ A x x, ♣ A x x: Partner has forced you to game on the basis of your opening bid. You would have a sound opening bid without one of the minor-suit aces. So you must make a mild slam try, not carrying the bidding past the game level, however. If a slam is reached, partner must take the initiative.

OPENER	RESPONDER
1 ◇	1 ♠
3 ♣	?

♠ Q J 10 x x x, ♡ Q J 10, ◇ K Q, ♣ Q x: Here we see a limitation to our general rule. There is lots of strength to spare, but some of it will be wasted. You are missing the ace-king of spades, ace-king of hearts, ace of diamonds, and ace-king of clubs. Partner's bidding normally shows 3½ to 4 honor-count. It is unlikely that he can take care of all those losers, or even all but one. Consequently, you should just bid four spades.

OPENER	RESPONDER
1 ◇	1 ♠
3 ♣	?

♠ K x x x x, ♡ x x x, ◇ K J, ♣ A x: The bidding is the same; your distribution is the same; your honor-count is the same; and your point-count is reduced. But now you have ample strength for a slam try, and even a direct slam bid would not be a bad gamble.

OPENER	RESPONDER
Pass	1 ♠
3 ♠	?

♠ A Q x x x, ♡ A Q x, ◇ A Q x, ♣ x x: You have almost 1½ honor-count more than enough to bid game, but you should just bid four spades. Why? Because partner's response is more limited than in most bidding sequences. He cannot have any extra strength. The most he can have is ♠ K J x x, ♡ K x x, ◇ K x, ♣ Q x x x, or ♠ K x x x x, ♡ x, ◇ J x x, ♣ A J x x. Add even a plus value somewhere, and he would either open the bidding or jump to four spades after passing.

SOUTH	WEST	NORTH	EAST
1 ◇	Double	Pass	1 ♠
Pass	4 ♠	Pass	?

♠ J x x x x, ♡ A x, ◇ x x x x, ♣ Q x. Bid six spades. Don't worry about diamond control. If partner can bid four spades, not knowing you have any honor strength or even a four-card spade suit (although he would be justified in gambling on your having a four-card spade suit), you must be cold for six. You do not have quite 1½ honor-count more than you have already shown, but your fifth spade is worth at least a plus value, and since partner must be distributional, you can promote your hand somewhat for having the right cards (no wasted strength in diamonds). With the king of hearts instead of the ace, bid five spades. It is better to use a five-spade bid as an invitation to a slam than as a demand for a slam if partner has diamond control. The odds are at least 10 to 1 against his having two diamond losers.

OPENER	RESPONDER
1 ♠	3 ♠
4 ♣	4 ♥
4 ♠	?

♠ K x x x, ♡ A x x x, ◊ x, ♣ K Q x x: You should have been uneasy when you bid three spades for fear partner would have to bid just four spades with something like ♠ A Q x x x, ♡ K x, ◊ x x x, ♣ A x x. Now that partner has shown a slam interest, however mild, you must not let the bidding die short of a slam. Since he has signed off at four, seven is scarcely biddable, and you should bid six directly. Where was your extra half honor-count? You would have a rather dubious three-spade bid without the queen of clubs or the king of spades. The equivalent of the extra honor strength is in your club fit[1] and excellent controls. Except for no-trump slams, we do not need 33 points in high cards. Usually we have two good suits for the preponderance of our tricks and controls in the other two. We like our hand when the strength is all in our two best suits or in side aces and kings, preferably aces. We dislike our hand when a lot of our strength is in queens and jacks of the wrong suits. Suppose that partner opens the bidding with one club and raises our one-heart response to three hearts. The following hands are listed in the order of preference:

♠ x x, ♡ A x x x x x, ◊ x x, ♣ K Q x
♠ K x, ♡ A x x x x x, ◊ x x, ♣ K x x
♠ A x, ♡ A x x x x x, ◊ x x, ♣ x x x
♠ K Q, ♡ A x x x x x, ◊ x x, ♣ x x x
♠ K Q, ♡ x x x x x x, ◊ K Q, ♣ x x x

The first hand is excellent. Even seven hearts may be cold. The fourth hand is not worth a slam try, while the fifth hand is not even strong enough for a slam try over a raise to four hearts.

OPENER	RESPONDER
1 ◊	1 ♠
4 ♠	?

[1] And I do mean club fit, even though partner may not have a long club suit. He should have at least A x x of clubs, as we shall see later.

♠ A J 9 x, ♡ x x x, ◇ x x, ♣ A x x x: According to the additional honor-count rule, you should make a slam try. This is the type of hand that it is easy to get pessimistic about. It is difficult to imagine how partner can dispose of all those losers. But counting losers is the wrong approach with this type of hand. Just imagine how much worse your hand might be—(♠ x x x x x, ♡ Q J x, ◇ x x, ♣ Q J x). Those two aces are very important cards, particularly when partner's hand is likely to be distributional. Remember, also, that a slam try is not a slam bid. You should show your ace of clubs by bidding five clubs, and leave the decision to partner. A typical raise to four spades would be ♠ K Q x x, ♡ x, ◇ A K Q x x x, ♣ K x. Partner would not take any stronger action *because he assumes that you will make another bid with as much as two aces.*

When partner shows a distributional hand, you do not need extra values as much as you need the right values.

OPENER	RESPONDER
1 ♡	2 ♡
4 ◇	?

♠ x x x x, ♡ A x x, ◇ K x x x, ♣ x x. Bid six diamonds. You have two key cards and four-card trump support for one of partner's suits. With as little strength as ♠ —, ♡ K Q x x x, ◇ A Q x x x, ♣ A x x, he will have a good play for *seven.*

SOUTH	WEST	NORTH	EAST
1 ◇	Pass	1 ♠	2 ♡
3 ♣	Pass	?	

♠ A x x x x, ♡ x, ◇ K x x x, ♣ K J x: This time you can almost visualize partner's hand. Five of each minor to the A-Q and a doubleton heart will result in a lay-down slam. For his free three-club bid, he should have a little more strength than that. Or, if he only has nine cards in the minors, he is pretty sure to have the king of spades or ace of hearts. This is a good hand, whatever the point-count may be, because there are no wasted or doubtful values.

OPENER	RESPONDER
1 ◇	1 ♠
3 ♣	3 NT
5 ♣	?

♠ J x x x x, ♡ A K 10, ◇ x x x, ♣ x x: Pass and hope that you are not too high already. The ace of hearts is a dubious value, and the king is worthless. Partner should have something like ♠ A K x x, ♡ —, ◇ A Q 10 x x, ♣ A Q x x, or ♠ A Q 10 x, ♡ x, ◇ A K J 10 x, ♣ A Q 10. With less strength in hearts and values elsewhere (♠ Q J x x, ♡ Q 10 x, ◇ K x x, ♣ J x x, or ♠ 10 x x x x, ♡ J 10 x x, ◇ K x, ♣ K x), you would gladly bid six.

OPENER	RESPONDER
1 ♠	2 ◇
2 ♣	3 ♣
3 NT	4 ♠
?	

♠ A Q J x x, ♡ J 10 x x, ◇ K x, ♣ K x: Again you should bid six, because partner has shown a good hand with a singleton heart, and you have no wasted strength other than the jack of hearts.

OPENER	RESPONDER
1 ♡	3 ◇
3 ♡	4 ♡
?	

♠ A x, ♡ K Q x x x x, ◇ K x, ♣ x x x: You should not give a second thought to passing. This is a tremendous hand. Just look at the bullish features! You have six hearts, not five. Your side strength is not in queens and jacks; it is an ace. Even your king is in partner's suit where it is of certain value rather than in clubs where it would only be of probable value. Your only problem is whether to bid six hearts immediately without giving information to the defense, or whether to show the ace of spades and try for seven. Nor is seven beyond the realm of possibility. If partner has ♠ x x, ♡ A x x, ◇ A Q x x x x, ♣ A x, there will be fourteen tricks off the top. And his hand is not even strong enough for a three-diamond response, according to most authorities!

A discussion of conventions has been delayed for two reasons. First, I did not want to confuse the issue we were considering—when to look for a slam, not how to go about bidding it. In the second place, a person can tie himself up in knots with conventions when he loses sight of the goal. When you have enough strength and enough controls for a slam, there is nothing wrong with just bidding it. In fact, it is desirable to bid it directly. Direct bidding makes the defense more difficult.

OPENER	RESPONDER
1 ♡	1 ♠
3 ♡	?

♠ A x x x x, ♡ K x x, ◇ A x x x, ♣ x. You have enough strength to bid six hearts, and you have an abundance of controls. The hand is too "thin" to consider a grand slam. A four no-trump bid can only help the opponents on defense.

The following hands show a tangible disadvantage in using Blackwood when it is not needed.

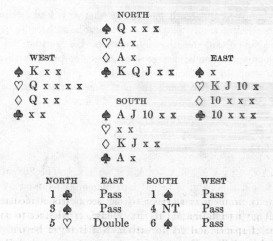

NORTH	EAST	SOUTH	WEST
1 ♣	Pass	1 ♠	Pass
3 ♠	Pass	4 NT	Pass
5 ♡	Double	6 ♠	Pass

The five-heart bid gives East a golden opportunity to make a lead-directing double. Had South bid six spades over three spades, West would probably have led a diamond, permitting South to make his contract with ease.

```
                    NORTH
                    ♠ K Q x x
                    ♡ K x x
      WEST          ◇ A              EAST
  ♠ x x             ♣ K Q x x x      ♠ x x
  ♡ Q 8 x x                          ♡ A J 10 x
  ◇ Q 9 x x         SOUTH            ◇ 10 x x x
  ♣ x x x           ♠ A J 10 x x     ♣ J 10 x
                    ♡ x x
                    ◇ K J x x
                    ♣ A x
```

NORTH	EAST	SOUTH	WEST
1 ♣	Pass	1 ♠	Pass
3 ♠	Pass	4 NT	Pass
5 ◇	Pass	6 ♠	

This time West apparently has no clue whether to lead a diamond or a heart. But a good player would lead a heart because he has gleaned important negative information. His partner did not double five diamonds! Either East does not care whether he gets a diamond or a heart lead, or else he prefers a heart lead. Remember these two hands the next time you are tempted to bid Blackwood "because it couldn't do any harm!"

```
        OPENER      RESPONDER
         1 ♡          1 ♠
         3 ♡           ?
```

♠ A Q 10 x x, ♡ K x, ◇ A x x, ♣ x x x: The "scientific" way to bid this hand is to bid four diamonds followed by five hearts. Now, if partner has at least second-round control of clubs, he is supposed to bid six. Whether this sequence is a *demand* that partner bid six with club control, or an *invitation* is quite a problem, but glossing over it and admitting for the sake of argument that the five-heart bid is a *demand*, I still do not like it. I greatly prefer an immediate six-heart bid. You have enough strength, and you have three key cards. There is not one chance in ten that the opponents can take the first two club tricks. Even if they are able to, they might not lead clubs without help from the bidding. The major disadvantage in bidding "scientifically" is that you are going to get to six anyway, in all probability, and you do not want to tell the opponents where your weak spot is. Give partner ♠ x x, ♡ A Q J x x x, ◊ K Q x, ♣ A x. An opening club lead would decrease his chances of bringing home the slam by about 25 per cent. Or if partner has second-round club control and the king of spades, a club lead would stop the overtrick.

OPENER	RESPONDER
1 ♡	1 ♠
4 ♣	?

♠ A Q x x x, ♡ J x, ◊ A x, ♣ 10 9 x x x: Bid six spades. There is almost nothing to be gained by a five-diamond bid. Why invite a club lead? But with a six-card spade suit, a grand slam may be biddable, and there is an excuse for a scientific approach.

Even when you do not help the opponents, attempts to be too scientific may create problems. Two strong players missed a slam with the following hands: ♠ A K Q x x x, ♡ Q J x x x, ◊ x, ♣ x; ♠ J x x, ♡ A K x x, ◊ A K x, ♣ x x x. The bidding was

OPENER	RESPONDER
1 ♠	2 ♡
4 ♡	5 ◊
5 ♡	Pass

I believe that opener was more at fault for missing the slam than responder, but let us look at the hand from responder's point of view. The hands must "add up" to six. Yet seven hearts is hardly biddable since opener needs a minimum of five key cards (ace-king-queen of spades, queen of hearts, and ace of clubs). So what is the purpose of the five-diamond bid? Will partner interpret this bid as a command to bid six if he has club control? Or will he look at his hand as a whole, paying particular attention to the diamond fit, and make a decision? Imagine opener's dilemma with ♠ A K Q 10 x, ♡ Q 10 x x x, ◊ x x, ♣ K Q, or ♠ A K 10 9 x, ♡ Q J x x, ◊ x x x, ♣ A. An immediate six-heart bid by responder will work out best 90 per cent of the time and it avoids any guesswork on opener's part.

For the record, I might state that I think most bids by the weaker of the two hands should be invitations rather than commands. When you have plenty of strength, you can bid a slam directly, gambling that partner will have the controls or that you will get a favorable lead. But when you do not have enough strength to bid a slam yourself, it is important to make a descriptive invitation, so that partner will know what he needs to bid six.

Ironically, the "hit or miss" method may solve problems that would be difficult with "scientific" bidding. You open the bidding with one spade and receive a two-diamond response. You look at ♠ A Q J x x x, ♡ —, ◇ K Q x x, ♣ A x x, and decide that there are all sorts of holdings that will give partner a good play for six diamonds, especially if he does not get a club lead. So you bid six diamonds. A good partner would bid seven with ♠ K x, ♡ x x, ◇ A J 10 x x, ♣ J 10 x x. He knows you might have been gambling on his having the ace of diamonds or the king of spades, but not both. You must have expected him to make six diamonds, even if he lost to one of these key cards. On the other hand, the immediate six-diamond bid shows a strong freak, and *no amount of side strength* will induce responder to bid a grand slam, although he may frequently return to six spades because of the match-point considerations.

Conventions

Now THAT you are impressed with the advantages of direct slam bidding (I hope), let us consider the necessary evil, conventions. The first one you think of—and probably the least necessary— is Blackwood. No other convention is so widely used, misused, and abused. I seriously recommend that you quit using Blackwood for three months in order to develop the natural skills that are so often pushed into the background. You will be surprised to discover how well you can get along. Keep track of all your slam hands, either bid or made, and see which ones would have been easier if you had used Blackwood. Also, note what other uses can be found for a four no-trump bid. Surely you wouldn't quit bidding four no-trump just because you were not using Blackwood!

Naturally, after three months you will go back to Blackwood, because Blackwood is useful with certain types of hands. But you won't use it so often. Furthermore, the fact that you only use it with some hands will enable partner to draw inferences from the fact that you use or fail to use it. The holder of a balanced hand should never use Blackwood because he cannot utilize the information about aces. Consequently, we have the inviolate rule that a player who has previously bid no-trump cannot ask for aces, although his partner, with an unbalanced hand, may use Blackwood or Gerber, depending upon the circumstances. The only problems arise when the partner of the no-trump bidder bids four no-trump. A good general rule is that a four no-trump bid by the weaker of the two partnership hands is a raise, while a four no-trump bid by the stronger of the two hands is Blackwood. A four no-trump bid by the opening two-bidder or the responder who makes a forcing take-out is Blackwood, because he is likely to have a strong distributional hand with which he can take control of the bidding.

OPENER	RESPONDER
1 ♠	3 ♦
3 NT	4 NT

This *is* Blackwood, although we could get the same result by following an earlier rule that four no-trump is not a raise when partner's previous no-trump bid was a minimum response to a forcing bid.

So much for whether four no-trump is Blackwood.

When should you use Blackwood? Jacoby says not to use Blackwood when you have a worthless doubleton, because if an ace is missing you won't know whether there are two quick losers or only one. A more inclusive rule is not to bid Blackwood unless you will know what to do over any response. If you are worried about the solidity of the trump-suit, distribution, degree of fit, or general strength, don't bid Blackwood. There must be a better bid. And don't try to make all the decisions. Be content to suggest a slam and let partner use his judgment whether to bid it or not. When you bid Blackwood, do not stop short of a slam unless two aces are missing. There is nothing more infuriating than for partner to take control of the bidding when he does not know what to do, especially when he jumps to four no-trump before either of you knows much about the other's distribution. After your Blackwood response, he signs off at five hearts or five spades, and you are pretty sure he could not even make a slam try if two aces were actually missing, because you have so many fillers. But you must pass. Some players get around this difficulty by signing off quickly when two aces are missing. When only one ace is missing, they think a while before signing off, so that partner will know he can bid again with extra values. Or they frequently think ten seconds before responding.

Even a kibitzer will know by the air of resignation or defiance whether responder has elected to show his aces despite having already overbid, or whether he has decided to cheat on his response. If you call the director, it turns out that you have an evil, suspicious mind. The opponents guessed right, but the hesitation had nothing to do with their final decision. Since there is little you can do about unethical tactics such as these, except through social pressure, the slow Blackwood bidders have become a sore spot among good players. If you want to retain their respect, pass when partner signs off, regardless of your hand, unless it contains a void.

You probably know most of the refinements to Blackwood. With four aces or no aces, respond five clubs, so that partner can ask for kings if he wishes. After cue bidding the opponents' suit, neither partner should show an ace or king in that suit.

SOUTH	WEST	NORTH	EAST
1 ♠	2 ◇	3 ◇	Pass
4 NT	Pass	?	

Bid only five diamonds with ♠ A x x x, ♡ J x x x, ◇ A, ♣ K Q J x or five hearts with ♠ A J x x, ♡ A x x x, ◇ —, ♣ Q x x x x, so that opener will know whether to bid six or seven with ♠ K Q x x x x, ♡ K Q x, ◇ x x x, ♣ A.

Similarly,

SOUTH	WEST	NORTH	EAST
1 ♡	1 ♠	3 ♡	Pass
?			

♠ —, ♡ K J 10 x x x x, ◇ A Q J x, ♣ K x, opener should

bid three spades to be followed by Blackwood. Then, if responder shows two aces and one king, opener will know they are the right aces and the right king, since the ace or king of spades would not be shown. Responder should show all his aces outside of spades, even though he cue bids four clubs over the three-spade bid. This is just an arbitrary rule. It would be just as logical not to show the ace of clubs again, but it is like deciding whether to drive on the left or the right side of the street. You need a rule, and it avoids confusion if you show all aces except aces in the *opponents'* suit after their suit has been cue bid.

When you bid four no-trump followed by five no-trump, you not only ask about kings; you announce that all the aces are accounted for. Partner may and should bid seven himself if possession of all the missing aces solidifies his hand. When you are considering a small slam, you should never bid four no-trump unless you can make an intelligent decision over partner's response, but you may bid four no-trump and a five no-trump just to show a grand slam interest, and without knowing what to do over partner's response to five no-trump. You hope partner can make the decision.

♠ K Q x x, ♡ x, ◇ A K Q x x x, ♣ K x; ♠ A x x x,
♡ A x x, ◇ x x x, ♣ A x x:

OPENER	RESPONDER
1 ◇	1 ♠
4 ♠	4 NT
5 ◇	5 NT
7 ♠	

Responder's three aces may be all opener needs to bid a grand slam. So responder shows his three aces indirectly. But if opener woodenly bids six spades in response to five no-trump, responder would have to pass. On rare occasions, you may bid five no-trump to find out about kings when an ace is missing, because you hope to reach six no-trump. But such hands are rare. When you bid five no-trump despite a missing ace, be sure that you have enough key cards (such as the king of trumps) so that partner will be unable to bid seven.

Cue bids have got themselves a bad name because of their

misuse. No expert has ever advocated a series of bidding where aces are shown automatically in a certain order, followed later by king-showing. But poor players have tried the mechanical approach, or even worse, have become so cue-bid conscious that any normal bid sounds to them like a cue bid, and even game-bidding is adversely affected. There are two basic rules for cue-bidding:

First, you don't cue-bid just because you have an ace; you only cue-bid because you have a reason, although the reason may be that partner has asked for a cue bid. Second, cue bids must not be allowed to interfere with game bidding, because game bids are much more frequent than slam bids. When you make an ambiguous bid which partner cannot recognize as a slam try, he must always be allowed to assume that you are trying to reach the best game contract until a later bid shows that you had a different objective. To call cue bids "ace-showing" is somewhat misleading, anyway. Even when attempting to reach game, you often bid a three-card suit where your strength is concentrated in an effort to get to or stay out of no-trump, depending upon where partner's strength is. When making a slam try, a cue bid serves many purposes. It elicits information about partner's controls, general strength, and location of strength, but at the same time you are telling him something about your hand. After you have got all the information you are strong enough to demand, he may volunteer more information if he thinks it will help you.

OPENER	RESPONDER
1 ♠	3 ♠
4 ♦	

In this case, four diamonds is obviously a slam try, since opener would not look for a five-diamond contract when responder has assured him that there will be a good play for four spades. The diamond bid may show a suit, or it may show the ace. But it should always show some diamonds, never a void or singleton, and seldom a doubleton. That is, the first cue bid by the stronger of the two hands should always show length. Thus partner can revalue his hand in terms of his fit. When cue bids merely show the lowest-ranking ace or void, they serve too limited a purpose. If all you want to do is show aces or find out about aces, you might as well adopt the wholesale method and use Blackwood. Over your four-diamond bid, responder should bid four hearts if he has the ace of hearts. This is the only automatic response in cue-bidding. When partner has made a slam try, you must show any ace which can be shown below the game level, assuming that your prior bidding was proper. Now, if opener re-bids four spades, he states, in effect, that his slam try was of the mild variety, and responder needs a maximum raise or a good fit to bid again. If opener refuses to bid four spades, but makes a further slam try, he has to have a stronger hand. His second cue bid merely shows a control, and responder should not worry about a fit for this suit.

There are a few arbitrary rules for cue-bidding. Opener would bid four clubs rather than four diamonds with ♠ A J 10 x x, ♡ K x, ◇ A x x, ♣ A x x, since, when other things are equal, he should bid his lowest-ranking suit. If opener were to bid diamonds first and clubs later, he would guarantee more diamonds than clubs. Over the four-club bid, if responder should have both red aces, he should bid four diamonds, the lower-ranking of the two; consequently a four-heart bid would deny possession of the ace of diamonds. The nice thing about cue-bidding is that while you are asking for information, you are giving information at the same time.

OPENER	RESPONDER
1 ♠	3 ♠
4 ◇	

The four-diamond bid demands a four-heart response if responder has the ace, but at the same time, it shows responder where a fit would be the most valuable. If he does not have the ace of hearts, he will sign off at four spades or take stronger action, depending to a large extent upon his diamond fit. Or, if he bids four hearts and you bid four spades, he will pass or bid again, depending upon his diamond fit as well as his general strength. Let's see how this works: ♠ A K x x x, ♡ A J x, ◇ A x, ♣ x x x.

OPENER	RESPONDER
1 ♠	3 ♠
?	

The proper bid is four hearts, not four diamonds. A heart fit will mean more to you than a diamond fit. If partner should have the king of hearts or diamonds, you would prefer the king of hearts. If he has the kings of both, you would rather he had a doubleton heart than a doubleton diamond. Suppose responder has ♠ Q x x x, ♡ K x, ◊ x x x, ♣ A K Q x, the bidding would proceed:

OPENER	RESPONDER
1 ♠	3 ♠
4 ♡	5 ♣
5 ◊	5 ♡
5 ♠	6 ♠

Note that four hearts was opener's only aggressive bid. The five-diamond bid was just a bid on the way to five spades which prevented responder from worrying about diamond control. It showed no extra strength. Exchange responder's heart and diamond holdings and he would simply bid four spades over four hearts. Without a heart fit, his hand would not be strong enough for aggressive action. Responder bid five hearts because opener had not limited his hand at that point, and the five-heart bid might have enabled opener to bid seven spades. However, it would have been pointless to show second-round club control by bidding six clubs after the sign-off bid of five spades. Once you can see that you have reached the end of your rope, quit cue-bidding.

♠ A K x x x, ♡ K x, ◊ K J x x x, ♣ x:

OPENER	RESPONDER
1 ♠	3 ♠
?	

You should bid four diamonds. Blackwood would turn out all right if partner showed three aces. But if he only showed two, what would you do then? You would hate to bid six spades and find partner with three small diamonds. With this hand, you can't afford *not* to show your long side suit. Suppose partner has ♠ Q x x x x, ♡ x x, ◊ A Q x, ♣ A x x. He will know that you have a diamond *suit*, since you are missing the ace. And he will know for certain that you are not cue-bidding a void! Knowing that your second suit is diamonds will enable him to value this hand very highly, and he would not think of signing off with a four-spade bid.

While you never make the first cue bid unless you want to suggest a slam, there are circumstances where your slam try, if any, must be a cue bid. Remember that the weaker of the two hands normally shows an ace rather than a second suit. For example:

SOUTH	WEST	NORTH	EAST
1 ♣	Double	Pass	1 ♠
Pass	4 ♠	Pass	?

If you bid five spades at this point, it means that you have enough general strength for a slam try but you have no ace outside of spades (you may or may not have the ace of spades). Or if the bidding were

OPENER	RESPONDER
1 ♠	2 ♢
3 ♠	5 ♣

it is unlikely that you would have either the ace of hearts or the ace of clubs. It is conceivable that you would fail to show one of these aces if it was your only ace, or if you stretched to make a slam try at all, but in that case you would be deliberately fooling your partner because you feared a loser elsewhere.

An immediate cue bid by responder should show no losers in the opponents' suit, excellent trump support for opener's suit, and at least two plus honor-count outside of the opponents' suit.

SOUTH	WEST	NORTH	EAST
1 ♡	2 ♢	3 ♢	

should show a hand of the following type: ♠ A K J x, ♡ Q x x x, ♢ A, ♣ J x x x, or ♠ K x x x, ♡ A x x x, ♢—, ♣ K J x x x. Responder's next bid should be a raise to four hearts. Now if opener has a good, sound opening bid outside of his diamond strength, he should be interested in a slam. Suppose that responder had a better hand; for example, add the queen of clubs to either hand. Now he should bid three diamonds followed by a five-heart bid at least, telling partner that he should bid six unless a substantial portion of his opening-bid strength was in diamonds. Suppose that opening bidder has ♠ Q x x, ♡ Q J x x x x, ◇ A K x, ♣ x.

SOUTH	WEST	NORTH	EAST
1 ♡	2 ◇	3 ◇	Pass

Opener should bid three no-trump! Despite the six-card suit and a singleton, it is imperative to bid three no-trump as a warning of considerable duplication. Responder cannot pass three no-trump with his void in diamonds and good heart support. But the three no-trump bid may slow him down a bit. He would have every right to bid six hearts over a three-heart re-bid with ♠ A x x x, ♡ A K x x, ◇ —, ♣ K 10 x x x.

The immediate cue bid as used here is quite rigid, and the opportunities for its use do not occur frequently. Many players are tempted to cheat a little in one way or another. For example, they sometimes cue-bid the opponent's suit with a small single-ton. This isn't too bad if responder has compensative values, except that if opener has the ace of the opponents' suit, he will not know whether it is a wasted card or not. Or if opener bids four no-trump responder will not know what to do; probably he should subtract an ace in responding to compensate for the loser in the opponents' suit which he has denied possession of. Much worse is the immediate cue bid without meaning—just as a forcing bid. There is no reason for this type of cue bid, since you can bid a new suit if all that you want to do is force. When you have A x or A x x of the opponent's suit and a strong hand, you should make your normal bid and cue bid the opponent's suit later, if at all. Only the immediate cue bid guarantees no losers in the suit. Even when your hand meets all the requirements for an immediate cue bid (good trump sup-port, no losers in the opponents' suit, sufficient honor-count), you should not make an immediate cue bid with a good side suit.

SOUTH	WEST	NORTH	EAST
1 ◇	1 ♡	?	

♠ A K Q x x, ♡ —, ◇ K x x x, ♣ Q x x x: You should bid either one spade or two spades and save the cue bid for later. Almost always your first efforts should be directed towards showing distribution and finding the proper trump suit; controls can be shown later. When partner opens a major suit for which you have good trump support, you don't need to find a better spot, and you can afford an immediate cue bid. When the opening bid is a minor, the first thing you should show is a good major suit. Failure to bid spades right away denies a spade *suit*. If you cue-bid hearts, all subsequent spade bids will be interpreted as cue bids.

As stated before, the first cue bid usually shows the ace, although it may occasionally show a side suit without the ace. Subsequent cue bids show aces or voids unless the suit has previously been bid, in which case they may show second-round control, usually the king. Nevertheless, it is proper to show first-round control under certain circumstances when you have only second-round control. The purpose of this unorthodox cue bid is to keep partner from worrying about two losers in the suit. The most frequent need for such a bid occurs when partner might worry about two losers in the opponents' suit if you merely bid five of your major. A similar need for reassurance is illustrated by the following hand: ♠ K Q x x x x x, ♡ x, ◇ A x x x, ♣ K; ♠ A x x x, ♡ J x x x, ◇ x, ♣ A Q x x. The actual bidding was

OPENER	RESPONDER
1 ♠	3 ♠
4 ◇	5 ♣
5 ♠	Pass

Opener knew that the ace of hearts was missing. Wouldn't responder be stymied with two or three losing hearts? Unless responder happened to have the king of hearts he would almost surely have to pass five spades. Opener should have bid five hearts over the five-club bid. Now responder would not worry about controls but would turn his attention to things that mattered. 7-4-1-1 hands are difficult to bid scientifically; in the example hand so much depended upon responder's diamond holding. But, in my opinion, the five-spade bid gave the partnership no chance to reach the slam unless it was unmakable. If responder has the king of hearts, he probably won't have enough cards elsewhere.

The raise to five of a major has several distinct meanings, depending upon the circumstances. When made by the weaker of two hands after strong bidding, it usually means that the hand is strong enough for a slam try but there is no more descriptive bid (no cue bid) available. Occasionally it means just the opposite! There are so many features to show that you can't show them all.

OPENER	RESPONDER
1 ♠	2 ♡
4 ♡	?

♠ Q x, ♡ 10 x x x x, ◇ A J x, ♣ A x x: If you were to bid five clubs, partner might worry about a diamond control; if you were to bid five diamonds, he might worry about club control. You can't show both aces without getting to six automatically. So you bid five hearts. Partner will be able to tell from his hand that you couldn't possibly be making a slam try without an ace. He will know that you have two aces, since if you had one ace you would show it. It is much more frequent for the stronger of the two hands to bid five of a major because he can't show all his features and he doesn't want to emphasize the importance of any particular control or concentration of strength.

OPENER	RESPONDER
Pass	1 ♠
3 ♠	5 ♠
?	

♠ K Q x x, ♡ x, ◇ K J x x x, ♣ x x x: Common sense tells you that opener could not be missing three aces. In fact, it is likely that he has all the aces, or all except the ace of spades. He doesn't have time to show them all. Or perhaps he has the ace of spades, two other aces, and a king, and he is afraid that if he shows you his two side aces, you would worry about control in the fourth suit. Whatever he has, he should expect you to bid six with this type of hand, because his five-spade bid shows that he is not worried about controls. Similarly, if the bidding were

RESPONDER	OPENER
Pass	1 ♠
3 ♠	4 ♡
4 ♠	5 ♠

opener probably has at least a first- and a second-round control in the minors. Of course, he is interested in your general strength and whether you have top cards or fillers, but the purpose of the four-heart bid is to call particular attention to your heart holding. When you bid five of a major after a series of strong bids, it is generally a request for partner to bid six, provided he has at least second-round control in the only unbid suit or the opponents' suit. Opener: ♠ K x, ♡ K Q x x, ◇ J x, ♣ A K J 10 x; responder: ♠ x x, ♡ A 10 x x x x, ◇ A Q x, ♣ Q x. Recommended bidding:

OPENER	RESPONDER
1 ♣	1 ♡
3 ♡	4 ◇
4 ♡	5 ♡
5 NT	6 NT

The five-heart bid was a command for opener to bid six if he had the ace of spades (which he wasn't strong enough to show over four diamonds) or a singleton spade. Even with the king, opener should not pass because the king would be a stopper half the time, even opposite small cards, and there is the chance that responder would have the queen of spades, making the king a sure stopper. However, since opener had a somewhat balanced hand, he chose to bid five no-trump to show that his spade control was the king. The meaning of five no-trump was obvious: opener wanted to play the hand so that his king of spades could not be led through. Responder, with the queen of clubs, had no hesitancy about raising to six no-trump. When the opponents have bid, an immediate bid of five of your major suit is a command that partner bid six with a first- or second-round control of the opponents' suit or pass without it.

SOUTH	WEST	NORTH	EAST
1 ♠	4 ♣	4 ♠	Pass
5 ♠	Pass	Pass	Pass

♠ A Q x x x x, ♡ A K J x x, ◇ —, ♣ x x; ♠ K J x x, ♡ x x, ◇ A Q 10 x x, ♣ x x: Opener asked a single question: Can you control clubs? If opener were not worried about clubs but merely concerned with responder's general strength, he should cue bid clubs so that responder could direct his attention elsewhere. Opener would bid five clubs in this same sequence with ♠ A Q x x x x, ♡ A J x, ◇ K J x, ♣ x. Now responder would probably bid the slam with ♠ K J x x, ♡ x x, ◇ A Q 10 x x, ♣ x x, but would sign-off with less top strength or poorer distribution.

We shall say more later about asking for second-round control. The examples shown were rather clear-cut, but in some sequences there is a disagreement whether a bid is a command that partner bid six with second-round control or an invitation to bid six provided he has second-round control and other values. In a very few cases there might be a disagreement whether you were showing second-round control or asking for it!

Cue bidding is such a complex subject that no amount of abstract discussion will make it clear. Following are examples of various common bidding sequences with advice on when to cue bid and when not to, when to accept an invitation and when to refuse it.

OPENER	RESPONDER
1 ◇	1 ♠
4 ♠	?

Remember that we said responder should make a slam try with as poor a hand as ♠ A J x x, ♡ A x x, ◇ x x, ♣ x x x x. He should bid five hearts. Suppose opener has ♠ K Q x x, ♡ K x, ◇ A K J x, ♣ A 10 x. Opener should simply bid five spades. With such poor distribution, he has a minimum raise to four. If all responder needs is a hand of this type for a slam, he should bid the slam himself. What does opener need to accept the invitation? Something like ♠ K Q x x, ♡ x x, ◇ A K Q J x, ♣ A x, or perhaps even better distribution; in other words, he needs playing tricks.

Let's look at another type of minimum slam try for responder after the triple raise. With A Q J x x of spades and nothing of importance on the side, he should bid five spades. Or with A Q x x of spades and the queen of diamonds. Yet ♠ A Q x x, ♡ Q x, ◇ x x, ♣ Q x x x x is not quite good enough, because two side queens are of less value than one queen in the right spot. Suppose that the bidding is

OPENER	RESPONDER
1 ◇	1 ♠
4 ♠	5 ♠
?	

and opener has ♠ K x x x, ♡ A Q 10, ◇ A x x x x, ♣ A. He should pass. In the first place, this was a minimum raise to four. In the second place, responder probably does not have the king of diamonds, or his slam try would be five diamonds. With the possibility of losing two diamond tricks or a diamond and a heart, or a diamond and a trump, or not being able to make the hand total twelve tricks, this is a good hand to pass. Give responder something like ♠ A Q x x, ♡ J x, ◇ Q x, ♣ x x x x x, and even the play for five will be skimpy. The point to be emphasized in this regard is that the five-spade or five-heart bid is not a command that opener bid six unless there will be two losing tricks off the top. It is an invitation for him to bid six with extra values in the form of playing strength.

In the following examples the bidding is the same, namely,

OPENER	RESPONDER
1 ◇	1 ♠
3 ♠	4 ◇
?	

(a) ♠ A J x x, ♡ K Q x, ◇ K Q J x x, ♣ x: Bid just four spades. In order for partner to have a lay-down slam, he must have, in addition to his ace of diamonds, at least the ace of hearts and the king-queen of spades or six spades to the king. With that much strength he will bid again over the four-spade sign-off.

(b) ♠ A J x x, ♡ A x x, ◇ K Q J x x, ♣ x: Not only do you bid four hearts, but even if partner signs off at four spades, you will carry the bidding to six.

(c) ♠ A J x x, ♡ A x, ◇ K Q x x, ♣ K x x: You bid four hearts on the way to four spades. If partner bids four spades, you will pass. If all that partner needs from you is second-round club control, he must jump to five spades over your four-heart bid. Incidentally, the proper opening bid was one no-trump.

(d) ♠ A J x x, ♡ A Q, ◇ K Q x x, ♣ K x x: Now you have an obligation to bid again even though partner signs off at four spades over your four-heart bid. Your proper bid would be four no-trump to show extra strength and the king of clubs. No-trump "cue bids" logically show the king and indicate a desire to play the hand so that the king will not be led through. Suppose responder's hand were ♠ K Q x x x x, ♡ x x x, ◇ A x, ♣ x x. He should probably pass the four no-trump bid because he has a minimum slam try and he is not interested unless you can go all the way.

(e) ♠ A x x x, ♡ A x, ◇ K Q J x x, ♣ K x: This is the type of hand that becomes very strong indeed upon hearing of the diamond fit. The extra diamond is of more value than the queen of hearts. Remember that the ideal slam hand is one where the strength is concentrated in two suits with just enough strength in the other suits to keep the opponents from cashing two tricks. Your hand would be even better with a singleton club, but I believe that this hand is worth a five no-trump bid, after your four-heart bid and partner's four-spade sign-off, rather than just four no-trump. However, it is a close decision, and no bid other than a pass to four spades could be severely criticized.

OPENER	RESPONDER
1 ◇	1 ♠
2 ♣	?

♠ Q 10 9 x x x, ♡ A x x, ◇ K J, ♣ A x: A leap to six spades would not be too bad, except that there is a better bid at your disposal. Bid three hearts. If partner can now bid four spades, bid six, of course. Even if he bids something else such as three spades or three no-trump, you will cue bid clubs and diamonds to show excellent controls and direct partner's attention to spades. Since you probably have the stronger of the partnership hands, and since you can start your cue bidding at a low level, you show your tripleton ace before your doubleton ace. In this case, it does not make too much difference, but partner will take his heart fit into consideration in deciding whether to bid three or four spades. Of course he will not know that you are interested in a slam when you bid three hearts. As we said before, cue bidding must not be allowed to interfere with game bidding, so partner will assume that you are showing a second suit with your three-heart bid and just making a game try. In fact, he may raise hearts with J x x x of hearts; he doesn't need the king to raise. While he will not know what your three-heart bid means at the time, he will know what you were doing when you cue bid on the next round.

OPENER	RESPONDER
1 ◇	1 ♠
2 ♠	?

♠ K 10 x x x, ♡ A x x x, ◇ K x, ♣ A x: Again, you should bid three hearts because of your excellent controls, but this is a minimum hand for a slam try. Unless partner jumps to four spades, you will settle for game. Even if he jumps to four spades, you will not be able to bid six; you can merely make one more try by bidding five clubs. Partner's jump to four spades shows a maximum raise, but he did not know that you were slam-minded, and he would not be paying too much attention to top strength and controls. He could have either ♠ A Q J x, ♡ Q 10 x, ◇ A J 10 x, ♣ J x, or ♠ A Q x x, ♡ K x, ◇ A Q x x, ♣ x x x, and you only want to be in slam with the latter type of hand.

OPENER	RESPONDER
1 ♡	1 ♠
3 ♡	?

(a) ♠ A Q 10 x x, ♡ K x, ◇ A x x, ♣ x x x: Remember the advice on this hand was to bid six hearts directly rather than call attention to your club weakness by "scientific bidding."

(b) ♠ A K Q x x, ♡ K x x, ◇ x x x, ♣ x x: This time the proper bid is to re-bid spades followed by a raise to five hearts. This clearly shows that you are strong in the majors, weak in the minors.

(c) ♠ A K J x x, ♡ x x x, ◇ A x, ♣ x x x: Bid four diamonds followed by five hearts. In these last two hands, you only had two key cards (ace of spades and king of hearts or ace of diamonds), and a direct slam bid would be too risky despite your general strength. But the fact that partner knows you would bid the slam directly with certain types of hands makes his decisions much easier.

♠ x, ♡ A J 10 x x x, ◇ K Q, ♣ K Q J x:

OPENER	RESPONDER
1 ♡	1 ♠
3 ♡	4 ◇
4 ♡	5 ♡
?	

Opener should pass. He knows that there is a club loser. Responder cannot have as much as the ace of spades, the king-queen of hearts, and the ace of diamonds, or he would bid the slam directly—whatever his club holding might be. Therefore, opener knows that the slam would depend upon a finesse at best, and there might be no play for it. Responder's hand: ♠ A K J x x, ♡ x x x, ◇ A J x, ♣ x x. The last three responder's hands all had enough general strength for a strong slam try. The major worry was lack of controls, although there was the ever-present danger of a misfit or duplication. The problem becomes more difficult as you reduce the general strength.

OPENER	RESPONDER
1 ♡	1 ♠
3 ♡	?

(a) ♠ A 10 9 x x, ♡ K x, ◇ A x x, ♣ x x x; (b) ♠ A K x x x, ♡ K x x, ◇ x x x, ♣ x x; (c) ♠ A K x x x, ♡ x x x, ◇ A x, ♣ x x x: These three hands are all slightly weaker in one way or another than the last example hands. In all these cases, there is much to be said in favor of just bidding four hearts. You miss a few good slams that way, but you stay out of serious trouble, and on the hands you play short of slam, you don't warn the opening leader to cash his tricks if he can. On the other hand, you hate to seal your partner's lips with a four-heart bid when he might really have a good hand. A possible solution is to raise to five with all skimpy slam tries without bothering to show where your strength is. Partner needs a maximum with good controls to bid six, and he must guess just where your strength lies. However, the opening leader must also guess where your strength is, which is a compensating advantage.

OPENER	RESPONDER
1 ♡	1 ♠
3 ♡	?

♠ A K J x x, ♡ x, ◇ K Q x x, ♣ Q x x: Bid three spades. If partner raises spades or bids four diamonds, you will make a slam try or slam bid. If he simply re-bids four hearts, it is better to pass rather than to gamble on the solidity of the heart suit. Much of your strength is of doubtful value.

OPENER	RESPONDER
1 ♡	1 ♠
3 ♡	?

♠ A K Q x x, ♡ x, ◇ A Q x, ♣ x x x x: Again you should bid three spades, but if partner bids four hearts, you must make another try by bidding five diamonds. If partner has a solid heart suit, he may be able to jump to six hearts.

SOUTH	WEST	NORTH	EAST
1 ♠	2 ♣	2 ♠	Pass
?			

♠ A Q x x x x, ♡ A K x, ◇ A, ♣ x x x: A five-spade bid would tell partner to bid six if he had first- or second-round control in clubs. But you are not strong enough for such a demand. Neither a singleton club nor the king will guarantee a good play for six spades. Besides, there is a slim possibility that the opponents could take the first three club tricks. You should bid three hearts, intending to bid five spades *only if partner can jump to four spades*.

SOUTH	WEST	NORTH	EAST
1 ♠	2 ♣	2 ♠	Pass
3 ♡	Pass	4 ♠	Pass
5 ◇			

would show a singleton or void in clubs and would simply ask responder about general strength outside of clubs while calling special attention to his heart fit.

Bidding two suits and raising a third suggests a short holding in the fourth suit. This is a natural inference. We can change this inference into a convention by making rules when this series of bidding guarantees a singleton or void. Goren's rule is that bidding two suits and raising a third with a jump bid along the line guarantees a singleton or void in the fourth suit. With ♠ A K x x, ♡ x x, ◇ A K Q x x, ♣ K x, you open one diamond and raise partner's one-spade response to four spades. With one less heart and one more club, you should jump to three clubs before raising to four spades in order to show a singleton heart. This series of bidding permits partner to bid five clubs with ♠ Q x x x x, ♡ x x x, ◇ x x, ♣ A J x, while he would pass an immediate four-spade bid. This convention is a fine idea, but care must be exercised not to use it unintentionally. I can still remember this hand from the long ago:

Opener: ♠ K x, ♡ A K Q x x, ◇ x, ♣ A K 10 9 x;
Responder: ♠ A 10 9 x x, ♡ x x, ◇ A x x, ♣ x x x:

OPENER	RESPONDER
1 ♡	1 ♠
3 ♣	3 ♠
4 ♠	6 ♠

A diamond was led, and there was no play for six spades; yet if opener had one more spade and one less club, the slam contract would have been a very fine one. (However, responder's proper bid was five diamonds). Opener had his singleton diamond all right, but this series of bidding has a slam connotation and suggests better spade support. Opener should re-bid four clubs over three spades; responder would make the waiting bid of four diamonds, and opener could *then* bid four spades, having already warned responder that his jump was based upon a powerful two-suiter. Suppose opener's hand was ♠ K x, ♡ A K Q x x, ◇ x x, ♣ A K Q x. There is no alternative to a three-club re-bid. Over three spades, he has a terrible problem. He would like to raise to four spades, but that would show a singleton diamond and better spade support. This is one of those hands for which there is no logical bid, but my preference is a four-club re-bid. With as much as Q x of diamonds and with less strength in clubs or hearts, opener should anticipate his difficulties by bidding two no-trump on the second round.

OPENER	RESPONDER
1 ◇	1 ♠
3 ♣	3 ♠ or 3 NT
5 ♠	

also guarantees a singleton or void in hearts, but shows an even stronger hand than would a jump followed by four spades. Responder only needs five or six points outside of hearts to bid six. Remember this hand from early in the chapter? ♠ A Q, ♡ K J x x, ◇ A K x x x, ♣ x x. We said that when partner opened one heart, you should bid in such a way as to demand a slam if he had first- or second-round control in clubs. The way you should plan the bidding is to jump in diamonds, bid spades, and support hearts at the five-level. But according to the rule just given, wouldn't that show a singleton club? Experts disagree on this point. I say no. If responder has controls in all the suits and enough strength to make an invitation beyond the game level *after jumping on the first round*, he should simply gamble on six himself. Whenever he jumps on the first round, the subsequent raise to five asks for control of the unbid suit. If he wants to show a singleton, *he must not jump on the first round*. With ♠ K x x, ♡ x, ◇ A Q J x x, ♣ A x x x, or ♠ K x x x, ♡ x, ◇ A Q 10 x x, ♣ A x x, he should bid two diamonds over his partner's opening spade bid. The subsequent bidding depends upon opener's re-bids. If the bidding continues

OPENER	RESPONDER
1 ♠	2 ◇
2 ♠	3 ♣
3 ♠	?

responder should bid five spades. A raise to four could not be recognized as a slam try, and furthermore, opener's failure to bid hearts or no-trump along the line is encouraging since it suggests no duplication in hearts. However, if opener had re-bid three no-trump over three clubs, responder would just bid four spades. The four-spade bid could be recognized as a slam try because responder obviously had trump support for a re-bid suit, and he would have bid four spades immediately over two spades if he were only interested in game. So opener should bid six with ♠ A Q x x x, ♡ J 10 x x, ◇ K x, ♣ K x, because so little of his strength is in hearts.

In my chapter on defensive bidding, I stressed the fact that there are many opportunities for two-way bids. Experts all agree that four no-trump should sometimes be Blackwood and sometimes be a natural bid. Why not treat five no-trump the same way? Culbertson's grand slam force is invaluable at times. A five no-trump bid asks partner to bid seven of the agreed suit if he has two of the three top honors. Either he or someone else suggested various sign-off responses which permit seven to be reached without the queen of trumps when there are less than four trumps outstanding. The only trouble with the grand slam force is that the opportunity to use it occurs so seldom. You can't use Blackwood to check on side aces, because a five no-trump bid would then be part of Blackwood. You can occasionally use the grand slam force after cue bidding. At least 90 per cent of the time you bid five no-trump, neither you nor partner will even think of the grand slam force because your subconscious minds will tell you that there are too many uncertain factors outside of the trump suit. However, when the bidding is

OPENER	RESPONDER	or	OPENER	RESPONDER
1 ♡	2 ◇		2 ♠	3 ♡
5 NT			3 ♣	4 ♡
			5 NT	

the five no-trump bid should be easily recognized as the grand slam force.

The purpose in having game-forcing bids is to get the maximum information before making the final decision and without fear of having the bidding stop abruptly. In other words, after a game-forcing bid, it is unnecessary to jump again below the game level merely to keep the bidding open. Any "unnecessary" jump should accomplish a purpose justifying the loss of a round of bidding. The usual reason for an unnecessary jump is to avoid trapping. Suppose partner opens the bidding at two no-trump and you have ♠ K Q x x x x, ♡ x x, ◇ Q 10 x, ♣ x x. You would have a guilty conscience if you made no effort to reach a slam; yet only the mildest sort of slam try is justified. A three-spade bid followed by five spades or four no-trump would be too strong a sequence; furthermore, five spades might conceivably be set. Since you are too weak to bid three spades followed by strong action later, you jump to four spades, leaving the initiative with partner.

OPENER	RESPONDER
1 ♣	1 ◇
2 ♠	?

♠ Q J x x, ♡ x x, ◇ A J 10 x x, ♣ x x: Again, you are
not strong enough to bid three spades and take aggressive action
later. You should jump to four spades so that partner with
♠ A K x x, ♡ —, ◇ K x x, ♣ A K x x x x, can bid six. But
with a slightly better hand (♠ Q J x x, ♡ x x, ◇ A x x x x,
♣ K x), you are too strong to jump to four spades. You must
bid three spades, and make a slam try or slam bid on the next
round.

OPENER	RESPONDER
1 ♡	1 ♠
3 ◇	?

♠ A x x, ♡ Q 10 x x x, ◇ Q J, ♣ 10 x x: In my opinion,
you had only a two-heart bid on the first round. However, when
partner bids three diamonds, you shouldn't get nervous; it looks
as though your overbid is going to pay off with interest. Your
excellent heart support, diamond fit, and spade control all point
toward an almost certain slam. Had partner bid three clubs,
you would just bid four hearts, because the queen-jack of
diamonds would be of doubtful value. But now that he has bid
three diamonds you are too strong for a four-heart bid. Also,
there is a psychological reason for bidding three hearts. Partner's jump is likely to be based upon a good spade fit. You want
to give partner a chance to support spades at the three-level.
He might be too strong to bid four spades over four hearts, and
you don't want to hear about his spade support for the first
time at the six-level. Suppose you bid three hearts and partner
now bids three spades. Now is the time to bid six hearts. These
hands must fit like a glove. Partner should then be able to bid
seven with ♠ K x x x, ♡ A K x x x, ◇ A K x x, ♣ —, since
he knows you don't have club strength for your bidding. (You
are too good a player to be encouraged by any club strength
other than the ace, and if you had the ace of clubs, you would
cue-bid it before jumping to six hearts.)

Avoiding trapping is not the only reason for an "unnecessary" jump. Another purpose is to show an independent trump suit so that partner can take control of the bidding.

♠ J 10, ♡ A K Q J x x, ◇ A x x, ♣ x x; ♠ A x x, ♡ x x x, ◇ K x, ♣ A K Q x x:

SOUTH	WEST	NORTH	EAST
1 ♡	1 ♠	3 ♣	Pass
4 ♡	Pass	4 NT	Pass
5 ♡	Pass	7 ♡	

The jump to four hearts guarantees a six-card suit as good as A K Q J x x, or K Q J 10 x x—or a seven-card suit headed by the A K Q, or K Q J. Even opposite a singleton there should be no losers in trumps (except for the ace which partner can find out about with Blackwood). Responder is able to count twelve top tricks with a long club or possible diamond ruff for the thirteenth. Before we leave this hand, note how the three-club bid simplified the subsequent bidding:

OPENER	RESPONDER
1 ◇	1 ♠
3 ♣	3 ♡
?	

With ♠ A K Q x, ♡ —, ◇ Q J 10 x x, ♣ A Q x x, you should bid four spades. The jump at this point shows good *spades*. It will take quite a bit of encouragement for partner to get enthusiastic with the poor spade suit he must have. With only A x x x in spades, you would not jump to four spades whatever your general strength might be. Remember, three spades is forcing, and if you are strong enough for more bidding, you can do it later.

On rare occasions, a spectacular jump is the easiest way to get an accurate picture of your hand. Partner should realize that you did not beat around the bush with a forcing bid, cue bid, Blackwood, etc., because the information obtained this way would be of no value to you.

OPENER	RESPONDER
1 ♣	1 ♡
5 ♡	?

With what sort of hand should you bid six? And what do you

need for a seven-heart bid? First, you should try to visualize partner's hand. He cannot have any losers in spades or diamonds —at least no quick losers—or he would have tried to find out whether you could take care of them. All you need to do is look at your club and heart holdings. With as good as five hearts to the ace-king, you should bid *seven*. Or five hearts to the ace and the king of clubs. With either of these two hands you would have a finesse for seven at worst, and probably a lay-down. Partner's actual hand: ♠ A, ♡ J x x x x, ◇ —, ♣ A K J x x x x. Can you think of a more logical way for him to bid? With the queen of hearts instead of the jack, he would be justified in using the grand slam force. An immediate bid of six hearts with the actual hand would be an insult to a good partner. Remember that the three top trumps could be missing.

SOUTH	WEST	NORTH	EAST
1 ♣	Pass	1 ◇	Pass
?			

♠ A, ♡ A Q, ◇ K J x x, ♣ A J x x x x: In my opinion, four diamonds is the only proper bid. A three-diamond bid is an underbid and a trap, while two hearts is a misbid. You don't want to get partner excited over a heart fit or worried over a lack of it. What you are really concerned about is partner's strength in clubs and diamonds, and a heart bid will only confuse the issue. Exchange the queen of hearts for a small diamond, giving you 6-5 distribution. Now you should jump to five diamonds.

Suppose you are fortunate enough to pick up this sort of hand: ♠ A, ♡ A K Q J 10 x, ◇ A, ♣ Q J 10 9 x. Naturally, you open the bidding with two hearts, and you get a two no-trump response. Your next bid should be three clubs. Partner bids three spades. At this point, many players would make the pointless and misleading bid of four diamonds. The correct bid is five hearts. You can make five hearts by yourself, and by bidding just clubs and hearts, you show where you want your partner's strength to be. He should bid six with ♠ J 10 x x x x, ♡ x, ◇ x x x x, ♣ K x, because he has one sure trick for you. Suppose that partner had made a positive response originally. For example,

OPENER	RESPONDER
2 ♡	2 ♠
3 ♣	3 NT
?	

After a bust response, the five-heart bid obviously meant that you could make five hearts all by yourself, since you would not gamble on picking up a trick in responder's hand. However, after a positive response, an immediate five-heart bid would not convey the same message—that you have eleven tricks in your own hand and need only one trick from partner in the right spot. Partner might think your five-heart bid was partially based upon his positive response, and he might pass with ♠ Q J 9 x x, ♡ x, ◊ J 10 x x, ♣ K x x. On the other hand, you should not gamble on his having the right cards, since he could easily have enough strength in spades and diamonds to justify his bidding without a club honor. The solution is to re-bid clubs, followed by five hearts. Once you show 6-5 distribution, partner would realize the value of the ace or king of clubs and the worthlessness of other cards he might have.

OPENER	RESPONDER
1 ♠	2 ♠
?	

♠ A K x x x x, ♡ A Q 10 x, ◊ —, ♣ K 10 9: This time a slam is not unlikely if partner has a strong raise with his strength in your three suits. The first step is to bid three hearts. If partner bids three spades or three no-trump, slam is too remote to consider, and you will settle for four spades. But if partner bids four spades or four hearts, you should bid five clubs to show the other suit. After a single raise, only a freak hand can justify a slam try, and it is much better to bid the suits that you have rather than the suits that you do not have.

OPENER	RESPONDER
1 ♠	2 ♠
?	

♠ K Q 9 x x x, ♡ A Q x x, ◊ —, ♣ A K x: Again, the correct bid is three hearts, hoping for a four-heart or four-spade bid. But if partner jumps to four spades, you should bid five spades. Partner's club fit is not so important this time, and by only mentioning hearts and spades, you emphasize the importance of cards in these suits. If partner raises three hearts to four hearts, you should simply bid six hearts. You will probably make seven if he has four hearts to the king and the ace of spades, but you won't need to bid seven to get a good board.

OPENER	RESPONDER
1 ♡	2 ♡
?	

♠ A x x, ♡ K Q x x x, ◇ A Q x x x, ♣ —: You could make a slam opposite holdings such as ♠ K x x, ♡ A x x x, ◇ J x, ♣ x x x x, or ♠ K x, ♡ J 10 x x, ◇ K x x x, ♣ x x x, but there is too much risk in passing the game level. The bidding might go

OPENER	RESPONDER
1 ♡	2 ♡
3 ◇	4 ♡
4 ♠	

only to find partner with ♠ J x x, ♡ 10 x x x, ◇ x x, ♣ A K J x, or ♠ x x, ♡ A x x x, ◇ x x x, ♣ A J x x. So the correct bid over two hearts is four diamonds. If partner has the two key cards, ace of hearts and king of diamonds, plus four-card support for either suit, he will jump to six. The other slam possibilities must be disregarded because of the risk of investigation.

The principle illustrated by these examples is so unfamiliar to the vast majority of players that it justifies repetition. *When you have a freak hand, bid the suits where you want partner's strength to be.* Do not draw his attention away from the important thing, strength in your suits, by cue bidding your voids and singleton aces.

One of the best indications of an expert bidder is that he is willing to leave some decisions to his partner. Ninety per cent of the players I know never think of making a slam try other than by Blackwood. If they feel optimistic, they bid a slam. If they feel pessimistic, they stop at game without even letting their partner know they have a good hand.

OPENER	RESPONDER
1 ♡	?

♠ A Q 10 x x, ♡ 10 x, ◇ K Q x, ♣ A Q x: The average player responds one spade. If opener re-bids a new suit or raises spades, responder goes on to six no-trump more or less by himself, telling his partner he should not open on such cheese if six no-trump does not make. If opener re-bids one no-trump or two hearts, the average responder turns pessimistic and stops at three no-trump. How much better it would be to respond two spades and re-bid three no-trump on the next round. If opener has 12 or 13 points, he will pass. If he has 15 or 16 points, he will bid six. As many players use the jump response, it is practically forcing to a slam. With a 20-point hand the jump response is a convenience, but you could get to six in a number of ways. It is with the 17- and 18-point hands that a jump take-out is necessary. When you have an independent suit or good support for partner's suit, you can make the jump take-out with less high-card strength than you would otherwise need, but lack of a fit for partner or an independent suit is no reason not to jump when you have a good enough hand.

OPENER	RESPONDER
1 ♡	?

♠ A Q J x x x, ♡ x, ◇ K x x, ♣ A Q x: Of course, this could be a bad misfit, but a two-spade response does not commit you to reaching a slam. Note how little partner needs: ♠ K x, ♡ A x x x x, ◇ A Q x, ♣ x x x will give you about a 75 per cent play for six spades, and another card, such as the jack of clubs, will give you a lay-down. If you only bid one spade, partner will re-bid one no-trump, and you will have quite a problem on the second round. Perhaps if you jump in one of your three-card minors, everything will turn out all right. Perhaps! But why make a series of confusing and ambiguous bids when one bid would do the job much better? Once you bid two spades, you can relax. Partner will take the initiative if he has key cards such as aces, kings, and spade honors.

OPENER	RESPONDER
1 ♡	?

♠ x x, ♡ A x x, ◇ A Q x x x x, ♣ A x: I know that even a suggestion of bidding three diamonds will shock the old-timers. This hand does not qualify for a jump take-out under any system or any point-count you have ever heard of. But it is a three-diamond bid in my book. What does partner need for a slam? Just a good five-card heart suit and the kings of spades and diamonds. The ace of spades, king of diamonds, and five hearts to the king-queen will be enough for *seven*. Of course, partner could have a pretty good hand with his cards all in the wrong places, but I do not believe it pays to be pessimistic. When the right 2½ honor-count (12 points) with a five-card suit in opener's hand is enough for thirteen cold tricks, the responding hand is worth a slam try. The safest and best time to make it is right away. If opener re-bids three no-trump, you must pass. Thirteen tricks may still be cold, but you can't risk another bid. At least you will have tried, which is more than the other players can say. If partner re-bids three hearts, you simply raise to four. Again, he may pass when you are cold for a slam. But sometimes partner does the right thing, and you will have given him a chance.

Not every 14-point hand with a six-card suit is worth a jump response. The best method of evaluation is what Culbertson calls plastic evaluation. Imagine a typical minimum or near-minimum opening bid with the cards favorably placed, and see if the combined hands will produce a lay-down slam. When they will, your hand is worth a slam try. When your hand is worth a slam try the moment partner opens the bidding, you should make a jump response unless there is a good reason not to. One reason for not jumping on the first round is that you want to show a singleton by bidding two suits followed by a strong raise of partner's suit. Another reason for not jumping immediately is that with a few hands you wish to retain control and find out what partner's normal re-bid would be, or you wish to avoid crowding the bidding because you want to get in several forcing bids to show your distribution below the decision-making level. Nevertheless, a very good general rule is to make a jump bid of some sort whenever you have 17 points or more in high cards, and very frequently with less. When you make a jump response with 12-16 points in high cards, it is because you have excellent distribution and controls so that if partner fits your hand well, you can make a slam even though he has a minimum opening bid.

OPENER   RESPONDER
1 ◇   ?

♠ x, ♡ A K Q x x x x, ◇ K x x, ♣ x x: Respond two hearts because partner needs only five diamonds to the ace-queen and the ace of clubs for a slam. Of course you would not jump if he opened any suit but diamonds. Suppose he has the ace-king-queen of spades, the ace-queen-jack of diamonds, and the queen-jack of clubs. He will probably insist upon a slam. So what? You would surely have reached a slam without the jump-response, and you will have plenty of company. With 19 points, partner will probably bid a slam, but he shouldn't get too exuberant with 16 or 17 points unless they are all top cards. Take another look at the 19-point hand: ♠ A K Q, ♡ x x, ◇ A Q J x, ♣ Q J x x. Opener should figure: "What a strong hand I have opposite a jump response! Almost too good to be true. Of course, the queen-jack of clubs are not worth much; side-suit queens and jacks seldom are. And the king-queen of spades are quite likely to be duplicated values. Still, 19 points are a lot of points, and there is something to be said for a blind, unscientific plunge of six no-trump. There may be 13 tricks with any lead, but there will surely be 13 tricks with a favorable lead. But if I want to bid scientifically, I must bid two spades. If partner keeps re-bidding hearts, I will bid four diamonds, followed by five hearts. Then if he cue-bids six clubs, I will try seven no-trump."

I do not want to dwell on this hand further. Perhaps the jump response gives you the best chance to stay out of a slam! But I am always suspicious of hands that purport to prove too much. Anyone can figure out logical ways of reaching the right contract whether it is five or seven when he sees both hands. All I contend is that the jump response does not hurt anything with this type of hand.

OPENER   RESPONDER
1 ♣   ?

♠ A K x x x, ♡ A x x, ◇ x, ♣ K x x x: I cannot see any excuse for not bidding two spades. What does partner need for six clubs? Something like ♠ Q x, ♡ J x x, ◇ A x x, ♣ A Q x x x. If you respond one spade, partner would re-bid one no-trump. At this point, even if you play three clubs as forcing, will partner visualize this good a hand? Or just ♠ A K x x x, ♡ x x, ◇ x, ♣ K J x x x? Much better bidding is

OPENER	RESPONDER
1 ♣	2 ♠
2 NT	3 ♣

after which opener cannot let the bidding die short of a slam. He does not have a lot of points, but he has a good club suit, not A x x, for example, and every honor in his hand other than the jack of hearts is a key card. These hands fit well, but the good fit is predictable during the bidding.

After a jump response, opener should usually bid the same as he would over a non-jump response, only at a higher level. However, a slam is often a good one or a bad one, depending upon the strength of the trump suit. For that reason, opener should tend not to re-bid his suit unless he has a six-card suit or a good five-card suit. A J 10 x x is satisfactory, but A J 8 x x is not. Partner will consider Q x x adequate support for a suit that has been re-bid. Also, opener should tend to bid where his high cards are.

OPENER	RESPONDER
1 ♣	2 ♡
?	

♠ 9 x x x, ♡ Q x, ◇ A x x, ♣ A K x x: Over a one-heart response you might have re-bid one spade, but a two-spade bid over two hearts, even with Q x x x of spades, would be very misleading. You must either bid two no-trump or three hearts. A raise is permissible because responder usually has a good heart suit for the jump. If not, he will re-bid three no-trump or raise clubs.

OPENER	RESPONDER
1 ♠	3 ♡
?	

♠ A K Q x x, ♡ K x x, ◇ K x x, ♣ x x: If partner had responded two hearts, you would raise immediately because a raise is more encouraging than a spade re-bid. After the jump response, a spade re-bid cannot be passed, so you should show your good spades, saving the heart raise till the next round.

Thus far, all of my suggestions have been fairly orthodox. Expert bidding as practiced by the top players of today is very good. It would take a lot of nerve to suggest that it all be junked in favor of something new and untried. On the other hand, there are certain hands that are hard to handle with the present bidding methods. I have a few suggestions for these hands. The suggested bids are "idle" bids which do not conflict with so-called normal bidding.

OPENER	RESPONDER
1 ♡	2 NT
3 NT	4 NT
?	

Has partner lost his mind? How can he bid over your three no-trump bid if he had a two no-trump response? Obviously he must not have had a normal two no-trump response. His four no-trump hand should show a balanced hand with 19 points or a good 18 points, slightly too much for a three no-trump response. What was the purpose of the two no-trump bid? To show that four no-trump was natural rather than Blackwood.

The two no-trump/four no-trump sequence can be made over any minimum re-bid. For example:

OPENER	RESPONDER	or	OPENER	RESPONDER
1 ♡	2 NT		1 ♡	2 NT
3 ♡	4 NT		3 ◇	4 NT

Because two no-trump is such an obvious limit bid, you are immediately aware of the fact that partner must be doing something unusual when he follows his two no-trump bid with aggressive action. Consequently, the two no-trump bid may be the beginning of other sequences to show similar hands with certain distributional features.

OPENER	RESPONDER
1 ◇	?

♠ J x x, ♡ K x x x, ◇ A K Q x, ♣ A x, or ♠ A x, ♡ Q x x, ◇ A J x x, ♣ A Q x x: A three no-trump response would show the honor-count, but it would not show the distributional support for diamonds. Failure to make some jump response will cause all sorts of difficulty later in the bidding. Nor is a jump response on a four-card suit, particularly a weak four-card major, very attractive. For one thing, partner will attach undue importance to his degree of fit with your suit, not knowing it is so puny. He will undervalue his side-suit strength. If partner cannot accept the slam invitation, it is hard to stop in a no-trump contract after a jump take-out and a minor-suit raise, a factor of importance in duplicate. My suggestion is to use the two no-trump response again, followed by a raise of opener's suit on the next round. If he bids anything else, he must have good enough distribution to make six diamonds a good gamble.

After

OPENER	RESPONDER
1 ◇	2 NT
3 NT	4 ◇

opener must bid four no-trump if he is not interested in a slam. Suppose partner opens the bidding with one heart and you have ♠ A J x x, ♡ A J x x, ◇ A x, ♣ K x x, or ♠ A K x, ♡ Q x x x x, ◇ K x, ♣ K Q x. A two no-trump response followed by a raise of partner's major suit could not be recognized as an "impossible" sequence. When you have about 17 points in high cards with distributional support for partner's *major*, you should give partner a double raise followed by a four-no-trump bid. The four no-trump bid cannot be Blackwood, since if you just had an ordinary double raise, you would have to pass partner's four-spade re-bid, and if you intended to bid Blackwood whatever partner did, you could bid it on the first round.

When I first wrote my article on impossible bids for *The Bridge World* in November, 1952, I suggested a two no-trump response followed by a new suit at the four-level to show implied support for opener's suit and a singleton in the new suit. Aside from the fact that this is a very artificial convention and would have to be announced, I have not had the proper hand for this convention in three years, and I now think this sequence could be used more profitably to describe a different type of hand. With ♠ A Q x x x, ♡ 10 x, ◇ K Q x, ♣ A Q x, you would respond two spades to an opening heart bid followed by a three-no-trump re-bid. Now exchange the king of diamonds for the ace, and the hand is slightly too strong for this sequence. Bid two no-trump followed by four spades! Or bid two no-trump followed by four clubs with ♠ A Q, ♡ Q x x, ◇ K x x, ♣ A Q J 10 x, All of these unusual sequences show 19 points or 18 good points, either in high cards alone or with one point for distribution.

Opener may be strong enough to bid a slam over the first response. This should not cause any serious difficulty. If he can bid a small slam directly, not knowing that responder has another bid up his sleeve, a grand slam should be a lay-down. Or even a slam try by opener will be sufficient to put the partnership in the grand-slam zone when opener's hand is balanced.

Opener: ♠ K Q x x x, ♡ A x x x, ◇ K x, ♣ A Q;
Responder: ♠ A J x, ♡ K 10 x, ◇ A Q J x, ♣ K 10 x:

OPENER	RESPONDER
1 ♠	2 NT
4 NT	7 NT

When opener's slam try may be based upon distribution, caution is necessary. Responder must then manage the bidding in such a way that it cannot stop short of a small slam while he investigates grand slam chances.

Opener: ♠ K Q x x x x, ♡ —, ◇ A 10 x x x, ♣ K x;
Responder: ♠ A J x x, ♡ A Q x x, ◇ Q x x, ♣ A x:

OPENER	RESPONDER
1 ♠	3 ♠
4 ◇	4 ♡
4 ♠	5 ♣
5 ◇	6 ♠

Opener signs off over the four-heart bid, and refuses to bid six over the strong five-club call. Responder consequently settles for six spades. However, keeping the responder's hand the same and changing opener's to: ♠ K Q x x x, ♡ K J x, ◇ A x, ♣ K Q x, the auction would end up differently, as follows:

OPENER	RESPONDER
1 ♠	3 ♠
4 ◇	4 ♡
4 ♠	5 ♣
6 ♠	7 ♠

Here responder admittedly has a close decision over six spades, but opener has jumped to the small slam without knowing about the ace of trumps, so the grand slam should be a good shot.

We shall finish off the chapter with a few miscellaneous hands which do not fit into any particular category.

OPENER	OPPONENT	RESPONDER
1 ◇	1 ♠	?

♠ x, ♡ —, ◇ K J 10 x x x, ♣ A Q J x x x: You should make no attempt to be scientific with this type of hand. Theoretically, asking bids should be useful, but as a practical matter, the opponents will do so much interference bidding that any attempt to get information would be futile. The correct bid is six diamonds. As it happens, the opponents have a good save in hearts but not in spades. But you gave them no chance to discover their heart fit. Furthermore, the opponents seldom sacrifice over this type of bidding, because they doubt that you know what you are doing. Another advantage in the leap to six is that the opponents often try to outguess you and figure that you are void in spades or expect a spade lead; consequently they lead a heart.

West: ♠ A K x x, ♡ x, ◇ A Q x x x, ♣ A x x; East: ♠ x x, ♡ x x, ◇ K x x, ♣ K Q x x x x:

SOUTH	WEST	NORTH	EAST
4 ♡	Double	Pass	5 ♣
5 ♡	Pass	Pass	6 ♣
Pass	Pass	Pass	

South committed the crime of bidding twice with his pre-empt and got the punishment he deserved. East could not jump to six clubs because West could have had a poorer hand or a doubleton heart. Nor could West bid a slam by himself. In other words, the pre-empt did just what it was designed to do, forcing each partner to guess. But South's five-heart bid made everything easy. West could make a forcing pass to show that he was still interested in a slam, and East was glad to accept the invitation. Just as in other competitive situations, the pass was more encouraging than a double would be. If West's hand were weakened substantially, he should double five hearts.

SOUTH	WEST	NORTH	EAST
Pass	Pass	3 ◇	3 ♠
Pass	?		

♠ Q x x, ♡ J 10 x x, ◇ —, ♣ A Q J x x x: You surely have a clear-cut slam try. You should bid four diamonds followed by a raise if partner re-bids four spades. All partner needs is a good five- or six-card spade suit, the king of hearts, and the king of clubs. Now take away a heart and give yourself a small diamond. This time partner needs the ace of hearts instead of the king. But if you just bid five spades, he would have to pass with two small diamonds. So you should bid four diamonds, but if partner only bids four spades, you should pass. The four-diamond bid implies spade support and shows a good hand, so partner could jump if he had a strong overcall.

OPENER	RESPONDER
1 ♠	2 ♠
3 ♡	5 ♡
?	

♠ A J x x x, ♡ K Q x x x, ◇ x, ♣ A x: The temptation is to pass without even thinking. It is true that you were not even sure of game when you bid three hearts, and you had no thought of a slam. On the other hand, partner could not assume that three hearts was a slam try, and he must have a pretty good hand to jeopardize game by trapping you this way. What can he have? There is only one hand I can think of consistent with his raise to two spades. King-queen-small of spades and five hearts to the ace. If he has that hand, you are cold for six hearts. If he has another type of hand, perhaps K x x of spades and six hearts to the ace, you will still have a finesse for the slam. The important thing is that his strength cannot be in the minors because he wouldn't bid as he did with minor-suit strength.

OPENER	RESPONDER
1 ♡	2 ♡
2 ♠	3 ◇
3 ♠	6 ♡

♠ A J 10 9 x, ♡ A K x x x x, ◇ x x, ♣ —; ♠ K x, ♡ Q x x, ◇ A x x x, ♣ x x x x: I will not contend that this is the soundest slam contract ever reached. Actually, it is a very good contract if a club is led, and only a fair contract if a diamond is led. However, the bidding calls for some comment. If opener had re-bid two no-trump after the heart raise, the three-diamond bid would show a five- or six-card diamond suit with a weak hand and weak heart support. But when opener re-bid two spades, showing at least nine cards in the majors, he could not logically be interested in a minor-suit contract; consequently, responder would not show a minor *suit*. The diamond bid had to be a cue bid. The three-diamond bid is equivalent to a four-heart bid, but it shows where some of responder's strength is. Suppose responder had cue bid opener's void. Then opener should simply bid four hearts. The only excuse for re-bidding spades was to show a continued interest in slam. Opener's bidding is rather optimistic since he needs a very good dummy with just the right cards. Certainly he could not risk another bid if responder had just jumped to four hearts over two spades.

OPENER	RESPONDER
1 ♠	?

♠ K x x x x, ♡ A Q J 10 x, ◇ —, ♣ Q J x: I have convinced several fine players that the proper response is three clubs! Whenever partner has the ace or king of the suit in which you make a jump take-out, he almost always manages to raise your suit either immediately or later. In any event, he will value that card highly and make a slam try with an otherwise minimum hand. There are too many possible sequences to attempt a detailed analysis, but this is the way you would like the bidding to develop:

OPENER	RESPONDER
1 ♠	3 ♣
3 ♠	4 ♠
5 ♣	5 ♡
5 ♠	6 ◇

In this sequence, the fact that you cue bid hearts before diamonds shows that you have a void in diamonds; otherwise you would cue bid diamonds first. Also, you must have a freak hand because you risk a pass to four spades, yet invite a grand slam after one more bid from partner. You hope that partner would just bid six hearts with the king of hearts and king of clubs, but go all the way to seven if his club honor were the ace. Fancy? A little. But the three-club bid is most likely to be useful in getting to or staying out of six.

OPENER	RESPONDER
2 ♠	4 ♠
?	

♠ A K x x x x, ♡ A K x x, ◇ A K, ♣ x: Bid five hearts. Nothing has been said yet about asking bids, but even if you had never heard of one, you should invent one on the spot. What can the five-heart bid mean? Partner has shown no first- or second-round controls. Yet you are still interested in a slam. You must be worried about his holding in your second suit. Third-round control is the most you can hope for. If he has the queen of hearts or a doubleton, he should bid six spades. Suppose partner had responded three spades instead of four spades. If partner were able to give a five-diamond response to Blackwood you would bid six hearts. A six-heart bid would have no purpose other than to invite a grand slam, and the obvious purpose of bidding hearts rather than some other suit is to show that it is a heart fit that you care most about.

Chapter 7

What's New at Bridge

BEFORE WE see what's new at bridge and what the trends are, it is necessary to study a little bridge history. I was not around in the early days of bridge, but our city library has quite a collection of old books by Reith, Lenz, Foster, and Culbertson. The following summary is based upon what I have read.

Undoubtedly, Culbertson has done more for bridge than any other three people. Not only did he introduce many revolutionary ideas which are now accepted as axioms; he was able, through clever showmanship and psychology, to sell those ideas to the public and make bridge popular with millions. Of course, the Culbertson system was not the *sole* creation of Culbertson. It was his explanation of how bridge was played by the best players of the day, including himself. Nevertheless, the Culbertson system was unique because of its employment of mathematical terms such as honor-count and playing tricks, and its breakdown of a complex subject into easily understandable parts.

In the years 1933–1935 Culbertson's position was unsuccessfully threatened by four very fine players, calling themselves the Four Aces. These were Howard Schenken, Oswald Jacoby, David Burnstine (Bruce), and Michael Gottlieb. At least two of them had played on Culbertson's teams in the past. Not only were the Four Aces fine players; they had an excellent system. Let us examine some of the differences between Culbertson's Blue Book of 1934 and the Four Aces' book of 1935. Culbertson said that a new suit by responder should not be forcing, not even the first response. Culbertson was never wishy-washy. Not only did he say the new suit should not be forcing; he argued very strenuously in favor of invitational, rather than forcing, non-jump responses. This permitted opening bids on 2½ honor-count without a re-bid. According to the Four Aces, a new suit by responder was absolutely forcing, at least on the first round. Culbertson used a two no-trump response or a double raise as a limit bid.

OPENER	RESPONDER
1 ♠	4 ♠

was stronger than

OPENER	RESPONDER
1 ♠	3 ♠

The Four Aces considered two no-trump as a forcing bid and employed the double raise with defensive strength and the triple raise with distribution just as we do today. Since opener was obligated to re-bid unless responder raised or bid one no-trump, opener needed somewhat more strength than Culbertson required, and opener had to prepare his re-bid by bidding the right suit first, including a possible three-card minor—again just as we do today. In many other respects, such as opening no-trump bids, action over a redouble, etc., the Four Aces recommended the treatment which is now almost universally adopted. Of course, it is not fair to compare a 1934 revision of a book written in 1930 with a new book written in 1935. Bridge was progressing rapidly in those days.

When Culbertson wrote his Gold Book in 1936, it was more "up to date" than anything previously written, since bridge books tend to reflect the practices of top players in general as well as the author's own ideas. Culbertson always made the claim that when better ideas were developed, he would incorporate them into the Culbertson system; and he did. He had managed to make his invitational responses work quite well when he was using them. Probably he decided they were not suitable for most players. Anyway, in 1936, Culbertson adopted the principle of forcing exploratory responses—I should say re-adopted, since Culbertson had suggested them long before, and then dropped them except as an optional feature in the Culbertson system. While Culbertson was able to swallow the first-round forces, he never liked all jumps and all new suit bids on later rounds as forces, and he held out for treating these bids as invitational.

A rough explanation of the basic difference between Culbertson and the majority of American experts is as follows: Culbertson likes to get into the bidding frequently, even with mediocre hands, to indicate leads, compete for part-scores, and occasionally steal the pot. These light hands cannot be re-bid round after round, and opener must be permitted to drop out of the bidding early in order to avoid a disaster. The other top players are inclined to let the small pots go. Once they enter the bidding, however, most bids are forcing or almost forcing, since opener is expected to have enough "strength in reserve" not to pass any enouraging or ambiguous bid.

The Goren-Schenken, Rock-of-Gibraltar style won in the United States by default, but the Culbertson style has apparently been adopted with success by the English players. In fact, much of their bidding seems to be straight from the old Blue Book. They use limit raises and limit two no-trump responses. They open light so far as defensive strength is concerned, but their offensive strength is sufficient for a *safe* re-bid so long as partner does not expect too much. Thus the English tend to open the bidding with ♠ K Q 10 x x x, ♡ A x, ◇ x x x, ♣ x x, or ♠ x, ♡ A K Q x x x, ◇ x x x, ♣ x x x. This type of bidding works particularly well when the responder has a good distributional fit and raises directly to game. The opening side makes game or takes a paltry set while the other side, which may be cold for game, cannot safely enter the bidding. Culbertson recommends opening ♠ x x, ♡ x x x, ◇ A K x x x, ♣ Q J x, or ♠ x, ♡ K J 10 x x, ◇ K Q J, ♣ x x x x in any position at duplicate, so he and the English have much in common. At least both schools open lighter than most Americans, although not necessarily on the same type of hands. Culbertson and the English seem to be worried less about "Preparedness" than the Americans. Culbertson recommends opening ♠ A K x x, ♡ x x x, ◇ A x x, ♣ x x x at duplicate without explaining what he would re-bid, but I am pretty sure that both he and the English would raise any suit response by partner. Culbertson and the English both tend to bid a four-card major and raise partner's response or re-bid two no-trump with a near-minimum hand in preference to preparing a re-bid by opening a minor suit. "Why bid a weak suit to prepare a safe re-bid when partner's or the opponent's bid may release us from the obligation to re-bid?" they ask.

The English bid more "naturally" than the Americans.

SOUTH	WEST	NORTH	EAST
1 ♠	Pass	2 ♣	Pass
?			

♠ A x x x x, ♡ Q x x, ◇ x x, ♣ A Q x: I am sure that Goren would recommend a two-spade re-bid. A raise to three clubs would be too encouraging a bid for this minimum hand. "It is better to lie about your suit than to lie about your hand," Goren says. The English bid three clubs since the club support is good and the spades are poor. If responder bids three no-trump and goes down, so what? The English seem to like skimpy game contracts and do a pretty good job of making them.

Another difference already hinted at between the American style and the English, or Culbertson style is in the constructive connotations of bids. The American tendency is to make many bids forcing or almost forcing. After an almost-force, partner must bid again with no particular values so as to give you another chance. A. Moyse, editor of *The Bridge World*, has attacked this style with his usual vigor:

OPENER	RESPONDER
1 ♡	1 ♠
2 ♣	?

Responder (according to many experts) must raise to three clubs with something like ♠ Q x x x, ♡ K x, ◇ K x x, ♣ x x x x to give opener a chance in case he had a very strong hand

OPENER	RESPONDER
1 ♡	1 ♠
2 ♣	3 ♣
?	

Other top players (and perhaps the same ones as in the last group) say opener must bid again on a minimum to give *responder* a chance in case he had ♠ K J x x x, ♡ A x,

◇ x x x, ♣ A Q x. In other sequences, when you have enough to bid game, you only bid two no-trump or raise to three of a major. Partner would be insulted if you bid the full value of your own hand or took his bidding seriously. "Don't you know I would bid game myself if I had my previous bids?" he asks. I am old-fashioned enough to believe that a raise should ask partner to bid again with extra values, not what he has already shown.

The English have poked fun at some of our weirdest ideas. In an amusing article in the July, 1952, *Bridge World*, Edmund Phillips asks why the following three-spade bid should be forcing, whether conventionally, inferentially, or "logically."

SOUTH	WEST	NORTH	EAST
1 ◇	2 ♣	Pass	Pass
2 ♠	Pass	3 ♠	

Opener may be competing with ♠ A K Q 10, ♡ K x, ◇ Q J 10 x x, ♣ 10 x, or he may be trying to get somewhere with ♠ A K Q 10, ♡ A, ◇ Q J 10 x x, ♣ 10 x x. If a raise to three is equivalent to a raise to game, responder must toss a coin with ♠ J x x x, ♡ Q x x x, ◇ K x x, ♣ J x. Obviously, Mr. Phillips believes responder should be able to raise to three spades as a chance-giving bid—despite Albert Morehead's opinion to the contrary.

NORTH: ♠ K J x x, ♡ J 10 x x x, ◇ A, ♣ Q 10 x;
SOUTH: ♠ x x x, ♡ A K, ◇ K 10 x x, ♣ A x x x: East-West vulnerable match-point duplicate:

SOUTH	WEST	NORTH	EAST
1 ◇	Pass	1 ♡	1 ♠
Pass	Pass	1 NT	Pass
2 ♣	Pass	2 NT	Pass
3 NT			

Mr. Moyse suggested and Mr. Phillips agreed that a double of one spade would be North's most logical action, but the question is how many no-trump North should bid if he fails to double. One no-trump is a gross underbid, especially at match points, since the mere fact that North bids does not indicate any interest in reaching game. Why did South bid two clubs? Does he want to play a minor-suit contract at duplicate with this hand? Obviously not, but his bid has the practical effect of giving North the choice between two clubs and three no-trump as a final contract. Even an optimistic raise to two no-trump has more to recommend it. Why did South bid again at all? To give North another chance, because he suspected that when North bid one no-trump, he really meant two no-trump (and North could not bid two no-trump because that would have meant *three* no-trump!). Nor was Mr. Phillips mistaken as to the latter point. According to Goren, and a large number of American experts, a two no-trump re-bid would be forcing.

The game of bridge would be much simpler than it is if everyone bid alike. Directors would have fewer problems; convention cards would not be needed; protest and ethics committees would not be so busy—and bridge would not be so much fun! Despite the convenience of enforced uniformity, people should have an opportunity to try out new theories and to persuade others. It must have been exciting in the early thirties when the leading exponents of various systems could challenge each other to matches with glory and the successful sale of their bridge books at stake. Till the Roth-Stone system came along, no one had made a serious attempt to challenge the basic Culbertson system since 1936. One person suggested a particular bid; another suggested a different way of evaluating a hand, but these differences were all minor. Culbertson himself kept suggesting minor changes from time to time. Reserving the whole opening two-level for powerhouse bids that come up infrequently must have bothered many people. Culbertson suggested the limit two-bid principle which makes the two-bid available for at least twice as many hands as formerly.

However, the strongest attack on the wastefulness of reserving the whole two-level for powerhouses came from Schenken. All game-going hands are shown by an artificial two-club bid, leaving an opening two-diamond, two-heart, or two-spade bid for another purpose. This other purpose is a mild pre-empt. The weak two-bid shows $1\frac{1}{2}$ to 2 honor-count with a good six-card suit. Preferably, most of the strength should be concentrated in this suit, and there should not be much length or strength in an unbid major. When holding a 6-4-2-1 distribution you should not have a maximum in honor-count because partner will pass with 2½ honor-count and a doubleton in your suit. Open two hearts with ♠ A x, ♡ K J 10 x x x, ◇ x x x, ♣ J x, or ♠ x, ♡ A K Q 10 x, ◇ J 10 x x, ♣ x x x. Pass or bid one heart in first or second position with ♠ Q x x, ♡ Q 10 9 x x x, ◇ A Q, ♣ J x. ♠ K Q J x x x, ♡ x x, ◇ K J 10 x, ♣ x is too strong for an opening two-bid in any position unless it is fourth hand, vulnerable. The following hands show how the weak two-bid can work at its best.

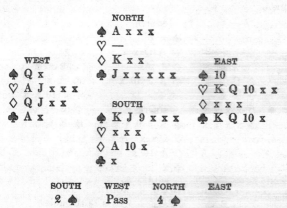

NORTH
♠ A x x x
♡ —
◇ K x x
♣ J x x x x x

WEST
♠ Q x
♡ A J x x x
◇ Q J x x
♣ A x

EAST
♠ 10
♡ K Q 10 x x
◇ x x x
♣ K Q 10 x

SOUTH
♠ K J 9 x x x
♡ x x x
◇ A 10 x
♣ x

SOUTH	WEST	NORTH	EAST
2 ♠	Pass	4 ♠	

Without the weak two-bid, West would open one heart and East would raise to four, shutting North-South out completely, just as the weak two-bid shut East-West out of the bidding.

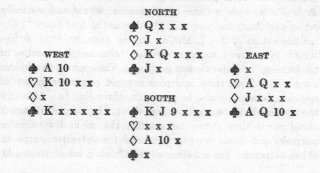

NORTH
♠ Q x x x
♡ J x
◇ K Q x x x
♣ J x

WEST
♠ A 10
♡ K 10 x x
◇ x
♣ K x x x x x

EAST
♠ x
♡ A Q x x
◇ J x x x
♣ A Q 10 x

SOUTH
♠ K J 9 x x x
♡ x x x
◇ A 10 x
♣ x

SOUTH	WEST	NORTH	EAST
2 ♠	Pass	3 ♠	Pass
4 ♠			

East-West are cold for six hearts but never enter the bidding. If you think West should be more aggressive, try exchanging the North and East hands and see what would happen. In fact, it is often dangerous for East to reopen, even when North passes. North can pass a good hand if it is not quite good enough for game.

NORTH
♠ x x
♡ A Q x x
♢ J x x
♣ A J 10 x

WEST
♠ Q 10 x
♡ K x
♢ x x x x
♣ x x x x

EAST
♠ A x
♡ J 10 x x
♢ K Q x
♣ K Q x x

SOUTH
♠ K J 9 x x x
♡ x x x
♢ A 10 x
♣ x

SOUTH	WEST	NORTH	EAST
2 ♠	Pass	Pass	Double
Pass	2 NT	Double	

According to the Four Aces, any under-game response other than a raise was forcing for one round. If partner opened two spades, you had to pass with ♠ —, ♡ Q J 9 8 x x, ♢ K Q x, ♣ K J x x, since a three-heart response would automatically get you too high and you might be doubled at four hearts. I like the suggestion of Joe I. McCabe in the January, 1955, *Bridge World*. Whenever responder wants to take complete control of the bidding, he responds two no-trump. The opening two-bidder must re-bid three clubs and pass any bid responder makes. If responder's suit is clubs, he passes the three-club bid. Although the opponents know what you are doing, they cannot do much about it. If they enter the bidding, the misfit for offensive purposes will mean a very fine hand for defensive purposes. When responder has a balanced hand with a lot of points, he bids three no-trump and opener will pass or re-bid his major, depending upon the type of hand he has. When responder has a singleton in his partner's suit and a long, solid minor suit for tricks, he bids two no-trump in order to take control of the bidding, and his subsequent three no-trump bid will be final.

I disagree with Mr. McCabe on one minor point. He suggests a two no-trump response followed by a raise as a pre-empt and an absolute command for opener to pass. An immediate raise is a better pre-empt than a delayed raise, since it shuts out cheap bids at the three-level, and while

OPENER	RESPONDER
2 ♠	3 ♠

should be weaker than

OPENER	RESPONDER
2 ♠	2 NT
3 ♣	3 ♠

I think that neither should be used as an out-and-out pre-empt, since such use (if properly announced) destroys the deceptive features of a raise. I would rather make the opponents guess whether my raise was strong or weak. Bid two no-trump followed by a raise in spades with ♠ A x, ♡ K Q x, ◊ A x x x, ♣ J 10 x x, or ♠ K x x, ♡ x x x, ◊ A x, ♣ A J 10 x x. Raise to three spades immediately with ♠ Q x x x, ♡ x x x, ◊ A K J x, ♣ x x, or ♠ Q x x x, ♡ x x, ◊ K x x x x, ♣ x x.

Won't partner be confused if you raise both as a constructive bid and as a pre-empt? Possibly, but if your left-hand opponent has a good hand, he will usually show it by bidding or doubling. It is too dangerous for him to make a trap pass because he knows that opener will probably pass, too. If he does not bid over three spades, he will probably pass even when opener re-bids four spades, and the undoubled penalty will be less than the part-score (at least) to which the opponents are entitled. Look again at the second example hand in this section.

Two clubs is the only strong two-bid, and two diamonds is the bust response. Provided responder has at least one ace or king, he normally makes a positive response with six or seven points. A fairly weak four-card major should be bid in preference to no trump.

Arguments have arisen as to whether the artificial two-club bid loses a round of bidding or gains a round of bidding. The answer varies from hand to hand. When the two-club bidder has a powerful, balanced hand, perhaps with a good major suit, the two-club bid saves a round of bidding. After

OPENER	RESPONDER
2 ♣	2 ◇
2 ♠	

for example, responder can give distributional information, having already made a bust response, while if the opening bid were two spades, he would have to bid two no-trump and decide whether or not to show his suit at a higher level. When opener has a two-suiter, particularly in the minors, the artificial two-club bid loses a round of bidding. The two-club bid works out very badly on distributional hands when an opponent pre-empts because opener will not have shown his suit, or suits, and responder cannot make an intelligent decision. These considerations probably influenced Jacoby in recommending a two-club bid on strong hands lacking a singleton or void, while recommending bidding two of your best suit on distributional hands. The artificial two-club bid for old-fashioned game-demand bids is satisfactory, but nothing to rave about. The advantage is in having two diamonds, two hearts, and two spades for another purpose.

There is one more important advantage in the weak two-bid system as modified by Stayman. It makes no-trump bidding more accurate. In the old days, you were forced to open three no-trump with ♠ A Q J, ♡ K Q x, ◇ A K Q x, ♣ A J 10, or ♠ A x, ♡ K x, ◇ A K Q J x x x, ♣ K x. Opposite the first hand, partner should bid four spades with ♠ x x x x x x, ♡ x x, ◇ x, ♣ x x x x x, or five spades with ♠ K x x x x x, ♡ x x, ◇ x, ♣ Q x x x. Opposite the second hand, partner should pass. Nor could you afford *not* to open three no-trump with the second hand since a two-diamond opening and a two no-trump response would send the lead through your hand and decrease your chances for game considerably. When using the weak two-bid, you open three no-trump with a long minor suit, and open two clubs followed by three no-trump with the strong balanced hand.

Another problem with the old style of bidding was that the two no-trump opening had to cover too wide a range of strength. Now you can open two no-trump with 22 or 23 points or bid two clubs followed by two no-trump with 24 or 25 points. Or, if you prefer, the requirements for these bids may be lowered one point. Some players like to use an opening three no-trump bid as a wild pre-empt, for example, ♠ K x x, ♡ x x, ◇ x, ♣ A K Q x x x x. Admittedly, this throws the auction into a state of confusion. I do not like this gambling three no-trump bid, since partner never knows what to do, and you often get a bad result when your side has the balance of strength. If you save a three no-trump opening for hands *at least* as good as the following, partner will have some idea what to do when the opponents compete: ♠ K, ♡ A x, ◇ J x x, ♣ A K Q x x x x, or ♠ A Q, ♡ J x, ◇ K x x, ♣ A K Q J x x: He can make penalty doubles with just a smattering of strength or raise to four no-trump with ♠ A x x, ♡ K x x, ◇ Q x x x x, ♣ x x, or bid six clubs with ♠ A x x x, ♡ x, ◇ A x x x x, ♣ x x x. (He can tell from his hand that your suit is clubs.)

The Roth-Stone System

THE SYSTEM developed by Al Roth and Tobias Stone is the first new one to gain many followers since the Culbertson system won long ago. A new bid, a new style, a new way of evaluating hands do not constitute a new system. Roth-Stone has a new *approach*, and it is developed expressly for play at duplicate. If you want to learn the system, you had better get their book. However, if you don't want to play the Roth-Stone system, you may still have to play against it. Even if the Roth-Stone system should go completely out of style, a discussion of how to play against players who psych frequently or who use super-sound free bids would be worth while.

Roth-Stone opening bids are "sounder" than normal; their minimum is about one point higher on an average than what Goren would require. Consequently, there are few, if any, stop-on-the-button bids such as

OPENER	RESPONDER	or	OPENER	RESPONDER
1 ♡	1 ♠		1 ◇	1 ♡
2 ◇	3 ♡		1 NT	3 ♡
Pass			Pass	

So far, just the American style of bidding, exaggerated.

Psych or "lead-directing" opening bids are an integral part of their system, and many of the peculiarities of Roth-Stone are devices to keep from getting too high or in the wrong suit after a psychic opening bid. The lead-directing bid is made in first or second position with no more than six points and at least Q 10 x x of the suit bid. The theory is that subsequent bidding will expose the nature of these hands and partner will know what to lead on defense. Occasionally, these bids will be an aid to offensive bidding, as when responder has a powerful hand with A Q x x of his partner's suit. The opponents' bidding exposes the psych, but opener must have at least the king four-long, which takes care of three potential losers. Suppose opener bids one heart with ♠ x x, ♡ K J 10 x, ◇ x x x, ♣ J x x x and responder raises to three hearts with ♠ A x x, ♡ A Q x x, ◇ J x, ♣ Q 10 x x. No harm is done in getting a trick too high, since the opponents are cold for four spades and may have some difficulty in getting there.

Naturally, when one opens with a lead-directing bid, he passes at his first opportunity. Responder must make some unorthodox bids to avoid getting in trouble. With four of his partner's major, responder must raise immediately, except with less than ten points. Over one heart he bids three hearts with ♠ A x, ♡ A x x x, ◇ A K J x x, ♣ x x, rather than three diamonds. (In fact, three diamonds shows a completely different type of hand.) The point is that responder must raise hearts so that if opener passes with a psych, at least the partnership will be playing in the best trump suit. A two no-trump response shows around 21 points rather than 13 or 14.

SOUTH	WEST	NORTH	EAST
•1 ◇	Double	?	

♠ A 10 x x, ♡ Q 9 x x, ◇ x x, ♣ A J x: I recommend a pass, whether you are playing Roth-Stone or not. In any system, if the bidding continues

SOUTH	WEST	NORTH	EAST
1 ◇	Double	Pass	1 ♡
Pass	Pass	?	

you would double. But playing Roth-Stone (or Bulldog), you would pass if the take-out doubler bids again or if your left-hand opponent jumps the bidding, for then it would be extremely likely that partner's bid was a psych. You pass quietly, and if the opponents bid to game, you still pass. You are able to make the best opening lead and declarer is apt to misguess the location of a few key cards.

Another radical bid in the Roth-Stone system is the artificial one no-trump response to a major-suit opening bid. A raise shows at least 10 points, counting distributional values conservatively, while the bid of a new suit at the two-level shows 11 points and obligates responder to bid again. So over one heart, bid one no-trump with ♠ x, ♡ x x, ◇ A Q J x x x, ♣ J x x x, or ♠ x x, ♡ K J 10 x, ◇ A x x x, ♣ x x x. The one no-trump bid over a major is forcing (consequently you lose out when one no-trump is the proper contract) and opener re-bids in a very odd manner. Since his opening major-suit bid guarantees at least a five-card suit, he only re-bids the suit to show six. Otherwise, he may be forced to re-bid a three-card minor. Over a minor-suit opening bid, any four-card major, however weak, may be bid, and a three-card major is frequently bid. Opener cannot raise without extra values, even with four trumps.

OPENER	RESPONDER
1 ◇	1 ♡
?	

Bid one no-trump with ♠ x x, ♡ K 10 x, ◇ A x x x x, ♣ A K x. Besides being too weak a hand for a raise, the trump support is insufficient. Trump support must be at least K Q x. Bid one no-trump with ♠ A Q J x, ♡ A Q x x, ◇ x x x, ♣ x x. Not even a one-spade bid is permissible, since it would deny four-card heart support! The moral from these last examples is that when the Roth-Stoners open a minor and re-bid one no-trump over a major-suit response, it does not pay to reopen with doubtful hands, since the opponents may be in a very bad contract. Once you bid, opener can "correct" or make a delayed raise with distributional support.

Roth-Stone uses many jump bids as pre-empts. An opening two-bid is weak, *even two clubs!* Jump overcalls are very weak. It seems as though Roth-Stone has abandoned Culbertson's rule of 2 and 3 for pre-empts and substituted a rule of 3 and 4, with playing tricks estimated quite optimistically. A jump in a new suit by responder is pre-emptive, and it really shows a terrible hand!

SOUTH	WEST	NORTH	EAST
1 ♡	Pass	3 ♣	

on ♠ x x, ♡ x x, ◊ x x x, ♣ Q J 10 x x x;

SOUTH	WEST	NORTH	EAST
1 NT	Pass	3 ♡	

on ♠ x, ♡ K J x x x x, ◊ x x x, ♣ x x x;

SOUTH	WEST	NORTH	EAST
1 ◊	1 ♡	2 ♠	

on ♠ J 10 9 x x x, ♡ x x, ◊ x x, ♣ Q J x.

Some of these bids may seem a bit unusual, but the most amazing part of Roth-Stone to me is the powerhouse free bid. Responder must have 11 points to make a free bid at the one-level, even if he is a passed hand! And opener needs a tremendous hand for a free bid. There is no stretching or shading permitted.

SOUTH	WEST	NORTH	EAST
1 ◊	1 ♡	?	

♠ K J 10 x x, ♡ x, ◊ J x x, ♣ K x x x: Pass!

SOUTH	WEST	NORTH	EAST
1 ◊	Pass	1 ♠	2 ♣
?			

♠ A x x x, ♡ K x, ◊ A K x x, ♣ x x x: Pass again!

And what keeps the Roth-Stone players from being stolen blind? After two passes, a reopening bid may be made *with no extra values.* At low levels, a Roth-Stone player *must* reopen unless he expects to obtain a good penalty by passing. How can we old-timers take advantage of this peculiarity? By passing with good defense and bidding with poor defense, once our side has entered the auction. The normal way for North-South to reach two spades with the following hands is

SOUTH	WEST	NORTH	EAST
1 NT	2 ♡	2 ♠	Pass
Pass	Pass		

South: ♠ A Q x, ♡ K x x x, ◇ A Q x, ♣ J 10 x; North: ♠ K J x x x, ♡ x, ◇ x x x, ♣ Q x x x: North is too weak for a free two-spade response (which is forcing) in Roth-Stone, so the bidding must be

SOUTH	WEST	NORTH	EAST
1 NT	2 ♡	Pass	Pass
Double	Pass	2 ♠	

Opener must reopen! Responder usually has a little strength because the opponents stopped bidding. But if East understands the system, he can pass with a good hand and collect a juicy penalty. The following hand illustrates the sort of trap East can set.

```
                        NORTH
                     ♠ x x x x
                     ♡ 10 x x x
        WEST         ◇ x x          EAST
     ♠ x x           ♣ x x x        ♠ A J 10
     ♡ x x                          ♡ A K x x
     ◇ K x x                        ◇ Q 10 x x
     ♣ A K Q x x x    SOUTH         ♣ 10 x
                     ♠ K Q x x
                     ♡ Q J x
                     ◇ A J x x
                     ♣ J x
```

Neither side vulnerable.

SOUTH	WEST	NORTH	EAST
1 ◇	2 ♣	Pass	Pass
Double	Pass	2 ♡	Double
Pass	Pass	2 ♠	Double

And with good defense, North is down three.

Why doesn't this sort of thing happen to the Roth-Stone players often enough to make them change their system? The first reason is that not many players understand Roth-Stone bidding well enough to set traps. Another reason is that the Roth-Stone players are pretty sharp and might get a hunch to pass, despite the system. Roth-Stone is not a system that poor or inexperienced players can use. Also, there is the element of fear. East might trap with a borderline hand, but in this case, he has a sure game. What if South does not bid? One can hardly call the director to protest the board because opener refused to fall into a trap as he was supposed to. Nevertheless, tactics such as these should be effective against anyone who carries "protection" to an extreme. Another plot that should work (East-West vulnerable):

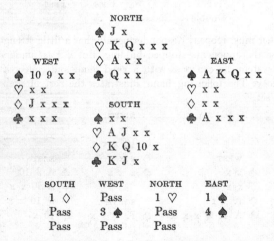

NORTH
♠ J x
♡ K Q x x x
◇ A x x
♣ Q x x

WEST
♠ 10 9 x x
♡ x x
◇ J x x x
♣ x x x

EAST
♠ A K Q x x
♡ x x
◇ x x
♣ A x x x

SOUTH
♠ x x
♡ A J x x
◇ K Q 10 x
♣ K J x

SOUTH	WEST	NORTH	EAST
1 ◇	Pass	1 ♡	1 ♠
Pass	3 ♠	Pass	4 ♠
Pass	Pass	Pass	

—300 for a top! If opener is not allowed to open one heart or raise to two hearts over one spade, he is fixed. Surely he has no double for four spades. And what can poor North think? With all the vulnerable bidding going on, his partner must have psyched. If this bidding is too rich for your blood, more prosaic sequences, such as an overcall followed by a skimpy raise, may be just as effective.

SOUTH	WEST	NORTH	EAST
1 ◇	1 ♠	Pass	2 ♠

creates problems for any North-South team, but if responder has refused to make a normal raise because of his requirements for free bids, he will have a very tough decision at the *three*-level with ♠ x x, ♡ K x x, ◇ K x x x, ♣ Q x x x, especially since Roth-Stone players *frequently* open three-card minors.

The "Bulldog" System[1]

COMPARED TO Roth-Stone, the Bulldog system is almost old-fashioned. Bulldog borrows many innovations from others, such as weak two-bids, weak no-trumps, pre-emptive responses, and lead-directing psychs, and there are many original ideas, such as the Rush Asking Bids. But the bread-and-butter bids, such as opening bids, single raises, and no-trump responses, retain their normal meaning. In fact, many of the Bulldog bids are more natural and less artificial than their Culbertson counterparts.

OPENER	RESPONDER
1 ♡	?

♠ x x x, ♡ A x, ◇ K J x x x, ♣ x x x: The orthodox bid is one no-trump, since two diamonds shows a better hand than this. (Roth-Stone requires a *much* better hand.) But the Bulldog theory is that a no-trump bid is undesirable with no strength in two unbid suits. If a no-trump contract is to be played, it should be played from the other direction. Besides, a two-diamond bid is superior to a no-trump response if opener has distributional support for diamonds. This may not be a clear-cut choice, even to a Bulldogger, but change the hand to ♠ x x, ♡ A x, ◇ K J x x x, ♣ x x x x, and he finds the thought of bidding one no-trump nauseating. (I agree.) In most bridge circles a sequence such as

OPENER	RESPONDER
1 ♡	2 ◇
2 NT	Pass

would even shock the kibitzers. But it is perfectly normal at

---

[1] Bulldog is a corruption of Bill-Doug. It was created by William (Bill) Hanna and Douglas (Doug) Steen.

Bulldog where the two-level responses are so light. A characteristic of Bulldog is that there are a large number of limit bids. Other players may agree that a bid is not forcing, while saying in the same breath that they would never pass. Bulldog players *do* pass.

It is my belief that no bridge ideas are the sole product of one or two minds. In the Los Angeles area, there has been a strong tendency toward major-suit raises with distributional support or with strength concentrated in aces and kings, despite the lack of adequate trump support. This tendency may have developed as a result of another one—only opening five-card majors or very strong four-card majors. Whatever the history may be, the better players raise one spade to two spades with ♠ 10 x x, ♡ A x x, ◊ A J x x, ♣ x x x, or ♠ x x x, ♡ A x, ◊ K x x x x, ♣ x x x. They would raise a one-heart response to three hearts with ♠ A x, ♡ Q J x, ◊ A K x x x, ♣ A x x. Bulldog may go farther than the local tendency in its preference for raising a major rather than bidding no-trump. One simply does not bid one no-trump over one club, one diamond or one heart with a doubleton spade or without some lead advantage. The ideal one no-trump response over one diamond is ♠ K x x, ♡ Q 10 x, ◊ x x x, ♣ Q 10 x x. With ♠ x x x, ♡ A x x, ◊ x x x, ♣ A x x x, the choice might well be one heart. The preference of a major-suit raise applies to opener as well. After opening one diamond, raise a spade response with ♠ J x x, ♡ A x, ◊ K Q x x, ♣ K x x x, or ♠ Q x x, ♡ A x x, ◊ A K x x, ♣ J x x.

Bulldog has adopted the weak no-trump. An opening no-trump bid, when not vulnerable, shows 12-14 points and a balanced hand, but vulnerable, 16-18 points are required. The Stayman convention is used with both the strong and the weak no-trump, with the point-count requirements for the responses adjusted accordingly. Nevertheless, it is difficult to find a 4-4 major-suit fit after an opening weak no-trump bid unless responder has a good hand. With a weak hand, he cannot risk Stayman because if he does not find the fit, he cannot guarantee a good play for two no-trump—or any other contract.

There are other problems. With a balanced 17- or 18-point hand, opener must often re-bid a three-card suit to avoid overbidding or underbidding. Suppose opener bids a minor and re-bids one no-trump over a suit response. This suggests a good hand (15-16 points) since one no-trump would normally be opened with 14 points or less. But perhaps the reason for not opening one no-trump despite a 13-point hand was that opener had a worthless doubleton. Probably Edgar Kaplan has the right idea. If you use the weak no-trump (which he uses whether vulnerable or not), you have to open one no-trump on all 12-14 point balanced hands—despite worthless doubletons or five-card heart suits. That way, a one no-trump re-bid will guarantee 15-17 points, and even a suit re-bid will suggest a better-than-minimum hand either in high cards or distribution. Kaplan believes that the difficulty of defending hands where nothing but no-trump is bid, plus the difficulty the opponents have in competitive bidding, compensates for the inferior contracts the weak no-trump causes you to reach. However, to get the maximum benefit from the weak no-trump, you have to make very light doubles of the opponents' overcalls. In other words, you have to be willing to shoot for tops when the occasions arise to make up for the bad boards you are bound to get. So unless you are very aggressive and very expert on defense, the weak no-trump will only bring you grief.

As for countermeasures, it pays not to be too aggressive in overcalling or doubling the weak no-trump in second position. An overcall should only be made with a very strong suit; a double should require about 15 points; and a two-club overcall should ask for a major-suit response. When the opportunity comes to re-open, tend to pass when the opponents are in one no-trump; tend to bid when they make a suit take-out.

Bulldog has attempted to define many bidding sequences as to point-count requirements and distribution that no one bothered to consider before. For example:

SOUTH	WEST	NORTH	EAST
1 NT	Pass	2 ♣	Double
?			

When the Stayman response is doubled, what should opener do? Bulldog says opener should bid something with two clubs, pass with three clubs, or redouble with four. The original feature of Bulldog which I like best is the Rush Asking Bid which will be discussed later.

Culbertson's Asking Bids

ELY CULBERTSON introduced an entirely new theory of slam bidding years ago, and later re-introduced it with improvements and refinements. Instead of both partners giving information which might or might not be useful, one partner asks and the other responds. The first asking bid is a new suit bid, usually at the four-level, after the trump suit is agreed upon. Without first- or second-round control, the response to the asking bid is a sign-off by returning to the agreed trump suit at the lowest level. With first- or second-round control, a positive response is given, showing outside controls at the same time. Repeat asking bids elicit more information. The asking bids work brilliantly on certain types of hands. But Culbertson makes asking bids a crutch rather than just another tool of the expert. He even suggests that the American experts would improve their slam bidding by dropping all the techniques developed in the last twenty years and relying upon asking bids almost exclusively. Take a typical sequence such as

OPENER	RESPONDER
1 ♢	1 ♠
3 ♠	?

The American expert can now show a second suit or a control or diamond support. He can make a strong slam try by carrying the bidding past the four-spade level, or he can be content with a mild slam try, leaving the initiative to his partner. Both players bid aggressively or conservatively, depending upon general strength, controls, and degree of fit. This sort of bidding is not easy; in fact, it is quite complicated, but it is the most accurate method of slam bidding yet developed. Using asking bids, the only way responder can ask about general strength is to jump to five spades. Any other bid results in his taking complete control of the bidding and leaving his partner no initiative. As recommended, asking bids crowd out too many natural bids. Furthermore, they are not practical. Where they seem to work most spectacularly, there would be no opportunity to use them in actual play. The following example hands are all from Culbertson's *Contract Bridge Complete*, published in 1954.

SOUTH: ♠ A K Q x x x, ♡ x x x, ◇ A x x x, ♣ —;
NORTH: ♠ 10 x x x x x, ♡ —, ◇ K x, ♣ 10 x x x x:

SOUTH	NORTH
1 ♠	3 ♠
4 ◇ ?	

The four-diamond bid asks for diamond control, and eight bids later South is able to bid the grand slam. Remarkable! First, congratulations to North for having the foresight to respond three spades. Had he carelessly bid four spades, there would not have been enough rounds of bidding left for the partnership to reach the cold grand slam. More remarkable is the fact that East and West, with 60 per cent of the high-card strength and excellent distribution, never entered the bidding. Perhaps they had a hunch that a club ruff would defeat five hearts or that they would be outbid anyway. Only once in a blue moon would North-South have five bidding rounds all to themselves with these particular hands.

SOUTH: ♠ A K Q x x, ♡ x, ◇ J x x x, ♣ A x x;
NORTH: ♠ 10 x x x x, ♡ A x x, ◇ A K Q x, ♣ x:

SOUTH	NORTH
1 ♠	3 ♠
4 ♣ ?	etc.

Seven spades is reached again. But let's give South a somewhat poorer hand, such as

(a) ♠ A K Q x x, ♡ x x, ◇ J x x, ♣ A x x, or
(b) ♠ A K Q x x, ♡ x, ◇ J x x x, ♣ Q x x.

Now opener would simply re-bid four spades after the three-spade response. It would not occur to him to make a slam try. Responder might bid again anyway; but if he should, the subsequent bidding would be guesswork. Let's see how the bidding would progress without asking bids. With the original hands the bidding might be:

OPENER	RESPONDER
1 ♠	2 ♢
3 ♢	3 ♡
3 ♠	5 ♠
6 ♣	6 ♡
7 ♠	

Perhaps this is the sort of bidding you dream up when you see both hands, but no fudging is necessary to reach six with the weaker hands *a* and *b*.

OPENER	RESPONDER	or	OPENER	RESPONDER
1 ♠	2 ♢		1 ♠	2 ♢
2 ♠	3 ♡		2 ♠	3 ♡
3 NT	5 ♠		4 ♢	5 ♠
6 ♠			6 ♠	

There must be something wrong with a system of bidding that is good for reaching seven but not good for reaching six.

OPENER	RESPONDER
1 ♡	1 ♠
4 ♣ ?	

♠ K Q x x, ♡ A K J x x, ♢ A x x, ♣ x: "If East responds four no-trump" (showing ace of spades and ace of clubs), "West has a biddable small slam," Culbertson says. Then he looks for other features necessary for the grand slam.

But suppose East held ♠ A x x x x, ♡ Q x, ♢ K x x, ♣ x x x (or much better). He must sign off with four spades since he has no first- or second-round club control. Although club control is not vital, West certainly cannot risk another bid over four spades. Culbertson refers to the normal sequence (a jump to three diamonds followed by a raise in spades), as dancing like a pig on a rope, but it will do the job. Asking bids put all your eggs in one basket. If partner continues to give the hoped-for response round after round, all is well. If he cannot, the consequences may be disastrous because there is not enough natural bidding upon which to base an intelligent decision.

The claim of asking bids is that specific, limited information is better than general information, and that grand slams, in particular, should not be bid without *certainty* of their success. However, it is not possible to eliminate "guesswork" in bidding, even with grand slams. Guesswork must be reduced to a minimum and based upon probabilities.

OPENER	RESPONDER
1 ♡	2 ♠
3 ◇	3 ♡
4 NT	5 ♠
?	

♠ x, ♡ K Q J x x x, ◇ A K x x x, ♣ x: Bid seven hearts. Of course, partner may have three little diamonds. But the probability of a diamond loser is negligible. Partner should have at least nine cards in the majors. If he has three of either minor, it is almost surely clubs. If he has three diamonds, he may have the queen. An asking bid in diamonds might be useful, but there is no crying need for it. In Culbertson's example, *responder* jumped to four no-trump over three diamonds and did not know what to do later. His trouble was that he was in too big a hurry to bid Blackwood. That sort of player will misuse whatever convention he adopts, but he should have a real field day with asking bids. Even with asking bids, some inferences are necessary.

OPENER	RESPONDER
1 ♠	2 ♠
4 ♣	5 ♣
6 ♠	

♠ A K Q x x, ♡ x, ◇ A x, ♣ K Q J x x: All opener knows is that responder's spade raise included the ace of clubs. The responding hand in Culbertson's example was ♠ J x x x, ♡ Q 10 x x, ◇ x x, ♣ A x x. The assumptions made by Culbertson were that responder held four spades and less than seven minor cards. I agree that if responder has four spades, the latter assumption is reasonable. But wouldn't responder bid two spades with ♠ J 10 x, ♡ Q 10 x x x, ◇ x x, ♣ A x x, or ♠ J 10 x, ♡ Q 10 x x, ◇ x x, ♣ A x x x? (I do not feel that the ten of spades is necessary, but adequate trump support makes this a "book" response.)

Better bidding would be

OPENER	RESPONDER
1 ♠	2 ♠
3 ♣	3 ♠
4 ♣	?

Now with the ace of clubs and four of either black suit, responder should bid five clubs, having already limited his hand with the three-spade bid. Opener would then bid six clubs, asking for a preference. With only three cards of both suits, responder would sign off at four spades rather than show the ace of clubs.

As I said earlier, I like the asking-bid principle. Asking bids would be all right if they did not interfere with normal bidding. If you like to use them, I suggest that you require that the first asking bid be a jump bid. Thus

OPENER	RESPONDER
1 ◇	1 ♠
4 ♣	

would be an asking bid with spades the agreed suit, as would

OPENER	RESPONDER
1 ♣	3 ♠
5 ◇	

Of course, this often takes away a round of bidding, but it is a round which could be more profitably employed otherwise.

Rush Asking Bids were originated by Courtland Rush, then of Los Angeles, and developed by William Hanna and Douglas Steen (Bulldog). Originally, the asking bid was an unusual jump, such as I suggested for Culbertson asking bids. The question asked was how many aces and kings partner had *outside* of the asked suit. Aces counted as two points and kings as one. A minimum response such as four diamonds over four clubs showed one point or less; four hearts would show two points, four spades three points, etc. After an opening two-club bid, the responses were geared higher so as to be able to show as little as one king outside the suit asked in.

Opener: ♠ A Q x x, ♡ K Q J x x x, ◇ —, ♣ K x x;
Responder: ♠ K x x x, ♡ x x, ◇ A x x x, ♣ A x x:

OPENER	RESPONDER
1 ♡	1 ♠
4 ◇	4 NT
6 ♠	

Or opener: ♠ A Q x x, ♡ K Q J x x x, ◇ —, ♣ K x x;
Responder: ♠ K x x x, ♡ A x, ◇ J x x x, ♣ A x x:

OPENER	RESPONDER
1 ♡	1 ♠
4 ◇	5 ◇
7 ♠	

Repeat asking bids were developed to discover third-round controls or strength in the asked suit. In order to use the repeat asking bids, it became necessary to make

OPENER	RESPONDER
1 ♠	3 ♠
4 ◇	

an asking bid instead of having to jump to five diamonds. The price of progress is high!

It would create a false impression to stop here after showing asking bids at their worst and cue bids at their best. Culbertson argued that cue-bidding, especially of the "promiscuous variety," is confusing even to experts. The following hand was bid by Howard Schenken and George Rapee and reported with approval by Goren. Certainly they are three of the best players to be found anywhere. And yet I wonder if their bidding was as good as it looks.

Rapee (opener):	Schenken:	RAPEE	SCHENKEN
♠ A K x x x	♠ x	2 ♠	3 ♡
♡ A x	♡ K Q x x x x	4 ♣	4 ♡
◇ A K x	◇ x x x	5 ◇	6 ♣
♣ A K J	♣ Q x x	7 NT	

The explanation was as follows: The four-heart bid must show at least a six-card suit headed by the king-queen, and the six-club bid showed a club honor, so Rapee could count 13 tricks, assuming a 3-2 heart break. Schenken could hardly have bid other than as he did. But did the four-heart bid guarantee K Q x x x x of hearts?

What would he bid with (a) ♠ x x, ♡ K Q 10 x x, ◇ Q x x, ♣ Q x x, or (b) ♠ x x, ♡ K Q J x x, ◇ J x x x, ♣ Q x, or (c) ♠ x, ♡ K J 9 x x x x, ◇ Q J x, ♣ x x? Perhaps he would not bid four hearts with the first hand, but I don't know what else he should bid. A four-spade preference would be *safe* enough but rather misleading. The four-club bid could easily create problems for responder, who might bid four hearts, not because he wanted to, but because he could not find a better bid. Over five diamonds I can't help wondering what Schenken would have bid without a club honor. More hearts? But wouldn't that show at least seven? Suppose opener had re-bid three spades to see what his partner's natural re-bid would be. Now with only a five-card heart suit and a smattering of strength in the minors, such as hand a, he would bid three no-trump. If he bid four hearts *over three spades*, opener *would have a right* to expect a good six-card suit. Then, just to make sure that the king or queen was not missing, he could bid five no-trump, the grand-slam force. Responder is likely to have a queen outside of hearts for his positive response, but it is not needed if the contract is seven *hearts*, since a long spade can be established by ruffs, or if worst comes to worst, there is always the club finesse to fall back on. As it happens, this came up in a total-point game (therefore, Rapee's seven no-trump bid gained an unimportant 160 points), but even at match-points, a seven-heart bid should earn a 70 per cent board. For that matter, a seven no-trump bid by opener would be a reasonable gamble at duplicate, since it would depend, at worst, upon a finesse.

The point of this example, whether or not you agree with my analysis, is that you should look at fancy bids with a critical eye. Whether it is a cue bid or an asking bid, ask yourself how the bidding would have progressed if a different response had been given, and be suspicious of forced bids at high levels. When partner is forced to bid, and when you leave him only one or two reasonable alternatives, don't assume that when he makes one of these bids he is showing additional features.

Psychic Bids

ANOTHER TREND in bridge is toward the modest psych. In the old days, psychs were of an audacious nature—like bidding on nothing to keep the opponents out of game, or bidding one's weakest suit in an effort to steal it from the opponents. This type of psych is very dangerous. It is unlikely to work against good competition, and likely to get you in trouble with a good partner. Consequently, audacious psychs have almost gone out of fashion. They are still used occasionally over a take-out double or over partner's pre-empt, but since everyone expects psychs in these two situations, the surprise element is missing. The psychs which have gained favor are the three-card major bids, used principally to inhibit unfavorable leads at no-trump.

OPENER	RESPONDER
1 ◇	?

♠ K J x, ♡ A x x, ◇ J x x, ♣ Q 10 x x: Instead of responding two clubs, followed by two no-trump over any minimum rebid, bid one heart. Hearts is the most likely weak spot, and a heart bid is fairly safe, since partner is unlikely to have good enough hearts to insist upon a heart contract. However, if he does, four hearts may be the best spot. A more dangerous psych is to respond one spade over an opening heart bid with ♠ x x x, ♡ 10 x x x x, ◇ Q x x, ♣ x x. If the opponents can make four spades, you may come out all right. If partner has a good hand, you will be sorry you bid at all.

Occasionally, a psych with a good hand is made to stop a sacrifice.

OPENER	RESPONDER
1 ♡	?

♠ A x, ♡ K x x x x, ◇ Q 10 x x, ♣ x x: At rubber bridge, you would toss science to the winds and bid four hearts. At duplicate, you don't want to bid four hearts and be down one; yet a temporary bid of two diamonds is likely to let the opponents get together in spades. They might attempt a four-spade sacrifice and surprise themselves by making it. A one-spade response followed by a raise in hearts is a fairly safe way to eat your cake and have it too.

An opening one-spade bid, third hand, with 11-13 points and a good three-card suit (like A J 9) has gained favor in the Los Angeles area, even among a few of the conservative old-timers. A one-spade bid is the toughest for the opponents to bid over, and it is hard for them to compete for a part-score. If they do buy the bid, a spade lead from partner will not hurt anything. If partner bids anything other than a spade raise, he will not be too disappointed. Even if he raises spades, the opponents are apt to misdefend and let you make an unmakable contract by not visualizing the trump situation.

Another old favorite that will be with us as long as the game of bridge, is the change-of-suit psych. A player bids one suit after another till the opponents get in the rhythm of doubling, whereupon he bids his real suit (seven or eight cards in length), and gets doubled again.

"Shooting"

OCCASIONALLY, one is justified in shooting, or trying for an unnatural result. Suppose you estimate that you have a 55 per cent score about three-quarters of the way through a tournament. Good sound bridge will not win, but two or three tops might do the job. I might add that I think you have a moral obligation to the other players not to shoot unless you have a fair score. Shooting is a little like eating another's food or using his property without permission—justifiable only in an emergency. The players who have earned good boards legitimately have a sort of vested interest in their scores and may properly resent your giving out 900-point sets to everyone who plays you late in the tournament. The type of shooting most people indulge in is rather futile, anyway. They play poker rather than bridge, and if they don't psych, they overbid outrageously. After a couple of hands of wild bidding, if a hand comes along which requires co-operation to bid, that co-operation will be missing because partnership confidence is gone.

Why do people invariably overbid when they are shooting? There are many better opportunities to shoot by underbidding. The typical player stretches when he has a close decision, even when he is not shooting, because of his rubber-bridge experience where optimism pays off. By taking the conservative choice in these situations, you can shoot without giving the opponents unreasonable odds. Just stop at three spades or play at a conservative minor-suit contract rather than attempting three no-trump on *close* hands, and hope that you will have one of the few plus scores. Never make a clear-cut underbid (or overbid) because of the possible cumulative effect of partner's doing the same thing. The best opportunity for shooting is in the play of the hands. When you see the cards, you can take calculated risks and adopt a play that is just as good as the ordinary play or only slightly inferior. This subject will be discussed in more detail in the section on play.

In championship play, usually two boards are played each round. I don't know why, but most players have an odd superstition that they need to get at least an average score each round. Thus, if they get a bad first board, they will go to any lengths to get a top on the other one. How often I can remember bidding a slam on the first board, only to have the opponents bid a slam on the second one, whether they had the cards for it or not! When you make up your mind to get a top at all costs, you are playing into your opponents' hands. It does not pay to try for tops or bottoms. You have a whole tournament to make up your points. Assume you are the one who gets the top on the first board. You have a psychological advantage over your opponents—most opponents, anyway. Let them shoot if they wish. You should play normal, sound bridge. The only way you might profitably deviate from normal is to bid a close game or slam if the opponents show an inclination to sacrifice. If you have just bid and made a difficult game or slam on the first board, the opponents are more likely to sacrifice against you when you bid strongly again.

Chapter 8

A Bridge Quiz

IN EACH CASE, you are South.

(1) ♠ 10 9 x, ♡ x, ◇ K Q J x x, ♣ K Q J x, neither side vulnerable:

SOUTH	WEST	NORTH	EAST
1 ◇	1 ♠	Double	Pass
Pass	2 ♡	Double	Pass
?			

(2) ♠ A K Q 10 x, ♡ A J x, ◇ x x, ♣ A K x:

SOUTH	WEST	NORTH	EAST
1 ♠	Pass	2 ♡	Pass
3 ♣	Pass	3 ♠	Pass
?			

(3) ♠ x, ♡ K Q x x, ◇ A Q 10 x x, ♣ Q 10 x:

SOUTH	WEST	NORTH	EAST
1 ♡	Pass	1 ♠	Pass
2 ◇	Pass	3 ♣	Pass
?			

(4) ♠ Q, ♡ A J 9 x x, ◇ K 10 x x x, ♣ A J:

SOUTH	WEST	NORTH	EAST
1 ♡	Pass	1 ♠	Pass
2 ◇	Pass	2 NT	Pass
?			

(5) ♠ x, ♡ A Q J 10 x, ◇ Q x x, ♣ J x x x, both sides vulnerable:

SOUTH	WEST	NORTH	EAST
Pass	1 ♠	Pass	2 ♠
Pass	Pass	2 NT	Pass
?			

(6) ♠ A x x, ♡ x x, ◇ A K x, ♣ K 10 x x x:

SOUTH	WEST	NORTH	EAST
1 ♣	1 ♠	3 ♣	3 ♠
?			

(7) ♠ K x x x, ♡ A 10, ◇ 10 x x, ♣ 10 x x x:

SOUTH	WEST	NORTH	EAST
Pass	Pass	1 ◇	1 ♡
1 ♠	2 ♡	3 ♣	Pass
?			

(8) ♠ 10 9 x, ♡ A x x x, ◇ A, ♣ A K Q x x:

SOUTH	WEST	NORTH	EAST
1 ♣	Pass	Pass	Double
?			

(9) ♠ A x x x, ♡ J x x, ◇ K J x x, ♣ x x, opponents vulnerable:

NORTH	EAST	SOUTH	WEST
1 ♡	Pass	2 ♡	4 ♠
Pass	Pass	?	

(10) ♠ A Q x, ♡ A K J x x, ◇ Q 10 x x, ♣ x:

SOUTH	WEST	NORTH	EAST
1 ♡	Pass	2 ◇	Pass
?			

(11) ♠ A K Q J x x, ♡ Q 9 x, ◇ K x x, ♣ A:

SOUTH	WEST	NORTH	EAST
1 ♠	Pass	2 ◇	Pass
?			

(12) ♠ A Q J x, ♡ 10 9 x x x, ◇ Q x x, ♣ x:

NORTH	EAST	SOUTH	WEST
1 ◇	2 ♣	?	

(13) ♠ K J, ♡ A J 10 x, ◇ x x, ♣ 9 x x x x, opponents vulnerable:

NORTH	EAST	SOUTH	WEST
1 ♣	1 ♠	2 ♡	2 ♠
3 ♣	3 ♠	3 NT	4 ♠
Double	Pass	?	

(14) ♠ K x, ♡ A K Q J 10 x x x, ◇ —, ♣ K x x:

SOUTH	WEST	NORTH	EAST
2 ♡	Pass	3 NT	Pass
?			

(15) ♠ x x, ♡ Q x x x, ◇ K 9 8 7 x, ♣ x x, neither side vulnerable:

EAST	SOUTH	WEST	NORTH
Pass	Pass	1 ◇	Pass
1 ♠	Pass	Pass	1 NT
Double	?		

(16) ♠ —, ♡ K J 10 x x, ◇ A K Q x, ♣ Q x x x:

SOUTH	WEST	NORTH	EAST
1 ♡	Pass	1 ♠	Pass
2 ◇	Pass	3 ♣	Pass
4 ♣	Pass	4 ♡	Pass
?			

(17) ♠ K x x, ♡ K J 10 x x x, ◇ K x, ♣ J x:

SOUTH	WEST	NORTH	EAST
Pass	Pass	1 ♣	1 ◇
2 ♡	Pass	Pass	3 ◇
?			

(18) ♠ x, ♡ x, ◇ A K Q J 10 x x x, ♣ x x x:

SOUTH	WEST	NORTH	EAST
1 ◇	1 ♠	Double	Pass
?			

(19) ♠ J, ♡ A 9 x x, ◇ x x x x, ♣ A K x x, both sides vulnerable:

NORTH	EAST	SOUTH	WEST
1 ♠	2 ♡	Double	Pass
2 ♠	Pass	?	

(20) ♠ A K x, ♡ x x x, ◇ K 10 x x, ♣ Q x x, opponents vulnerable:

SOUTH	WEST	NORTH	EAST
Pass	1 ◇	2 ◇	Pass
2 ♠	Pass	3 ♠	Pass
?			

(21) ♠ x x x, ♡ 10 x x x x x, ◇ 9 x x, ♣ Q, you are vulnerable:

WEST	NORTH	EAST	SOUTH
1 ◇	Pass	1 ♠	Pass
3 ◇	Double	Pass	?

(22) ♠ K Q x x, ♡ A 10 x, ◇ x, ♣ K Q 10 x x, you are vulnerable:

SOUTH	WEST	NORTH	EAST
1 ♣	Pass	1 NT	2 ♡
?			

(23) ♠ x x, ♡ A J 10 9 x, ◇ x, ♣ J 10 x x x:

NORTH	EAST	SOUTH	WEST
1 ◇	1 ♠	Pass	2 ♠
2 NT	Pass	?	

(24) ♠ 10 9 x, ♡ —, ◇ A x x, ♣ A K J x x x x:

NORTH	EAST	SOUTH	WEST
1 ♠	Pass	3 ♣	Pass
3 ♡	Double	?	

(25) ♠ x x, ♡ K x x x, ◇ A x x, ♣ A J x x:

EAST	SOUTH	WEST	NORTH
1 ♡	Pass	1 ♠	Pass
2 ♡	Pass	Pass	2 ♠
Pass	?		

(26) ♠ A K x x, ♡ K Q x, ◇ K 10 x x, ♣ J x:

SOUTH	WEST	NORTH	EAST
1 ◇	Pass	2 ♣	Pass
2 NT	Pass	4 ◇	Pass
4 NT	Pass	5 ◇	Pass
?			

(27) ♠ A 10 8 x x, ♡ J x x, ◇ A K 10 9, ♣ x, both sides vulnerable:

EAST	SOUTH	WEST	NORTH
1 ♣	Double	1 ♡	Double
1 NT	?		

(28) ♠ x, ♡ K J x x, ◇ K J 9 x x, ♣ A K Q:

EAST	SOUTH	WEST	NORTH
1 ♠	Double	3 ♠	Pass
Pass	Double	Pass	4 ♡
4 ♠	?		

(29) ♠ Q 10 x x, ♡ A Q x x x, ◇ x, ♣ Q x x, neither side vulnerable:

NORTH	EAST	SOUTH	WEST
Pass	1 ♣	Pass	1 ◇
Pass	1 NT	?	

(30) ♠ K x x x, ♡ A x x, ◇ x x, ♣ Q 10 9 x, opponents vulnerable:

WEST	NORTH	EAST	SOUTH
1 ◇	Pass	1 ♡	Pass
2 ♡	Pass	Pass	?

(31) ♠ Q 9 x x x, ♡ K 10, ◇ K 10 x x, ♣ x x x, both sides vulnerable:

WEST	NORTH	EAST	SOUTH
1 ◇	Pass	1 ♡	Pass
2 ♡	Pass	Pass	?

(32) ♠ K Q 9 x x, ♡ x x x, ◇ 10, ♣ K Q x x, neither side vulnerable:

SOUTH	WEST	NORTH	EAST
Pass	Pass	1 ◇	Double
?			

(33) ♠ x, ♡ Q x x, ◇ Q 10 x, ♣ A K J 10 x x:

SOUTH	WEST	NORTH	EAST
1 ♣	1 ♠	2 ♡	2 ♠
3 ♣	3 ♠	3 NT	4 ♠
?			

(34) ♠ x, ♡ K J x x, ◇ K x, ♣ A Q J x x x, you are vulnerable:

EAST	SOUTH	WEST	NORTH
1 ♠	Double	Pass	3 ♡
Pass	4 ♡	4 ♠	Double
Pass	?		

(35) ♠ x, ♡ A K x x, ◇ Q x x, ♣ K J x x x:

WEST	NORTH	EAST	SOUTH
1 ♠	Pass	Pass	Double
2 ◇	Double	2 ♠	?

(36) ♠ A J, ♡ Q 10 x, ◇ K x x x, ♣ 9 8 x x, opponents vulnerable:

EAST	SOUTH	WEST	NORTH
1 ♣	Pass	1 ◇	Double
2 ♣	Double	Pass	2 ♡
Pass	?		

(37) ♠ x x x, ♡ x x x, ◇ Q x x x x, ♣ x x, neither side vulnerable:

WEST	NORTH	EAST	SOUTH
3 ♡	Double	Pass	?

(38) ♠ K J 10 x x x, ♡ A x, ◇ Q x, ♣ K x x, opponents vulnerable:

NORTH	EAST	SOUTH	WEST
1 ♡	Double	Redouble	Pass
Pass	2 ◇	?	

(39) ♠ 10 9 x, ♡ A Q, ◇ A K 9 x x x, ♣ 10 x:

NORTH	EAST	SOUTH	WEST
1 ♣	2 ♠	Double	Pass
3 ♣	Pass	3 ◇	Pass
3 NT	Pass	?	

(40) ♠ x x x, ♡ A K J 10, ◇ A K 10 x, ♣ J x, you are vulnerable:

WEST	NORTH	EAST	SOUTH
Pass	Pass	1 ♡	Pass
1 ♠	2 ♣	2 ♠	?

(41) ♠ Q J x, ♡ Q, ◇ Q J 9 x x, ♣ A Q 10 x:

NORTH	EAST	SOUTH	WEST
Pass	1 ◇	Pass	2 ♣
2 ◇	Double	?	

(42) ♠ A K, ♡ A K Q x, ◇ K J 9 x x, ♣ K x:

EAST	SOUTH	WEST	NORTH
3 ♠	3 NT	Pass	4 ♡
Pass	4 ♠	Pass	5 ♣
Pass	?		

(43) ♠ A K x, ♡ K x x x x, ◇ A K Q x, ♣ x:

	SOUTH	WEST	NORTH	EAST
	1 ♡	1 ♠	2 ♠	Pass
	3 ◇	Pass	4 NT	Pass
	5 ◇	Pass	6 ♡	Pass
	?			

(44) ♠ x, ♡ x, ◇ A K Q x x x x x, ♣ x x (strong two-bids):

NORTH	EAST	SOUTH	WEST
2 ♡	Pass	?	

(45) ♠ 10 x x x x, ♡ x x, ◇ K x x, ♣ x x x:

NORTH	EAST	SOUTH	WEST
1 NT	Pass	Pass	2 ♡
Double	Pass	?	

(46) ♠ K x x x, ♡ J 9 x x, ◇ J x, ♣ K x x, both sides vulnerable:

NORTH	EAST	SOUTH	WEST
1 NT	Double	Pass	2 ◇
Pass	Pass	?	

In the remaining hands, you are using the weak no-trump bid (12-14 points).

(47) ♠ K x x, ♡ 10 x x, ◇ K x x, ♣ Q x x x:

NORTH	EAST	SOUTH	WEST
1 NT	2 ♡	?	

(48) ♠ K x x, ♡ 10 x x, ◇ K x x, ♣ Q x x x:

NORTH	EAST	SOUTH	WEST
1 NT	Double	Pass	2 ♡
Pass	Pass	?	

(49) ♠ x x x, ♡ x x, ◇ K J 9 x, ♣ A 9 8 x:

NORTH	EAST	SOUTH	WEST
1 NT	2 ♠	?	

(50) ♠ K Q 10 x x, ♡ x x, ◇ x x, ♣ Q 10 9 x:

NORTH	EAST	SOUTH	WEST
1 NT	Double	2 ♠	3 ♣
Pass	Pass	?	

Answers to Quiz Questions

(1) Bid two spades, which is the cheapest and most flexible bid available, assuming that you decide to pull the double. Partner will not have much support for either minor suit at the three-level after he has doubled both majors. It is possible that the opponents were hopelessly out on a limb, but it is too dangerous to leave the double in with your hand. In addition to the fact that you have no quick tricks, your spade length means that partner's spade tricks will go to waste since East will have a singleton spade at most. Look at it this way: Wouldn't you rather try for eight tricks at spades than for seven tricks at hearts? Or to take a more pessimistic view, wouldn't you rather try for seven tricks at spades than for six tricks at hearts? In actual play, hands like these are a test of ethics as well as judgment. It is extremely difficult not to be influenced by the enthusiasm of partner's double.

(2) Bid five spades. It is tempting to bid five hearts so that if partner has the king of diamonds, it cannot be led through. However, a five-heart bid would guarantee a singleton diamond, while a five-spade bid asks for diamond control. You hope that partner will bid five no-trump with the king of diamonds so that you can raise to six no-trump.

(3) Bid three no-trump. A three-diamond bid would be both pointless and misleading. Partner might take you to four hearts, figuring you for 5-5 or 6-5 distribution.

(4) Bid three no-trump. Again a three-diamond bid would be misleading; it would show your distribution all right, but would suggest a hand of the following type: ♠ x, ♡ K Q x x x, ◇ A K x x x, ♣ x x, or even ♠ —, ♡ A K x x x, ◇ K x x x x x, ♣ x x. Responder would and should pass the three-diamond bid with ♠ A J x x x, ♡ x, ◇ Q J x, ♣ K 10 x x. In other words, the three-diamond bid should show a lack of enthusiasm for a no-trump contract. With a hand well

suited for no-trump, containing fillers in the black suits, the proper bid is to raise to three no-trump.

(5) Bid three clubs. It is tempting to bid three hearts despite the fact that partner has asked you to bid a minor suit, and perhaps you would risk a heart bid if you could do so at the two-level. When you consider the type of hand partner probably has (♠ x x x x, ♡ x, ◊ K J x x, ♣ K Q x x), you can see the danger of spade forces in a heart contract.

(6) Bid five clubs. If partner has a singleton spade, as the opponents' bidding tends to indicate, you should have an excellent play, if not a lay-down, for five clubs and a very poor play for three no-trump.

(7) Bid three diamonds. A pass would be very conservative; partner's three-club bid probably should be considered forcing. On the other hand, a club raise would be too aggressive.

(8) Redouble. Even though partner has passed, you may have the better hands. A one-heart bid would prevent partner from bidding a five-card spade suit, and it would not enable him to co-operate with you later in the bidding. Suppose that partner holds ♠ x x x x x, ♡ K x x, ◊ x x x, ♣ x x. If you redouble, partner will bid as high as two spades if necessary, and he will double if the opponents bid three diamonds. If you only bid one heart instead of redoubling, you will have to bid the whole hand by yourself.

(9) Pass unless your partner has never psyched in his life. If you consider the bidding and the vulnerability carefully, you will realize that things are just too good to be true. You would have doubled a two-spade bid.

(10) Bid two spades. Three diamonds is an underbid, and four diamonds does not show where your strength lies. How can you tell partner to bid a slam with ♠ K x x , ♡ x x, ◊ A K x x x, ♣ x x x, but to stop short with ♠ x x x, ♡ x x, ◊ A K x x x, ♣ K x x? Only by bidding two spades, followed by a vigorous diamond raise.

(11) Bid three hearts. The same principle is involved here as in the last problem. You wish to reach a slam if partner has ♠ x x, ♡ K x x, ◊ A Q J x x, ♣ x x x, but not if he has ♠ x x, ♡ x x x, ◊ A Q J x x, ♣ K x x. Unless something startling takes place, you should bid just four spades next round.

If partner has a close decision whether or not to bid over four spades, he will evaluate strength in your suits more highly than strength in an unbid suit.

(12) Bid two diamonds. Then if partner can bid again, you should have an easy decision. If you bid two hearts or two spades, you may lose control of the bidding. For example, over two hearts or two spades, suppose partner re-bids two no-trump. You can hardly afford to leave him there; and any bid you make at this stage, even three diamonds, is forcing.

(13) From the discussion of the last problem, you might infer that I disapprove of the two-heart bid. Not at all! This time the excellent club fit provides a safety factor if you don't find a fit in hearts. If partner has as little as ♠ x x, ♡ K Q x x, ◇ x x x, ♣ A K x x, or ♠ x x x, ♡ K Q x, ◇ x x, ♣ A K x x x, you would have a good play for four hearts, which could never be reached unless you bid hearts at this point. Even if partner has a somewhat better hand, including a biddable heart suit, a spade raise on your left would effectively gum up the works since partner could not bid hearts at the three-level. To get back to the original problem, should you leave the double in? I think you should. It is true that partner's club strength will be wasted, but his double must show something besides solid clubs. He should have a trick in diamonds, and he should be short in hearts. You can reasonably expect two heart tricks and a trump trick with your own hand. Wouldn't you be ashamed of yourself for pulling the double if partner should have something like ♠ x, ♡ x x, ◇ A Q 10 x, ♣ A Q J 10 x x, which is just about what you should expect from his bidding? As for your club length, partner should have guessed that when you bid three no-trump rather than doubling the vulnerable opponents, and in any event, his double must show strength outside of clubs.

(14) Bid four hearts. It is almost inconceivable that partner will pass this bid or that you will miss a cold slam if he does. The important thing is to make a minimum bid at this point in order to avoid reaching a hopeless grand slam through a misunderstanding of some kind.

(15) Bid two diamonds. Your hand is too weak to stand one no-trump doubled, and partner is marked with diamond length and strength; otherwise why would he pass the one-diamond bid with a good hand? Similarly, if the bidding had gone

EAST	SOUTH	WEST	NORTH
Pass	Pass	1 ◇	Pass
1 ♡	Pass	1 NT	Double
Pass	?		

you should bid two diamonds.

(16) Pass. Partner has shown a good hand by this sequence of bidding, but the hands will not fit. You have too much strength in diamonds opposite partner's singleton or void.

(17) Pass. You have told your story. As it happens, partner has a good double of three diamonds.

(18) Bid two diamonds. Resist the temptation to bid more just because you have eight solid tricks. When so many high cards are missing, the bidding is extremely unlikely to die at two diamonds, and partner would be justified in expecting some side strength if you jump. Over three diamonds, he would surely bid at least six with ♠ Q J 9 8 x, ♡ A Q x, ◇ x x x, ♣ A x.

(19) I recommend a three-heart bid. According to the "book," the three-heart bid says that you want to play hearts despite the opponent's bid. In other words, you would be exposing a probable psych. The trouble is that the opponents do not psych vulnerable overcalls at the two-level very often, and you seldom get the type of hand with which you want to play the opponent's suit at a high level. It is more useful to bid three hearts in this position as an "I've shot my wad" bid, meaning that you have too much strength to pass but that whatever partner bids now is likely to be dropped. If you don't like the three-heart bid, your best alternative is a raise to three spades. A two no-trump re-bid with a single heart stopper would be very dangerous and misleading.

(20) The answer depends upon the personalities of the players. You should realize at once that somebody does not have his bid. More than likely it is partner. Without the king of diamonds, you would have no clue. It would be almost impossible for you to stay out of a slam with ace-king of spades and queen of clubs. But that king of diamonds is just one high card too many. When I held this hand, I naively bid four clubs followed by five spades over partner's four-spade bid. Partner held ♠ Q x x x x x, ♡ J 10 x x x, ◇ —, ♣ x x, and he was

rather disgusted that I had not passed three spades or at least passed four spades. His bidding looked dangerous on the surface, but when I had passed originally, it seemed to him that the opponents must be cold for game. His bid might gum up the works for the opponents or enable us to reach a good sacrifice. Surely the opponents' vulnerable bidding and my hand would give me a clue as to what was going on. The opponents remained unpredictably passive until we reached the five-level, which made the psych a little harder to catch. Of course partner could have passed my two-spade bid, but that would have given the whole show away too early.

(21) Pass. The only thing that worries you is how partner can make a penalty double when you have three diamonds. However he *has* made a penalty double; it can't be anything else. How could partner possibly make a take-out double at this level with unfavorable vulnerability when responder's hand is unlimited? Partner holds ♠ J 10 9 x, ♡ x, ◇ K J 8 x, ♣ A K 10 x. He reached the reasonable conclusion that he could not afford to trap any longer since responder could hardly have another bid.

(22) Double. This is simply a matter of judgment. There is a good chance to beat the opponent's two tricks, since partner shows a balanced hand with nine or ten points.

(23) Bid three spades. A three-heart bid should show a six-card suit to the queen-jack with no side strength; in other words, it would be a sign-off bid. Over your three-spade bid, partner will bid three no-trump with ♠ A Q x, ♡ x x, ◇ A K J 10 x, ♣ K Q x, but he should bid four hearts with his heart and club holdings reversed. What can your three-spade bid mean unless it is a club-heart two-suiter with a fair hand?

(24) Bid four clubs. A preference bid of three spades would be misleading. Partner might figure that your jump shift was based upon strong spade support instead of a long club suit. Also the four-club bid shows that you have a very unbalanced hand; otherwise you would pass in order to give partner a chance to bid three no-trump. (In a sequence such as this, a pass to three hearts does not guarantee heart support. Only a redouble tells partner that you want to play the hand in hearts.) It happened that partner held ♠ A K Q J x, ♡ A

Q x x, ◇ J x, ♣ Q x, which was more than he actually needed to take control with Blackwood and bid seven no-trump, knowing that the queen of clubs would solidify the long suit.

(25) Pass, although a raise to three spades could be right. In rubber bridge, partner would not bid two spades without a good hand. The risk would not be worth while. Consequently when he does bid, you must raise. But in duplicate he may hold ♠ A Q 8 x x x, ♡ x, ◇ 10 9 x x x, ♣ Q x. It is not likely that the spade response on your left was a psych, for two reasons: first, psychs are infrequent enough that it does not pay to assume a bid is a psych unless the evidence is pretty strong; second, psychs are most often made when responder has a good fit for opener's suit. Because of your heart holding, it seems unlikely that responder had a good heart fit.

(26) Pass. You have too much of your strength in the wrong spot to be interested in a slam. Don't adopt the attitude that you have to bid a slam because you have passed the three no-trump (or four no-trump) level. It is true that you will probably lose to the pairs playing three no-trump, but you can at least beat the pairs who bid six and fail to make it. Perhaps partner's hand is so freakish that no one else will play three no-trump either.

(27) Pass. This is automatic. You can't double one no-trump since you have a minimum take-out double and no club strength. But you should not get in partner's way. Perhaps he can double. In any event, you have already described your hand, and there is no excuse for bidding at this stage.

(28) Pass. Again the same principle is involved. Your previous bidding described this hand perfectly. You don't think the opponents can make four spades, and you don't think partner can make five hearts, but he knows this without your telling him again. If you pass, partner will bid five hearts with ♠ x x, ♡ A x x x x x, ◇ x x, ♣ x x x, or five clubs with ♠ x, ♡ Q x x x x, ◇ x x, ♣ J x x x x, but if you should double again, he would pass. Even if you and your partner both pass and you defeat the opponents a trick or two, you shouldn't have a bad board. For that reason, a double is a bad percentage bid.

(29) Bid two diamonds. Your distribution makes a competitive bid a good gamble, since your previous pass will prevent partner from being misled. Of course there is some risk in enter-

ing the bidding at all, but the main point is that you should bid two diamonds if you bid at all. A double would not show this type of hand; it would indicate a good balanced hand with club strength. A two-diamond bid should be easier for partner to read than a two-club bid, since partner should have a few diamonds.

(30) Double. This is a safer and more flexible bid than two spades with a weak spade suit. With such well-placed strength, I would re-open with a double even if vulnerable.

(31) Pass. Too much of your strength is in the opponents' suits for a reopening bid. Partner has a good spade fit (K J 10 x), but even so, both red kings are in the wrong spot, and two spades is down two. Also, because of the position of your red kings, the opponents are cold for four hearts.

(32) Pass. By passing now and bidding your spades later, you show a pretty good hand. Furthermore, if the opponents unsuspectingly bid to the two-level, you should have a good double with your shortage of diamonds and king-queens behind dummy's aces.

(33) Pass. Incidentally, I don't like the three-club bid at all. My preference is for a raise to three hearts or a pass. But to get back to the problem, it is very bad to "double for partner" in a situation like this. If one of the opponents is short in clubs, you have almost no defensive strength; furthermore your three-card heart holding cuts down your defensive possibilities in hearts. While you don't need strength in spades for a double, a double should show strength *in at least two suits*. Partner has bid strongly, and perhaps he will double four spades. But *you* certainly should not double since you have *less* defensive strength than partner can reasonably expect. (See hand 13.)

(34) Pass. Partner should not double in this spot without a reason. Either he has part of his strength in spades, or he has a four-card heart suit with a minimum hand for his previous bidding. With something like ♠ x x, ♡ A x x x x, ◇ A x, ♣ 10 x x x, he should pass, and of course you would bid five hearts.

(35) Double. Apparently you are doubling for partner as I advised you not to do in problem 33. But there is a difference. Your double of one spade was a take-out double; consequently

you are hardly likely to have much strength in spades. The double merely confirms a good hand—good enough for a take-out double in second position. If you pass, partner may figure you for a nine- or ten-point hand and fail to double even with spade strength and a fair hand. The double serves a purpose. It shows *more* defensive strength than partner would have a right to expect without the double.

(36) Bid four hearts. Partner must have a weak hand to pull the double, but even so, he should have an excellent play for game because your strength is so well placed. His hand is ♠ Q 10 x x, ♡ K 9 x x x x, ♢ A x, ♣ x. Could he conceivably have less?

(37) Pass. This is your only chance for a plus score. If you can make four diamonds, partner will raise you to game, and you will be down one. Even at rubber bridge, I believe it pays to pass with this type of hand and hope for a small plus score rather than a certain minus (and possibly a severe penalty), but in duplicate, the pass is right even if the opponents make their contract 40 per cent of the time.

(38) Pass. The opponents may be out on a limb. If partner is unable to double, he must bid something, and you can still bid spades (but over two hearts you should bid three spades). Even with the vulnerability reversed, I think the pass is correct in order to show a somewhat balanced hand with scattered strength.

(39) Bid five clubs. Whatever you do, don't pass. Partner almost surely has a singleton spade. He also has a good club suit and the king of hearts, but he is depending upon you to stop spades. Since you doubled spades without a stopper, you must not allow partner to play no-trump.

(40) Bid five clubs. It is difficult to imagine how the other players have found their bids, but one thing is certain: partner has a good club suit for his vulnerable overcall. Another thing seems almost certain to me: the opponents have nine spades between them; responder could not have scraped up a bid without a five-card suit, and opener could not have had enough high cards to raise except for the fact that he had four-card support. So three no-trump is hardly the right spot for you. On the other hand, partner cannot lose more than one club trick and one spade trick at a club contract.

(41) Redouble. Theoretically a redouble means that you want partner to stay put at two diamonds, but one never gets the proper hand for such a bid. It is more useful to use the redouble merely as a strength-showing bid. Partner, with his void in diamonds, will surely pull himself to his longer major suit. If he bids two hearts, you simply bid two spades, having already indicated a good hand by your redouble. If partner bids two spades, raise to three spades.

(42) Just bid five hearts. What did you have a right to expect of partner for his four-heart bid? A six-card heart suit, since it would have been too dangerous for him to bid a five-card suit when your three no-trump bid might have been based upon a long minor suit with little or no heart support. But what does partner need in high cards for his four-heart bid? Absolutely nothing. In fact, the poorer his hand, the more reason for him to bid. With ♠ x x, ♡ 10 x x x x x, ◇ x x, ♣ x x x, particularly with ♠ x x, ♡ x x x x x x x, ◇ x, ♣ x x x x, his hand would look pretty hopeless at no-trump, but with queens in the minor suits, he would pass, hoping that those queens would solidify your hand. What is the purpose of this discussion? To make you realize that partner could be without high cards; consequently when you are willing to push the bidding to the five-level opposite a hand with no high cards, then partner must realize that an ace is all that he needs for a slam. Remember that an ace is more than a trick. It is a control and an honor which will promote honors in your hand. On the other hand, the five-club bid might not show the ace. You could not blame partner for having bid five clubs over four spades with a two-suiter (♠ x, ♡ 10 x x x x x, ◇ x, ♣ Q J x x x). Some players would bid five clubs; others would bid five hearts, figuring that hearts were agreed upon. Experts could disagree upon the proper bid over four spades with a two-suiter. But *no* good player with an ace in his hand would fail to bid six hearts over your return to five hearts.

(43) Bid six no-trump. It is not often that it pays to override partner's decision on a hand of this type. But what can he have for his bidding? Remember, he is missing an ace. Can he have *less* than ♠ —, ♡ A Q x x x, ◇ x x x, ♣ K Q J x x?

(44) Bid four no-trump. There is nothing you can accom-

plish by delaying. More than likely, partner is void in diamonds. You are going to place the contract in six diamonds or seven diamonds depending upon how many aces partner shows. Over seven diamonds, partner might be able to bid seven no-trump with five or six top tricks and a diamond. However, the important thing is to get the four no-trump bid in before something disastrous happens. Like what? Like the opponents' getting together for a sacrifice or at least crowding you (with partner's help perhaps) past the four no-trump level. In actual play, partner held ♠ A x, ♡ A Q J 10 x x, ◊ —, ♣ K Q 10 x x. Getting to, and buying the bid at, six diamonds was worth a cold top. West had a good spade suit but not good enough to bid for the first time at the five-level.

(45) Pass. Partner's double is for penalties. He holds ♠ A x, ♡ K Q 9 x, ◊ A J x, ♣ K J x x.

(46) Double. You should have an excellent play for a one-trick set, possibly more, and not too good a play for game. West's bid was a rescue bid, and he may not have even a good suit. It is less dangerous to double West's two-diamond bid (which is not a voluntary bid on his part) than to double an immediate two-diamond overcall by East, who would be more apt to have a long, solid suit. If the opponents had not been vulnerable, you should have redoubled on the previous round. If partner could not double two diamonds after your redouble, you would bid two no-trump rather than try for a two-trick set.

(47) Pass. This is slightly too close to double. The high-card strength is approximately evenly divided, with East's strength over partner's, and East should have a good suit. Furthermore, if he goes down, your plus score will probably be all right, since you have no assurance that you can make anything your way or even that the hand will be opened at the other tables.

(48) Double. This time there is less chance of a six-card trump suit than in the previous example. The double is close, but you figure to beat two hearts.

(49) Double, because of your minor-suit spot cards and the possibility of a heart ruff. From this and the previous example, you can see that I believe in close doubles when you play the weak no-trump. As I said before, you have to be aggressive to make the bid pay off.

(50) Pass. You are sure of beating three clubs, but you don't have much defense against the red suits. It looks as though your bidding has maneuvered the opponents into a very bad contract. Since you couldn't expect to make much your way, be content to settle for a plus score (it may be 150 points). With ♠ K Q 10 x x, ♡ Q x, ◇ Q x, ♣ x x x x, you would double, because this time you wouldn't care if the opponents should run out. You would double any bid at the three-level with this hand.

Chapter 9

Is Duplicate Really Different?

WHY ARE there always one or two rubber-bridge games going on in some corner of the club while an important tournament is being held? Let's ask one of the better players why he is not downstairs competing for glory.

First, he mentions a personal quarrel he had with some officer of the Bridge League back in 1939. Since he does not know us very well, he refrains from commenting upon the worthlessness of masterpoints in general, or that Mrs. Jones, with over 500 points, can't follow suit. Finally he gets around to his real reason for preferring rubber bridge, or for not liking duplicate.

"I was playing a four-spade contract at one of those Friday night rat races a few months ago. The dummy had four spades to the king-nine and I had five to the ace-ten. Since I had two losers outside the trump suit, I naturally took the safety play, a first-round ducking finesse. I got a cold bottom! Every other declarer had banged down the ace and king, making five. Now you know that isn't bridge. Any system of scoring that penalizes the correct play is ridiculous."

Rubber-bridge players with weak hearts or high blood pressure, stop here! In this chapter I recommend some very dangerous and unusual plays. There is no answer to the rubber-bridge player's comment on match-point scoring except that those who are accustomed to it like it. More skill is involved in determining when to adopt a safety play than there is in merely executing it. The important consideration in duplicate is how often you expect a play to work—hence the probability of its working this time —not how much (in total points) it could gain or lose.

NORTH
♠ 10 9
♡ J 5
◇ K Q 10 9 6 2
♣ A K 4

SOUTH
♠ A K J 8
♡ Q 10 9
◇ J 3
♣ J 10 9 6

NORTH	SOUTH
1 ◇	1 ♠
2 ◇	2 NT
3 NT	

The opening lead is the four of hearts to East's king. West ducks the seven of hearts return, playing the deuce. It is almost certain that three more heart tricks will be run by the opponents as soon as the lead is lost. Combined with the trick already lost and the ace of diamonds, that is one too many. At rubber bridge, the proper play would be to try for four spade tricks and four club tricks without touching the diamonds. Declarer's chances would not be good, but it would be worth a try with so much to gain, so little to lose. In duplicate, there is much more to lose. Down one should be almost an average board, while down two would surely be a cold bottom. The odds are greater than three to one that attacking the black suits will lose a trick rather than gain a trick, which means that playing to make the hand will result in three bottom boards for every top. When the odds are so unfavorable, it is better to play safe for eight tricks. The fact that the contract is for nine tricks is immaterial, since it is the contract everyone will reach.

NORTH
♠ A J 10 7
♡ 8 7 3 2
◇ A 8 4
♣ 9 8

SOUTH
♠ 6 3
♡ A K Q 6 5
♢ K 7 6
♣ A 4 2

SOUTH	NORTH
1 ♡	1 ♠
1 NT	2 ♡
4 ♡	

The opening lead is a small diamond. Upon winning with the king, you draw the opposing trumps in three rounds and finesse the ten of spades. East wins with a king and returns a diamond, knocking out the ace. Your proper play is to re-enter the South hand with the ace of clubs for another spade finesse in order to get rid of the losing diamond. Risky? Of course it is risky. If the finesse loses you will be down one in a cold contract, but, more often than not, the second spade finesse will work.

NORTH
♠ K Q 8 5
♡ J 7 4
♢ A Q 8
♣ Q J 8

SOUTH
♠ A J 9 6 4 2
♡ A K 6
♢ 7
♣ K 9 5

SOUTH	NORTH
1 ♠	3 ♠
4 ♣	4 ♢
4 ♡	5 ♠
6 ♠	

West leads the ace of clubs and continues the suit. In rubber bridge you would draw the outstanding trumps, then cash the ace and king of hearts, hoping to drop the queen. Only if the queen failed to drop would you resort to the diamond finesse.

In duplicate, the possibility of dropping the queen of hearts is not strong enough to justify the risk of going down an extra trick. Only one heart should be cashed before finessing the queen of diamonds. In this case six spades is not quite as obvious a contract as four hearts was in the last example (a factor to be discussed later), so you should go to *reasonable* lengths in an effort to make your contract. With one more heart in the dummy and one less card in the minors, you might cash the top hearts. Now the queen is more likely to fall, and there is a better chance that if the diamond finesse loses, East won't have a heart to return.

What about safety plays in duplicate?

You should seldom make them in a normal contract. By "safety plays," I mean playing in such a way as to lose a trick with average breaks in order to avoid losing additional tricks with bad breaks. Of course you should still play suits *correctly*, i.e., lead the queen first with Q x x x x opposite A K 9 x or with Q x x x x opposite A J 9 x x. At least you should play suits correctly when you have time, controls, and entries. It appeals to my sense of irony to see declarer, particularly when he is an opponent, go down in a cold contract because he has taken "a safety play." There is often a big difference between the best way to play a suit and the best way to play a hand.

North: A J x; South: K 9 x x x: The safety play to lose only one trick with this holding is to cash the ace, re-enter the south hand, and lead toward the jack. This holds the loss to one trick except against a 5-0 break. Simply finessing the jack on the first round, preserving the possibility of taking a marked finesse later through East's ten, if he started with Q 10 x x, gives you a much better chance to run the suit without loss. It only loses when East has the singleton queen. Taking the safety play at duplicate is like betting even money on a ten-to-one long shot.

When two plays are almost equally likely to work, adopt the safer. At a no-trump contract, dummy has a seven-card diamond suit to the ace-king-jack opposite your worthless doubleton. Dummy has no outside entries, and you can afford to lose the lead. Finesse the jack on the first round rather than play for the queen to drop. Even if the finesse loses, you won't lose the whole suit. However, the true safety play is to duck the first trick entirely so as to guard against West's holding four diamonds. That possibility is too remote to play for in duplicate, unless there is some indication of unusual distribution. In the following example, the clue is from the bidding (both sides vulnerable):

```
                     NORTH
                  ♠ 9 7 5 4
                  ♡ 6
     WEST         ◇ A K J 6 4 3 2         EAST
  ♠ —             ♣ 8                  ♠ A J 10 8 3 2
  ♡ 9 8 5 3                            ♡ A Q 10 7 2
  ◇ Q 10 9 7                           ◇ —
  ♣ Q 10 7 5 3      SOUTH              ♣ 9 5
                  ♠ K Q 6
                  ♡ K J 4
                  ◇ 8 5
                  ♣ A K J 6 2
```

EAST	SOUTH	WEST	NORTH
1 ♠	1 NT	Pass	3 NT
4 ♡	Double	Pass	4 NT

The opening lead is a heart to the ace, and declarer wins the second trick with the jack of hearts. East's vulnerable bidding should be based upon eleven cards in the majors. Under these circumstances, a safety play in the diamond suit is called for. Notice also that the contract is better than normal, a factor we shall discuss later.

```
  NORTH
♠ A x x
♡ A K Q x x
◇ K x x
♣ x x

  SOUTH
♠ Q x x
♡ x x
◇ A Q 8 x x
♣ K x x
```

NORTH	SOUTH
1 ♡	2 ◇
3 ◇	3 NT

The opening lead is the jack of spades. You resist the impulse to play low, and caution is rewarded when East's king falls under the ace. When you lead the king of diamonds, West drops the nine. It is not possible to get a count on the hand. However, the spades apparently are divided 6-1, increasing the probability of a 4-1 diamond break. Although there is no clear-cut correct play, my inclination would be to finesse the eight of diamonds on the next round. If you are ever to indulge in safety plays in normal contracts and without adverse bidding, this is the time.

NORTH
♠ Q J x x
♡ A
◇ 10 8 x x x
♣ Q x x

SOUTH
♠ A K x x
♡ x x x
◇ A K 9 x
♣ x x

SOUTH	NORTH
1 ♠	2 ◇
3 ◇	3 ♠
4 ◇	4 ♠

The opening lead is the queen of hearts. The ace wins and you play the queen of spades and a low spade to the king, as both opponents follow suit. At this point your contract is cinched unless West has all the outstanding diamonds. The correct play at rubber bridge would be to lead the third round of spades to dummy's jack and return a diamond, finessing the nine if East plays small. You would be willing to concede two clubs and a diamond trick, since one losing heart could be ruffed, and the other could be discarded on a long diamond. The deep finesse in diamonds is obviously too likely to cost a trick to be the right play at duplicate. Surely you would just cash the ace and king. However, there is a better line of play than this for duplicate. You can't afford to ruff one heart and pull three rounds of trumps since if the opponents could win a diamond trick they would be in a position to cash a heart trick as well as the top clubs. You must either ruff no hearts before attacking diamonds or must ruff two hearts. The recommei de I play is to win the second trump in your hand, ruff a heart, lead a diamond to the ace, and ruff the other heart. Then you attempt to return to your hand with the king of diamonds (unless West has dropped an honor on the first round, in which case you would finesse the nine) to draw the opponent's last trump. If West can ruff your king of diamonds, you will be down one, but for this to happen, West must have started with three trumps and one small diamond (about a 7 per cent chance). The recommended play enables you to make six whenever diamonds are 2-2, unless West has the doubleton queen-jack, and when West has a singleton diamond honor and doubleton trump (a combined chance of at least 35 per cent).

NORTH
♠ x x
♡ K x
◇ A K 10 9 7 6
♣ A J x

SOUTH
♠ A 10 x
♡ A 10 x
◇ J 5
♣ 10 x x x x

NORTH	EAST	SOUTH	WEST
1 ◇	1 ♠	1 NT	Pass
3 NT			

A spade is led, and you hold up until the third trick, upon which West discards a heart. The correct rubber bridge play would be to attack the diamonds by cashing the ace and king. You wouldn't mind losing a diamond trick to *West*, and you wouldn't want to risk losing to *East's* singleton or doubleton queen. The better play in duplicate is to take a first-round diamond finesse.

This play will gain (a trick) twice as often as it will lose (several tricks).[1]

In the last two hands, it was recommended that you jeopardize your contract in order to play for an overtrick because the odds were so favorable. Unless the odds are favorable, you should play safe for your contract, since a plus score tends to be slightly better than average. On almost every board, one or two pairs fail to reach the proper contract. This means that a small premium is paid for not making a serious error in the bidding. When you bid three no-trump and make three, you beat any team that stops in a part-score, settles for a trifling penalty, passes the hand out, or reaches an unmakable slam. Sometimes it seems inconceivable that any of these things might happen, but they do. By just bidding properly and not making some obvious error, you can average 55 per cent. If you fail to make a cold contract by playing for an overtrick, you lose to all the declarers in part-scores and abnormal contracts as well as to those doing the normal thing. You shouldn't mind getting an occasional bottom if you can average two tops for every bottom through the same line of play, but you don't want to risk your 55 per cent score for an additional 45 per cent without proper odds. For example:

NORTH
♠ K x
♡ A x x
♢ Q J x x x x
♣ x x

SOUTH
♠ A J 10 x x x
♡ K x x
♢ K x
♣ K Q

SOUTH	NORTH
1 ♠	2 ♢
2 NT	3 ♡
3 ♠	4 ♠

[1] The finesse gains if West holds Q 8 4 3, Q 8 4 2, Q 8 3 2, Q 4 3 2, Q 8 4, Q 8 3, Q 8 2, Q 4 3, Q 4 2, Q 3 2 (ten distributions). The finesse loses if East holds Q, Q 8, Q 4, Q 3, Q 2 (five distributions).

You got to four spades, but what a struggle! A heart lead forces your king. A spade is led to the king followed by a low spade return, East playing small. Should you finesse? The finesse has just about the same chance of losing a trick as of gaining a trick (an overtrick). But when it loses, you won't make your contract, since a heart return will establish four tricks for the defenders. Playing the ace of spades followed by the king of diamonds, if the queen of spades doesn't drop, gives you a much better play for your contract. While four spades is the normal contract, a few pairs may reach inferior contracts of two spades, three no-trump, or five diamonds. Making just four spades will beat these pairs, while going down one may lose to them. If everyone were in four spades you could afford to gamble on the finesse, but in order to take advantage of your contract, you should adopt the line of play most likely to insure it.

Many times, with eight trumps, it is proper to play the ace and king rather than finesse for the queen when you can't afford to lose the lead. This is not a true safety play. You are not sacrificing to guard against a bad break, but are adopting a percentage play against normal distribution. For example:

NORTH
♠ K x x
♡ A x
♢ x x x
♣ J x x x x

SOUTH
♠ A J x x x
♡ x x
♢ A K Q J
♣ Q x

Opening lead against four spades is the king of hearts. The ace wins, and you lead the king of spades and a low spade, East following with a low spade. A spade finesse would put all your eggs in one basket. Even if the spade finesse is on, you may come out just as well not to take it. In other words, if spades are 3-2 and diamonds are 3-3, or if the defender with the long spade is also long in diamonds, you can discard your heart loser from dummy and ruff a heart before the defenders can do anything about it. Playing the ace gains when West has the doubleton queen and loses when East has the queen four-long. These possibilities are equal and cancel each other out. The crucial holdings are when the queen is three long. If you knew that East had the queen you would always finesse; if you knew that West had it you would refuse to finesse. In the long run you will come out better to cash the ace and try for a heart ruff; but this is not a safety play. You are not giving up a play for an overtrick to insure your contract since there is no play for an overtrick and no way to insure your contract.

Thus far we have been discussing the play at normal contracts and with normal defense, particularly in regard to the opening lead. The term "normal contract" is a loose one. Arbitrarily, I'll define it as a contract that over 80 per cent of the pairs in a particular field should reach. That means that if you play exactly the same as all other declarers in the same contract, you will get somewhere between a 40 per cent and a 60 per cent board. In that type of contract, you should be willing to take risks to make more tricks than the others, provided the odds are in your favor. You should welcome the opportunity to make a play that will give you two good boards to every bad one, rather than accept a 50 per cent or 55 per cent board without a struggle. If the other pairs have the philosophy expounded here, or if they do not see a safety play, a safety play is a big gamble and a bad gamble, while an unsafe play gets an average board.

Contracts do not fit neatly into a normal-abnormal classification. You must guess what others are doing, and you will often guess wrong. Still, you must try to evaluate your contract and let that evaluation influence your play. The better the contract, the safer you play. When just making the contract will be worth an 80 per cent score, only very good odds should induce you to risk the contract for an overtrick. On the other hand, when the contract is poor or unusual, you should go to any lengths to beat or tie the normal result.

NORTH
♠ A K J 10 x x
♡ x
♢ A 10 8 x
♣ J x

SOUTH
♠ Q x
♡ K J x
♢ J 9 x x
♣ A K x x

NORTH	SOUTH
1 ♠	2 NT
3 ♠	3 NT
Pass	

The opening lead is a small heart, your king capturing the queen. Partner's pass to three no-trump was a gamble. The normal bid is four spades. At a spade contract there will be just two losers unless East has both the king and queen of diamonds. If the other teams are making eleven tricks at spades, you might just as well be down two as to take ten tricks at no-trump. Fortunately, you don't have to put your hopes on a long shot—finding both diamond honors off side. There is a 50 per cent play for eleven tricks at no-trump by leading a low club toward the jack at trick two. If West has the queen, you get a top. If East has the queen, you lose a few tricks, but probably no match points, since you were going to get a bottom anyway.

NORTH
♠ J x x x
♡ J
♢ K x x x x
♣ x x x

SOUTH
♠ A K 9 8 x
♡ A 10 8
♢ x x
♣ x x x

(neither side vulnerable)

EAST	SOUTH	WEST	NORTH
1 ♡	1 ♠	4 ♡	4 ♠
Double			

West leads the four of hearts. East plays the queen, and you win with the ace. How do you like your contract? Not very well, do you? The opponents have an excellent chance to set you three tricks. On the other hand, if you are "lucky" enough for the spades to split 2-2, or if the king of diamonds is on side, then you surely could have set four hearts. In that event, even a three-hundred-point set would be a bad result. Nor can you expect many teams to be in the same boat, since partner's four-spade bid was quite optimistic. Is there any distribution of the opponents' cards which could make four spades a good sacrifice? If there is, you must play for it. Your best chance is that West has a singleton spade. The correct play is to ruff a heart and return the jack of spades, intending to let it ride if not covered. The four hands might be:

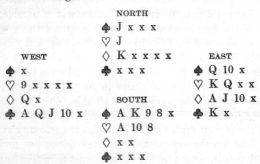

```
                       NORTH
                    ♠ J x x x
                    ♡ J
     WEST           ◇ K x x x x          EAST
  ♠ x               ♣ x x x           ♠ Q 10 x
  ♡ 9 x x x x                         ♡ K Q x x
  ◇ Q x                SOUTH          ◇ A J 10 x
  ♣ A Q J 10 x       ♠ A K 9 8 x      ♣ K x
                     ♡ A 10 8
                     ◇ x x
                     ♣ x x x
```

The double spade finesse is not a bad play even at rubber bridge when you consider the bidding, but at duplicate, it is a mandatory play.

```
  NORTH
♠ 10 8
♡ x x
◇ Q x x
♣ A K x x x x
  SOUTH
♠ A J 7 x x
♡ A Q 10
◇ A J x
♣ x x
```

SOUTH	NORTH
1 ♠	2 ♣
2 NT	Pass

The opening lead is a small heart. East plays the jack, and you win with a queen. You and your partner were not playing the same system on this hand. Everyone else will get to three no-trump. Furthermore, you can see that three no-trump is cold if clubs break 3-2. So instead of ducking a club at this point, as the three no-trump players will do, you must hope and assume that clubs split 4-1. If you could be sure of taking the same number of tricks as everyone else, you would be satisfied to play the hand normally. You would get a top when the clubs broke 4-1 or a bottom when they broke 3-2. However, if the clubs are going to break 4-1, as you hope, there is no point in subjecting yourself to the hazard of better-than-average defense. Instead, lead a club to the ace and return the ten of spades.

NORTH
♠ A K x x
♡ x x x
♢ K 10 x
♣ K x x

SOUTH
♠ x
♡ A x
♢ A J 9 8 x
♣ A x x x x

SOUTH	NORTH
1 ♢	1 ♠
2 ♣	3 ♢
5 ♢	

You win the king of hearts lead, take a quick heart discard on the king of spades, and are now ready to draw trumps. If the diamonds can be picked up without loss, then the hand would be cold for ten tricks at no-trump (630), but only twelve tricks at most in diamonds (620). While five diamonds should be the most popular contract, there will be some pairs in three no-trump, or conceivably six diamonds. Consequently, if you play diamonds the normal way by finessing through East, and if the finesse works, you will get about a 30 per cent board. You'd really prefer having the finesse fail so that the optimists would get a bad result. The only trouble is that if the finesse fails you won't automatically get a 70 per cent board to make up for the 30 per cent board you would get if the finesse were on. To illustrate this point, assume that there are ten other pairs playing your direction. Six of them will bid five diamonds the same as you, and four will bid three no-trump. When the finesse works, you tie for bottom with six others and get three match points out of a possible ten. Suppose the finesse fails. You beat or tie the three no-trump bidders, depending on how the heart suit splits. In other words, you may just get five points instead of seven. Your over-all expectancy would be about 45 per cent. Rather than settle for a line of play which will average a 45 per cent score, you should finesse diamonds the other way. Suppose you take a first-round finesse through West. When this play works, you get a cold top (100 per cent), and of course you get a bottom when it fails for an over-all average of 50 per cent. Now I realize that the problem is not quite as simple as stated. There is the problem of whether or not the clubs will break. A first-round finesse through West is not quite as good a play to bring in the diamond suit without loss as cashing the king and finessing through East. On the other hand, playing West for the queen of diamonds gives you a better chance to bring in an overtrick against a 4-1 club break. The assumption was that the three no-trump bidders would play East for the queen of diamonds, since that is the best play to take five diamond tricks. Whenever declarer is in an optimistic contract such that just making it will assure him of a good board, he should adopt the percentage play to make his contract.

NORTH
♠ K x x
♡ K x
◇ x x x x
♣ x x x x

SOUTH
♠ A J 10 9 x
♡ A x x
◇ A Q
♣ A 10 x

SOUTH	NORTH
1 ♠	2 ♠
3 NT	

The opening lead is a small diamond, East playing the jack. At this point, you have nine tricks cold, and an overtrick if you guess the spades right. How many tricks will the four-spade bidders take? Presumably they will not get the diamond lead, and they will lose a diamond, two clubs, and possibly a spade. They will take nine or ten tricks, depending upon how they guess the spades. You will also take nine or ten tricks, depending upon how you guess the spades. Nine tricks at no-trump beat nine tricks at spades; ten tricks at no-trump beat ten tricks at spades. If you guess spades the same way as the declarers in four spades, you automatically get a good board. The normal play in spades is to ruff the third round of hearts, then play the king of spades and finesse the jack on the next round. Playing at no-trump, you should also finesse through East by playing the king and finessing the jack. Suppose that East had played the king of diamonds at the first trick. You would have the same tricks at no-trump as before, but with the diamond finesse on, the four-spade bidders would take ten or eleven tricks depending upon how they guessed spades. You could only take nine or ten tricks at no-trump. Your only chance for a good board is to guess the spades right while the spade bidders guess the spades wrong. Their normal play in spades would be the same whether the diamond finesse worked or not. Since they will play East for the queen of spades, you will play West for the queen. Naturally you take a first-round finesse so as to be able to pick up the queen four-long. If East has a singleton, the odds are four to one that it will be a small card rather than the queen.

In the last example, the proper play depended upon what happened at the first trick. When the opening lead gave declarer a trick, he played one way. When it did not give him a trick, he played another way. It happened that declarer was worried more about beating declarers in another contract than beating declarers in his own contract. However, the opening lead also has an important influence upon the play of "normal" contracts.

NORTH
♠ J x x x
♡ x x x
◇ K Q 10 x
♣ A x

SOUTH
♠ A Q 9 x x x
♡ A x x
◇ J x
♣ Q x

SOUTH	NORTH
1 ♠	2 ◇
2 ♠	3 ♠
4 ♠	

West leads a small club, and you make the percentage play of ducking to your queen. Playing the ace only gains when East has both black kings. Fortunately, East can only put up the jack, so you win the trick in your hand. Now what is the correct way to play the spade suit? If anyone has the notion that banging down the ace is the best way to bring in the suit without loss, now is the time to dispel that notion. The finesse is three times as good a play with a combined holding of ten cards. Since the ten is missing, you should lead the jack, intending to let it ride unless covered. This enables you to pick up the suit without loss when East has all three trumps. Pardon the digression! I have been talking about the best way to play the *spades*, not how to play the *hand*. West's lead gave you a trick you could not possibly have made by yourself. Probably West's lead was logical, since an aggressive lead was called for by the bidding. Nevertheless, many players refuse to lead from kings and would have made a waiting lead or tried the unbid major. You may consider yourself lucky. By cashing the ace of spades and starting the diamonds, you have an excellent play for eleven tricks. This will beat all North-South teams that got a heart lead. If the spade finesse would have failed, you will get a very good board indeed. It would be foolish to push your luck too far by risking the spade finesse before the ace of diamonds is knocked out. After a favorable lead, don't jeopardize your good board with a risky line of play.

NORTH
♠ x x x
♡ x x x
◇ A J 10 x x
♣ K Q

SOUTH
♠ A x x
♡ A K
◇ Q 9 x
♣ A J 10 x x

SOUTH	NORTH
1 ♣	1 ◇
2 NT	3 NT

West leads the king of spades. This time you are not concerned with what can be made at another contract, since everyone should arrive at three no-trump. In all probability, the king of spades is a normal lead. The question is when you should take the ace of spades. If you take the first trick, you might take all thirteen tricks, or you might be set if you take the diamond finesse. If you win the second spade trick, the diamond finesse can "safely" be taken, since if East has a third spade to return, spades must split 4-3. If you had a hunch that the diamond finesse was not going to work, you would probably hold up till the third round to be sure of making ten tricks. Let's assume there are just three teams playing the hand, team No. 1 winning the first trick, team No. 2 winning the second trick, and team No. 3 holding off till the third round. Let's see how each team will fare. Fifty per cent of the time the diamond finesse works, and team No. 1 gets a top (two points) by taking all the tricks. About five per cent of the time, the diamond finesse will be off, but East will have no spade to return because West started with six. Again team No. 1 gets a top. Twenty per cent of the time the diamond finesse will be off and the spades will be split 5-2, in which case team No. 1 will get a bottom. Twenty-five per cent of the time, the diamond finesse will fail, but spades will be split 4-3, and team No. 1 will tie with team No. 2 for half a point. Fifty-five per cent times 2 plus 25 per cent times ½ equals 1.225 match points or 61.25 per cent, which is team No. 1's expectancy.

Team No. 2 wins the second trick. Fifty-five per cent of the time (when the diamond finesse works or when East has a singleton), team No. 2 beats team No. 3 and loses to team No. 1 for one match-point. Twenty per cent of the time, when the diamond finesse is off and spades are 5-2, team No. 2 gets a top. The other 25 per cent of the time, team No. 2 ties with team No. 1 for half a point. Total expectancy: 1.075 points out of 2 or 53.75 per cent.

Team No. 3 gets a zero whenever the diamond finesse works or when East has a singleton spade. When spades split 5-2, team No. 3 loses to team No. 2 and beats team No. 1. The only time team No. 3 gets a top is when the diamond finesse is off and the spades split 4-3. Team No. 3's expectancy is only 35 per cent. Actually the problem is even more complicated than this. I conveniently had the same number of teams (one) adopting each line of play.

As a child, did you ever play the game where, at the same instant, two people make a sign with their hands to indicate rock, scissors, or paper? Rock smashes scissors; scissors cut paper; paper covers rock. If you knew what the other person was going to do, you could always win. Similarly, if you knew what line of play most of the other teams would adopt, you could make the play that would give you the best percentage. If a majority of the teams would hold up two rounds, you would hold up one round. This play would beat the field whenever the diamond finesse worked or whenever spades were split 5-2. Winning the first trick would be like bidding a grand slam when everyone else was in game. It would be better to try to beat the field by 30 points than to risk more to beat the field by 60. On the other hand, if most declarers would hold up one round, you should win immediately. You would get a cold top about 55 per cent of the time, and you would tie with the field whenever spades split 4-3. My preference, not knowing what the field will do, is to win immediately. It is strange that such a bad play at rubber bridge can be a good play at duplicate.

Perhaps you got lost in this long discussion. Don't worry about it; no harm is done. The figures I used for percentages were only approximate anyway. I did not want to complicate the discussion by considering the possibility that *East* was long in spades or that the suit might block. The point is this: There were two distinct lines of play available. You could win the first spade trick, hoping the diamond finesse would work; or you could hold off, hoping the diamond finesse would fail. But if you were to hold off, how long should you hold off? Taking the first spade trick would be the best play at least half the time, and it might get you a few points even if it failed because spades might be blocked, or some declarers would not hold off long enough. It is better to adopt a play which clearly gives you at least a 50 per cent chance for a top, plus a chance for a few more points, than to adopt a line of play which will clearly be inferior 50 per cent of the time and which may be no better some of the rest of the time. I would rather bet that a finesse will work than bet that it will not work *and* have to guess the distribution of a suit.

In this example, the king was led, which prevented you from counting the suit. I believe you should be able to turn to West and ask, "Does your partner generally high-low with three small cards?" or "Does he play a compulsory next-to-highest card whenever you lead the king?" but such questions are not customary. You must guess about the distribution. What if North goes into a long huddle before leading, and finally lays down the deuce of spades? Although you presumably know the distribution, you should definitely win the first trick. If West had a problem (and it is usually a problem whether the opening leader should lead his own suit against three no-trump with a weak hand or try to find his partner's strength), you can assume you have been fixed if the diamond finesse is off. Without a spade lead, twelve tricks are cold. If you win immediately, and the diamond finesse works, West's good guess on the opening lead will not hurt you.

As I mentioned in an earlier chapter, the best spot for shooting is in the play of the hands. There is no way to estimate the effects of weird bidding on a particular hand, and it is almost impossible to start shooting in the bidding without having partnership confidence suffer. In the play of the hand, you can calculate the risks involved, and there are many opportunities to adopt a different line of play from the normal that is almost as good as the normal—sometimes just as good. In the last hand, for example, most people will not take the ace of spades at the first trick because of their rubber-bridge habits. Winning the first spade trick is like shooting with the odds in your favor. Suppose you are in a four-spade contract in which you will make either ten or eleven tricks, depending upon whether you guess the location of the queen of trumps. Dummy has ♠ K x x; you have ♠ A J 10 9 x. Most teams will play the king and finesse the jack on the next round. This is the percentage play because it works when West has the singleton queen as well as when East has the queen. If you are shooting, you should lead the jack and let it ride for a first-round finesse. This is almost as good a play as the percentage play.

Suppose that you open the bidding with two no-trump and partner raises to three with a six-card diamond suit headed by the king and no other card in his hand above an eight-spot. Your diamond holding is A 10 x. The normal play is to cash the ace, then duck the ten to guard against a 3-1 break, provided that you can afford to lose the lead. If you are shooting, play the king on the second round, assuming that West follows suit. Not only do you make one more diamond trick this way if the suit splits 2-2; you have an additional entry to the dummy to finesse something else.

You can shoot by being either optimistic or pessimistic.

NORTH
♠ K x x
♡ A K
◊ A J 10 x x x
♣ A x

SOUTH
♠ 10 x x
♡ J 10 x
◇ K Q x
♣ J 9 x x

Opening lead against three no-trump is the eight of clubs. You duck, and East wins with the queen, returning a small club. You have nine cold tricks, and you can't try for a tenth without seriously endangering your contract. If you are shooting, you lead a diamond to your king followed by a low spade lead to the king. The ace should be on-side 50 per cent of the time, and you will get a top. The odds are slightly in your favor because you will not get a bottom quite 50 per cent of the time. Even if the ace of spades is over the king, the spade suit may be blocked, in which case your play will not cost anything.

NORTH
♠ A J
♡ x
◇ J 10 x x
♣ A Q 10 9 x x

SOUTH
♠ Q 10 x
♡ A 7 x x x x
◇ Q 9
♣ K J

NORTH	SOUTH
1 ♣	1 ♡
2 ♣	2 NT
3 NT	

West leads the king of hearts, East playing the nine. When East discards at the second trick, you know that West's lead was from K Q J 10 8 of hearts. In other words, it was a normal lead despite your heart bid. If the spade finesse works, you have nine tricks. Unfortunately, the spade finesse has to be taken before the club suit is run. If you are shooting, you don't take the spade finesse. You hope that down one will be a top with everyone else going down three.

The following hand illustrates another excellent situation for shooting.

NORTH
♠ Q J x x
♡ A K J x x x
◇ x
♣ x x

SOUTH
♠ A K 10 x x
♡ x x
◇ A x
♣ J x x x

Opening lead against your four-spade contract is the king of diamonds. You win and cash the ace of spades, lead a heart to the ace, and return the queen of spades to your king, both opponents following suit. The normal play at this point is to lead a heart to the king and ruff a heart if the queen does not drop. This way you are assured of taking eleven tricks, and you will take twelve or thirteen tricks if the hearts break favorably. An alternate play is to finesse the jack of hearts. Even if it loses, you will still make your contract. The finesse gains when West's original heart holding is Q x x or Q x x x. It loses when East has the doubleton or tripleton queen. These possibilities are so nearly equal that, for practical purposes, there is no difference. Most players adopt the "normal" play, not because they have figured out the percentages, but for a psychological reason. They know that eleven tricks are cold, and they cannot stand the thought of taking ten tricks when all the weak players will take from one to three more tricks. The satisfaction of beating them by one trick when the finesse works would not equal the humiliation of losing to them by two or three tricks when the finesse fails. If you have a thick skin or a sympathetic partner, situations such as this offer an excellent opportunity for shooting.

Chapter 10

Defense

DEFENSE, even at rubber bridge, is difficult. The defenders have many unpleasant guesses to make without sufficient information to guide them. In order to defend with any logic or consistency, the defenders must use signals. These, in turn, may be more valuable to declarer than to the defenders. However, defense at duplicate is incomparably more difficult. In rubber bridge, the objective of the defense is clear-cut. Set the contract. Overtricks are relatively unimportant. In duplicate, you cannot permit yourself the luxury of attempting to set every contract. The following example illustrates how these different objectives influence the defense.

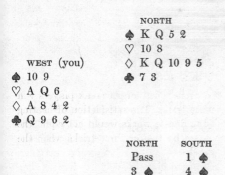

```
                        NORTH
                        ♠ K Q 5 2
                        ♡ 10 8
     WEST (you)         ◇ K Q 10 9 5
     ♠ 10 9             ♣ 7 3
     ♡ A Q 6
     ◇ A 8 4 2
     ♣ Q 9 6 2

                        NORTH    SOUTH
                        Pass     1 ♠
                        3 ♠      4 ♠
```

The opening lead is the ten of spades. Dummy's queen wins, and declarer wins the next trick with the ace of spades, dropping partner's jack. Declarer's jack of diamonds knocks out your ace.

What next? In rubber bridge, there is no problem. You return a club—any club. If partner has the ace, he will return a heart since you must have either the ace-queen of hearts or the ace of hearts and king of clubs in order to set the contract. Notice all the alternatives that present themselves at duplicate. First, you may decide that partner doesn't have the ace of clubs, but has the king of hearts. In that case a heart lead would be necessary to prevent an overtrick. Or if declarer has A K x of clubs, even the ace of hearts would be lost by not cashing it. Let's say you decide to risk a club lead anyway and find partner with the ace. But what does he return? He decides to return a club, playing you for the king. You cannot blame him particularly. He is worried about overtricks, too. That is to say you cannot blame partner for returning the club unless you made it easy for him by leading the *nine*, a play you would never think of at rubber bridge. However, if you carelessly led the deuce of clubs, you still have a feeble alibi. "I would have led the king if I had had it. Therefore I couldn't have it, and I was afraid to lead the nine for fear you would duck with the king."

The point is that defense at duplicate can be complicated. Three or four alternate lines of play exist where there was only one logical defense at rubber bridge.

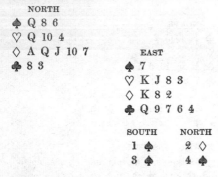

The same type of problem is involved with this deal. What risks should one take to set the contract? West leads the nine of hearts. Declarer shrugs his shoulders and calls for the queen. You cover and he wins with the ace. He lays down the ace of trumps followed by the diamond finesse. At this point you can set the contract with a club return provided partner has the ace, but in view of the strong bidding, the odds are in favor of South's having the ace of clubs. In the long run, you will come out ahead in duplicate by cashing the jack of hearts, and there is a remote possibility that partner can ruff the third round. If declarer is a good rubber-bridge player whom you would like to play with some day, it is better to lead the club. The satisfaction of making the percentage play (to take the maximum number of tricks, but not to beat the contract) will not compensate you for his look of intense disgust—especially when partner has the ace of clubs and he looks to declarer for a nod of sympathy.

In the last two example hands, you were concerned with obtaining the maximum number of tricks, not necessarily with setting the contract. But when the opponents are in a contract such that just making it will give them a good board, you should go all out to set it.

North-South vulnerable:

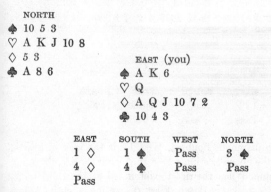

```
       NORTH
♠ 10 5 3
♡ A K J 10 8
◇ 5 3                    EAST (you)
♣ A 8 6                 ♠ A K 6
                        ♡ Q
                        ◇ A Q J 10 7 2
                        ♣ 10 4 3

       EAST    SOUTH    WEST    NORTH
       1 ◇     1 ♠      Pass    3 ♠
       4 ◇     4 ♠      Pass    Pass
       Pass
```

Partner opens the nine of diamonds. There is one remote legitimate chance of defeating the contract, finding partner with the queen-nine of clubs. But the bidding indicates that partner is not likely to have even a queen. A fine swindle play exists. By ducking the diamond lead, you preserve an entry to partner's hand—provided he has the eight of diamonds. The plot is to win the first round of trumps and return the queen of hearts to get a ruff later. Declarer can foil this plot by leading a diamond back at trick two—or if he has the eight of diamonds, he can let you carry on with your scheme, giving him an over-trick in the process. However, even the best of players may not see what is going on, and *it is worth the gamble* because you can see that four spades bid and made will be a lower board. Some teams may not reach game, while other players with your hand might take the five-diamond sacrifice (which obviously goes down only three tricks). Probable South hand: ♠ Q J 9 8 x x, ♡ x x, ◇ K x, ♣ K Q x.

Do you remember the hands on play where it was neces-sary to assume you were in the optimum contract and play accordingly? The same principles apply on defense. Both vulnerable.

<pre>
                    NORTH
                    ♠ K 7 6
                    ♡ Q 7 3
     WEST   ◇ 10 8
     ♠ Q J 8 4 2   ♣ Q 10 9 4 2
     ♡ J 10
     ◇ A Q 7
     ♣ J 8 5
</pre>

EAST	SOUTH	WEST	NORTH
1 ♡	2 ◇	Double	Pass
Pass	Pass		

Against two diamonds doubled, West leads the jack of hearts, covered by the queen and king. East then leads the ace, dropping declarer's nine. When the good eight is led at the third trick, declarer ruffs with the king, West discarding a club. A low trump is led, West winning with the queen as East drops the nine. The nine must be a singleton, since declarer would not ruff with the king from K 6 5 4 3 2. Since East left the double in despite his six-card suit and singleton diamond, he surely has either the ace of clubs or the ace of spades. So how should West defend? First, he should cash the ace of diamonds to get rid of dummy's ten so that a heart lead by East will establish the seven of trumps. The average East player cannot tell what is going on well enough to give an intelligent signal, and will probably discard a heart. Now here is where the duplicate and rubber-bridge defenders take different paths. The rubber-bridge player leads the queen of spades. East may have either ace, but the spade lead has less to lose and more to gain. If East has the ace of spades (two or three long), a two-trick set will result, while the ace of clubs will only produce a one-trick set. Or suppose that East has both the ace of spades and the king of clubs (giving declarer ♠ x x, ♡ 9 x, ◇ K J 6 5 4 3 2, ♣ A x). Now a spade lead results in a three-trick set while a club lead loses two tricks for a difference of 600 points! Or if partner gets mad and plays the king, the club return will lose four tricks! Why isn't the spade return correct at duplicate? Because many players would bid two spades with West's hand instead of doubling. Four hearts would then be reached by momentum. West can count six heart tricks, two diamond tricks, and two spade tricks, at least, if his partner has the ace of spades. Neither a one- nor a two-trick set will be good if four hearts is cold. Therefore, unless West wants to play for an improbable three-trick set (which he should do only with a *very* expert partner—one who would automatically discard a small spade with nothing in spades), he should hope that his partner's ace is in clubs. Two hundred points will be more than enough for an excellent board if four hearts cannot be made. West should play declarer for ♠ A x, ♡ 9 x, ◇ K J 6 5 4 3 2, ♣ K x.[1]

Now change the vulnerability so as to make only North-South vulnerable. Unless East discards a small spade on the ace of diamonds, West should return the queen of spades, as in rubber bridge, to try for a two-trick set.

[1] Note that if West tries to avoid committing himself and returns a spade before cashing the ace of diamonds, declarer can make his contract by leading the king of clubs immediately. If East holds off, South continues the king and seven of spades, discarding his last club.

NORTH
♠ K 6
♡ K Q 9 8
◇ 8 6 2
♣ K J 10 7

WEST
♠ 9 5 2
♡ 3 2
◇ J 9 7 3
♣ A 8 6 4

EAST
♠ A 7 4
♡ 7 6 4
◇ K Q 10 5
♣ Q 9 2

SOUTH
♠ Q J 10 8 3
♡ A J 10 5
◇ A 4
♣ 5 3

SOUTH	NORTH
1 ♠	2 ♣
2 ♡	4 ♡

The opening lead is a small diamond, the queen forcing the ace. Declarer pulls trumps in three rounds and leads a spade to the king. East wins and returns a small diamond. West returns a low club. Now, South has to guess correctly or be set. There are several interesting features about this hand. Declarer could have avoided this situation by ducking the first trick. The question we are concerned with is whether this risky line of defense is justified. I believe that it is. It is true that if declarer puts up the king of clubs he will make an overtrick and a top, but most declarers I know would rather not be faced with this "opportunity." If East makes a practice of underleading his diamond for a club return whether he (East) has the ace or queen of clubs, he will profit in the long run. If East is a timid sort of player who will only make this play when he has the ace of clubs—that is, when he has nothing to lose—he will not do very well, because declarer will know which way to play. Or if declarer is a stranger, so that building up a reputation for the future is not a consideration, East should make the play anyway. Declarer will reason that good defense would always go this way when East had the ace of clubs but either East or West might lose his nerve if East does not have the ace. In other words, declarer will probably misguess. Whatever West's philosophy may be, he has no choice but to underlead his ace of clubs. It is a matter of partnership co-operation. East did not underlead his diamond trick just to have West cash the ace of clubs.

```
                    NORTH
                 ♠ A K 7 6
                 ♡ 9 7
    WEST         ◇ 8 4 3            EAST       SOUTH  NORTH
♠ Q J 10 8 3  ♣ 8 7 6 3       ♠ 9 4 2         1 ♡    1 ♠
♡ 8 5 4                        ♡ J 3           4 ♡
◇ J 2           SOUTH          ◇ K 10 9 7 5
♣ Q 10 5      ♠ 5             ♣ A 9 4
              ♡ A K Q 10 6 2
              ◇ A Q 6
              ♣ K J 2
```

More important than any other quality of a defender is the
ability to tell which tricks will vanish unless a vigorous effort
is made to obtain them and which tricks declarer is bound to
lose eventually. A good defender must know when to be aggressive, attempting to establish or cash tricks, or when to be passive,
waiting for them to fall in his lap while declarer does all the
guesswork.

West leads the queen of spades. Dummy wins with a king
and cashes the ace for a diamond discard. Next, a low club
is led, the jack losing to the queen. At this point, with dummy
quite barren, West has nothing to lose by returning another
spade. Whatever tricks the defenders have cannot possibly
escape, and unless declarer makes a good guess at the tenth
trick he will wind up with only nine tricks. Notice that with any
return other than a spade declarer can hardly avoid taking
ten tricks.

```
                    NORTH
                 ♠ K 4 2
                 ♡ K Q 6 5
    WEST         ◇ A Q J            EAST
♠ A J 7 6     ♣ K 7 3          ♠ 9 3
♡ A 4 2                        ♡ 8
◇ 10 6 5 3      SOUTH          ◇ K 7 4 2
♣ Q 6         ♠ Q 10 8 5      ♣ A J 10 8 5 4
              ♡ J 10 9 7 3
              ◇ 9 8
              ♣ 9 2
```

NORTH	EAST	SOUTH	WEST
1 NT	2 ♣	2 ♡	3 ♣
3 ♡	Pass	Pass	Pass

The opening lead is the queen of clubs and a club continuation when dummy ducks. Declarer ruffs the third round with the nine of hearts. He then leads a low heart to the queen and returns a heart to the ten. West wins with the ace and returns a heart. Next, declarer finesses the jack of diamonds. East should not return the nine of spades. Everything indicates that a passive policy is best. Declarer is marked with a total of six cards in the spade and diamond suits (since he obviously had five hearts and two clubs). However those six cards are distributed, a diamond discard will do declarer no good and a spade lead is very unlikely to do the defenders any good. A diamond return by East, preferably the seven,[2] letting declarer guess his own spade suit, will probably result in a two-trick set.

These hands have illustrated conditions where a passive policy was best. One hand was entryless, so that a passive policy would force the declarer to play away from the other hand, or else the defenders could determine from counting that no useful discard could be obtained. The following hands illustrate the necessity for an attacking policy: Declarer has an established or nearly established suit, usually in the dummy, which will provide discards for losers in the concealed hand,

```
                        NORTH
                        ♠ A Q 5 3
                        ♡ 9 6
                        ◇ Q J 10 8
        WEST            ♣ Q 9 4
        ♠ 8 7
        ♡ K Q 7 2
        ◇ A 7 3
        ♣ K J 10 5
```

SOUTH	WEST	NORTH	EAST
1 ♠	Double	Redouble	Pass
Pass	2 ♣	3 ♠	Pass
4 ♠			

[2] Figure out for yourself how declarer should play if he knows East has four diamonds. Can you see why I hedged by saying a spade return was *very unlikely* to help the defenders?

The opening lead is a trump. Declarer pulls two rounds, dropping East's jack. Next, a diamond is led, the king forcing West's ace. West can count five spade tricks for declarer, three diamond tricks, a heart ruff, and one or two aces—unless the defense can gather in the setting tricks off the top, resulting in a duplication of values for declarer. West knows that South has at least three hearts, and probably four, from East's failure to bid hearts in response to the double. If declarer has the ace of hearts and the ace of clubs he will make five, whatever the defenders do. (He cannot get rid of all of his hearts.) On the other hand, if he does not have the ace of clubs, it will be necessary to lead clubs to prevent declarer from taking ten tricks. In other words, even though you think from the bidding that declarer has the ace of clubs, it cannot hurt to lead a club, preferably the king followed by the jack, and it may gain. South's hand might be: ♠ K 10 9 x x, ♡ A J 10 x, ◇ K x, ♣ x x. After losing two club tricks, he must still lose a heart eventually. Even if he has the ace of clubs, the club return will not lose anything. A heart return, on the other hand, can scarcely gain, whether South has the ace or not.

NORTH
♠ K J 8 5
♡ 8 7
◇ Q J 10 3
♣ 6 5 3

WEST (you)
♠ 9 7
♡ Q 9 6 3
◇ A 8 6
♣ Q 9 7 2

SOUTH	NORTH
1 ♠	2 ♠
3 ♠	4 ♠

The opening lead is a trump; South pulls two rounds and leads a low diamond from the board, playing the nine from his hand. You win with the ace and can see that a shift is necessary. Which suit should you shift to? Very definitely, you should lead a club. Declarer's strength is equally likely to be in hearts or clubs, but since the board has three small clubs there is more to be gained from a successful club switch. South's hands might be any of the following:

A	B	C
♠ A Q x x x	♠ A Q x x x	♠ A Q x x x
♡ A J x	♡ A K x	♡ x x
◊ 9 x	◊ K 9 x	◊ K 9 x
♣ A J x	♣ x x	♣ A K x

In hands A and B the club switch gains; in hand C it does not matter.

```
        NORTH
     ♠ 5
     ♡ A Q J 3               EAST (you)
     ◊ J 10 4             ♠ 8 6 4
     ♣ Q J 10 6 3         ♡ 7
                          ◊ A Q 9 8 5 2
                          ♣ K 8 7
```

NORTH	EAST	SOUTH	WEST
1 ♣	1 ◊	1 ♠	Pass
2 ♣	Pass	3 ♡	Pass
4 ♡	Pass	Pass	Pass

The opening lead is a seven of diamonds, your ace dropping declarer's king. Declarer will be able to take a ruffing finesse through your queen of diamonds for one discard. One spade discard is not likely to do him any good, but a club discard will if he is missing the ace. So you lead a club, preferably the king. South's hand: ♠ A K Q x x, ♡ K 10 x x x, ◊ K, ♣ x x.

```
                    NORTH
                 ♠ K 6 5 4
                 ♡ A 8 3
        WEST     ◊ 9 8 4              EAST
     ♠ A 10 9 3 2   ♣ A 6 2       ♠ Q J 7
     ♡ J 6                        ♡ 9 5 2
     ◊ A 10 5                     ◊ K J 7 2
     ♣ K 10 3        SOUTH        ♣ 9 7 4
                  ♠ 8
                  ♡ K Q 10 7 4
                  ◊ Q 6 3
                  ♣ Q J 8 5
```

WEST	NORTH	EAST	SOUTH
1 ♠	Pass	2 ♠	Pass
Pass	Double?	Pass	3 ♡

Your opening lead is the ace of spades. Declarer must now be out of spades and can discard a loser on the king. There is no point in attacking the club suit. If declarer wishes to discard a club on the king of spades, it is too late to prevent him. However, it may not be too late to get your diamond tricks. If you are going to risk a diamond lead, it is much better to lead low than to lead the ace.

After your lead of a low diamond and the gathering in of three diamond tricks, you should turn passive again and lead a spade.

The forcing game is very similar to passive play. For instance, the hand at the top of page 353 might be termed a forcing game because West plugged away at one suit, making declarer ruff each time. But we usually speak of a forcing game only on a hand in which we expect declarer to lose control and therefore be unable to cash some of his winners. If declarer has a five-card suit and we make him ruff a few times we call it a forcing game. If he has a seven-card suit and we make him ruff a couple of times we just call it defending passively.

```
                    NORTH
                 ♠ K 8 3 2
                 ♡ 8 7 6
       WEST      ◇ J 4            EAST
    ♠ A J 10 9   ♣ Q 9 5 4     ♠ Q 6 4
    ♡ A K J                    ♡ Q 10 2
    ◇ 8 3                      ◇ 9 7 5 2
    ♣ J 8 7 6       SOUTH      ♣ A 10 2
                 ♠ 7 5
                 ♡ 9 5 4 3
                 ◇ A K Q 10 6
                 ♣ K 3
```

WEST	NORTH	EAST	SOUTH
1 ♠	Pass	2 ♠	3 ◇
Pass	Pass	Double	

The opening lead is the king of hearts. Even though partner plays the ten, you should shift to spades. It is very improbable that partner will have four spades and four hearts (and still double diamonds). With any other distribution, the spade shift can hardly lose. Notice that persistent spade leads will prevent declarer from making his thirteenth heart, while a heart continuation will give him eight tricks.

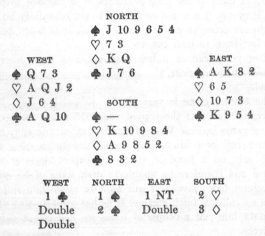

NORTH
♠ J 10 9 6 5 4
♡ 7 3
◇ K Q
♣ J 7 6

WEST
♠ Q 7 3
♡ A Q J 2
◇ J 6 4
♣ A Q 10

EAST
♠ A K 8 2
♡ 6 5
◇ 10 7 3
♣ K 9 5 4

SOUTH
♠ —
♡ K 10 9 8 4
◇ A 9 8 5 2
♣ 8 3 2

WEST	NORTH	EAST	SOUTH
1 ♣	1 ♠	1 NT	2 ♡
Double	2 ♠	Double	3 ◇
Double			

The bidding is a little strange, but is given as it actually occurred.

The opening trump lead to stop heart ruffs is normal. But upon seeing the board, the defenders should abandon leading trumps or trying for ruffs in order to shorten declarer's trumps, for if North trumps with a high diamond it will cost him a trump trick. The actual defense consisted in leading trumps twice, and giving East a fourth-round heart ruff. Spade and club leads at every opportunity would have resulted in South's winning just five trump tricks instead of five trump tricks and a heart.

Opening Leads

CULBERTSON has a table of opening leads listed in order of preference. The top of a sequence is generally the most desirable lead, since it is both attacking and safe. Other leads are less desirable because they are either less aggressive or more dangerous. However, you must consider many factors in choosing the opening lead. Perhaps a trump lead is indicated by the bidding. If it is indicated strongly enough, you should lead a trump whatever your hand is. If the decision is close, you will not lead a trump if you have another *good* lead, or if a trump lead might cost a trump trick. A trump lead is dangerous with a singleton trump or unguarded honor. Normally, it is proper to lead partner's suit, but you should sometimes prefer a trump lead or a lead from a sequence. Even the proper card of a suit to lead depends upon the bidding. Usually, you lead the queen from Q J 9 x x, but sometimes you should lead fourth-best.

When should a trump be led? Almost invariably you should lead a trump when the opponents sacrifice at a high level. Your side has most of the high cards. The only place the opponents are likely to pick up an undeserved trick is by a ruff you could have prevented. In general, lead trumps when you have most of the high cards and the opponents must be bidding on distribution. Lead a trump when you can tell that the opponents' suits are stacked against them. Also, lead a trump when dummy must be bidding on ruffing values. The trump lead is most effective when dummy has three trumps. This holding may be indicated by his showing a preference. Almost everyone leads a trump when he has a strong holding in declarer's side suit—something like K J 10 x. You should also lead a trump when you are short in the side suit and have reason to believe partner has strength in it.

SOUTH	WEST	NORTH	EAST
1 ♡	Pass	1 ♠	Pass
2 ◇	Pass	2 ♡	Pass
3 ♡	Pass	Pass	Pass

West (you) holds ♠ Q J 10 8, ♡ x x x, ◇ x x, ♣ A J 8 x. The proper lead is a trump, not a spade. The entire hands are:

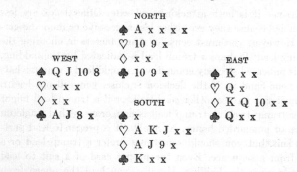

NORTH
♠ A x x x x
♡ 10 9 x
♢ x x
♣ 10 9 x

WEST
♠ Q J 10 8
♡ x x x
♢ x x
♣ A J 8 x

EAST
♠ K x x
♡ Q x
♢ K Q 10 x x
♣ Q x x

SOUTH
♠ x
♡ A K J x x
♢ A J 9 x
♣ K x x

With any lead except a trump, declarer gets two diamond ruffs and makes his contract.

Just as it is important to know whether to be aggressive or passive after you see the dummy, it is often valuable to be able to tell beforehand. With a good sequence like K Q J x, you can be aggressive without danger. The problem arises when the most aggressive lead you have is from K x x, K J x x, or Q x x. You must then anticipate how the play will go. When the opponents bid just one suit:

OPENER	RESPONDER
1 ♠	2 ♠
3 ♠	4 ♠

you should usually play it safe. Lead a trump or top-of-nothing. When the dummy has bid no-trump, you should again make a passive lead. Dummy will not provide discards for declarer's losers very often, and you merely take the guess out of the suits when you lead them. When the bidding is

OPENER	RESPONDER
1 ♠	2 ♣
2 ♠	4 ♠

you should tend to be more aggressive, since the dummy may have a good club suit to discard losers on. If you have very good clubs (Q J 9 x) or very short clubs so that partner may have them stopped, you can be reasonably passive, but with three small clubs or (even worse) K x x or Q x x of clubs, you must make the most aggressive lead possible in an effort to cash your tricks fast. Even underleading A J x may be justified. Incidentally, a lead away from a king is a much better lead than its reputation would indicate. It is likely to accomplish something by setting up a fast trick, and it is less likely to cost a trick than a lead from the queen. Even if the opponents win the first trick cheaply, the king may not be lost.

Usually you should make an aggressive lead against a small slam in a suit and a passive lead against a no-trump slam. Even against slams, it pays to listen to the bidding.

OPENER	RESPONDER
1 ♠	2 NT
3 ♠	4 ♠
6 ♠	

Since dummy has bid no-trump, you should make a passive lead. When the bidding is one no-trump, four no-trump by responder, six no-trump by opener, you should make as safe an opening lead as possible. You should not lead a king from K Q x. When the bidding is

OPENER	RESPONDER
1 NT	3 ♦
3 NT	5 NT
6 NT	

the slam may have been bid on 30 points in high cards and a long diamond suit. Now, you should make as aggressive a lead as possible. Another factor to consider is how good a hand you have. When you have six or seven points and the opponents are in a no-trump slam, it is unlikely that you will hit anything of value in partner's hand. An aggressive lead can only lose a trick. I still remember the following hand: ♠ 9 x x, ♡ J x x x, ◇ A 10 9 8, ♣ J x. The bidding was

OPENER	RESPONDER
1 ◇	1 ♠
2 NT	6 NT

Surely my partner would not have much. So I wanted to find the safest possible lead. A spade lead might pick up my partner's queen, and a lead from a jack against a slam is always likely to cost a trick. Laying down the ace of diamonds would probably surrender my double stopper. So by the process of elimination, I led the ten of diamonds, the only safe lead. The trouble with the lead was that it was too good! It was the only lead that did not lose a trick or avoid a guess for declarer. While it did not lose a *trick*, it lost the *contract*. The whole hand:

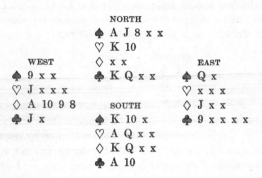

NORTH
♠ A J 8 x x
♡ K 10
♢ x x
♣ K Q x x

WEST
♠ 9 x x
♡ J x x x
♢ A 10 9 8
♣ J x

EAST
♠ Q x
♡ x x x
♢ J x x
♣ 9 x x x x

SOUTH
♠ K 10 x
♡ A Q x x
♢ K Q x x
♣ A 10

Declarer decided to avoid a two- or three-trick set at any cost, so instead of playing the king and ten of spades from his hand, which is the percentage play to run the spade suit, he finessed spades the other way! The point of this example is rather subtle. Don't lead from A 10 9 8 unless you have the queen of spades!

Most authorities say that leading an ace against a small slam is good, bad, or indifferent, without differentiating between aces. It is usually very bad to lead an ace of a suit the opponents have bid unless it was a jump bid and apt to be artificial. But an ace is a perfectly good lead when it is of an unbid suit. If the opponents' suits break well, cashing the ace may prevent an overtrick. If their suits break badly and they have a loser in them, it will be a good thing to have cashed the ace early before declarer could get rid of the suit. When the bidding is

OPENER	RESPONDER
1 ♢	1 ♠
3 ♣	3 ♠
4 ♠	6 ♠

do not lead the ace of diamonds or spades. You should cash the ace of hearts if you have it, and it is all right to cash (or possibly underlead) the ace of clubs, since clubs are often a three-card suit, and occasionally a phoney suit.

Let us consider leads at no-trump. Usually it pays to be aggressive when defending against a game or part-score contract. Suppose you are on lead against three no-trump (the bidding having gone one no-trump by opener, three no-trump by responder) with ♠ J 10, ♡ x x x, ◇ Q x x x x, ♣ J x x. You should lead a spade in preference to a diamond. You have not enough entries to make a diamond lead a good bet. The only time a diamond lead is likely to pay off is when partner has four diamonds so that you will have an entry within the suit. Rather than play for such an improbable holding, lead a spade. Partner probably has five or more spades and a few high cards. The opponents may not bid a good minor suit, while they would at least suggest a major-suit contract with a good major suit in either hand. Tend to lead a major suit against three no-trump whenever you have a close choice.

Again you are on lead against three no-trump with ♠ K Q 10 x x, ♡ x x x, ◇ x x x, ♣ x x. At rubber bridge you should lead your fourth-best spade, since you have no entries. The spade suit cannot be brought in unless partner has the ace or jack. Leading the king loses when partner has the doubleton ace and declarer has J 9 x x. At duplicate you should lead the king. You can't afford to concede a trick to dummy's doubleton jack or two tricks to declarer's A J x just to improve your chances of beating three no-trump slightly. Some players go so far as to lead the king from K Q 9 x x with or without entries. This is the best play to avoid conceding a trick to the jack, but loses heavily when partner has the doubleton or singleton ace or jack.

It doesn't pay to look for killer leads. *Perhaps* the best lead against three no-trump from ♠ A J x, ♡ Q 10 x, ◇ K 10 x, ♣ 9 8 x x at rubber bridge is the jack of spades. You hope to find partner with five spades to the king or queen. At duplicate, just lead the nine of clubs.

Occasionally, you should make an unreadable lead. Suppose you decide to lead from the 9 7 5 4 3 of spades. Lead the seven spot. Partner will be able to tell that it is not fourth-best, yet he will know from the bidding that you have at least four (the opponents cannot profitably hide major suits). Or suppose you are on lead against one no-trump with ♠ K J 10 8, ♡ K 5, ◇ J 6 3, ♣ A J 3 2. You decide to play passively and wait for the spade leads from partner. The safest lead is a diamond, but the three might look like fourth-best and encourage partner to return the suit. The jack is too good a card to throw away, so you lead the six. Similarly, if you lead from 10 x x, the middle card is best. The reason for these unorthodox leads is that partner tends to return your suit almost automatically when it looks like fourth-best. The lead of second-best can be recognized immediately as something odd and will put him on the alert.

What do you lead against three no-trump with ♠ x x, ♡ A Q 10 6 3, ◇ x x x, ♣ x x x? It should depend upon where you think the king of hearts is. If there is an opening one no-trump bid on your right, lead the six. Declarer should have the king. Even if he wins the opening lead with the jack or nine, when partner gets on lead and returns a heart, you should be able to take four tricks. But suppose the bidding was one spade (on your left), a one no-trump response, and a raise to three no-trump. The king of hearts is much more likely to be in dummy, so you should lead the queen. You hope the suit will be distributed as follows:

$$
\begin{array}{ccc}
& \heartsuit \text{ K x x} & \\
\heartsuit \text{ A Q 10 x x} & & \heartsuit \text{ x x} \\
& \heartsuit \text{ J x x} &
\end{array}
$$

Even with the opening no-trump bid on your right, you should lead the queen against three no-trump with the following hand: ♠ A x, ♡ A Q 10 x x, ◇ K x x, ♣ J x x. It looks as though partner will have no cards, and you must defend this hand alone. If you have to make all the heart leads from your own hand, the queen is the right lead to shut out the jack. (Even leading the ace would be all right!) A jack doubleton in the dummy is more likely than a king doubleton in declarer's hand. Of course, defending against one no-trump, you would lead fourth-best, since you expect partner to win a trick and return hearts for you. In fact, you might not lead hearts at all in order to try for *five* heart tricks.

A six-card suit headed by the A K Q 10 must be the most popular lead against no-trump in anybody's book. Yet I remember defending a hand where it was improper to lead the suit at all. ♠ x, ♡ A K Q 10 x x, ◊ Q 10 x x, ♣ x x:

SOUTH	WEST	NORTH	EAST
1 ♡	1 ♠	Double	1 NT
Double	Pass	Pass	Pass

The biggest surprise was that the opponents stayed in one no-trump doubled, although, as it happened, they had no better spot. Anyway, East was clearly marked with four or five hearts to the jack, and partner probably had a singleton. So, in order to be able to run the suit, it was necessary to lead something else —a spade, naturally—and wait for partner to lead hearts. What is the point in showing such a hand? It is to keep you from thinking in a groove. Don't memorize a table and follow it blindly. Don't settle your bridge arguments by turning to a book, which must, of necessity, give general rules. Ask a good player for his opinion after stating all the facts, and if he is *really* a good player, he will agree with you! (Warn him in advance.)

Here is one more example of how it pays to think rather than memorize:

SOUTH	WEST	NORTH	EAST
1 ♡	Pass	1 ♠	Pass
1 NT	Pass	2 NT	Pass
3 NT	Pass	Pass	Double

You (West) hold ♠ A 9 2, ♡ Q x, ◊ J 10 8 x x x, ♣ x x. Partner's double asks for a spade lead, but which spade should you lead? You should lead the nine! Dummy's spade holding is Q 10 5 4, and partner has K J 8 7. If you lead the deuce, the suit will be blocked. If you lead the ace, you give up an entry necessary for two spade leads through dummy. If you could see the dummy, you would surely lead the nine in case declarer should have the doubleton eight. It should not be hard to visualize the spade distribution before the dummy comes down. The ace could be the right lead to pick up declarer's singleton honor, although it is unlikely that he will have an honor when partner doubles and your spade holding is so strong. The only really bad lead is the "normal" lead of the deuce.

Conventional Leads

STANDARD leads and plays are what I would call tactical signals. They show what you have in a particular suit without attempting to suggest a general line of defense. For example, whenever you have a suit, regardless of length, headed by a three-card sequence (three touching cards topped by an honor), lead the top card unless it is the ace. With an incomplete sequence (K Q 10, Q J 9 x, J 10 8 x x, etc.) the conventional lead is still the top card. At a suit contract, the lead of a suit headed by a two-card sequence (Q J x x) is not very desirable unless it is partner's suit. However, if you do lead the suit, you should lead your top card, since you cannot expect to bring in the whole suit, and you want to take your tricks fast.

With a holding headed by the ace-king or ace-king-queen, lead the king first, then the queen if you have it. There are two exceptions to this rule. When you have a very strong suit and you want partner to play his highest card, lead the ace against a no-trump contract. By leading the ace from A K J 10 x, you can find out right away who has the queen. The other exception is with the blank ace-king at a suit contract. To show this specific holding, lead the ace, then the king.

An interior sequence is a sequence topped by a higher card (A J 10 9, K 10 9 x x, etc.). The lead from such a holding is seldom made against a suit contract, but is a good lead against no-trump. The proper lead is the top of the sequence such as the jack or the ten. If you lead the jack from K J 10 9 x and someone wins with the queen, you should play the king the next time the suit is played.

By definition, a sequence must be headed by an honor. Cards such as 9 8 7 x x, A 9 8 x x, K 9 8 7, etc. are not sequences, interior or otherwise. Nevertheless, many players lead the nine from such holdings against no-trump. Leading the nine from a nine-high suit, regardless of length, tells partner whether there will be time to establish it. The fourth-best lead might encourage partner to keep leading the suit despite declarer's triple stopper, when a shift to a weaker spot should be made. However, the advantage of leading the nine to show no honors is lost when the nine is also led from K 9 8 x or Q 9 8 x x. When the nine is led and dummy has J 10 x, East should refuse to cover the ten with the queen unless he also has the king. Why encourage partner unduly, or why put up the queen when declarer may have the ace-king alone? That is, East can afford to duck, and should duck if he does not have to worry about a lead of the nine from K 9 8 x, in which case it may be best to play the queen and force declarer either to take his ace right away or give up his double stopper. On the other hand, leading the nine gains when the suit is distributed as follows:

10 x	J x	J 10 x	K 10 x
A 9 8 x x Q x x	A 9 8 x x Q x x	A 9 8 x x Q x x	J 9 8 x Q x x
K J x	K 10 x	K x	A x x

In the first, second, and fourth examples, if the fourth-best were led, the seven would be a crucial card, but East would not know to play the seven if he had it (assuming that Dummy played small). In the third example, East should not cover Dummy's honor whether the lead was from a nine-high suit or an ace-nine-eight holding. Several more examples could be given to show the advantages of leading the nine from A 9 8 (x x). East can handle the ambiguity created by the practice of leading the nine from a nine-high suit, or a suit headed by A 9 8 or J 9 8—so long as he doesn't have to worry about K 9 8 or Q 9 8. My recommendation, therefore, is to lead fourth best whenever you have the king or queen; lead the nine any other time you have the eight.

Before leaving the subject of sequences, let us consider how you should play from a sequence when not on lead. When partner leads a low card and second hand plays low, you must play the lowest of equal top cards. Thus, if partner leads the deuce and dummy plays the three, you should play the jack from Q J x. Playing the jack denies possession of the ten. Or if dummy plays low from Q x x, you may finesse by playing the nine, but not the ten, with K 10 9. However, when you are not obligated to play a high card, you should play the top of a sequence if you can spare it. Thus, if partner leads the king, you guarantee the jack or a singleton if you play the queen. If partner leads low and dummy plays the ace, you may drop the queen to show at least the jack and probably the ten. Playing the jack denies possession of the queen, since if you can afford to play one, you can afford the other. Similarly, when you discard a king, it shows a solid suit, missing the ace.

The conventional lead from a four-card suit or longer, not headed by a sequence, is the fourth-best. Next time the suit is played, if you don't have to play a high card to force an honor or win the trick, play fifth-best, then sixth-best. If you lead the four and play the deuce the next time, partner knows you started with a doubleton or a five-card suit, and he should be able to tell your distribution within three cards. If partner leads a suit, you should return your original fourth-best card with an original holding of four or more, but return your top card with less than four. The preferred lead is also the small card from a three-card holding headed by the jack or better, whether or not partner has bid the suit. Some players go farther and lead low from *any* three-card holding in partner's suit, but they are in a minority. Lead the top card of a worthless tripleton, followed by the middle card, and lead the top card of any doubleton. With a suit headed by the ace, lead the ace against a suit contract if you think someone has a singleton or when the bidding indicates that the king will not be in the dummy. Otherwise, lead low. These are the "rules" on leads. Pretty easy, aren't they? The problem is when not to follow the rules. There are two types of exceptions:

You lead differently in order to take the maximum number of tricks in a suit or to give partner information and guide the defense.

```
                    NORTH
                 ♠ A K Q J 6
                 ♡ 10 6 5
    WEST         ◇ A 3              EAST
 ♠ 9 3           ♣ K Q J         ♠ 10 8 5      SOUTH  NORTH
 ♡ K 7 2                         ♡ A J 9 4      1 ♠    1 NT
 ◇ Q 7 2           SOUTH         ◇ 9 8 6        3 NT
 ♣ 10 8 6 4 2    ♠ 7 4 2         ♣ A 9 3
                 ♡ Q 8 3
                 ◇ K J 10 5 4
                 ♣ 7 5
```

West leads his fourth-best club, East winning with the ace. East
can count eight winners in the dummy; consequently, drastic
action is called for. A diamond shift would not work unless West
has as good as the king-jack-ten, while a heart shift would be
profitable if he has as good as three to the king. But East must
be careful which heart he leads. If he leads a low heart, declarer
will duck and the suit cannot be run. East must lead the jack of
hearts. The thumb rule for this is to assume that dummy's honor
is in your own hand, and make the lead you would make if that
were the case. You must be able to visualize the same situation
from other angles. In principle, the same combination is involved
in the next hand:

```
                    NORTH
                 ♠ A K Q J 8
                 ♡ Q 7 3
    WEST         ◇ A 6             EAST
 ♠ 7 4 3         ♣ K J 7        ♠ 6 2
 ♡ K J 8                        ♡ A 9 6 4      NORTH  SOUTH
 ◇ 7 5 2          SOUTH         ◇ J 10 9 3     1 ♠    1 NT
 ♣ A 9 4 3       ♠ 10 9 5       ♣ Q 8 6        3 NT
                 ♡ 10 5 2
                 ◇ K Q 8 4
                 ♣ 10 5 2
```

West leads a low club and declarer makes the error of ducking.
East wins with a queen and returns the jack of diamonds.
Declarer wins on the board with the ace and returns the king

of clubs. West wins with the ace and must switch to a heart. Naturally, he leads the jack. If he were desperate enough he might lead the jack from king, jack, deuce, hoping partner would have the ace, ten, or the ace, nine, eight. Following are three combinations where West must not lead fourth-best.

(a)	(b)	(c)
K x x	A J x	J x x
A Q 10 x x x x	Q 10 7 x K 8 x	Q 10 7 x K 8 x x
J x x	9 x x	A 9

Normally, with a doubleton, the correct lead is the top card. There are two reasons for this: It is a conventional lead, showing distribution, and if the doubleton is a doubleton honor, leading the honor helps to unblock the suit. However, when you lead trumps, unblocking is seldom a consideration, and it is usually of more value to declarer than to partner to know your exact holding. You have a better chance of taking a trump trick later if you lead low than if you lead your honor. And, for another reason we will soon see, it is better to lead low from a doubleton honor in trumps, if you are going to lead the suit at all.

```
                    NORTH
                  ♠ 8 6
                  ♡ 10 8
                  ◇ K 9 7 6 5
     WEST         ♣ Q 10 7 4        EAST
   ♠ A J 5                        ♠ 10 3
   ♡ Q J 9 7 3                    ♡ A 5 2          SOUTH  NORTH
   ◇ J 2             SOUTH        ◇ Q 10 8 3        1 ♠    1 NT
   ♣ 9 6 3         ♠ K Q 9 7 4 2  ♣ K J 5 2         3 ♠
                   ♡ K 6 4
                   ◇ A 4
                   ♣ A 8
```

West leads the queen of hearts taken by East's ace. East decides, logically enough, that a trump return is called for. If he leads the ten, declarer will play the queen. West will be unable to win with the ace and return the suit without losing a trump trick. However, if East leads his small spade, West can win the queen with his ace and return a spade to cut down dummy's

ruffing power without losing a trump trick. How will West know
he will not lose a trick? He will not know, but he figures to come
out even at worst by preventing a ruff.

A similar situation in a side suit exists in the following hand:

```
                        NORTH
                        ♠ 9 5 4
                        ♡ 10
        WEST            ◇ 10 9 8 7 6        EAST
        ♠ A 10 8 6 2    ♣ J 7 6 3           ♠ J 3
        ♡ A Q 5                             ♡ J 9 8 6 4 3 2
        ◇ 5             SOUTH               ◇ Q 2
        ♣ K 9 5 2       ♠ K Q 7             ♣ Q 10
                        ♡ K 7
                        ◇ A K J 4 3
                        ♣ A 8 4
```

SOUTH	WEST	NORTH	EAST
1 ◇	Double	2 ◇	2 ♡
2 NT	3 ♡	Pass	4 ♡
Double	Pass	5 ◇	Pass
Pass	Double		

West leads a diamond, won by declarer. Declarer plays another
diamond, the ace of clubs, and a small club, ducked in dummy.
East can see that a club trick is about to be developed for a
discard and must return a spade to establish a trick before it is
too late. But he must lead a small spade, not the jack.

Under opening leads, second-best leads from short suits or
long suits without high cards were recommended. The first hand
in this chapter was a good example of when not to lead fourth-
best. A low card suggests you want the suit returned. The lead
of an eight or nine suggests a switch. Suppose dummy has
K x x of hearts and you have 10 8 4 2. Dummy also has a solid
diamond suit, so you must take whatever heart tricks you can
right away or lose them. You should lead the eight or ten. If
you lead low, partner might play the jack from A J x when a
low card was called from dummy.

Other times partner can tell from the bidding that you cannot have certain holdings, and you can use a little ingenuity

to avoid giving him problems. Suppose partner has opened the bidding at one heart and you have given a double raise, but the opponents buy the bid for four spades. From 9 7 4 2 of hearts, your proper lead is the nine. Partner knows you could not give a double raise on three hearts to the nine-spot. If he holds A J 10 x x, and dummy holds K x x, you don't want him to finesse the ten and let declarer win with the singleton queen. Farfetched? No, I have been faced with this sort of problem many times when the deuce was led. Of course, you would have no choice but to lead the deuce if your bidding had not already indicated your distribution. Another example: In some way, perhaps by your failure to give a preference, the bidding has indicated to partner that you do not have four hearts. However, it will be important for partner to know whether you have three hearts or two. If he leads the suit, you have no problems. Suppose, however, that you must break the suit. With 7 2, lead the seven, but with 7 4 2, lead the deuce just as you would from J 4 2. There are other occasions where a non-standard lead is called for, but we shall consider them under the next topic, signaling.

Signaling

THE WHOLE subject of signaling appears quite complicated. There are signals for partner to continue or discontinue a suit. There are signals merely to show the location of a high card. There are signals to show distribution, and suit preference signals. In addition to these are conventional signals in leading and following suit, already discussed, and at times it is better not to signal, since declarer will be in a better position to take advantage of the information than partner will. The problem is which of the many messages partner intends to put across. Many times he must anticipate your problems and make the signal which will be most useful to you. Although discussed under a separate sub-topic, discarding is a form of signaling, too. As a general rule, when there are no unusual factors present, signaling is for the purpose of telling partner whether or not to continue his suit. Sometimes you don't know yourself. As a general rule, a low card is not as definite a signal as a high card. A low card may mean "shift," or "I can see no reason why I should encourage you to continue the suit," while a high card almost always means, "It looks to me as though you ought to play this suit some more." The ideal situation would be to have the two, four, six, eight, ten of a suit each time. Then you could play whichever card you wanted to show the various stages of enthusiasm you had for partner's play. But, unfortunately, a nine will often be your lowest card when you want to request a shift, while other times a three may be a signal for a continuation, or perhaps you would like the suit continued but you can't afford more than the deuce. Or you may have the choice of two cards. One appears to be a violent signal for a continuation, the other for a definite shift. But you don't know for sure yourself. You would like to play a non-committal card and let partner use his own judgment. As a general rule, don't signal with a card that may cost you a trick by playing it. Partner must consider the possibility that you can't spare a bigger card.

How do you tell partner which suit to shift to? Ordinarily, his common sense will tell him whether to be aggressive or passive by suits.

```
                    NORTH
                    ♠ A 5 4
                    ♡ 6 5 3
      WEST          ◇ K J 8 7 3
  ♠ 8 6             ♣ K 6
  ♡ A K 10 4
  ◇ 9 6 2
  ♣ J 8 7 3

              SOUTH     NORTH
                1 ♠       2 ◇
                2 ♠       3 ♠
                4 ♠
```

You lead the king of hearts and partner plays the deuce. Which suit should you shift to?—for you must shift. If partner has diamond tricks he cannot lose them. A diamond lead might easily permit declarer to pick up partner's queen without guess work. On the other hand, if declarer has the ace-queen of diamonds, or even just the ace, you must cash the club tricks now or you will lose them. Incidentally, if your clubs were headed by the ten spot (or lower), you should lead a high club rather than a low one. You don't want partner to play the jack with A J x (x x) if declarer ducks in dummy. The south hand might be ♠ K Q 10 x x x, ♡ x, ◊ A Q x, ♣ 10 x x, or ♠ K Q x x x x, ♡ Q x x, ◊ A Q x, ♣ x. From the bidding, partner almost has to have a high card somewhere. But if he has no high cards whatsoever and three small hearts, he should play his middle heart to prevent you from shifting. Then he should play his highest heart on the next round so that if you have a trick to cash you would cash it rather than play the third round of hearts, expecting partner to win with the queen or ruff.

```
                          NORTH
                        ♠ A 8 6
                        ♡ 8 6 4
         WEST           ◊ K Q 5
        ♠ 9 3           ♣ K 8 7 3
        ♡ A K 9 5 3
        ◊ 9 8 6
        ♣ 10 6 5

                        SOUTH    NORTH
                          1 ♠      2 ♣
                          2 ♠      3 ♠
                          4 ♠
```

Again you lead the king of hearts and partner plays the deuce. But this time you lead your ace of hearts anyway. Partner has merely indicated that from his point of view, a heart continuation is not mandatory. There are many holdings with which a heart continuation on your part will be the wisest course. There is no distribution of the heart suit which would permit declarer to win an undeserved trick in hearts by a heart continuation. Declarer's hand might be:

(a) ♠ K Q 10 x x x, ♡ Q J 10 x, ◊ A x, ♣ x, or

(b) ♠ K J x x x x, ♡ Q x, ◊ A x, ♣ A x x (notice that declarer makes six if hearts are not continued), or

(c) ♠ Q J 10 x x, ♡ J x x, ◊ A x, ♣ A Q x (remember partner must not play the queen from Q x).

```
                    NORTH
                    ♠ 9 4
                    ♡ 8 7 6
                    ◇ K 10 8 5 3
    WEST            ♣ A Q 2
    ♠ K 8 7 6 3
    ♡ Q J 5
    ◇ 4
    ♣ 9 6 5 3
```

EAST	SOUTH	WEST	NORTH
1 ♡	2 ◇	2 ♡	3 ◇

Your opening lead is the queen of hearts which holds the trick, partner playing the deuce. In this case, the deuce is not merely a non-committal play since partner has several higher hearts at his disposal— and could even overtake if he wanted to. The switch called for must logically be a club. If partner wanted spades led, he could easily have overtaken the first trick and led them himself, but the club situation is such that if clubs are led at all, you must lead them. And rather than lead your fourth-best, you should lead a higher club so that partner, with K 10 x of clubs, will not play the ten if declarer plays small from the dummy. Fortunately, partner has ♠ 10 x x, ♡ A K 10 9 2, ◇ x x x, ♣ K J x, leaving declarer with ♠ A Q J, ♡ 10 x, ◇ A Q J x x x, ♣ 10 x x. (I don't like the two-diamond overcall with A Q J of spades, but the opponents do not always follow my system.) Note that the club shift, followed by a low heart to your jack and another club lead, is the only way to set the contract.

Remember the most common use of a high- or low-card signal is to indicate a continuation or a shift. The next most common signal is to show distribution. Outside the trump suit, high-low to show two or four or six of a suit, and play your cards in the normal order to show an odd number. You should not signal every time you follow suit, but only when you think that exact knowledge of your distribution will be important to partner, as when he has a high card in the suit and wonders how long to hold off.

```
                    NORTH
                    ♠ K Q J 6
                    ♡ 6 5
        WEST        ◇ K Q 3              EAST
♠ 9 8 4 2           ♣ 9 7 6 5     ♠ A 10 7 3   SOUTH   NORTH
♡ Q 10 7                          ♡ J 2          1 ♡     1 ♠
◇ 9 8 4             SOUTH         ◇ A J 7 5       2 ♡
♣ A 10 4            ♠ 5           ♣ J 8 3
                    ♡ A K 9 8 4 3
                    ◇ 10 6 2
                    ♣ K Q 6
```

The opening lead is the nine of diamonds. Dummy plays the queen, and since East cannot afford to win and return the suit, he merely plays the encouraging seven. If declarer should lead the king of spades from the dummy at this point, East would have a tough guess, but declarer does not know who has the ace of spades and does not know which hand to play from first. So declarer leads the ace and king of trumps, followed by a low spade. West plays the nine to avoid any possible ambiguity (if he plays the four, for example, East will not know for sure where the deuce is; if declarer has it, West will have played his lowest card to show three), and East wins the first trick. As a result, declarer is down one. If the South and West hands were changed to West: ♠ 9 8 2, ♡ Q 10 7, ◇ 9 8 4, ♣ K Q 6 4; South: ♠ 5 4, ♡ A K 9 8 4 3, ◇ 10 6 2, ♣ A 10, West would have played the deuce on the first spade lead, and East would have held off till the second round.

There will be many more examples of distributional signals for hold-offs, so no more examples will be given here. Following is an unusual use of the distributional signal:

```
                    NORTH
                    ♠ Q J 8 3
                    ♡ Q J 7             SOUTH   NORTH
        WEST        ◇ A J 10 5            1 ♠     3 ♠
♠ 7 5               ♣ Q 4        EAST     4 NT    5 ◇
♡ A K 9 5 4                      ♠ 10     6 ♠
◇ 8 7 6                          ♡ 10 8 6 2
♣ J 8 2             SOUTH        ◇ 9 3 2
                    ♠ A K 9 6 4 2  ♣ K 9 7 6 3
                    ♡ 3
                    ◇ K Q 4
                    ♣ A 10 5
```

The opening lead is the king of hearts. Does East want the heart suit continued? He cannot possibly tell since he does not know the distribution. He wants his partner to cash the ace if it will hold; otherwise he had better shift. Since East cannot know whether he wants a continuation or not, West should not expect him to try to guess. Instead, East should show his distribution so that West will know what to do. If East plays the eight or ten to show an even number of cards, West will shift to a trump (his safest lead), and eventually declarer must lose a club.

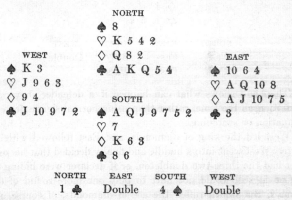

```
                     NORTH
                     ♠ 8
                     ♡ K 5 4 2
      WEST           ◇ Q 8 2           EAST
   ♠ K 3             ♣ A K Q 5 4       ♠ 10 6 4
   ♡ J 9 6 3                           ♡ A Q 10 8
   ◇ 9 4             SOUTH             ◇ A J 10 7 5
   ♣ J 10 9 7 2      ♠ A Q J 9 7 5 2   ♣ 3
                     ♡ 7
                     ◇ K 6 3
                     ♣ 8 6
```

NORTH	EAST	SOUTH	WEST
1 ♣	Double	4 ♠	Double

This hand illustrates the distributional signal in the trump suit; which is to high-low with three trumps. After West's optimistic double, he leads the jack of clubs. Declarer wins with the queen and leads a trump. After a long hesitation, he plays the ace and leads back the jack. When West wins, he would have a real problem if it were not for signals. He is fairly sure declarer has another club. (Otherwise, wouldn't he have taken a quick discard before giving up the lead?) Nevertheless, without signals, West would not even be *sure* that his partner was out of clubs, and he would not know whether or not his partner had a trump left. It would be rather embarrassing to lead back a club, giving declarer an impossible contract if East should have enough tricks to set the contract right off the top. If East knows his signals, he will have high-lowed to show three trumps, *and by implication that he wants to ruff with one of them,* so West obediently leads a club, and the ruff sets the contract.

NORTH
♠ Q 8 7
♡ A 8 6 5
◇ Q 6 5
♣ J 10 8

WEST
♠ A 9 5 4
♡ 7
◇ A K 10 9 7
♣ A 9 4

EAST
♠ K J 2
♡ 9 4
◇ J 8 3 2
♣ Q 7 6 3

SOUTH
♠ 10 6 3
♡ K Q J 10 3 2
◇ 4
♣ K 5 2

NORTH	EAST	SOUTH	WEST
Pass	Pass	3 ♡	Double
Pass	Pass	Pass	

This hand shows what can happen if a defender shows distribution all the time, rather than using normal signals for continuation or switching.

West led the king of diamonds, and East followed with the three. West went into a huddle and finally decided that his partner had the three-two doubleton, or if declarer were hiding the deuce, it still would not hurt to play one more round of diamonds. But South ruffed the ace of diamonds, of course, and obtained a useful spade discard. East should have been even more anxious than normal to play the deuce of diamonds because of his spade holding.

At no-trump, you don't want to encourage partner with a worthless doubleton in his suit, so you should refuse to give him a high-low. If partner leads an honor (other than the ace), you should play your next-to-highest card unless you want a switch so badly that you are willing to mislead partner as to your holding in his suit. Or if partner leads the suit which you believe is the best one to develop, and if dummy puts up an honor which you cannot beat, you should play your next-best card. If you have not been using this signal, you certainly should try it. It works surprisingly well. Partner can tell later in the hand whether or not you have a card left to lead to him if you gain the lead. There is one important exception to this rule. Whenever partner leads a king at no-trump and you have the jack, play it. If partner is leading from A K 10, he will know you don't have the queen when you play the jack. Playing the jack makes it easy for partner when he has led from K Q 10. Unless he sees the jack, he may shift to another suit.

The suit-preference signal is very simple. *When a card cannot logically be a come-on or shift signal, and when it cannot be for the purpose of showing distribution*, then playing an unnecessarily high card asks for a shift to (or shows an entry in) a higher-ranking suit, while an unnecessarily low card asks for a shift to a lower-ranking suit. Usually there are only two logical choices. The lower-ranking suit may be hearts if only hearts and spades are logical leads.

```
                    NORTH
                    ♠ 6 4
                    ♡ J 3 2
      WEST          ◇ A J 10 7 4 2     EAST
  ♠ K J 9 5 2       ♣ Q 6            ♠ Q 10          SOUTH   NORTH
  ♡ 10 7 6                           ♡ 9 8 4          1 ♣     1 ◇
  ◇ 8 3             SOUTH            ◇ K 9 5          2 NT    3 NT
  ♣ A 5 3           ♠ A 8 7 3        ♣ 9 8 7 4 2
                    ♡ A K Q 5
                    ◇ Q 6
                    ♣ K J 10
```

West leads the five of spades and overtakes his partner's ten at the second trick to continue the suit. At this point West has the king, nine and deuce left. He cannot afford to lead the deuce, since, as in the actual case, declarer might have the ace-eight left, but the king and nine are equals. West should return the nine, his lower card, to show that his entry is in the lower-ranking suit, clubs. Now, declarer leads the queen of diamonds and West plays the eight to show a doubleton. (It may not seem necessary to show the distribution here, but if South has one more diamond, leaving East with the doubleton king, he does not want East to risk a hold-off, since it could gain nothing.) East wins the second round with the king and, with no signals to guide him, would undoubtedly return a heart. (After all, the heart return could not lose unless declarer had four hearts to the ace, king, queen.) But if East trusts his partner's play of the nine of spades he will return a club.

```
                    NORTH
                    ♠ 6 2
                    ♡ 8
      WEST          ◇ K 10 8 7 3    EAST
 ♠ 10 8 7 5 4       ♣ K J 9 5 4     ♠ Q 9 3        SOUTH   NORTH
 ♡ A J 9 6 2                        ♡ K 7 5 4      1 ◇     2 ♣
 ◇ 6 4              SOUTH           ◇ 9 2          3 NT    4 ◇
 ♣ 7               ♠ A K J          ♣ A 10 8 2     4 ♠     5 ◇
                    ♡ Q 10 3
                    ◇ A Q J 5
                    ♣ Q 6 3
```

West leads the seven of clubs, which East has no trouble in reading as a singleton. Ruffing situations such as these offer the most
frequent opportunities for the use of suit preference. East returns the deuce of clubs in order to show a possible entry in
hearts. Without any high cards in either suit he would return
the eight (non-committal). Upon ruffing the club West can
underlead his ace of hearts for another ruff. Admittedly, this
takes lots of partnership confidence.

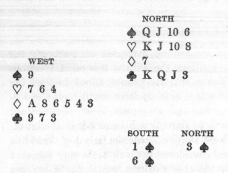

```
                    NORTH
                    ♠ Q J 10 6
                    ♡ K J 10 8
      WEST          ◇ 7
 ♠ 9               ♣ K Q J 3
 ♡ 7 6 4
 ◇ A 8 6 5 4 3
 ♣ 9 7 3
                    SOUTH   NORTH
                    1 ♠     3 ♠
                    6 ♠
```

You lead the ace of diamonds which holds. If partner has a
trump trick (very unlikely) he will get it without any effort on
your part. If he has the ace of hearts or the ace of clubs you
may get another trick if you grab it right away; otherwise you
are fighting for a lost cause. Leading another diamond cannot

do any good. In this case, partner's card should be a suit-preference signal. If he plays something like the ten or jack of diamonds, lead a heart; if he plays a very low diamond, lead a club.

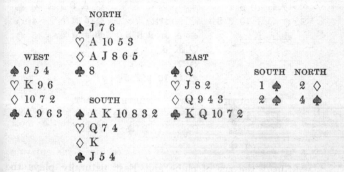

```
                 NORTH
                 ♠ J 7 6
                 ♡ A 10 5 3
     WEST        ◇ A J 8 6 5      EAST
  ♠ 9 5 4        ♣ 8              ♠ Q
  ♡ K 9 6                         ♡ J 8 2        SOUTH   NORTH
  ◇ 10 7 2       SOUTH            ◇ Q 9 4 3       1 ♠     2 ◇
  ♣ A 9 6 3      ♠ A K 10 8 3 2   ♣ K Q 10 7 2    2 ♠     4 ♠
                 ♡ Q 7 4
                 ◇ K
                 ♣ J 5 4
```

West leads the ace of clubs and East plays the ten. There is no reason why a club continuation should be out of the question. In fact, a club continuation is very logical when East plays the ten. East may have two purposes. He might want to shorten the dummy's trumps, or he simply might have nothing in diamonds and hearts that he wants led through. Compare this with the last hand where a shift was mandatory. Remember, as long as a continuation is conceivable a high card should ask for it. A high card will at least show strength in the suit, in some cases suggesting a trump switch. At least 90 per cent of the time a message to continue or shift is adequate with a good partner, because if he is to shift he will know what to shift to. In this case, if East were to play a spectacularly high card like the king, some players consider this a suit-preference signal. I have my doubts as to the utility of this treatment. How often do you have good enough clubs that you can afford to throw the king—yet good enough hearts to demand a heart shift?

NORTH
♠ Q J 5
♡ J 8
◊ A K 9 8 4
♣ 8 6 3

WEST
♠ 10 4
♡ Q 10 5 2
◊ Q J 10 6 3
♣ A K

EAST
♠ 7 6 2
♡ A 9 7 4 3
◊ 5 2
♣ J 4 2

SOUTH
♠ A K 9 8 3
♡ K 6
◊ 7
♣ Q 10 9 7 5

SOUTH	WEST	NORTH	EAST
1 ♠	Double	Redouble	2 ♡
Pass	Pass	2 ♠	Pass
4 ♠			

West leads the ace of clubs and East naturally plays the deuce. When West continues with the king, East knows West has led from the ace-king doubleton and would like to find an entry to East's hand to get a ruff. East should now play the jack—after all, the jack is now worthless except as a signal. When this hand was played, East thoughtlessly played the four and West decided his partner did not have the ace of hearts. He led the queen of diamonds, hoping that his partner could ruff.

We have covered the orthodox signals and will now look at some special situations where inferences can be drawn from partner's play.

NORTH
♠ A K J 7 4
♡ Q J 6 3
◊ J 8 6
♣ 7

WEST
♠ Q 9 3
♡ 7 4
◊ A 9 3 2
♣ Q 10 6 4

EAST
♠ 10 6 5 2
♡ 9 8
◊ K Q
♣ A 9 8 5 2

SOUTH
♠ 8
♡ A K 10 5 2
◊ 10 7 5 4
♣ K J 3

SOUTH	WEST	NORTH	EAST
1 ♡	Pass	1 ♠	Pass
2 ♡	Pass	4 ♡	

East wins the opening club lead. His best chance to set the contract is to find his partner with the ace of diamonds. But what will happen if he merely leads the king and queen of diamonds? West will play the nine on the first trick, a smaller one the next time, waiting for a third diamond lead. East should foresee this unsatisfactory development and avoid it. He should lead the queen of diamonds followed by the king. West will realize that his partner is trying to convey a message by the unorthodox order of playing his diamond honors. And it should not be very hard to figure out what this message is. Incidentally, this is a good example of why it does not pay to be fancy. If you frequently lead the ace from ace-king-queen, or lead the wrong card from a sequence, thinking it will not matter, when you need to put across a special message partner will not pay any attention. It will be a case of hollering "wolf" too often.

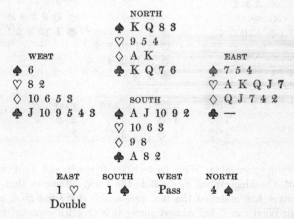

```
                         NORTH
                      ♠ K Q 8 3
                      ♡ 9 5 4
      WEST            ◊ A K            EAST
    ♠ 6              ♣ K Q 7 6       ♠ 7 5 4
    ♡ 8 2                            ♡ A K Q J 7
    ◊ 10 6 5 3         SOUTH         ◊ Q J 7 4 2
    ♣ J 10 9 5 4 3   ♠ A J 10 9 2   ♣ —
                      ♡ 10 6 3
                      ◊ 9 8
                      ♣ A 8 2
```

EAST	SOUTH	WEST	NORTH
1 ♡	1 ♠	Pass	4 ♠
Double			

East doubles the strong bidding, hoping that his partner can read it as a request for an unusual lead. West obligingly leads the jack of clubs. Upon ruffing this trick, East leads the jack of hearts. West should *not* play the eight. Why did East lead the jack? It is apparent when the jack holds the trick that he must hold some higher honors. The jack play must show that he holds the ace, king, queen, jack, and is thinking of underleading them the next time, hoping to find partner with the ten. (If West has 10 8 x of hearts the underlead is necessary!) Perhaps you have never seen anything like this before, but logically, what else could East have in mind? Furthermore, whether West plays a low card or a high card, East will certainly continue to play hearts. There is no need to encourage him. If West plays the eight and East trusts him, he will lead a small heart at the second trick, giving declarer his contract with an overtrick. If East merely plays small and then ruffs the third round for another club return, declarer will be down two.

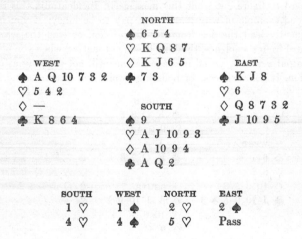

NORTH
♠ 6 5 4
♡ K Q 8 7
♢ K J 6 5
♣ 7 3

WEST
♠ A Q 10 7 3 2
♡ 5 4 2
♢ —
♣ K 8 6 4

EAST
♠ K J 8
♡ 6
♢ Q 8 7 3 2
♣ J 10 9 5

SOUTH
♠ 9
♡ A J 10 9 3
♢ A 10 9 4
♣ A Q 2

SOUTH	WEST	NORTH	EAST
1 ♡	1 ♠	2 ♡	2 ♠
4 ♡	4 ♠	5 ♡	Pass

Both vulnerable: West leads a small spade and East wins with the king. When East holds the trick, he knows that his partner has underled the ace, presumably for some good reason. What can it be? Almost surely it is to get a diamond ruff. The "safe" return of the jack of clubs would show either no imagination or no confidence in partner. If East is careful, he will return the seven or eight of diamonds. However, once West gets his ruff, he should play passively, signal or no signal, by laying down the ace of spades.

```
                    NORTH
                 ♠ Q 7 3
                 ♡ A 9
                 ◇ 10 9 6 4
     WEST        ♣ K 10 7 4
  ♠ 9 6 4
  ♡ 10 7 3
  ◇ K J 2
  ♣ J 9 6 2
```

```
     SOUTH     NORTH
     1 NT       3 NT
```

West leads a club. East wins with the ace and returns the eight
of diamonds. South ducks, allowing West's jack to win. What
should West now return? He should definitely return the nine
of spades rather than a heart. Assume for a moment that East
holds a five-card heart suit to the king. In that case he would
have led a heart back himself. In other words, if East had a
heart suit worth developing he could have afforded to return a
heart. On the other hand, if he had good spades he would not
have been able to return a spade. For instance, the whole hand
might be:

```
                    NORTH
                 ♠ Q 7 3
                 ♡ A 9
     WEST        ◇ 10 9 6 4        EAST
  ♠ 9 6 4        ♣ K 10 7 4     ♠ K J 10 5
  ♡ 10 7 3                      ♡ J 6 4 2
  ◇ K J 2          SOUTH        ◇ 8 7 5
  ♣ J 9 6 2     ♠ A 8 2         ♣ A 5
                ♡ K Q 8 5
                ◇ A Q 3
                ♣ Q 8 3
```

```
                        NORTH
                        ♠ Q 10
                        ♡ 10 6                East-West vulnerable
          WEST          ◇ Q J 10 6            EAST
          ♠ K 5         ♣ J 9 7 5 4           ♠ 8 7 2
          ♡ A Q J 7 2                         ♡ K 4 3
          ◇ A K 7 2     SOUTH                 ◇ 8 3
          ♣ 6 2         ♠ A J 9 6 4 3         ♣ K Q 10 8 3
                        ♡ 9 8 5
                        ◇ 9 5 4
                        ♣ A
```

NORTH	EAST	SOUTH	WEST
Pass	Pass	1 ♠	Double
2 ♠	3 ♣	Pass	3 ♡
Pass	4 ♡	4 ♠	Double

The opening lead is the king of diamonds, East playing the eight. West continues the ace and a third round to give his partner a ruff. At this point East returns the king of hearts rather than a low heart because he may want to remain on lead. West follows with the queen. What can he mean by that play? If all he wanted was a heart continuation, he could overtake with the ace and play hearts himself. If his hearts are so good that he can afford to waste the queen, yet lets East hold the trick, he must want East to play a suit that West cannot afford to play. And what can that be? A trump or a club? A trump, naturally. The deuce of hearts would call for a club switch. If declarer finesses the trump lead, West gives his partner another diamond ruff (East has carefully ruffed the diamond with the seven and returned the deuce of spades) to kill a winner, and declarer is unable to get either a heart ruff or a discard.

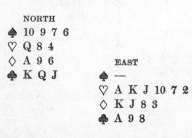

```
     NORTH
♠ 10 9 7 6
♡ Q 8 4
◇ A 9 6             EAST
♣ K Q J             ♠ —
                    ♡ A K J 10 7 2
                    ◇ K J 8 3
                    ♣ A 9 8
```

EAST	SOUTH	WEST	NORTH
1 ♡	1 ♠	Pass	2 ♠
Double	3 ♠	Pass	Pass
Pass			

West leads a low heart, East winning with the ten. East cashes the king, while West discards a low club. With anyone but an expert for a partner East should lead a low heart rather than the ace at trick three. He wants his partner to ruff and return a diamond before the ace of clubs is knocked out. With an expert partner, leading the ace of hearts provides a two-way play for a set. West will know that East has no particular desire to be on lead after the hearts are cashed. He will trump the third round automatically and lead back a diamond *unless* he has a trump holding such that an over-ruff threat will promote a winner. If he allows the third heart trick to hold, East should cash the ace of clubs and lead the fourth round of hearts.

Many times it pays to hold off with a trump trick until partner is out of trumps so that you can see his discard and know what to lead. A somewhat similar situation is presented in the following hand:

```
                  NORTH
                  ♠ J 10 x x
                  ♡ K x x
     WEST         ◇ x                    EAST        NORTH  SOUTH
♠ x x             ♣ K Q J x x       ♠ x               Pass    1 ♠
♡ Q x x x                           ♡ A J 10 x x      3 ♠     4 ♣
◇ Q x x x         SOUTH             ◇ J x x x x        4 ♠     5 ♠
♣ A x x           ♠ A K Q x x x     ♣ x x             6 ♠
                  ♡ x
                  ◇ A K x
                  ♣ x x x
```

West led a trump, won in the dummy by the ten, and the king of clubs was returned. West, of course, did not know what South's club holding was and was afraid to hold off. If he did risk holding off one round, however, he could have held off till the third round, since East would have high-lowed. And on the third round—that is, if declarer would have had enough nerve to continue leading clubs before leading another round of trumps—East would discard a high heart. As it was, West won too soon and guessed wrong, returning a diamond.

Discards

DISCARDING is related to signaling in many respects. Discarding a high card shows some strength in a suit. Sometimes the strength is a stopper; other times it is a suit that can be profitably developed. In the latter case, particularly at no-trump, it is usually better to discard a small card in a suit you don't want developed and partner can infer that you want another suit led. In addition to the signaling problem, you must hold the right cards to keep declarer from developing suits of his own. Cowardly discarding does not pay. As a general proposition, both defenders cannot guard all the suits. It is a mistake to try. One defender should decide early which suit he will retain and start discarding the other. This lets partner know what is expected of him.

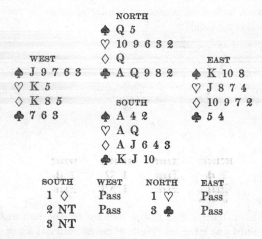

```
                          NORTH
                          ♠ Q 5
                          ♡ 10 9 6 3 2
                          ◇ Q
        WEST              ♣ A Q 9 8 2        EAST
        ♠ J 9 7 6 3                          ♠ K 10 8
        ♡ K 5                                ♡ J 8 7 4
        ◇ K 8 5            SOUTH             ◇ 10 9 7 2
        ♣ 7 6 3           ♠ A 4 2            ♣ 5 4
                          ♡ A Q
                          ◇ A J 6 4 3
                          ♣ K J 10
```

SOUTH	WEST	NORTH	EAST
1 ◇	Pass	1 ♡	Pass
2 NT	Pass	3 ♣	Pass
3 NT			

West leads his fourth-best spade; declarer puts up the queen from the dummy and wins the third round with his ace, discarding a heart from dummy. Then he runs the club suit. On the third club trick East has to make a decision. If declarer

has the ace-king-small of hearts, East must retain at least three
hearts and throw away the diamond suit. If declarer has five
diamonds to the ace-king, East must retain all his diamonds
and discard his hearts. East decides to keep his diamonds and
throws away three hearts. Now look at West's hand for a moment. He must find two discards. If he cautiously plays safe,
throwing away one of his spades to keep both kings guarded,
declarer can play safe too. All he has to do is to duck the queen
of diamonds. He does not care who has the king, because West
has not retained enough spades to bother him. When East starts
throwing away hearts, West must keep his doubleton king, but
should unguard his king of diamonds so as to keep all his
spades. Declarer must now make a lucky guess. His contract
has not been handed to him on a silver platter. Earlier, if East
had decided to throw diamonds and keep his hearts, West
would keep his king of diamonds guarded but blank his king
of hearts.

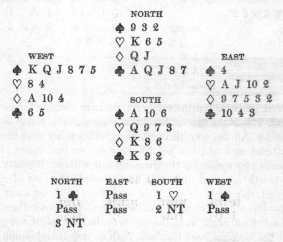

```
                        NORTH
                        ♠ 9 3 2
                        ♡ K 6 5
                        ◇ Q J
       WEST             ♣ A Q J 8 7        EAST
  ♠ K Q J 8 7 5                        ♠ 4
  ♡ 8 4                                ♡ A J 10 2
  ◇ A 10 4              SOUTH          ◇ 9 7 5 3 2
  ♣ 6 5                 ♠ A 10 6       ♣ 10 4 3
                        ♡ Q 9 7 3
                        ◇ K 8 6
                        ♣ K 9 2
```

NORTH	EAST	SOUTH	WEST
1 ♣	Pass	1 ♡	1 ♠
Pass	Pass	2 NT	Pass
3 NT			

West leads the king of spades and continues the suit, declarer winning the second round. West's very first discard on
the club suit is the ten of diamonds, guaranteeing the ace.
After this play East should hop up with his ace on the first
heart lead so as not to let declarer steal a single trick. Imagine

for the moment that declarer had the ace of diamonds and West only the king. In this case West should not play the ten of diamonds. In fact, it is doubtful whether he should signal at all. Declarer may have to guess which of two or more finesses to take, and there is no point in showing him the right path. If West fails to play the ten of diamonds, East should not go up with the ace of hearts on the first heart return. As I said, West probably should not signal, but if he does, he should discard a small spade and then the ten of diamonds. His failure to discard the ten of diamonds *immediately* logically shows just diamond strength or a stopper. West would not throw a good spade away if he had a quick entry.

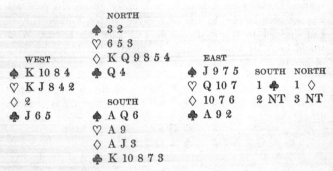

West leads his fourth-best heart, declarer winning the second round. This is the type of hand that puts a mental strain on the defender. All the way through, West will wonder who has the last heart and whether he will ever get on lead again. West discards two spades on the diamond suit without difficulty. On the fourth round of diamonds East discards the nine of clubs, guaranteeing the ace, and West can afford to throw away two clubs. His other discard should be the ten of spades rather than a heart. East might have the queen or declarer might not guess that the king has been blanked. With no defensive bidding and no signal in spades, declarer is unlikely to guess right. Imagine that South had the ace of clubs and East had the king. On the fourth round of diamonds East would not signal in clubs and West would know that he did not have the ace—or possibly that he had the ace but no heart to return. In either case,

West would give up hope of setting the contract and would concentrate on holding down the overtricks. That means he would retain the guarded jack of clubs as long as possible and the king-ten of spades.

```
                      NORTH
                   ♠ 6 2
                   ♡ 10 8 7 4
                   ◇ K Q 9 4
    WEST            ♣ K 6 5         EAST
 ♠ A 10 7 5 3                    ♠ 8 4           SOUTH  NORTH
 ♡ Q J 5                         ♡ K 9 3          1 NT   2 NT
 ◇ 8 3                           ◇ 10 7 6 2       3 NT
 ♣ 7 4 3           SOUTH         ♣ A 10 9 8
                   ♠ K Q J 9
                   ♡ A 6 2
                   ◇ A J 5
                   ♣ Q J 2
```

Remember, we have urged that it does not pay to be a coward in discarding. If we have a long suit set up or a long suit which is likely to be set up at no-trump, we do not throw it away. When we do throw it away, the inference is that we do not want it led back. In the above hand, West leads his fourth-best spade, East's eight losing to declarer's nine. If South were shrewd enough to lead a club right away, East probably would win and return a spade, allowing declarer to make an overtrick. But if declarer cashes his diamond tricks, on the third and fourth diamonds West should discard spades to show that he doesn't want them returned. When East wins with the ace of clubs he will shift to a heart and hold declarer to his contract.

```
                      NORTH
                   ♠ A K 9 8
                   ♡ J 7
    WEST            ◇ Q 3           EAST
 ♠ Q J 2           ♣ K Q 10 9 5   ♠ 10 4         NORTH  SOUTH
 ♡ Q 6 5 2                        ♡ 10 8 4 3      1 ♣    2 NT
 ◇ K 9 8 7         SOUTH          ◇ 10 6 4 2      3 NT
 ♣ 7 3             ♠ 7 6 5 3      ♣ A 6 4
                   ♡ A K 9
                   ◇ A J 5
                   ♣ J 8 2
```

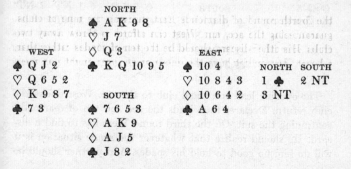

In this hand we see another example of the extent to which an honor should be guarded. West leads the seven of diamonds won by dummy's queen. East wins a club trick with his ace and returns a diamond, declarer winning with the ace. On the third round of clubs, West discards a heart. On the fourth round of clubs, East discards a diamond. From East's failure to play a high heart, not to mention the bidding, West can place declarer with at least the ace, consequently nine tricks. So the problem is to hold down the overtricks. He discards a small diamond. On the fifth club, East discards his last diamond. This clearly shows he does not expect to gain the lead in time to make saving a diamond worth while. And, for that matter, any other discard would involve some risk. For instance, the discard of a small spade would cause the ten to fall under the ace and permit a finesse through West if declarer should have the jack. West is forced to keep his spades and his king of diamonds—therefore blanks down to the doubleton queen of hearts. This is all logical, not double dummy, but it takes an expert partnership not to blow a trick on this type of defense.

In the next hand West has to make an early decision in order to direct the partnership to correct line of defense.

NORTH
♠ K Q 8 5
♡ 6 4
◇ K J 9 8 4
♣ Q 3

WEST
♠ J 10 6
♡ J 5 2
◇ Q 6
♣ K 9 8 6 2

EAST
♠ 9 7 3 2
♡ K Q 9
◇ 7 5 2
♣ A 7 4

SOUTH
♠ A 4
♡ A 10 8 7 3
◇ A 10 3
♣ J 10 5

SOUTH	NORTH
1 ♡	1 ♠
1 NT	2 NT
3 NT	

The opening lead is a small club to the ace. West ducks the club return. Declarer then leads the ace and ten of diamonds, continuing the suit. On the third round West has to find a discard. He should realize that whatever the spade situation is it will do him no good to hold his spades. And partner should be told early that he must hang on to them; consequently, a small spade is discarded. On the fourth round of diamonds, East discards the nine of hearts and West discards another spade. On the fifth round of diamonds East has to show real partnership confidence and discard the queen of hearts. (Notice that if he throws away his small clubs, South can cash the ace of spades and throw East in with the ace and another heart.) It is the same principle, again. One partner saves one suit and the other partner saves another. If West makes wishy-washy discards, throwing a heart, then a club, then a spade, for example, East will have no idea what to do.

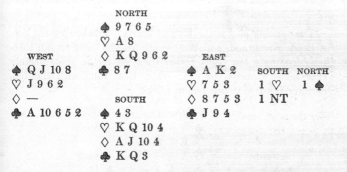

West leads the queen of spades. East overtakes and continues the suit. On the fourth spade trick East must find a discard. His correct discard is the three of diamonds. This lets his partner know that he has no stopper in diamonds. (His partner could not reasonably expect him to have anything else stopped.) If he throws the three of diamonds, West should cash his ace of clubs. Otherwise, West will lead a low club, hoping to find his partner with a club honor and a diamond trick.

Because of the peculiar nature of trumps where one may play a trump or not, unless trumps are led, inadequately guarded trump holdings may be promoted to tricks through an uppercut or overruff. An "uppercut" is a ruff by one defender so that if declarer overruffs, a trump trick is established for partner. An overruff (or threat of overruff) makes declarer ruff so high that he cannot draw trumps without loss of an extra trick. These two plays are very similar, as you can see from the following two examples:

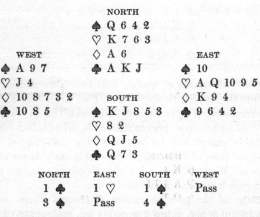

```
                     NORTH
                   ♠ Q 6 4 2
                   ♡ 9 7 6 3
      WEST         ◇ A K Q 10      EAST
    ♠ A 9 7        ♣ A           ♠ 10              NORTH  SOUTH
    ♡ K Q 10 8 2                 ♡ A 5             1 ◇    1 ♠
    ◇ J 5 2        SOUTH         ◇ 9 4 3           3 ♠    4 ♠
    ♣ J 8        ♠ K J 8 5 3     ♣ Q 9 7 6 4 3 2
                 ♡ J 4
                 ◇ 8 7 6
                 ♣ K 10 5
```

The opening lead is the king of hearts overtaken by the ace. A heart is returned, and West continues the third round, carefully leading a low heart rather than the ten to show partner that he is expected to ruff. When East ruffs with the ten, declarer must lose two trump tricks.

```
                     NORTH
                   ♠ Q 6 4 2
                   ♡ K 7 6 3
      WEST         ◇ A 6           EAST
    ♠ A 9 7        ♣ A K J       ♠ 10
    ♡ J 4                        ♡ A Q 10 9 5
    ◇ 10 8 7 3 2   SOUTH         ◇ K 9 4
    ♣ 10 8 5     ♠ K J 8 5 3     ♣ 9 6 4 2
                 ♡ 8 2
                 ◇ Q J 5
                 ♣ Q 7 3
```

NORTH	EAST	SOUTH	WEST
1 ♣	1 ♡	1 ♠	Pass
3 ♠	Pass	4 ♠	

The opening lead is the jack of hearts. Declarer ducks and ducks again on the second trick, but East wins with the queen and returns a low heart. Again, whatever declarer may do, he must lose two trump tricks, and in this case must also lose a diamond trick.

```
                    NORTH
                    ♠ 10 9 5
                    ♡ K Q J 6 3
        WEST        ◇ 7 6              EAST
   ♠ K Q J 7        ♣ 6 5 4       ♠ 8 6 3 2
   ♡ 9 4                           ♡ A 10 8 5
   ◇ A 9 8 4 2      SOUTH          ◇ J 3
   ♣ 10 8           ♠ A 4          ♣ Q J 2
                    ♡ 7 2
                    ◇ K Q 10 5
                    ♣ A K 9 7 3
```

SOUTH	WEST	NORTH	EAST
1 ◇	1 ♠	Pass	2 ♠
3 ♣			

West leads the king of spades, declarer holding up till the second round. Declarer then leads a low heart to the board, West playing the nine. East holds off, signaling with the ten. Declarer then leads a low diamond, finessing the ten, and West wins with the ace. If West merely returns a spade, declarer ruffs, cashes the ace-king of clubs, the king-queen of diamonds and ruffs a diamond. East could ruff or overruff, but it would be with his high trump. However, West should not return a spade. He should lead a heart and East will return another heart, assuring the defenders of two trump tricks. Notice that if declarer had won the first spade trick, the defenders would have had to cash their spade winner before starting the uppercut-overruff treatment. Otherwise, South would simply discard his losing spade on the heart lead from East.

```
                    NORTH
                    ♠ K 4
                    ♡ A 9 7 3
        WEST        ◇ Q J            EAST
   ♠ Q 9 8 7 3 2    ♣ K 9 7 6 3   ♠ J 6
   ♡ J 4                           ♡ 10 6 5         SOUTH   NORTH
   ◇ K 6 4 2        SOUTH          ◇ 8 7 3          1 ♡     2 ♣
   ♣ J              ♠ A 10 5       ♣ A Q 10 8 2     2 ◇     4 ♡
                    ♡ K Q 8 2
                    ◇ A 10 9 5
                    ♣ 8 4
```

West leads the jack of clubs. When dummy ducks, a very fine play on East's part is to overtake with the queen to play the ace and another one. He can determine that one discard from declarer's hand (if declarer has a singleton club) cannot do him any good. As it is, the overruff threat sets up a trump trick for the defenders which, combined with the diamond trick they get later, will set the contract.

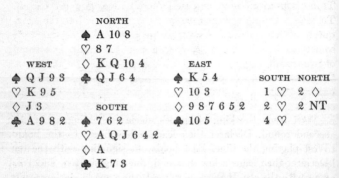

```
                  NORTH
                ♠ A 10 8
                ♡ 8 7
  WEST          ◇ K Q 10 4      EAST
♠ Q J 9 3       ♣ Q J 6 4     ♠ K 5 4         SOUTH  NORTH
♡ K 9 5                       ♡ 10 3            1 ♡    2 ◇
◇ J 3           SOUTH         ◇ 9 8 7 6 5 2     2 ♡    2 NT
♣ A 9 8 2     ♠ 7 6 2         ♣ 10 5            4 ♡
              ♡ A Q J 6 4 2
              ◇ A
              ♣ K 7 3
```

West leads the queen of spades, dummy playing the ace, East the five, and declarer the deuce. Next, declarer finesses trumps, losing to the king. At this point West has a problem, but proper inferences should lead him to the correct line of play. In the first place, it is virtually certain that declarer does not have the king of spades, for with that card he would have won in his hand to preserve a tenace over West's jack. And he could be pretty sure declarer has the singleton ace of diamonds, or three diamonds to the ace, or a singleton spade. With one or more spade losers and a doubleton ace of diamonds he would have attempted to take a quick discard before finessing trumps. The problem is to cash the top tricks without losing anything. Remember, from West's point of view, South may have three diamonds to the ace, a seven-card heart suit, and a singleton spade. In that case, it will be necessary to cash the ace and king of clubs or lose one of them. West cashes the ace of clubs and partner plays small. (This is hardly the time for East to start a high-low to show a doubleton.) Next, West leads a low spade to his partner's king, and a spade is returned. Now, it is obvious that there are no more side tricks to be won. This is the situation to look for an uppercut. West returns the thirteenth spade, East ruffs with a ten, and the nine of trumps will eventually become a winner.

Refusal to Ruff

THERE ARE many obvious cases where it does not pay to ruff. To take a simple example, suppose the declarer has the king-queen of trumps and West has the ace-jack. Declarer ruffs something with his queen. If West merely discards he is assured of two trump winners. If he overruffs his jack may be picked up. Of course, declarer might misguess anyway. However, it is particularly important not to overruff with a holding like A 10 x or A 9 x when declarer ruffs with an honor. It does not normally pay to ruff a low card when the hand which plays after it can also play a low card rather than a winner. Nor does it often pay to ruff with a high trump. It is generally better to wait until the lead can be obtained in a side suit so that the trump can be cashed, drawing two for one. Following are two obvious examples where it does not pay to ruff.

	NORTH		
	♠ Q J 6		
	♡ Q J 9 8 4		
WEST	◊ A 7 6 5	EAST	
♠ K 8 5	♣ 4	♠ 10 7 4 2	SOUTH NORTH
♡ 6		♡ K 10 2	1 NT 2 ♣
◊ Q J 10 9 4 3	SOUTH	◊ —	2 ♡ 4 ♡
♣ K 8 7	♠ A 9 3	♣ J 10 6 5 3 2	
	♡ A 7 5 3		
	◊ K 8 2		
	♣ A Q 9		

West leads the queen of diamonds, and dummy plays low. If East ruffs, it will cost him a trump trick while South follows suit with a loser.

In the following hand, East should refuse to overruff so as to force declarer to lose control.

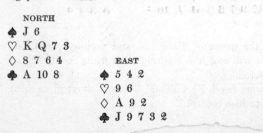

```
                    NORTH
                 ♠ A 9 4
                 ♡ A 10
   WEST          ◇ A K 5 4        EAST
♠ J              ♣ 10 8 7 5    ♠ K 5 3 2      NORTH  SOUTH
♡ J 8 7 2                      ♡ Q 6 5        1 NT   2 ♣
◇ J 7 3             SOUTH       ◇ 10 9 6       2 ◇    2 ♠
♣ K Q J 4 2      ♠ Q 10 8 7 6   ♣ A 9 3       4 ♣
                 ♡ K 9 4 3
                 ◇ Q 8 2
                 ♣ 6
```

Declarer ruffs the second club trick, followed by the ace and king of hearts, a heart ruff, the ace of diamonds, the queen of diamonds, and a heart ruff with the nine of spades. If East overruffs with the king, it will be his last trick. If he discards a diamond instead, declarer must lose two tricks. In this case East should refuse to overruff in order to retain control.

Entries

THE FIRST group of hands deal with the problem of preserving partner's entries, which is particularly important when defending against no-trump. The subject of unblocking will not be taken up here, because it does not differ much from the declarer's problems of unblocking. When partner leads top of a sequence you overtake with a doubleton honor to prevent the suit from being blocked, and the play of next to top when partner leads a suit at no trump serves the double purpose of signaling and unblocking. Occasionally, you must refuse to return fourth-best of partner's suit if your spot cards are large enough to block the suit. What we are most concerned with in this section is preserving partner's entries outside his own suit.

```
   NORTH
♠ J 6
♡ K Q 7 3
◇ 8 7 6 4           EAST
♣ A 10 8         ♠ 5 4 2
                 ♡ 9 6
                 ◇ A 9 2
                 ♣ J 9 7 3 2
```

SOUTH   NORTH
1 NT   3 NT

West leads the ten of spades and dummy wins with the jack. Declarer leads a low diamond from the board. East should definitely play the ace in order to return a spade (the deuce). In this case there is a double purpose in hopping up. For one thing, West will not be able to lead a spade if he has the king without giving up another trick in the suit. Even if East had the jack to force the queen at trick one so that the question of *who* led the spade was unimportant, he would still want to rush in and lead a spade before his partner's entry was knocked out. The following hands are all typical examples of why it pays to rush in:

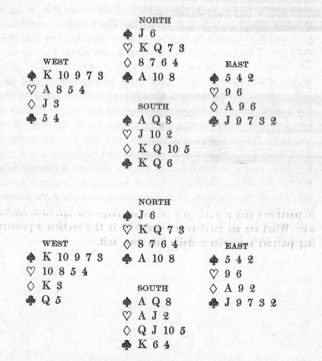

```
                    NORTH
                    ♠ J 6
                    ♡ K Q 7 3
    WEST            ◇ 8 7 6 4         EAST
♠ K 10 9 7 3        ♣ A 10 8     ♠ 5 4 2
♡ A 8 5 4                          ♡ 9 6
◇ J 3               SOUTH          ◇ A 9 6
♣ 5 4               ♠ A Q 8        ♣ J 9 7 3 2
                    ♡ J 10 2
                    ◇ K Q 10 5
                    ♣ K Q 6
```

```
                    NORTH
                    ♠ J 6
                    ♡ K Q 7 3
    WEST            ◇ 8 7 6 4         EAST
♠ K 10 9 7 3        ♣ A 10 8     ♠ 5 4 2
♡ 10 8 5 4                         ♡ 9 6
◇ K 3               SOUTH          ◇ A 9 2
♣ Q 5               ♠ A Q 8        ♣ J 9 7 3 2
                    ♡ A J 2
                    ◇ Q J 10 5
                    ♣ K 6 4
```

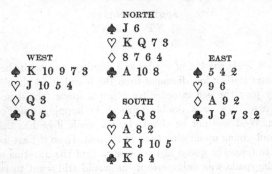

NORTH
♠ J 6
♡ K Q 7 3
◇ 8 7 6 4
♣ A 10 8

WEST
♠ K 10 9 7 3
♡ J 10 5 4
◇ Q 3
♣ Q 5

EAST
♠ 5 4 2
♡ 9 6
◇ A 9 2
♣ J 9 7 3 2

SOUTH
♠ A Q 8
♡ A 8 2
◇ K J 10 5
♣ K 6 4

In the first hand, if East ducks, declarer may guess to shift to hearts and knock out West's entry. In the second example, if East plays small, his partner's king of diamonds will be forced out and again he will have no entry. The person who ducks in this second example feels triumphant when he sees the third example. "You see, that's just what I was afraid of," he says. "If I hop up with the ace of diamonds my partner's queen drops on the second round and I give them an overtrick." But he is 100 per cent wrong. Do *you* always play for the queen to drop when your right-hand opponent hops up with the ace? Playing this hand in rubber bridge, you should (after holding off till the third round of spades), because you don't mind losing to East and can't risk losing to West. But in duplicate it is a close problem, and it is much better to give declarer a chance to go wrong. Besides, a doubleton queen holding by partner is only one possibility of many. If in the second example East had the king and West had the ace, it would be vital for East to hop right up with the king on the first diamond lead. This is a much tougher play to make, but it is still correct.

NORTH
♠ 8 2
♡ A 10 4
◇ K Q 7
♣ J 10 7 4 3

WEST
♠ Q 9 7 6 4
♡ Q 8 6
◇ 10 9 6
♣ A 8

EAST
♠ J 10 5
♡ K 9 5 2
◇ 8 3 2
♣ K 5 2

SOUTH
♠ A K 3
♡ J 7 3
◇ A J 5 4
♣ Q 9 6

SOUTH	NORTH
1 ◇	1 ♡
1 NT	2 NT
3 NT	

The opening lead is a spade and the key play on the hand is for East to hop up with the king on the first club lead from the board. If West has a singleton honor, it is just too bad!

NORTH
♠ 7 3
♡ A J 10 6 5
◇ K 9 7
♣ A Q 4

WEST
♠ Q 9 6 5 2
♡ K 3
◇ J 6 4 3
♣ 9 6

EAST
♠ A J 4
♡ Q 9 2
◇ 10 5
♣ 10 7 5 3 2

SOUTH
♠ K 10 8
♡ 8 7 4
◇ A Q 8 2
♣ K J 8

SOUTH	NORTH
1 ◇	1 ♡
1 NT	3 NT

This hand illustrates another way of preserving an entry into partner's hand. West leads a low spade and East plays the jack. Declarer cannot afford to hold up and risk losing the whole spade suit, especially when all he needs is a diamond break for nine tricks. When the partner of the opening leader has ace-queen-small of his partner's suit, the play of the queen is standard. The play of jack from ace-jack-small, is riskier, since it may give declarer an undeserved trick with the queen, but in a hand like this where partner is almost bound to be entryless, the play of the jack is an insurance play.

```
                      NORTH
                    ♠ A 7 4
                    ♡ 10 9 5 4
        WEST        ◇ K Q 9 6        EAST
    ♠ J 6 5 3       ♣ 8 7        ♠ Q 10 8 2      SOUTH  NORTH
    ♡ K 7 3                      ♡ 8 2            1 ♡    1 ♠
    ◇ 5 3           SOUTH        ◇ A 8 4          1 NT   2 ♡
    ♣ K 10 9 2      ♠ K 9        ♣ Q J 6 4        3 ♡    4 ♡
                    ♡ A Q J 6
                    ◇ J 10 7 2
                    ♣ A 5 3
```

West leads the five of diamonds, and East should play the eight. The diamond lead could hardly be a singleton, since South would not re-bid one no-trump with a five-card diamond suit. Assuming that the diamond lead is from a doubleton, East must save his only entry until his partner is ready to ruff.

```
                      NORTH
                    ♠ Q 5 3
                    ♡ 10 7 6
        WEST        ◇ K Q 8 7 3        EAST
    ♠ 7 2           ♣ 9 5          ♠ K J 9 6 4
    ♡ J 9 5 3                      ♡ K 8 4
    ◇ A 9 4         SOUTH          ◇ 5
    ♣ 8 7 6 4       ♠ A 10 8       ♣ A 10 3 2
                    ♡ A Q 2
                    ◇ J 10 6 2
                    ♣ K Q J
```

WEST	NORTH	EAST	SOUTH
Pass	Pass	1 ♠	1 NT
Pass	2 NT	Pass	3 NT

Many times with a suit headed by the ace you must duck a round or two, saving the ace as an entry after the suit has been set up. Ducks with a king-queen, or king-jack, as in the above hand are less frequent. The opening lead is a spade which East must duck whether or not dummy plays the queen. If he plays an honor, declarer will duck and the suit cannot be established and run. When declarer wins with the ten he must guess which minor-suit ace to knock out. If declarer leads the jack or ten of diamonds, West is called upon to exercise his judgment. Conceivably, he should hold off till the third round to prevent the run of the diamond suit. Actually, of course, it would not work in this case. And, for that matter, West's percentage play is to go in with the ace immediately. He can assume that his partner has one entry, and if the spades are continued before it is knocked out, partner should be able to set the contract, whether diamonds are run or not.

In the next group of hands the problem will be to destroy the declarer's entries rather than to preserve partner's.

Certain standard combinations present no problem. Suppose dummy has a six-card suit headed by the ace-jack-ten with no outside entries. You are West. When declarer leads low toward the board, you should play your honor if you have a doubleton king or queen. The suit may be distributed as follows:

<pre>
              A J 10 x x x
        K x   Q x x
              x x
</pre>

If you were to play small, partner could prevent the run of the whole suit by ducking when the ten was finessed, but your carelessness would cost you a trick. If you had K x x or Q x x, you would play small, and partner should duck with his doubleton honor. Suppose an otherwise entryless dummy has A J 10 x x of a suit. Now it is correct for West to play an honor even from a tripleton holding. If declarer has a doubleton, he can win nothing but the ace. If he thinks West is splitting his honors, declarer may duck and finesse the next round for *no* tricks.

When dummy has A J 10 x and no outside entries, West should play an honor whenever the suit is split 4-3-3-3 in order to hold declarer to two tricks. More of these combinations could be given, but they are easy to figure out when they occur, provided you are alert and watching for them.

```
                    NORTH
                 ♠ J 7 6
                 ♡ 5 4
    WEST         ◇ A J 10 9 6 5      EAST
 ♠ K 10 4 2   ♣ 7 2              ♠ Q 8 3        SOUTH   NORTH
 ♡ Q 10 8                        ♡ J 9 7 6 2     1 ♣     1 ◇
 ◇ 8 3 2         SOUTH           ◇ K 7           2 NT    3 NT
 ♣ K 8 3      ♠ A 9 5            ♣ Q 6 4
                 ♡ A K 3
                 ◇ Q 4
                 ♣ A J 10 9 5
```

West leads his fourth-best spade, dummy plays small, and East should play the eight. Declarer wins with the nine, but has no entry to the dummy within the spade suit. Next, declarer leads the queen of diamonds and East bravely ducks. Declarer finesses diamonds again, and the dummy is completely dead. East's play may look risky, but declarer cannot see his hand, and is almost bound to finesse again, once he has led the queen. A better line of play for declarer after the play of the first spade trick (indicating East is trying to cut down on his entries —hence probably has the king of diamonds) is to lead a low diamond to the nine, and if it holds, use this entry for a club lead in an effort to develop the club suit. Naturally, if the nine of diamonds loses to the king, declarer will later overtake the queen in order to run the suit.

```
    NORTH
 ♠ 3
 ♡ A J 10 4
 ◇ K 10 8 6 5 4      EAST
 ♣ 9 6            ♠ 8 7 6
                  ♡ K Q 7 3
                  ◇ J 9 3
                  ♣ J 8 5
```

	SOUTH	WEST	NORTH	EAST
	2 ♠	Pass	3 ◇	Pass
	3 ♠	Pass	4 ◇	Pass
	4 ♠	Pass	5 ♡	Double
	6 ♠	Pass	Pass	Pass

West leads the nine of hearts, North plays the ten, and you (East) win with the queen. Decide what you would return. A small heart is the indicated play! Declarer's most probable diamond holding is the doubleton ace—possibly the doubleton ace-queen. His purpose in ducking was to save the ace of hearts as an entry to the diamond suit after it was established by a ruff. You can make up hands in which it would be fatal to return a heart, but in almost every case you will find they are not consistent with the bidding or it would be illogical for declarer to duck the opening lead. He could hardly have been *counting* on a heart return! Probable South hand: ♠ A K Q J 10 x, ♡ x x, ◇ A x, ♣ A Q x.

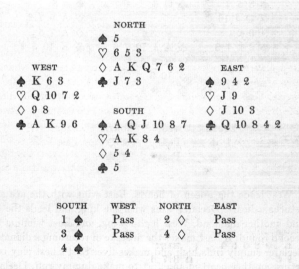

NORTH
♠ 5
♡ 6 5 3
◇ A K Q 7 6 2
♣ J 7 3

WEST
♠ K 6 3
♡ Q 10 7 2
◇ 9 8
♣ A K 9 6

EAST
♠ 9 4 2
♡ J 9
◇ J 10 3
♣ Q 10 8 4 2

SOUTH
♠ A Q J 10 8 7
♡ A K 8 4
◇ 5 4
♣ 5

SOUTH	WEST	NORTH	EAST
1 ♠	Pass	2 ◇	Pass
3 ♠	Pass	4 ◇	Pass
4 ♠			

The opening lead is the king of clubs, East playing the four. West's percentage play is to shift to a diamond. If South has a singleton diamond he may get rid of a losing club, but if diamonds are not led he would get rid of some heart losers later on the diamonds. Dummy wins with the ace and takes a spade finesse. West wins and leads another diamond. This prevents declarer from using the diamond suit. The diamond play is a sort of insurance play. It might permit declarer to get rid of a quick loser (if he should have a singleton diamond) but it prevents him from discarding several eventual losers on the diamonds later. About the only time the diamond lead would turn out badly is when South is void of diamonds. This is a fairly common play, making dummy use up its entries to its long suit before trumps are drawn.

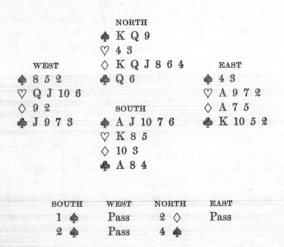

NORTH
♠ K Q 9
♡ 4 3
♢ K Q J 8 6 4
♣ Q 6

WEST
♠ 8 5 2
♡ Q J 10 6
♢ 9 2
♣ J 9 7 3

EAST
♠ 4 3
♡ A 9 7 2
♢ A 7 5
♣ K 10 5 2

SOUTH
♠ A J 10 7 6
♡ K 8 5
♢ 10 3
♣ A 8 4

SOUTH	WEST	NORTH	EAST
1 ♠	Pass	2 ♢	Pass
2 ♠	Pass	4 ♠	

West leads the queen of hearts. East wins with the ace and returns a heart. Declarer wins with the king and leads the ten and another diamond, West high-lowing, and East winning the second round. If East makes the mistake of returning a diamond, declarer simply ruffs high and makes five. East's best play is to return another heart in an effort to make dummy ruff. Declarer can still make his contract, but not an overtrick, by refusing to ruff—or even by ruffing and leading a diamond back from the board. However, declarers have been known to misplay when given an opportunity. If he concedes a club trick and tries for a cross-ruff, partner's eight of spades will be a winner.

```
                        NORTH
                        ♠ A 5
                        ♡ J 8
        WEST            ◇ K Q 5              EAST
        ♠ 10 4 3        ♣ Q J 10 9 4 3       ♠ 8 6
        ♡ 9 6 5 4 2                          ♡ K Q 10 7
        ◇ J 7 2         SOUTH                ◇ A 10 3
        ♣ 8 5           ♠ K Q J 9 7 2        ♣ A 7 6 2
                        ♡ A 3
                        ◇ 9 8 6 4
                        ♣ K
```

EAST	SOUTH	WEST	NORTH
1 ♡	1 ♠	Pass	2 ♣
Pass	2 ♠	Pass	3 ♠
Pass	4 ♠		

The opening lead is a small heart, the ten forcing the ace.
Declarer next leads the king of clubs. East thinks longingly of
ducking but decides he cannot afford to. (He's right! If he
ducks, declarer makes five.) East wins and cashes his heart trick
and must now lead back the three of diamonds. His only hope
of setting the contract is that his partner has the jack of diamonds. The ace of spades is an entry to the dummy, but if
partner has three spades, the only entry to the dummy after
trumps are drawn is in the diamond suit.

```
                        NORTH
                        ♠ A K 9 5
                        ♡ Q 7
        WEST            ◇ J 4 3              EAST
        ♠ Q 10 6 4      ♣ A 8 7 3            ♠ J 3
        ♡ K 10 8 3                           ♡ J 6 5 2
        ◇ K Q 8 7       SOUTH                ◇ —
        ♣ 6             ♠ 8 7 2              ♣ Q J 10 9 5 4 2
                        ♡ A 9 4
                        ◇ A 10 9 6 5 2
                        ♣ K
```

NORTH	EAST	SOUTH	WEST
1 ♣	3 ♣	3 NT	

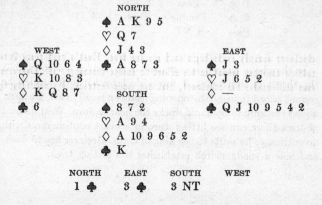

The opening lead is a club, declarer winning with the king. A low spade is led to the ace, followed by a diamond return. Naturally, declarer plays the nine and West can either hold up now or later. He decides to win immediately and must return the king of hearts. This knocks out declarer's last side entry and he is unable to bring in the diamond suit. Leading the king this way is a sure play when the ace is doubleton. In this case where the other hand has a doubleton, more luck is needed. If declarer had the jack of hearts he could throw the queen from the dummy.

```
                    NORTH
                    ♠ 7
                    ♡ 8 4
        WEST        ◇ K Q J 9 8 6 2        EAST
     ♠ 4 2          ♣ A 7 6             ♠ K Q 10 8 5 3
     ♡ Q J 7 3 2                        ♡ K 9 6
     ◇ 5 4          SOUTH               ◇ A 10
     ♣ K 10 9 3     ♠ A J 9 6           ♣ 5 4
                    ♡ A 10 5
                    ◇ 7 3
                    ♣ Q J 8 2
```

EAST	SOUTH	WEST	NORTH
1 ♠	Pass	1 NT	2 ◇
2 ♠	Double	Pass	3 ◇
Pass	3 NT		

In the above hand it is not possible to destroy the entry, but the threat of destroying it forces declarer to duck a trick he cannot afford to lose. The opening lead is a small heart. Declarer allows the king to hold and ducks the heart return. West on lead at trick three can see little future in a heart continuation with no entries, so he shifts to the king of clubs. Declarer has to duck, and now a spade switch establishes the setting trick.

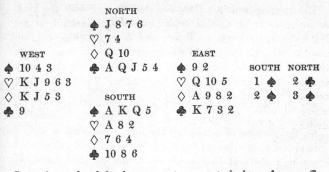

```
                    NORTH
                  ♠ J 8 7 6
                  ♡ 7 4
   WEST             ◇ Q 10             EAST
♠ 10 4 3           ♣ A Q J 5 4      ♠ 9 2          SOUTH  NORTH
♡ K J 9 6 3                         ♡ Q 10 5        1 ♠    2 ♣
◇ K J 5 3           SOUTH            ◇ A 9 8 2       2 ♠    3 ♠
♣ 9               ♠ A K Q 5         ♣ K 7 3 2
                  ♡ A 8 2
                  ◇ 7 6 4
                  ♣ 10 8 6
```

Sometimes the defenders cannot prevent declarer from ruffing, gaining an entry in the process, but they can force declarer
to ruff sooner or later than he desires. The opening lead is West's
singleton club. Declarer wins with the ace and draws three
rounds of trumps followed by the ten and another club. East
wins the third round of clubs, cashes the ace of diamonds, and
shifts to a heart. Perfect defense! Declarer cannot get a ruff
before the fourth defensive trick is cashed. If he goes to the
board with a trump lead, he loses his ruff, necessary for the
tenth trick. If East had led a heart before cashing the ace
of diamonds, South would duck. Then West would have to lead
away from his king of diamonds. He should make this play, but
why should East make it hard for him? On the other hand, if
East gets overly encouraged by his partner's signal in diamonds
and continues diamonds instead of shifting to a heart, declarer
will win the heart return, ruff a diamond, and discard his heart
losers on the clubs.

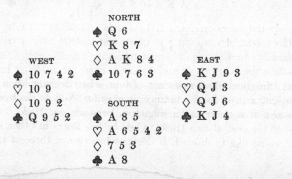

```
                    NORTH
                  ♠ Q 6
                  ♡ K 8 7
   WEST             ◇ A K 8 4          EAST
♠ 10 7 4 2        ♣ 10 7 6 3        ♠ K J 9 3
♡ 10 9                              ♡ Q J 3
◇ 10 9 2           SOUTH            ◇ Q J 6
♣ Q 9 5 2        ♠ A 8 5            ♣ K J 4
                  ♡ A 6 5 4 2
                  ◇ 7 5 3
                  ♣ A 8
```

NORTH	EAST	SOUTH	WEST
1 ◇	Double	Redouble	1 ♠
Pass	Pass	2 ♡	Pass
3 ♡	Pass	4 ♡	

West leads a small spade, covered by the queen, king and ace. At trick two, declarer leads a diamond, putting in the eight-spot. Only a club return will set the contract. The diamond duck, for the purpose of setting up the fourth diamond, is obviously to obtain a club discard (no use to discard a spade, since a spade can be ruffed). If East carelessly cashes his high spade before returning a club, declarer will ruff the third round of spades, pull two rounds of trumps, and discard his club loser on the long diamond, while East ruffs with his high trump. If East returns the club before cashing his spade winner, declarer will be unable to pull two rounds of trumps in order to use his long diamond and still get a spade ruff. On the thirteenth diamond, East will not ruff with his high trump. He will win the spade return and cash the high trump, leaving declarer with another spade loser.

```
                    NORTH
                 ♠ Q
                 ♡ K Q 8 5 2
                 ◇ A 8 7 5
    WEST         ♣ J 9 4              EAST
 ♠ 5 4                             ♠ 8 7 6 2
 ♡ A 9 6                           ♡ J 10 3
 ◇ K 9 3 2          SOUTH          ◇ J 10 4
 ♣ Q 10 7 3      ♠ A K J 10 9 3    ♣ K 8 6
                 ♡ 7 4
                 ◇ Q 6
                 ♣ A 5 2
```

	SOUTH	NORTH
	1 ♠	2 ♡
	2 ♠	2 NT
	4 ♠	

In about three cases out of four, when declarer leads toward K Q x (x x) in the dummy, it pays for West to duck with the ace. If declarer has a singleton, he steals one trick, but often at the cost of two tricks, when he has losers in other suits he would like to discard. If declarer has two or three of the suit, he may have difficulty getting back to his hand to lead the suit again. The opening lead is a trump, declarer overtaking in order to draw trumps. Next, he leads a low heart. If West ducks, declarer cannot return to his hand without setting up tricks for the defense. Change the hand slightly, giving East the ace of hearts three-long, and king of diamonds. Now a duck of the heart trick is devastating. For that matter, East should hold up whether he has the king of diamonds or not, assuming that West signals his distribution. For all he knows, declarer has the king of diamonds, in which case a diamond return would not force the ace. Then ducking would be the only play to hold declarer to ten tricks. Inexperienced players are inclined to grab the ace right away when it is over the king-queen. The correct play is to hold up till the second round when declarer has a doubleton, as shown by partner's distributional signal. The hold-up gives declarer one less *usable* entry to dummy when he plans to ruff out his suit. Besides, if you duck fast, declarer may waste an important entry to his hand just to lead up to the remaining honor.

The following hands show the influence of entries on the play of other suits.

```
                    NORTH
                 ♠ K Q 8 6 4
                 ♡ Q 9 3
                 ♢ 5
     WEST         ♣ J 7 3 2           EAST
  ♠ A 9                            ♠ J 10 5 2     SOUTH  NORTH
  ♡ K 10 8 5 2                     ♡ A J 7 4        1 ♢    1 ♠
  ♢ J 7 6          SOUTH           ♢ 10 3           3 ♢
  ♣ Q 8 6        ♠ 7 3            ♣ K 5 4
                 ♡ 6
                 ♢ A K Q 9 8 4 2
                 ♣ A 10 9
```

The opening lead is a heart, declarer ruffing the second round. Trumps are drawn followed by a spade lead, which West ducks. The jack of clubs is then led from the dummy. Normally, East would cover. But he can see that the lead will never be in dummy again. So he plays low, and South must lose two club tricks.

		NORTH			
		♠ K J 10 8 6			
		♡ A 10 5 4			
WEST		♢ K 8	EAST		
♠ A 4 3		♣ K 6	♠ 9 7 2	NORTH	SOUTH
♡ K J 6			♡ Q 9 8 3	1 ♠	2 ♢
♢ 3 2		SOUTH	♢ 10 7 5 4	2 ♡	2 NT
♣ J 8 5 4 2		♠ Q 5	♣ A 10	3 NT	
		♡ 7 2			
		♢ A Q J 9 6			
		♣ Q 9 7 3			

West leads his fourth-best club. East wins the king[3] with the ace and returns a heart. West wins with the jack and returns the king, declarer being forced to duck. West realizes the futility of continuing hearts, since his partner cannot have an entry. So he shifts to a club, hoping that his partner has the ten. The defense thus takes two clubs, two hearts, and a spade.

		NORTH			
		♠ A 8			
		♡ 9 6			
WEST		♢ A J 10 9 4	EAST		
♠ 9 2		♣ 8 7 6 4	♠ K J 5 4	SOUTH	NORTH
♡ K 10 7 5 2			♡ Q J 4	1 ♠	2 ♢
♢ 6 5 3		SOUTH	♢ K 8 2	2 NT	3 NT
♣ J 3 2		♠ Q 10 7 6 3	♣ Q 10 9		
		♡ A 8 3			
		♢ Q 7			
		♣ A K 5			

West leads a heart, declarer ducking the first two tricks. West knows that establishing the hearts with no entry would be a waste of time. When declarer plays small to the second trick he

---

[3] Of course it is a mistake, or at least a greedy play, for declarer to put up the king of clubs at the first trick.

overtakes his partner's queen in order to lead a spade—his only reasonable hope. The spade lead is a "killer." East knocks out the ace and holds up one round with the king of diamonds, leaving the dummy high and dry.

The next few hands illustrate reasons for hold-up plays other than for entry purposes.

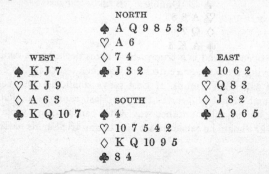

```
                       NORTH
                       ♠ K 7 3
                       ♡ 8
        WEST           ◇ A K Q J 5 4        EAST
        ♠ A 10 2       ♣ A 9 6              ♠ 7 6
        ♡ A K Q 10 3                        ♡ J 9 5
        ◇ 10           SOUTH                ◇ 7 6 3 2
        ♣ Q 8 7 3      ♠ Q J 9 8 4          ♣ J 10 5 2
                       ♡ 7 6 4 2
                       ◇ 9 8
                       ♣ K 4
```

NORTH	EAST	SOUTH	WEST
1 ◇	Pass	1 ♠	2 ♡
3 ♠	Pass	4 ♠	

West leads the king of hearts and continues with the queen. Dummy ruffs and returns the king of spades. If West wins, he is helpless. Declarer has control of every suit, can pull trumps and discard his losers on the diamonds. But if West plays small, declarer has problems. He cannot run the diamond suit till trumps are drawn, and he cannot draw trumps without West's cashing his heart tricks.

```
                       NORTH
                       ♠ A Q 9 8 5 3
                       ♡ A 6
        WEST           ◇ 7 4                EAST
        ♠ K J 7        ♣ J 3 2              ♠ 10 6 2
        ♡ K J 9                             ♡ Q 8 3
        ◇ A 6 3        SOUTH                ◇ J 8 2
        ♣ K Q 10 7     ♠ 4                  ♣ A 9 6 5
                       ♡ 10 7 5 4 2
                       ◇ K Q 10 9 5
                       ♣ 8 4
```

WEST	NORTH	EAST	SOUTH
1 NT	2 ♠	Double	3 ◇
Pass	Pass	Double	

West leads the king of clubs and a low club. East returns a trump; South finesses the ten. West should duck this trick. Whether declarer tries for a heart ruff or tries to bring in the spade suit, his plans can be easily foiled. But suppose West wins the diamond trick and returns a heart (as good a play as any). Declarer ducks in the dummy. Then, if a trump *is not led*, declarer will obtain a heart ruff. If a trump *is* led, he draws trumps, finesses the queen of spades and ruffs out the suit with the ace of hearts still an entry.

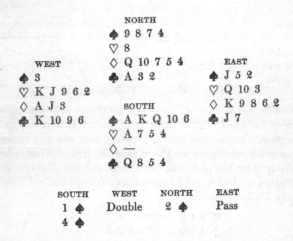

NORTH
♠ 9 8 7 4
♡ 8
◇ Q 10 7 5 4
♣ A 3 2

WEST
♠ 3
♡ K J 9 6 2
◇ A J 3
♣ K 10 9 6

EAST
♠ J 5 2
♡ Q 10 3
◇ K 9 8 6 2
♣ J 7

SOUTH
♠ A K Q 10 6
♡ A 7 5 4
◇ —
♣ Q 8 5 4

SOUTH	WEST	NORTH	EAST
1 ♠	Double	2 ♠	Pass
4 ♠			

The opening lead is a trump. East gives declarer his contract by playing the jack, since declarer then has ten tricks by cross-ruffing with high trumps. If East plays small, he can overruff the fourth round of hearts. Perhaps East cannot see that far ahead, but to put it another way, what can he gain by playing the jack? Should he expect to set up a trump trick in his partner's hand?

```
                    NORTH
                  ♠ K Q 5 4
                  ♡ J 7 3
        WEST      ◇ 9 8              EAST
      ♠ 7         ♣ Q 9 8 4        ♠ 10 3        SOUTH   NORTH
      ♡ 10 8 4 2                   ♡ A Q 6       1 ♠     2 ♠
      ◇ A Q 10 6          SOUTH    ◇ J 5 3 2     3 ♠     4 ♠
      ♣ J 6 5 2         ♠ A J 9 8 6 2   ♣ K 10 7 3
                        ♡ K 9 5
                        ◇ K 7 4
                        ♣ A
```

West leads his deuce of hearts, East winning with the ace. Since declarer might have the ace-king-queen of diamonds for a heart discard, East returns the queen of hearts, certain that his partner has the king. The heart return is the only play to give declarer the contract. Unfortunate? No. East had a 100 per cent safe play. He should play the queen at the first trick. If it held the trick, as he expected it would, he could continue with the ace and a small one. In the actual situation he would avoid a disaster.

```
                    NORTH
                  ♠ K Q 9 8 7
                  ♡ A Q 6
        WEST      ◇ 10 8 6 3        EAST
      ♠ 5         ♣ 7              ♠ 10 2        SOUTH   NORTH
      ♡ J 10 9                     ♡ K 7 5 3     1 ♠     3 ♠
      ◇ Q J 7 4 2        SOUTH     ◇ K 9         4 ♠
      ♣ K 9 5 2        ♠ A J 6 4 3   ♣ A 10 8 6 3
                        ♡ 8 4 2
                        ◇ A 5
                        ♣ Q J 4
```

It takes stamina to be a good defender. The opening lead is the jack of hearts, declarer going right up with the ace. The ace and king of spades are played, followed by the lead of a low club. In this case, If East ducks, all is well. But East should not be careless. He should duck fast! That is to say, he should not give away the fact that he has the ace. Declarer might have had

K J x instead of Q J x. And why should East risk ducking at all? Because he has no reasonable chance of setting the contract unless his partner can win this trick. Declarer is marked with three hearts (possibly one) by his play of the ace at the first trick, and ducking the club figures to come out even at *worst*.

Lead Values

IN THE next group of hands, we shall consider cases where it is much more important for one defender to be on lead than it is for the other. We will consider the symptoms of the situation, and various devices of the defenders to give each other the lead or to prevent declarer from passing tricks to the opponent of his choice.

```
        NORTH
     ♠ K 10 8 4
     ♡ A 7 5
     ◇ 10
     ♣ J 10 8 6 2            EAST
                          ♠ 9 2
                          ♡ 8 2
                          ◇ J 9 8 7 5 4
                          ♣ K 7 3
```

SOUTH	WEST	NORTH	EAST
1 ♠	Double	3 ♠	

West leads the king of hearts. When declarer ducks in dummy, East should not try to show a doubleton. He should play the deuce to let his partner know he does *not* have the jack. So West shifts to a trump. After playing a couple of rounds of trumps, with West discarding a heart on the second round, declarer leads a low club from the board. Without question, East's proper play is to go up with the king. Partner's shift at the second trick marks declarer with the jack of hearts. It is vital for East to obtain the lead to set up a heart trick before the club suit is established. Hopping up with the king of clubs is not even risky—not if partner and declarer are strong players.

Declarer is marked with the ace or king of diamonds. Why? Because partner neither led a diamond originally nor shifted to a diamond. If declarer had six spades to the A Q J, the ace or king of diamonds, and the ace of clubs, he would not have passed at three spades. And if partner had the ace of clubs singleton? Then he would have 6-5 distribution and would not have sold out so cheaply. The complete hand:

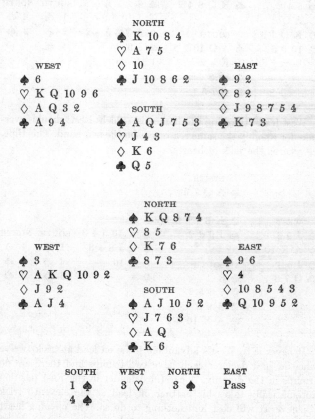

```
                    NORTH
                    ♠ K 10 8 4
                    ♡ A 7 5
        WEST        ◇ 10            EAST
        ♠ 6         ♣ J 10 8 6 2    ♠ 9 2
        ♡ K Q 10 9 6                ♡ 8 2
        ◇ A Q 3 2   SOUTH           ◇ J 9 8 7 5 4
        ♣ A 9 4     ♠ A Q J 7 5 3   ♣ K 7 3
                    ♡ J 4 3
                    ◇ K 6
                    ♣ Q 5
```

```
                    NORTH
                    ♠ K Q 8 7 4
                    ♡ 8 5
        WEST        ◇ K 7 6         EAST
        ♠ 3         ♣ 8 7 3         ♠ 9 6
        ♡ A K Q 10 9 2              ♡ 4
        ◇ J 9 2     SOUTH           ◇ 10 8 5 4 3
        ♣ A J 4     ♠ A J 10 5 2    ♣ Q 10 9 5 2
                    ♡ J 7 6 3
                    ◇ A Q
                    ♣ K 6
```

SOUTH	WEST	NORTH	EAST
1 ♠	3 ♡	3 ♠	Pass
4 ♠			

West leads the king, then the queen of hearts. East should ruff the second round and lead a club, since the trump is good for nothing else, and it is inconceivable that it will be to West's advantage to remain on lead.

NORTH
♠ K J 9 8
♡ 9 7 6
♢ 9
♣ K Q 8 4 2

WEST		EAST		
♠ 5 4 2		♠ 6	SOUTH	NORTH
♡ A Q 8		♡ J 10 5 3	1 ♠	2 ♣
♢ K Q J 8		♢ A 7 6 5 4 2	2 ♠	3 ♠
♣ 10 9 6	SOUTH	♣ J 3	4 ♠	

SOUTH
♠ A Q 10 7 3
♡ K 4 2
♢ 10 3
♣ A 7 5

West leads the king of diamonds, which East should over-take for roughly the same reasons as on the last hand. This time, he returns the jack of hearts.

NORTH
♠ A Q 7 6
♡ —
♢ K 8 7 6 3
♣ J 9 6 2

WEST		EAST		
♠ J 9 2		♠ K 10 5 4 3	SOUTH	NORTH
♡ A K 10 4		♡ Q J 8 4 3	1 ♣	1 ♢
♢ J 5 4		♢ Q 10	2 ♣	2 ♠
♣ Q 7 3	SOUTH	♣ 4	3 ♢	5 ♣

SOUTH
♠ 8
♡ 7 6 5 2
♢ A 9 2
♣ A K 10 8 5

It never is to West's advantage to be on lead at trick twelve when he and declarer each have two trumps and there are no trumps in the dummy. A careful defender in the East position automatically takes his partner off lead at the eleventh trick whenever it will cost him nothing to do so. The opening heart lead is ruffed, followed by the top diamonds, another heart ruff, the ace and a spade ruff, a heart ruff, a spade ruff, a heart ruff, and a spade ruff with the ace. The position is now

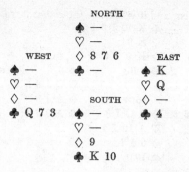

NORTH
♠ —
♡ —
◇ 8 7 6
♣ —

WEST
♠ —
♡ —
◇ —
♣ Q 7 3

EAST
♠ K
♡ Q
◇ —
♣ 4

SOUTH
♠ —
♡ —
◇ 9
♣ K 10

Declarer leads a diamond, and East should overruff his partner's three-spot. If West had held the four of clubs instead of the three, he should have underruffed when South ruffed with the ace. He could then follow suit to the next diamond lead, allowing his partner to ruff with the three-spot.

NORTH
♠ A 8 6
♡ A J 9 8
◇ A 7
♣ A Q 9 6

WEST
♠ 9 3 2
♡ 10 3
◇ Q J 10 3
♣ J 8 4 2

EAST
♠ Q J 10 5
♡ 5 2
◇ 9 6 4 2
♣ K 10 5

SOUTH
♠ K 7 4
♡ K Q 7 6 4
◇ K 8 5
♣ 7 3

	NORTH	SOUTH
	1 ♣	1 ♡
	4 ♡	4 NT
	5 ♣	6 ♡

Declarer wins the diamond opening lead in the dummy, pulls two rounds of trumps, and cashes the ace and king of spades. If East is a strong player he will follow suit with an honor each time. The possibility of an end-play will have haunted him ever since the first look at the dummy. Declarer will cash the king of diamonds and ruff a diamond, then lead a low spade. East must play his carefully-retained five-spot in order to allow his partner to win the trick.

```
                    NORTH
                    ♠ K 10 7 6 4
                    ♡ K 9
   WEST              ◇ K 9 7 4        EAST
   ♠ 5 3            ♣ 8 6            ♠ 9              SOUTH  NORTH
   ♡ 6 3                            ♡ Q J 8 5 2      1 ♠    2 ♡
   ◇ Q 10 3          SOUTH          ◇ A J 8          3 ♡    3 ♠
   ♣ K Q J 7 3 2    ♠ A Q J 8 2     ♣ A 9 5 4        4 ♡    4 ♠
                    ♡ A 10 7 4
                    ◇ 6 5 2
                    ♣ 10
```

Declarer ruffs the second round of clubs followed by the king of hearts, ace of hearts, a heart ruff, a spade to the ace, a heart ruff, a spade to the queen, and a low diamond lead. If West is on his toes, he will play the ten (or the queen), and declarer must lose three diamond tricks. If he ducks, declarer puts in the seven spot for an end-play on East. In the previous example hand, a defender had to anticipate the end-play attempt before the hand was stripped. It is very easy to tell what is going on when declarer has stripped his hand and dummy down to one side suit and trumps. If the lead comes from dummy in this situation, so that you can't see declarer's holding, you can avoid the end-play (provided it is avoidable) by playing your highest card other than the ace or king. As in this example, the highest card, the queen, would have worked just as well as the ten. Sometimes the highest card is the only one to avoid the end-play.

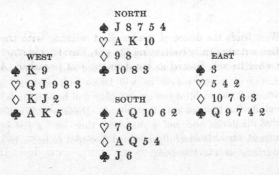

```
                    NORTH
                    ♠ J 8 7 5 4
                    ♡ A K 10
   WEST              ◇ 9 8            EAST
   ♠ K 9            ♣ 10 8 3         ♠ 3
   ♡ Q J 9 8 3                       ♡ 5 4 2
   ◇ K J 2          SOUTH            ◇ 10 7 6 3
   ♣ A K 5          ♠ A Q 10 6 2     ♣ Q 9 7 4 2
                    ♡ 7 6
                    ◇ A Q 5 4
                    ♣ J 6
```

SOUTH	WEST	NORTH	EAST
1 ♠	Double	Redouble	2 ♣
Pass	2 ♡	2 ♠	Pass
3 ♠	Pass	4 ♠	

The opening lead is the king of clubs, East playing the nine. West should visualize the possibility of being endplayed with the king of trumps and should avoid it by the simple expedient of leading a low club at the second trick. East will have no difficulty in figuring out what is expected of him. A diamond return is marked.

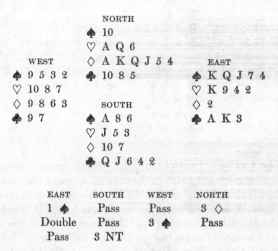

```
                    NORTH
                 ♠ 10
                 ♡ A Q 6
      WEST       ◇ A K Q J 5 4       EAST
   ♠ 9 5 3 2     ♣ 10 8 5         ♠ K Q J 7 4
   ♡ 10 8 7                        ♡ K 9 4 2
   ◇ 9 8 6 3     SOUTH             ◇ 2
   ♣ 9 7         ♠ A 8 6           ♣ A K 3
                 ♡ J 5 3
                 ◇ 10 7
                 ♣ Q J 6 4 2
```

EAST	SOUTH	WEST	NORTH
1 ♠	Pass	Pass	3 ◇
Double	Pass	3 ♠	Pass
Pass	3 NT		

West leads the deuce of spades. East winning with the jack. Before automatically continuing the suit, East should start figuring what he will discard as the diamond suit is cashed. Almost any way he looks at it, he will be endplayed, forced to lead a heart into the A-Q unless he unguards his king of hearts—which declarer would surely be able to guess. There is one hope —that his partner has the nine of spades. So East shifts to a low spade at trick two! If he leads an honor, declarer will duck and have a certain end-play. However, if declarer ducks the low spade, West wins and breaks up the end-play with a heart return. Now, even if he plays the ace, declarer is helpless, since East has his small spade as an exit card, and of course West will save his spades since he has nothing else worth saving.

Declarer has motives other than end-plays for losing the lead to one opponent rather than the other. If they are of unequal ability, he may prefer losing the lead to the weaker player, who probably will not know what to do. Particularly at no-trump, one hand may be dangerous on lead while the other is not.

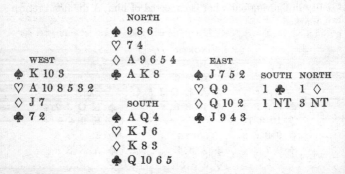

West leads his fourth-best heart; East's queen forces the king. Declarer leads a club to the ace and returns a low diamond. If East is alert, he will put up the ten. Otherwise, declarer plays the eight, losing to West, the non-danger hand. If South had led the first diamond trick toward the board, the defenders would have to be careful to see that on the way back East did not play the ten, losing to West's jack. Best play is for West to play low (no use losing the only trick in the suit by hopping up with the jack when partner has Q x x) and for East to play the queen on the way back. But if East is only a fair player, it might be worth while for West to hop up with the jack at the first diamond trick. And what if the diamond suit were as follows?

A 9 x x x

Q x   J 10 x

K 8 x

If declarer should lead a low diamond from the board, East would have to play the ten while West unblocked. If declarer should lead low from his hand, West would play low, since he would be allowed to hold the trick if he went up with the queen. The ace would win, and East would be compelled to play the *jack* when the suit was led back in order to present declarer with a guess. If he were to play the ten, declarer would duck; he would have no alternative. But if the jack were played, he might play the king, figuring West for the Q-10 left. These suit distributions and plays should be memorized. Of course, there are other holdings presenting avoidance and defense against avoidance problems, but if you learn these, the others will be easy.

The last hand of the group is a fancy hand. And yet, good defense is marked, once declarer provides the opportunity.

West leads the ten of hearts. East over-takes the nine in order to continue the suit. When he holds the second trick, he knows declarer has the blank ace left. So he could return the king, queen, or three with equal effect. He returns the queen as suit preference, showing an entry in the middle-ranking suit. West must discard the ace of diamonds to keep from making his partner a liar. This defense holds declarer to eight tricks. Even if West does not interpret the queen of hearts as a suit-preference play, he should throw the ace of diamonds at rubber bridge in the very reasonable hope that declarer has a worthless doubleton.

Counting

THE DEFENDERS should attempt to figure the distribution of the unseen hands on every deal. Usually, they start out with an approximate picture of the distribution as a result of the bidding. Later, as partner signals to show distribution, or as one hand shows out of a suit, an exact picture can be obtained.

```
                    NORTH
                  ♠ Q 7 3
                  ♡ K 10 8 4
      WEST        ◇ 8 7 6 4        EAST
  ♠ 6 5 2         ♣ J 5        ♠ J 10
  ♡ A 7 2                      ♡ Q 9 5 3    SOUTH NORTH
  ◇ A 10 3         SOUTH       ◇ Q J 9 5 2   1 ♠    2 ♠
  ♣ 9 8 6 2      ♠ A K 9 8 4   ♣ K 4         4 ♠
                  ♡ J 6
                  ◇ K
                  ♣ A Q 10 7 3
```

West leads a trump. Declarer wins in his own hand, leads a trump to the queen, and returns the jack of clubs. South wins the king with the ace, cashes the queen, and ruffs a small club. He leads a diamond from the board, upon which the queen, king, and ace are played. West is able to count the South hand as having started with five of each black suit, leaving him three red cards. East's play of the queen of diamonds guarantees the jack, so West returns a diamond. Since declarer ruffs, he must have two hearts left. When he leads a low heart toward the board, West can duck with no risk whatsoever. Declarer now has a chance to misguess the hearts. However, if South had followed to the second round of diamonds and ruffed the third, West would hop right up with the ace of hearts.

```
                 NORTH
                 ♠ 10 9 3
                 ♡ A 10 5 3
                 ◇ 7 6 4
 WEST            ♣ A Q 8        EAST
♠ K J 7 4                      ♠ Q 8 6 2      SOUTH   NORTH
♡ Q 6                          ♡ 9 8 2         1 NT    3 NT
◇ K 9 5 3 2       SOUTH        ◇ J 8
♣ 5 2            ♠ A 5         ♣ 10 9 7 4
                 ♡ K J 7 4
                 ◇ A Q 10
                 ♣ K J 6 3
```

The opening lead is a small diamond, the jack forcing the
queen. South cashes his four club tricks; West and dummy
discard diamonds. Declarer leads a heart to the ace and finesses
the jack on the way back. When West wins this trick, what can
he tell about South's distribution? He knows that he started
with four clubs and the A Q 10 of diamonds. By inference, he
knows South also had four hearts. (With only K J x of hearts,
declarer would not play his hearts in such a way as to leave a
good heart stranded in the dummy.) Consequently, South must
have a doubleton spade. If the doubleton is Q x, West can lead
the king or a low card with equal effect. If the doubleton is A x,
South must lead an honor so as to avoid an end-play. So if
West has been counting, he will return the king of spades to
cover both possibilities.

```
                 NORTH
                 ♠ A 10 9 7
                 ♡ Q J 6
 WEST            ◇ 7 6 5 4
♠ K 8 3          ♣ A 6
♡ K 7 4
◇ A K 10
♣ 10 9 8 4
```

```
      SOUTH        NORTH
       1 ◇          1 ♠
       2 ◇          3 ◇
       3 NT
```

The bidding does not follow our system, but the hand is
completely crazy. In other words, assuming that South holds
three diamonds and North holds four diamonds, which East
declarer South lacks. Declarer runs a club to the jack and
covers heart diamonds, it is always difficult to defend against
this kind of bidding. South may have a long minor suit or less

West leads the ten of clubs; East plays the queen, and South wins with the king. South tosses out the jack of diamonds. West wins (East discarding a small spade) and plays another club. Declarer plays a diamond from dummy; West wins and plays a club; declarer wins and plays a diamond; West cashes his good club. At this stage, West has taken four tricks and merely wishes to find a safe exit. East's first discard was a small spade, followed by a small heart, and a small spade. Dummy has discarded two small spades. South discarded a small heart on the fourth club. West should lead the king of spades! Declarer is known to have held nine cards in the minors and has discarded a heart. Would declarer blank the ace of hearts? No, because the heart finesse may give him his ninth trick. Besides, East's spade discard at trick two is an indication that he started with five. He would not voluntarily reduce himself to fewer spades than the dummy. West can be sure that South has the doubleton ace of hearts and a singleton spade left. West should lead the king in case the singleton is the queen. South's hand: ♠ Q, ♡ A x x, ◇ Q J 9 x x x, ♣ K J x.

```
        NORTH
     ♠ K Q J 7 6
     ♡ J 5 4
     ◇ K 6 3
     ♣ J 8
                              EAST
                           ♠ 10 8 5 4
                           ♡ A 10 6
                           ◇ A 10 8 5
                           ♣ 7 4

        SOUTH    NORTH
         1 NT     2 ♠
         3 NT
```

The bidding does not follow our system, but neither player looks completely crazy. In other words, assume that declarer has less than 21 points. West leads the nine of diamonds, which East ducks to South's jack. Declarer leads a club to the jack and returns another diamond. It is always difficult to defend against this type of bidding. South may have a long minor suit or lots of points. However, assuming that partner has not ducked with a club honor, declarer has a minimum of nine points in clubs, three in diamonds, four in spades (he would have knocked out the ace of spades before the ace of diamonds if he did not have it); therefore, he cannot have the king and queen of hearts. You must hop right up with the ace of diamonds before he can steal eleven or twelve tricks (yes, you should have been counting declarer's tricks as well as his points) and lead the low heart, knowing that he cannot afford to play the king if he has it. South's hand: ♠ A x, ♡ K x x, ◇ Q J x x, ♣ A K Q x.

The following hand hardly fits into any of the other categories. It illustrates an important point: When you hold your hand near your body and don't separate your suits, declarer can't tell what you have. Don't worry about some fantastic double-dummy play.

```
                  NORTH
                  ♠ A J 6
                  ♡ 9 8 3
  WEST            ◇ K 7 6          EAST
♠ 7 5 2          ♣ Q 8 4 2        ♠ Q 8 4 3
♡ Q J 10 6 4 2                    ♡ K 7        SOUTH  NORTH
◇ 8 2             SOUTH           ◇ J 10 3      1 NT   3 NT
♣ A 3            ♠ K 10 9         ♣ 10 9 7 5
                  ♡ A 5
                  ◇ A Q 9 5 4
                  ♣ K J 6
```

Declarer ducks the opening heart lead and wins the second trick, noting the fact that East has unblocked. He can see two possibilities for his ninth trick, a successful spade finesse, or finding East with the ace of clubs and no heart to return. To combine both possibilities, he plans to finesse the spade towards East. To add one more chance, a sucker play, he leads the ace of diamonds, a diamond to the king, and returns the jack of spades. He has no intention of letting it ride unless East hesitates. East should play low without the flicker of an eyelash. There are times when it is difficult to tell whether to cover or not. This is not such a time. Declarer cannot afford a backward or pseudo finesse at this stage when its loss would entail a three-trick set—not when he has other plays available. (If declarer has the ten, there is little point in covering.) But if East starts to figure this all out after the jack is led, he might just as well cover.

Deception

MOST deception on defense is of the negative variety. You don't start a complicated series of plays to fool the declarer. You simply refuse to signal more than necessary and avoid defending in such a way that declarer has no chance to misplay.

```
                    NORTH
                    ♠ A 8
                    ♡ K Q 10 9 7 6 5
        WEST        ◇ A 8            EAST      SOUTH  NORTH
        ♠ J 9 5 3   ♣ A 3            ♠ 10 2    Pass   2 ♡
        ♡ J 2                        ♡ A 8 4   2 ♠    3 ♡
        ◇ J 10 9 3                   ◇ Q 5 4 2 4 NT   5 ♠
        ♣ Q 7 5     SOUTH           ♣ J 10 6 4 6 NT
                    ♠ K Q 7 6 4
                    ♡ 3
                    ◇ K 7 6
                    ♣ K 9 8 2
```

Declarer wins the diamond lead with the king and leads a low heart to the queen. A good defender in East's position would play low automatically. Ducking will make no difference if declarer has the jack of hearts, but it will make a great deal of difference if the heart is a singleton. If East wins, declarer has no choice but to lay down the king of hearts later, which will drop the jack. If East ducks, declarer will have to guess whether to play the king to smother the jack or to play low for the ace to fall doubleton.

```
                    NORTH
                    ♠ K Q J 7 3
                    ♡ A J 10
    WEST            ◊ K 9                EAST
    ♠ 10 8 2        ♣ K Q 3             ♠ A 9 5        NORTH  SOUTH
    ♡ 9 5 4 3                           ♡ K 6           1 ♠    2 NT
    ◊ J 10 8 4      SOUTH               ◊ 7 5 3 2       5 NT   6 NT
    ♣ 8 4           ♠ 6 4               ♣ 9 6 5 2
                    ♡ Q 8 7 2
                    ◊ A Q 6
                    ♣ A J 10 7
```

South wins the opening diamond lead and leads a spade to
the board. The jack wins, and declarer returns to his own hand
with a club. When he leads a spade, East ducks again. Now,
declarer is afraid that spades are split 4-2, so he abandons the
suit for the heart finesse. There is nothing illogical about declarer's play. However, if East had won with the ace of spades
on either round, declarer could not have misguessed. He would
have tried the spade suit first (which he could do then without
risk), resorting to the heart finesse only if needed.

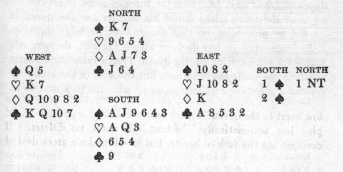

```
                    NORTH
                    ♠ K 7
                    ♡ 9 6 5 4
    WEST            ◊ A J 7 3             EAST
    ♠ Q 5           ♣ J 6 4              ♠ 10 8 2       SOUTH  NORTH
    ♡ K 7                                ♡ J 10 8 2      1 ♠    1 NT
    ◊ Q 10 9 8 2    SOUTH                ◊ K             2 ♣
    ♣ K Q 10 7      ♠ A J 9 6 4 3        ♣ A 8 5 3 2
                    ♡ A Q 3
                    ◊ 6 5 4
                    ♣ 9
```

West opens the king of clubs and continues the suit. Declarer
ruffs the second trick. A trump is led to the king, followed by
an unsuccessful trump finesse. West exits with another club.
Declarer pulls East's last trump and leads a diamond to the ace
for a heart finesse. Of course East drops the king of diamonds.

West wins the king of hearts, and exits with his last club. When declarer leads a diamond towards the board, West does not hop up with the queen. He plays the eight. Now, declarer may duck, figuring East's play of the king was from king-queen doubleton. There is nothing fancy about this play; it scarcely deserves the term "deception." It is simply giving declarer a chance to misguess.

```
                      NORTH
                    ♠ A J 9
                    ♡ K 8 6 3
       WEST         ◇ K 7 4 2         EAST
  ♠ K 10 3          ♣ 9 8          ♠ Q 8 6 2      SOUTH  NORTH
  ♡ 9 5                            ♡ J 10 4        1 ♡    2 ◇
  ◇ 10 6 3                         ◇ A 9           3 ◇    3 ♡
  ♣ Q 10 6 4 2      SOUTH          ♣ K 7 5 3      3 NT    4 ♡
                    ♠ 7 5 4
                    ♡ A Q 7 2
                    ◇ Q J 8 5
                    ♣ A J
```

In this hand West can see that just letting declarer alone will not be enough. His opening lead is a club, the king forcing the ace. Declarer pulls three rounds of trumps and gives up a diamond trick, East returning the three of clubs. West can see no more defensive tricks unless his partner has the queen of spades. So proceeding on that assumption, he leads the king. If he leads small or lets declarer attack the suit, declarer will finesse the nine, driving out the queen. Then a subsequent finesse will hold his spade losers to one. But the lead of the king may mislead a green declarer into going up with the jack next time.

```
                      NORTH
                    ♠ A Q 10 7 3
                    ♡ 8 5
       WEST         ◇ A Q 4          EAST
  ♠ K J 6           ♣ 7 6 3         ♠ 9 5 2        SOUTH  NORTH
  ♡ 10 7 6 3 2                      ♡ K Q 9         1 ♣    1 ♠
  ◇ 7 5             SOUTH           ◇ J 10 6 3 2   1 NT    3 NT
  ♣ K Q 10         ♠ 8 4           ♣ 5 2
                    ♡ A J 4
                    ◇ K 9 8
                    ♣ A J 9 8 4
```

West leads a heart, the queen losing to the ace. Declarer does not know that East has the king of hearts, so from his point of view, it would be dangerous to lose the lead to East. He leads a diamond to the ace and returns a club, finessing the nine. West knows that he has clubs under control. It will not pay him to be a cheapskate and win with the ten, because, if declarer gets discouraged with his club suit and shifts to spades, he will be tremendously successful. If West wins with the king or queen of clubs and returns a spade, declarer surely will not take the deep spade finesse and may not even finesse the queen, because he hopes to run the club suit. With logical play by declarer, he will be held to nine tricks.

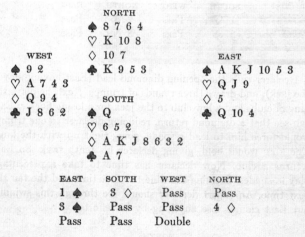

```
                    NORTH
                 ♠ 8 7 6 4
                 ♡ K 10 8
    WEST          ◇ 10 7                    EAST
 ♠ 9 2            ♣ K 9 5 3             ♠ A K J 10 5 3
 ♡ A 7 4 3                              ♡ Q J 9
 ◇ Q 9 4                                ◇ 5
 ♣ J 8 6 2        SOUTH                 ♣ Q 10 4
                 ♠ Q
                 ♡ 6 5 2
                 ◇ A K J 8 6 3 2
                 ♣ A 7
```

EAST	SOUTH	WEST	NORTH
1 ♠	3 ◇	Pass	Pass
3 ♠	Pass	Pass	4 ◇
Pass	Pass	Double	

Again, the key to successful defense is not to be niggardly. South ruffs the second spade trick and leads a low diamond to the ten-spot. West guesses correctly by hopping up with the queen and returning the suit. Declarer runs off a few more diamonds for good measure, then leads a low heart to the eight-spot. East knows that declarer is playing him for A J x or A Q x. Why spoil his fun? If East wins with the nine, declarer will have no alternative but to play the king next time—which will hold. So East should play the jack to allow the subsequent finesse of the ten.

```
                        NORTH
                        ♠ K 10 9
                        ♡ Q 8 5
        WEST            ◇ Q 7 6          EAST
  ♠ A 8 4 2            ♣ A J 4 2        ♠ Q J 5
  ♡ 7                                   ♡ 10 4 2
  ◇ K 10 8 4 3 2       SOUTH            ◇ A J 9 5
  ♣ 10 5               ♠ 7 6 3          ♣ Q 8 3
                        ♡ A K J 9 6 3
                        ◇ —
                        ♣ K 9 7 6
```

SOUTH	WEST	NORTH	EAST
1 ♡	Pass	2 ♣	Pass
3 ♣	Pass	3 NT	Pass
4 ♡			

Declarer ruffs the opening diamond lead (East having played the jack), and draws three rounds of trumps. Next, he plays the king of clubs and a low club to the jack for a losing finesse. East can see that a diamond return, reducing declarer to one trump, would force him to lead a spade, going right up with the king. The king would hold, giving declarer his tenth trick. So East returns a club. Now declarer has time to take a percentage play in spades, finessing the nine the first time and the ten the next time. An expert declarer should see through this swindle, but East cannot lose anything by his efforts.

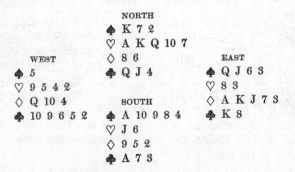

```
                        NORTH
                        ♠ K 7 2
                        ♡ A K Q 10 7
        WEST            ◇ 8 6            EAST
  ♠ 5                  ♣ Q J 4          ♠ Q J 6 3
  ♡ 9 5 4 2                             ♡ 8 3
  ◇ Q 10 4             SOUTH            ◇ A K J 7 3
  ♣ 10 9 6 5 2         ♠ A 10 9 8 4     ♣ K 8
                        ♡ J 6
                        ◇ 9 5 2
                        ♣ A 7 3
```

EAST	SOUTH	WEST	NORTH
1 ◇	1 ♠	Pass	4 ♠

West leads the four of diamonds, and East gathers in the ace and king. East can see one more trump trick for sure, but declarer will probably take a safety play in trumps, finessing the ten on the second round *unless he is afraid of a ruff.* So East returns the three of hearts, hoping declarer will read it as a singleton and bang down the ace-king of spades.

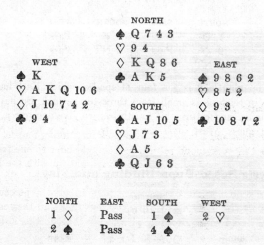

NORTH
♠ Q 7 4 3
♡ 9 4
◇ K Q 8 6
♣ A K 5

WEST
♠ K
♡ A K Q 10 6
◇ J 10 7 4 2
♣ 9 4

EAST
♠ 9 8 6 2
♡ 8 5 2
◇ 9 3
♣ 10 8 7 2

SOUTH
♠ A J 10 5
♡ J 7 3
◇ A 5
♣ Q J 6 3

NORTH	EAST	SOUTH	WEST
1 ◇	Pass	1 ♠	2 ♡
2 ♠	Pass	4 ♠	

West leads the king of hearts, and East plays the *eight.* East is gambling that his partner does not have a six-card suit or that a sluff and ruff will not aid declarer. The purpose is to induce dummy to trump high by making it appear that East has a doubleton. Dummy trumps the third round of hearts with the queen and finesses the ten-spot. West wins with the king, and declarer must still lose another trump trick.

```
                    NORTH
                    ♠ 3
                    ♡ A 10 5
      WEST          ◇ A Q J 8 6 3      EAST
    ♠ J 8 4         ♣ J 6 3          ♠ A K 9 6 5 2
    ♡ K 8 7 6 3                      ♡ J 9
    ◇ 9 4 2         SOUTH            ◇ 10 7
    ♣ K 8           ♠ Q 10 7         ♣ Q 5 2
                    ♡ Q 4 2
                    ◇ K 5
                    ♣ A 10 9 7 4
```

NORTH	EAST	SOUTH	WEST
1 ◇	1 ♠	2 ♣	Pass
2 ◇	Pass	2 NT	Pass
3 NT			

The opening lead is the four of spades, which East has no
trouble in reading as small from three to the jack. So he wins
with the *ace* and returns his fourth-best to give declarer a very
difficult guess. West *could* have led from K x x for all *South*
knows.

Analysis Based Upon Bidding and Play

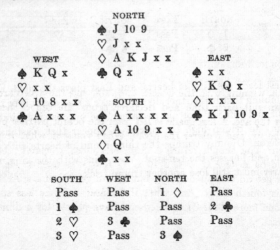

```
                    NORTH
                    ♠ J 10 9
                    ♡ J x x
      WEST          ◇ A K J x x      EAST
    ♠ K Q x         ♣ Q x            ♠ x x
    ♡ x x                            ♡ K Q x
    ◇ 10 8 x x      SOUTH            ◇ x x x
    ♣ A x x x       ♠ A x x x x      ♣ K J 10 9 x
                    ♡ A 10 9 x x
                    ◇ Q
                    ♣ x x
```

SOUTH	WEST	NORTH	EAST
Pass	Pass	1 ◇	Pass
1 ♠	Pass	Pass	2 ♣
2 ♡	3 ♣	Pass	Pass
3 ♡	Pass	3 ♠	

WEST leads the ace of clubs and a small club to his partner's king. East returns a spade, and West wins with the queen. At this point West is almost certain that declarer has five of both majors, consequently a singleton diamond. The natural play is to return a diamond and let declarer guess his own heart suit. Since declarer's singleton diamond happens to be the queen, this play works out very badly. Upon winning with the queen, declarer simply leads another low spade to the board. Now he has an entry in trumps to get four discards on the dummy's diamond suit. Can West foresee this development? Yes, he should at least be aware of the possibility. Normally, a heart return would be more dangerous than a diamond return, but not this time. East is marked with either the ace or the king-queen of hearts. If declarer had as good as five hearts to the ace-queen, he would open the bidding.

```
                        NORTH
                        ♠ A 9 5 4
                        ♡ A K 3
        WEST            ◇ A J 8 7
  ♠ K J 10 8 2          ♣ Q 9
  ♡ 8 6
  ◇ 5 4
  ♣ K J 8 3
```

SOUTH	WEST	NORTH	EAST
1 ♡	1 ♠	2 ♣	Pass
2 ◇	Pass	6 ◇	

You lead a trump. Declarer wins and draws two more rounds, partner following suit. Next, declarer plays three rounds of hearts, winning with the queen, the king, and the ace. Partner follows suit each time and declarer drops the ten of hearts under the ace. A low spade is led from the board, partner playing the six, and declarer the seven. When you win, what do you return? You should return a club, of course. Declarer's hand should be ♠ Q 7 x, ♡ Q J 10 x, ◇ K Q x x, ♣ A x. He can never get rid of a spade loser, but he can get rid of a club loser on his fourth heart. And what if declarer had one less spade and one more club? Then he would have played for a dummy reversal.

NORTH
♠ J 10 8 4
♡ K 6 4
◇ 8 7 3
♣ A Q 10

WEST
♠ A 9 3
♡ A 10
◇ J 10 9 6 5 4 2
♣ 7

EAST	SOUTH	WEST	NORTH
1 ♠	4 ♡	4 ♠	5 ♡
Double			

The opening lead is a club, declarer winning with the jack. West hops right up with the ace on the first trump lead and must find an entry to his partner's hand for a ruff. East has played a low club, showing no strength there. South undoubtedly has an unbalanced hand and may easily have a void. With a six-card spade suit to the king-queen and a singleton heart, East would not have doubled five hearts; he would at least have passed the decision around to his partner. But with a five-card spade suit and the A K Q of diamonds, a penalty double would look logical to him. West's best chance of finding an entry to his partner's hand is to underlead the ace of spades. It happens that this is the only play to set the contract. South's hand: ♠ Q, ♡ Q J 9 x x x x, ◇ —, ♣ K J x x x.

NORTH
♠ J 9 8 6 2
♡ K 10 6 5
◇ A 4
♣ 5 4

EAST
♠ 7
♡ 9 3
◇ K Q 10 7 6 3
♣ K J 6 2

NORTH	EAST	SOUTH	WEST
Pass	2 ◇	2 ♠	Pass
3 ♠	Pass	4 ♠	

West leads the nine of diamonds, dummy winning with the ace. Declarer cashes the ace and king of trumps, West following suit. South then leads the jack of diamonds, West playing the eight, and East the queen. (The deuce is missing.) East leads the deuce of clubs, declarer playing the ten and West the ace. West returns the seven of clubs, East's king dropping South's queen. Declarer is an excellent player. What should East return? A heart return is correct! South's hand: ♠ A K Q 10 x, ♡ A x x, ◇ J x, ♣ Q 10 3. South made a very fine play by dropping the ten and queen of clubs. But as he pointed out, East has already shown up with enough cards for his weak two-bid and is marked with a doubleton heart. If the only problem were to guess the location of the queen of hearts, declarer would play West for it anyway. The important thing is not to let declarer avoid a heart loser if he is missing both the queen and jack. There is no way to tell whether declarer is false-carding, and, if so, in which suit.

Don't let partner make a mistake!

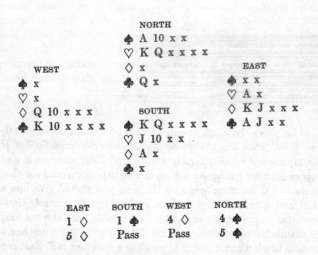

	NORTH	
	♠ A 10 x x	
	♡ K Q x x x x	
WEST	◇ x	EAST
♠ x	♣ Q x	♠ x x
♡ x		♡ A x
◇ Q 10 x x x	SOUTH	◇ K J x x x
♣ K 10 x x x x	♠ K Q x x x x	♣ A J x x
	♡ J 10 x x	
	◇ A x	
	♣ x	

EAST	SOUTH	WEST	NORTH
1 ◇	1 ♠	4 ◇	4 ♠
5 ◇	Pass	Pass	5 ♠

West leads his singleton heart. Suppose East returns a heart at trick two. West will ruff and return a diamond. After all, East opened and re-bid diamonds. To avoid this, East should cash his ace of clubs at trick two. West would play small because he wants a heart ruff. If declarer had the singleton ace of diamonds and a doubleton club, failure to cash the ace of clubs before leading a heart would cost the defenders two tricks. Cashing the ace of clubs is an automatic play for an expert. The average player forgets about his partner's problems and expects him to play double dummy.

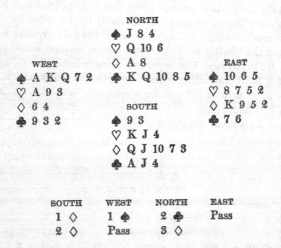

NORTH
♠ J 8 4
♡ Q 10 6
◇ A 8
♣ K Q 10 8 5

WEST
♠ A K Q 7 2
♡ A 9 3
◇ 6 4
♣ 9 3 2

EAST
♠ 10 6 5
♡ 8 7 5 2
◇ K 9 5 2
♣ 7 6

SOUTH
♠ 9 3
♡ K J 4
◇ Q J 10 7 3
♣ A J 4

SOUTH	WEST	NORTH	EAST
1 ◇	1 ♠	2 ♣	Pass
2 ◇	Pass	3 ◇	

West plays the king, queen, and ace of spades, declarer ruffing. South then lets the queen of diamonds ride on a finesse. If East wins and returns the eight of hearts, West should win and return another spade. As a general rule, whenever you see that declarer has no more losers on the side, you should give him a sluff and a ruff, since it may cause him to lose control. However, the important point is that East should not take the king of diamonds till the third round. The average defender has a mental block when it comes to yielding a sluff and ruff. East can make it easy on his partner by holding off till the dummy is out of trumps. Then, whether West is thinking or not, he will return a spade because it is an automatic play.

```
        NORTH
    ♠ K Q 8
    ♡ Q 9 7
    ◇ K J 6 3              EAST
    ♣ 6 5 4            ♠ 10 2
                       ♡ A J 10 8 6 5 3
                       ◇ Q 10 4
                       ♣ 7
```

WEST	NORTH	EAST	SOUTH
Pass	Pass	3 ♡	3 ♠
Pass	4 ♠		

West leads the deuce of hearts, and East, unable to tell whether or not it is a singleton, plays the ace. Declarer ruffs, cashes the ace of clubs and three rounds of trumps (West following suit each time). Then declarer leads a low club from the board, putting in the nine when East discards a heart. West wins with a jack and leads the ace and another diamond. When East wins the queen on a finesse, what should he return? He should return a diamond to break up the impending squeeze. From the play he should know the location of every card in the deck. The complete hand is:

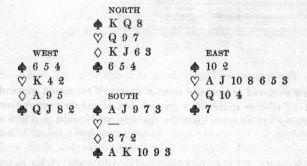

```
                    NORTH
                ♠ K Q 8
                ♡ Q 9 7
    WEST        ◇ K J 6 3          EAST
♠ 6 5 4         ♣ 6 5 4        ♠ 10 2
♡ K 4 2                        ♡ A J 10 8 6 5 3
◇ A 9 5         SOUTH          ◇ Q 10 4
♣ Q J 8 2   ♠ A J 9 7 3        ♣ 7
            ♡ —
            ◇ 8 7 2
            ♣ A K 10 9 3
```

Declarer could make his contract once East has played the ace of hearts, but the line of play adopted by declarer is not unreasonable. The important problem is for the defense. There is more to this hand than meets the eye. When this hand was played, West saw the squeeze coming up, that is, if East should fail to return a diamond upon winning with the queen. However, he assumed that his partner would see the squeeze, too, and break it up. No matter how good a player is, he will have mental lapses, some players more than others. Even with Schenken as a partner, if there is a way to prevent him from making a mistake, do so. How can West break up the squeeze all by himself? One way is to underlead the ace of diamonds. Suppose he is afraid his partner will duck with Q x x. Then he must return the king of hearts!

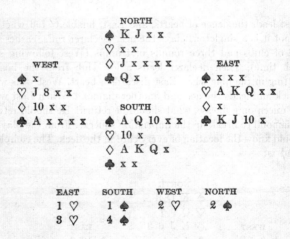

		NORTH		
		♠ K J x x		
		♡ x x		
WEST		◇ J x x x x		EAST
♠ x		♣ Q x		♠ x x x
♡ J 8 x x				♡ A K Q x x
◇ 10 x x		SOUTH		◇ x
♣ A x x x x		♠ A Q 10 x x		♣ K J 10 x
		♡ 10 x		
		◇ A K Q x		
		♣ x x		

EAST	SOUTH	WEST	NORTH
1 ♡	1 ♠	2 ♡	2 ♠
3 ♡	4 ♠		

The opening lead is the deuce of hearts won by East's queen. The key play of the hand is for East to lead the *ace* at trick two. Try to visualize East's problem when he can only see his own hand and dummy. If declarer has the ace of clubs, a club lead at trick three would be fatal. In the actual hand, failure to lead a club at trick three would be just as disastrous. East would like his partner to give him a suit-preference signal on the second round of hearts. However, West would probably play his next-smallest heart at trick two without thinking, if East were to make the normal play of cashing the king. The play of the ace should jar West out of his lethargy. If he now plays his smallest remaining heart, East can return a club with a slightly greater degree of assurance than he would otherwise.

```
                    NORTH
                  ♠ Q J 3
                  ♡ K 6
                  ◊ 9 7 2
                  ♣ Q J 10 6 3
    WEST
  ♠ 4
  ♡ Q 10 9 7 4 3
  ◊ J 6 5
  ♣ A K 4


        SOUTH    WEST    NORTH    EAST
          1 ♠     2 ♡     2 ♠     Pass
          4 ♠
```

Your opening lead is the king of clubs, partner playing the deuce. What should you play next? Obviously, a diamond shift is called for. Suppose the play goes as follows: A low diamond is led at trick two, and partner's queen forces the ace. South plays a spade to the jack and a low spade to the ace. Next, he leads a club, forcing you to take the ace. Now what? If you lead a diamond, you may find that declarer has false-carded with A K x of diamonds, and you will lose your heart tricks. Theoretically, there should be no problem. Partner should follow with his higher or lower remaining club-spot on the second round of clubs as a suit-preference play. We have all (on rare occasions, of course) played with a partner who would carelessly play the wrong club in this situation—or one whose play could not be relied upon as being an intentional signal. This hand illustrates that there are two ways to obtain a reputation of being a fine player. The first way is to make your lead on the assumption that partner was showing a suit preference. If your play works, congratulate him on making it easy for you by his brilliant signaling. After all, you want partner and the opponents to realize it was no accident that you made the proper lead. If partner thinks fast, he will take credit for his signal whether he intended one or not. If your play fails, deliver a withering blast at such carelessness so that people all over the room will know (a) this misfortune was not your fault, and (b) was not the standard of bridge to which you are accustomed.

But suppose you prefer to build your reputation the hard way—by winning. You had a chance to avoid any problems if you were farsighted enough. You should lead the jack of diamonds at trick two. Normally, the jack would be a losing play since it could give declarer the whole suit if partner had just the king or queen. This time, with a club suit staring you in the face, you don't mind establishing a few more tricks for declarer. The idea is to find out where partner's cards are and to cash out fast. By leading the jack, you give partner a chance to signal (assuming he has four or more diamonds). If he has the ace of hearts and only the king *or* queen of diamonds, he will play small. If he would overtake your jack with A Q x x or K Q x x, it really does not matter, since you had no chance with this partner anyway. Admittedly, the play of the jack is not a sure thing. Partner may have A Q x, or K Q x of diamonds, for example. However, the play of the jack can hardly lose, and it may avoid a problem.

AS406	To Market, to Market	Allen Richards	.95
AS274V	Airing in a Closed Carriage	Joseph Shearing	.95
AS273V	Mignonette	Joseph Shearing	.95
AS109X	How the Old Woman Got Home	M. P. Shiel	.95
AS157V	The Pipe Dream	Julian Symons	.95
AS37	Big Shot	Lawrence Treat	.95
AS121	Murder in Trinidad	John W. Vandercook	.95
AS80X	A Dying Fall	Henry Wade	.95

True Crime for Connoisseurs
Authors: Charles Boswell and Lewis Thompson

Each book in this original true crime series deals with actual crimes by members of a particular profession. Titles published to date:

AS357	Advocates of Murder	$ .95
AS506	Business of Murder	.95
AS436	Curriculum of Murder	.95
AS446	Harvesters of Murder	.95
AS316	Practitioners of Murder	.95

Collier Mystery Classics

General Editor: *Anthony Boucher,* critic and author
This series includes distinguished mystery novels—some of them long out of print—as well as books about true crimes and an occasional collection of short stories. Each work is selected by Anthony Boucher and has a special introduction written by him. Titles published to date:

AS584V	No Good From a Corpse	Leigh Brackett	.95
AS262V	The Blind Barber	John Dickson Carr	.95
AS511V	The Clay Hand	Dorothy Salisbury Davis	.95
AS448V	Pity for Pamela	Mary Fitt	.95
AS416Y	Mr. Pottermack's Oversight	R. Austin Freeman	.95
AS500	Oscar Slater: The Great Suspect	Peter Hunt	.95
AS308Y	Hamlet, Revenge!	Michael Innes	.95
AS418V	Arms for Adonis	Charlotte Jay	.95
AS554V	I Am the Cat	Rosemary Kutak	.95
AS528V	The Master of the Day of Judgment	Leo Perutz	.95
AS417	Uncle Abner: Master of Mysteries	Melville Davisson Post	.95
AS447	The Footprints on the Ceiling	Clayton Rawson	.95
AS546	The Wedding Guest Sat on a Stone	Richard Shattuck	.95

IF YOU ENJOYED READING THIS BOOK, YOU'LL BE INTERESTED IN THESE OTHER COLLIER BOOKS ON
Social Science